Basic
ENGLISH
Grammar and Composition
Level F

Master the Basics One Step at a Time

edited by
Bearl Brooks
and
Marie-José Shaw

Student's Edition

ESP Publishing, Inc.
Jonesboro, Arkansas

The Authors: Basic English Grammar and Composition is a compilation of language arts materials written by professional classroom teachers.

Book Design: Bearl Brooks

Editors: Bearl Brooks and Marie-José Shaw

Cover Design: Nancy Baldridge

Graphic Arts Credits: Nancy Baldridge, Donna Bearden, Tim G. Brasher, Tammy M. Cope, Margie Luster, Donna Morrow, Barry L. Prine, James D. Redding, Jetta Skillern, Robin Sydorenko, Judy Warren

Student's Edition

Order number: EGC-F

ISBN 0-8209-0646-8

Published by
ESP Publishing, Inc.

Copyright © 1990

The Alphabet — Vowels and Consonants

The alphabet is divided into vowels and consonants.

There are five main vowels. They include "a," "e," "i," "o," and "u." The letters "y" and "w" are sometimes vowels.

EXAMPLES: a. famous ➔ a   o   u   d. style ➔ y   e
   b. ruler ➔ u   e   e. idea ➔ i   e   a
   c. welcome ➔ e   o   e   f. music ➔ u   i

There are 21 consonants. They include "b," "c," "d," "f," "g," "h," "j," "k," "l," "m," "n," "p," "q," "r," "s," "t," "v," "w," "x," "y," and "z."

EXAMPLES: a. license ➔ l   c   n   s   d. history ➔ h   s   t   r
   b. among ➔ m   n   g   e. guest ➔ g   s   t
   c. itself ➔ t   s   l   f   f. wonder ➔ w   n   d   r

A Add the missing vowels.

1. l__o__nesome
2. r____w
3. v____sit
4. ____ther
5. gh____st
6. p____ssible
7. tom____to
8. ____normous
9. countr____
10. m____dern

11. f____nally
12. qu____t
13. pr____mise
14. nons____nse
15. hab____t
16. mach____ne
17. zer____
18. c____stle
19. perh____ps
20. surpr____se

21. bl____nket
22. m____nute
23. ____mbrella
24. welc____me
25. j____wel
26. separ____te
27. cr____wd
28. wr____te
29. t____nnel
30. str____nger

31. adv____nture
32. v____luable
33. sk____
34. d____zen
35. sm____rt
36. bab____
37. abs____nt
38. underst____nd
39. t____cket
40. ____pinion

B Add the missing consonants.

1. in__f__ormation
2. ____untest
3. ____ovie
4. a____ult
5. ____ourney
6. ____ourself
7. ____oldier
8. pia____o
9. mis____ake
10. te____ephone
11. ____eason

12. a____ard
13. to____ether
14. ____eadline
15. e____cuse
16. ____omedian
17. un____ess
18. ____elevision
19. na____ure
20. flowe____s
21. ____ungry
22. ____ontinue

23. po____ato
24. re____ember
25. ____usiness
26. diffi____ult
27. ____agic
28. ____ebra
29. high____ay
30. ____ey
31. ____uddenly
32. in____eresting
33. progra____

34. he____o
35. ____oliday
36. fore____er
37. e____ucation
38. ____obody
39. encyclope____ia
40. re____ort
41. ____uick
42. break____ast
43. outli____e
44. alpha____et

Unit 1 cont'd ➔

Long Vowels

"A," "e," "i," "o," and "u" are vowels. "Y" may also be a vowel.

A long vowel sound says its own name.

EXAMPLES:

ā	ē	ī	ō	ū
ate	me	five	go	use
cake	we	find	old	cute
game	hero	right	home	rule

 What are the sounds of the long vowels in these words?

1. advice	_ī_	26. night	___	51. postage	___	76. music	___
2. idea	___ ___	27. nobody	___ ___	52. identical	___	77. knife	___
3. bold	___	28. opinion	___	53. phase	___	78. cave	___
4. change	___	29. potato	___ ___	54. hesitate	___	79. awake	___
5. cute	___	30. basement	___	55. parachute	___	80. tomato	___ ___
6. danger	___	31. quite	___	56. legal	___	81. chrome	___
7. deadline	___	32. prize	___	57. hibernate	___ ___	82. company	___
8. educate	___	33. crude	___	58. quiet	___	83. hyphen	___
9. became	___ ___	34. safely	___ ___	59. site	___	84. item	___
10. escape	___	35. shape	___	60. obligate	___	85. jersey	___
11. excuse	___	36. surprise	___	61. vacant	___	86. lotion	___
12. favorite	___	37. strange	___	62. kind	___	87. pavement	___
13. famous	___	38. used	___	63. ashamed	___	88. nature	___
14. finally	___ ___	39. telephone	___	64. place	___	89. pronoun	___
15. ghost	___	40. vacation	___ ___	65. notebook	___	90. secret	___
16. grade	___	41. vine	___	66. stupid	___	91. station	___
17. giant	___	42. zero	___ ___	67. sign	___	92. strike	___
18. globe	___	43. motto	___	68. silent	___	93. sunshine	___
19. joke	___	44. confuse	___	69. hike	___	94. total	___
20. key	___	45. truth	___	70. echo	___	95. student	___
21. later	___	46. ignore	___	71. state	___	96. style	___
22. lonely	___ ___	47. pace	___	72. wife	___	97. ache	___
23. mistake	___	48. zone	___	73. stone	___	98. title	___
24. newspaper	___	49. combine	___	74. table	___	99. race	___
25. lake	___	50. notice	___	75. time	___	100. both	___

Short Vowels

"A," "e," "i," "o," and "u" are vowels. "Y" may also be a vowel.

A short vowel does not say its own name. Study the following examples of short vowels.

a	e	i	o	u
cat	jet	fit	rob	hug
lap	red	rip	pop	us
stab	well	fill	shop	bump

 Identify the short vowel in each word.

_u_ 1. bug	___ 26. adopt	___ 51. problem	___ 76. twenty
___ 2. ugly	___ 27. product	___ 52. fifty	___ 77. alley
___ 3. film	___ 28. program	___ 53. utter	___ 78. ankle
___ 4. arrest	___ 29. finger	___ 54. puzzle	___ 79. valley
___ 5. back	___ 30. walnut	___ 55. rid	___ 80. flashlight
___ 6. rotten	___ 31. melon	___ 56. gallon	___ 81. bluff
___ 7. buckle	___ 32. multiply	___ 57. rung	___ 82. whistle
___ 8. cabin	___ 33. humble	___ 58. saddle	___ 83. wreck
___ 9. important	___ 34. canyon	___ 59. seldom	___ 84. flat
___ 10. kitchen	___ 35. wrist	___ 60. fish	___ 85. lemon
___ 11. cell	___ 36. ship	___ 61. castle	___ 86. net
___ 12. lodge	___ 37. central	___ 62. signal	___ 87. flock
___ 13. chapter	___ 38. mental	___ 63. shrink	___ 88. drill
___ 14. mixture	___ 39. chef	___ 64. sixty	___ 89. chop
___ 15. clever	___ 40. mumps	___ 65. chest	___ 90. slippery
___ 16. collect	___ 41. native	___ 66. solve	___ 91. candy
___ 17. notice	___ 42. company	___ 67. bulb	___ 92. staff
___ 18. debt	___ 43. orbit	___ 68. struggle	___ 93. test
___ 19. design	___ 44. passenger	___ 69. summer	___ 94. yellow
___ 20. direct	___ 45. sunlight	___ 70. ant	___ 95. belt
___ 21. piano	___ 46. lesson	___ 71. swift	___ 96. stand
___ 22. draft	___ 47. picture	___ 72. robin	___ 97. switch
___ 23. echo	___ 48. plant	___ 73. thunder	___ 98. ranch
___ 24. fashion	___ 49. tunnel	___ 74. pump	___ 99. timber
___ 25. ditch	___ 50. prison	___ 75. fix	___ 100. winter

Unit 2 cont'd

"y" and "w" as Vowels

The letters "y" and "w" may function as both vowels and consonants.

The letter "y" has a consonant sound in the word "yellow." The letter "y" has a vowel sound in the word "my."

The letter "w" has a consonant sound in the word "wait." The letter "w" has a vowel sound in the word "how."

A Underline the words in which the "y" has the vowel sound.

1. <u>sky</u>	16. yes	31. twenty	46. type
2. young	17. tryout	32. cycle	47. myth
3. lyric	18. mystery	33. typical	48. bygone
4. you	19. fly	34. rhythm	49. boy
5. bicycle	20. by	35. year	50. dynamite
6. system	21. yell	36. hymn	51. style
7. pygmy	22. symbol	37. your	52. antonym
8. yacht	23. yawn	38. tyrant	53. syllable
9. hybrid	24. lazy	39. yesterday	54. gym
10. yoke	25. ugly	40. berry	55. funny
11. homonym	26. yolk	41. yourself	56. ready
12. yo-yo	27. synonym	42. sly	57. xylophone
13. plenty	28. yonder	43. yearn	58. gypsy
14. yak	29. county	44. cry	59. yearly
15. yard	30. canary	45. yarn	60. yeast

B Underline the words in which the "w" has a vowel sound.

1. <u>below</u>	11. white	21. crow	31. walrus
2. wish	12. we	22. blow	32. cow
3. bowl	13. how	23. weed	33. wind
4. rows	14. chow	24. allow	34. welcome
5. water	15. wisdom	25. vowel	35. howl
6. flow	16. blower	26. flower	36. throw
7. what	17. owl	27. wild	37. brown
8. war	18. wolf	28. grow	38. work
9. towed	19. town	29. frown	39. with
10. walk	20. worm	30. waste	40. crown

Vowel Digraphs

A vowel digraph occurs when two letters are used to spell a single vowel sound. Many vowel digraphs spell a long vowel sound. The most common vowel digraphs are "ai," "ea," "ee," and "oa."

A long "a" sound is usually spelled by "ai."
EXAMPLE: train   tail
A long "e" sound is usually spelled by "ea."
EXAMPLE: scream   dream
A long "e" sound is usually spelled by "ee."
EXAMPLE: queen   seen
A long "o" sound is usually spelled by "oa."
EXAMPLE: loaf   throat

A Complete each word by adding "ai," "ea," "ee," and "oa."

1. fr __ee__ ze	21. tr _____ n	41. p _____ n	61. gr _____ n
2. cl _____ m	22. w _____ st	42. scr _____ n	62. sn _____ l
3. b _____ tle	23. t _____ d	43. l _____ ves	63. _____ sy
4. _____ ch	24. _____ k	44. g _____ ning	64. p _____ ce
5. sl _____ p	25. r _____ ning	45. s _____ son	65. r _____ ch
6. t_____ cher	26. c _____ l	46. t _____ se	66. cl _____ n
7. l _____ n	27. kn _____	47. ch _____ se	67. p _____ nut
8. b _____ t	28. l _____ der	48. m _____ ning	68. _____ ten
9. sp _____ k	29. r _____ lroad	49. thr _____	69. gr _____ dy
10. bl _____ ch	30. cl _____ ring	50. expl _____ n	70. r _____ son
11. sm _____ red	31. t _____ th	51. pl _____ se	71. h _____ ting
12. s _____ ms	32. ch _____ r	52. g _____ t	72. r _____ red
13. pr _____ cher	33. c _____ t	53. _____ st	73. m _____ ting
14. tr _____	34. fr _____ dom	54. w _____ ks	74. r _____ d
15. s _____ p	35. k _____ p	55. n _____ rby	75. w _____ ken
16. f _____ lure	36. b _____ st	56. wh _____ l	76. n _____ dless
17. sh _____ ts	37. d _____ r	57. f _____ ding	77. w _____ l
18. g _____ ls	38. r _____ m	58. j _____ l	78. m _____ lbox
19. sp _____ ker	39. _____ tmeal	59. l _____ king	79. _____ ming
20. _____ gle	40. _____ th	60. succ _____ d	80. r _____ ding

B What is the main vowel sound of each word?

1. green __e__	6. leak _____	11. oat _____	16. peach _____
2. meat _____	7. deer _____	12. sail _____	17. neat _____
3. tail _____	8. coal _____	13. seen _____	18. nail _____
4. eel _____	9. needle _____	14. rail _____	19. peel _____
5. pain _____	10. team _____	15. oak _____	20. see _____

Unit 3 cont'd

Diphthongs

Two vowel sounds blended together in a single syllable form a diphthong. The two most common diphthongs are "ou" and "oi."

EXAMPLES: a. ouch   c. soil
                 b. cow   d. toys

A Each of the following sentences contains a word with the diphthong "ou." The diphthong "ou" may be spelled as "ou" or "ow." Complete each word correctly.

1. C__ou__nt the money again.
2. H_____ did you do it?
3. The gr_____nd was too wet.
4. The _____l hooted.
5. Alex pl_____ed the garden.
6. "A" is a v_____el.
7. Don't sh_____t!
8. The cat chased the m_____se.
9. He ordered a p_____nd of beef.
10. All_____ me to introduce myself.
11. I want br_____n shoes.
12. Milk comes from c_____s.
13. The dog h_____led all night.
14. This candy is s_____r.
15. _____r teacher is Ms. Maddox.
16. The ball rolled d_____n the hill.
17. The music is too l_____d.
18. Her h_____se is next door.
19. It s_____nded like an explosion.
20. Where is my t_____el?
21. A circle is r_____nd.
22. Ginger and I went to t_____n.
23. Eric is pr_____d of his good trade.
24. The bride wore a long g_____n.
25. Smile; don't fr_____n.
26. This word is a n_____n.
27. Chris cleaned the c_____nter.
28. The queen wore a gold cr_____n.
29. The actor took an extra b_____.
30. I like to fish for tr_____t.

B Each of the following sentences contains a word with the diphthong "oi." The diphthong "oi" may be spelled as "oi" or "oy." Complete each word correctly.

1. The child played with the t __oy__
2. The people rej_____ced at the news.
3. Who is that b_____?
4. The storm destr_____ed the crops.
5. Dad changed the car's _____l.
6. Kings and queens are r_____alty.
7. Don't touch the p_____son.
8. Kent j_____ned the Scouts.
9. What was that n_____se?
10. He av_____ded my question.
11. The v_____age lasted six months.
12. The penny is a copper c_____n.
13. Christmas is a j_____ous holiday.
14. Did you enj_____ the show?
15. The man had a deep v_____ce.
16. The snake c_____led and struck.
17. Peter is l_____al and trustworthy.
18. She p_____nted at the blue one.
19. The s_____l was rich in minerals.
20. You've made a wise ch_____ce.

The Schwa Sound

The schwa (ə) is used to mark a soft vowel sound. The schwa sound occurs in an unstressed syllable.

EXAMPLES: a. mezh′ər   measure   c. ā′ b ə l   able
          b. par′ə graf   paragraph   d. ə frād′   afraid

 Each respelling contains a schwa sound. Rewrite the word described by respelling.

1. sėr′tən li   _certainly_
2. ə kount′ _____
3. pas′ən jər _____
4. kwī′et _____
5. jī′ent _____
6. en′jən _____
7. his′tə ri _____
8. kəm plēt′ _____
9. ə buv′ _____
10. al′fə bet _____
11. tel′ə fōn _____
12. hol′ə dā _____
13. ə grē _____
14. frīt′ən _____
15. lōn′səm _____
16. dis′tənt _____
17. pō′əm _____
18. sel′dəm _____
19. pər haps′ _____
20. hī′fən _____
21. bā′kən _____
22. dol′ər _____
23. ā′prən _____
24. lī′ən _____
25. trav′əl _____
26. bil′yən _____
27. ō′shən _____
28. sig′nəl _____
29. ə krôs′ _____
30. jung′gəl _____

31. lem′ən _____
32. mə shēn _____
33. ə dapt′ _____
34. un′yən _____
35. sə plī′ _____
36. pāv′mənt _____
37. ə genst′ _____
38. uv′ən _____
39. pe tā′tō _____
40. də rekt′ _____
41. el′ə fənt _____
42. fash′ən _____
43. prod′əkt _____
44. ə liv′ _____
45. thou′zənd _____
46. kab′ən _____
47. rot′ən _____
48. lis′ən _____
49. ī′lənd _____
50. bās′mənt _____
51. kə lekt′ _____
52. gōl′dən _____
53. sil′vər _____
54. sit′ə zən _____
55. ə riv′ _____
56. kich′ən _____
57. wiz′dəm _____
58. kot′ən _____
59. mul′tə plī _____
60. sev′ən tē _____

61. kə nãr′i _____
62. en′ər jē _____
63. kol′ə ni _____
64. ə dorn′ _____
65. pə rād′ _____
66. sī′ləns _____
67. priz′ən _____
68. sə pōz′ _____
69. wel′kəm _____
70. sē′zən _____
71. kum′pə nē _____
72. an′sər _____
73. prob′lem _____
74. strān′jər _____
75. sər priz′ _____
76. bot′əm _____
77. ə lou′ _____
78. frō′zən _____
79. prə vīd′ _____
80. sud′ən _____
81. sen′təns _____
82. yü′nyən _____
83. tə môr′ō _____
84. rē′əl _____
85. moun′tən _____
86. ter′ə bəl _____
87. ə rith′ mə tik _____
88. ə hwīl′ _____
89. vā kā′shən _____
90. wėr′kə bəl _____

Unit 4 cont'd

Matching Vowel Sounds

"A," "e," "i," "o," and "u" are vowels.

A long vowel sound says its own name.

EXAMPLES: take   me   right   fold   ruler

A short vowel sound does not say its own name.

EXAMPLES: at   let   it   pot   cut

 In each row underline the words which contain the same vowel sound as the first word.

1. rug . . . . . <u>hut</u>   rule   <u>dumb</u>   <u>tub</u>   huge   <u>funnel</u>
2. so . . . . . . nobody   bold   none   owner   on   pole
3. list . . . . . tide   quit   missed   wider   visit   with
4. cute . . . . suit   cube   sudden   up   tube   rude
5. leaf . . . . eagle   center   east   key   neat   help
6. late . . . . . rain   have   straight   shape   sofa   maid
7. hot . . . . hold   job   solve   top   note   not
8. ice . . . . . mile   kitten   side   license   night   written
9. rat . . . . . male   cabin   match   cave   blank   ask
10. let . . . . . led   seldom   spend   better   even   test
11. ghost . . . . lonely   locate   open   drop   joke   cot
12. shut . . . . rush   adult   bugle   hunger   using   lucky
13. ticket . . . . thick   rich   skip   tile   while   hit
14. speak . . . sleep   get   reason   bed   beast   seed
15. vine . . . . . prize   quiet   sit   pride   riddle   idea
16. came . . . . bat   safe   potato   escape   famous   ran
17. under . . . unless   tunnel   uncle   umbrella   usually   fuse
18. lip . . . . . . sing   tie   fit   magic   hilly   white
19. sea . . . . . met   greed   me   easy   bee   fed
20. use . . . . . usual   you   cup   tune   used   stuff
21. wet . . . . . nest   fence   feet   melt   spell   real
22. lake . . . . . train   cable   pattern   cab   frame   game
23. ride . . . . . tried   trick   island   bride   is   light
24. kid . . . . . kite   didn't   chicken   isle   sip   mitt
25. old . . . . . . piano   word   tomato   vote   boat   dot
26. at . . . . . . fate   sad   ample   map   fat   stay
27. us . . . . . . bus   glue   hunt   but   mule   mud
28. stop . . . . . load   lot   robber   rope   mop   knot
29. acre . . . . . grade   remain   cats   pane   day   sat
30. time . . . . . rip   ripe   high   suffix   find   die

Vowels Before "r"

It is very difficult to hear the sound of a vowel before "r." There are no rules to help you spell a word which contains a vowel plus "r." You must learn how such words are spelled.

EXAMPLES:
- a. sorrow
- b. secure
- c. fir
- d. luxury
- e. berry
- f. effort
- g. sparrow
- h. solitary

 Add the missing vowels.

1. advent_**u**_re
2. airp____rt
3. c____reful
4. dess____rt
5. en____rmous
6. fav____rite
7. f____rever
8. forw____rd
9. gen____ral
10. hist____ry
11. h____rry
12. imp____rtant
13. inf____rmation
14. int____resting
15. m____rket
16. s____rve
17. ____rder
18. ret____rn
19. sep____rate
20. tow____rd
21. t____rrible
22. av____rage
23. f____rious
24. b____rber
25. g____rden

26. b____rrel
27. b____rder
28. b____rden
29. c____rbon
30. c____rpenter
31. c____rrot
32. ch____rm
33. ch____re
34. c____rtoon
35. cl____rk
36. coll____r
37. conf____rm
38. c____rtain
39. dep____rt
40. dist____rt
41. mod____rn
42. en____rgy
43. expl____re
44. f____rmal
45. g____rbage
46. fut____re
47. f____replace
48. et____rnal
49. aw____re
50. h____rrible

51. g____rment
52. j____rsey
53. h____rbor
54. h____rdware
55. h____rd
56. h____rse
57. ins____re
58. p____rfume
59. platf____rm
60. f____rnace
61. p____rse
62. reg____rd
63. sc____rf
64. sc____rn
65. sh____rk
66. sh____rtage
67. st____rch
68. w____rehouse
69. p____rachute
70. w____rse
71. w____rkable
72. f____rmer
73. f____reign
74. ch____rge
75. w____re

76. m____rble
77. m____rcy
78. n____rve
79. n____rth
80. ____rbit
81. n____rmal
82. p____rtner
83. p____rform
84. rem____rk
85. ____rchard
86. res____rt
87. ret____re
88. sc____rlet
89. s____rvice
90. s____rprise
91. t____rdy
92. th____rn
93. v____rb
94. s____rrender
95. evap____rate
96. w____rry
97. t____rget
98. ign____re
99. p____rpose
100. sh____re

Unit 5 cont'd →

Consonant Sounds

Most consonants make their own sounds. Some, however, spell their sounds in many different ways. The "k" sound may be spelled as "k," "c," "ck," or "ch." The "f" sound may be spelled as "f," "ph," or "gh." The "s" sound may be spelled as "s" or "c." The "z" sound may be spelled as "z" or "s." The "j" sound may be spelled as "j" or "g." The "ks" sound is often spelled with an "x." The "q" is usually followed by a "u"; "qu" spells the "kw" sound.

EXAMPLES:
  a. "chorus" begins with "k" sound
  b. "phone" begins with "f" sound
  c. "cereal" begins with "s" sound
  d. "zebra" begins with "z" sound
  e. "gentle" begins with "j" sound
  f. "tax" ends with "ks" sound
  g. "quit" begins with "kw" sound

A What is the beginning sound of each word?

_b_ 1. battle
____ 2. quit
____ 3. daughter
____ 4. circus
____ 5. decision

____ 6. favorite
____ 7. hardware
____ 8. fireplace
____ 9. ghost
____ 10. reward

____ 11. cabin
____ 12. phase
____ 13. luxury
____ 14. zebra
____ 15. center

____ 16. giant
____ 17. sorrow
____ 18. multiply
____ 19. phony
____ 20. tooth

B Answer each question.

1. What is the sound of the "g" in "general"? _j_
2. What is the sound of the "ph" in "elephant"? ____
3. What is the sound of the "qu" in "quite"? ____
4. What is the sound of the first "c" in "collection"? ____
5. What is the sound of the "p" in "important"? ____
6. What is the sound of the "z" in "zookeeper"? ____
7. What is the sound of the "j" in "juice"? ____
8. What is the sound of the "s" in "usually"? ____
9. What is the sound of the "g" in "target"? ____
10. What is the sound of the "gh" in "enough"? ____
11. What is the sound of the first "n" in "information"? ____
12. What is the sound of the "s" in "suddenly"? ____
13. What is the sound of the "x" in "taxable"? ____
14. What is the sound of the "ch" in "choir"? ____
15. What is the sound of the "b" in "handbook"? ____
16. What is the sound of the "l" in "lonesome"? ____
17. What is the sound of the "s" in "newspaper"? ____
18. What is the sound of the "qu" in "question"? ____
19. What is the sound of the first "t" in "together"? ____
20. What is the sound of the "j" in "journey"? ____
21. What is the sound of the "c" in "century"? ____
22. What is the sound of the second "s" in "surprise"? ____

Comprehension Check

(A) Add the vowels. Then rewrite each word.

1. b _a_ g ____bag____
2. r __st _____
3. sk __ _____
4. f __ld _____
5. c __t _____
6. __p _____
7. m __nth _____
8. __c __ _____
9. g __rl _____
10. __w __y _____

11. fl __ _____
12. w __x _____
13. sm __ll _____
14. w __st _____
15. g __ft _____
16. c __w _____
17. p __nd _____
18. s __v __n _____
19. d __nc __ _____
20. s __st __r _____

21. b __d __ _____
22. th __nk _____
23. __nd _____
24. fr __st _____
25. sm __k __ _____
26. l __nch _____
27. __x __t _____
28. c __rr __t _____
29. r __c __rd _____
30. s __rr __ _____

(B) Underline the words which contain long vowel sounds.

1. <u>kind</u>
2. bus
3. race
4. catch
5. close
6. mule
7. deep
8. nest
9. take
10. bright
11. back
12. east
13. sold
14. chain
15. rice
16. box
17. tree
18. age
19. cube
20. west

(C) Underline the words which contain short vowel sounds.

1. <u>fun</u>
2. desk
3. save
4. meat
5. brick
6. watch
7. with
8. must
9. chat
10. rip
11. chase
12. shell
13. list
14. happen
15. ice
16. zipper
17. sand
18. stop
19. time
20. sky

(D) Identify the sound of the main vowel in each word.

_ĕ_ 1. check
____ 2. drop
____ 3. crave
____ 4. truck
____ 5. letter
____ 6. night
____ 7. ribbon
____ 8. stay
____ 9. wrestle
____ 10. staff
____ 11. cost
____ 12. best

____ 13. state
____ 14. size
____ 15. stop
____ 16. greed
____ 17. laugh
____ 18. butter
____ 19. over
____ 20. visit
____ 21. fast
____ 22. throw
____ 23. trail
____ 24. music

____ 25. cheese
____ 26. runner
____ 27. high
____ 28. twelve
____ 29. brush
____ 30. open
____ 31. hold
____ 32. smile
____ 33. bless
____ 34. brick
____ 35. off
____ 36. lace

Test 1 cont'd

Comprehension Check (continued)

(E) The scrambled word in the parentheses contains the schwa sound. Unscramble each word and then use it to complete the sentence.

(vene)   1. One is an odd number and two is an __*even*__ number.

(nvree)   2. I have _____ been to the Rocky Mountains.

(batsen)   3. Only two students were _____ on Tuesday.

(lseitn)   4. I want you to _____ to this song again.

(dorre)   5. In what _____ should I put these books?

(prblmoe)   6. How did you work the math _____ on page 67?

(lbeieev)   7. I can't _____ you said that to Ms. Henderson.

(leoppe)   8. The _____ must vote for responsible leaders.

(dsstere)   9. What will we have for _____ tonight?

(brnibso)   10. The packages were decorated with blue _____ .

(mercaa)   11. I'll take your picture with my new _____ .

(wteerns)   12. California, Washington, and Oregon are _____ states.

(ptatesoo)   13. I like steak, salad, and baked _____ .

(wlyare)   14. The _____ defends his client in court.

(ddsuenly)   15. _____ it began to rain.

(F) Add the missing vowels.

1. f _i_ rst
2. n __ rth
3. c __ rt
4. f __ r
5. m __ re
6. doct __ r
7. c __ rtain
8. supp __ r
9. h __ rt
10. ch __ rry
11. s __ re
12. low __ r
13. f __ rm
14. st __ re
15. b __ rry
16. w __ rk
17. st __ r
18. st __ ry
19. b __ rk
20. t __ rkey
21. c __ rk
22. b __ rn
23. sh __ rp
24. numb __ r
25. e __ rly

Write a paragraph about your most important possession. Underline the words which contain the schwa sound.

_____
_____
_____
_____
_____
_____
_____
_____
_____

Matching Consonant Sounds

A consonant sound may be made by a single consonant, or it may be made by a combination of two or more consonants.

EXAMPLES:
  a. *"Breeze" and "breathe" begin with a "br" blend.*
  b. *"Knew" and "knight" begin with an "n" sound.*
  c. *"Grade" and "crowd" end with a "d" sound.*
  d. *"Yes" and "chance" end with an "s" sound.*

A In each row underline the words which begin with the same consonant sound as the first word.

1. history......honest	<u>habit</u>	heir	<u>hunger</u>	honor	<u>house</u>
2. confident....career	cleanser	change	capital	center	kitten
3. breakfast....brush	blouse	bug	brother	biggest	bread
4. knock......key	knee	know	needle	new	crazy
5. flood.......favor	flea	flame	frozen	flower	flexible
6. wise.......work	whistle	wait	wrong	while	wonderful
7. piano.......pencil	protect	press	perhaps	pleasant	pal
8. thick.......thin	thought	terrible	thousand	truth	thimble
9. circus......circle	chew	sudden	season	suds	strange
10. slice.......separate	sleeve	slow	straight	sled	small
11. proof.......person	praise	poison	play	prize	pout
12. shy........shout	sleep	shade	secret	shine	shoulder
13. freedom.....forever	frame	frighten	future	fragile	frost
14. dream......dread	dry	discover	drink	dozen	drown
15. challenge...chance	country	cheap	castle	chilly	choose
16. black.......brown	blend	bless	business	blond	battle
17. machine....music	magic	night	nonsense	mistake	middle
18. street......strong	stand	student	stretch	struggle	scale
19. tremble.....trust	towel	treatment	thank	trouble	tell
20. please......play	prowler	plane	powder	plum	position

B In each row underline the words which end with the same consonant sound as the first word.

1. exercise.....<u>is</u>	nonsense	<u>cause</u>	<u>prize</u>	famous	<u>was</u>
2. advice.......business	was	enormous	surprise	license	size
3. absent.......added	habit	helped	cut	minute	caught
4. against.....honest	guess	breakfast	honesty	guest	house
5. enough......if	roof	through	laugh	stuff	of
6. cabin........some	explain	none	lining	in	find
7. bridge.......edge	hug	huge	log	large	fudge
8. escape......up	hoped	help	rip	mapped	stop

17

Unit 6 cont'd

Consonant Blends

A consonant blend occurs when two consonant letters spell one sound.

Common Consonant Blends

bl	ch	pl	th	pr	fl	br	cr	sh
sp	fr	sc	gl	gr	st	sn	sk	wh
		sw	str	thr	tch	dr		

EXAMPLES: a. withdraw c. threaten
b. teaspoon d. gravity

 Supply the consonant blends.

1. _bl_anket
2. um____ella
3. ____eat
4. ____ampede
5. under____and
6. lu____icate
7. toge____er
8. ma____ine
9. ____eese
10. ____atter
11. ____eater
12. ____ought
13. in____oduce
14. ____ip
15. ____ashlight
16. un____easant
17. runni____
18. Engli____
19. any____ere
20. ru____ing
21. everythi____
22. in____ument
23. ____ontier
24. sub____itute
25. accom____ish

26. ____ange
27. breakfa____
28. ____ead
29. an____em
30. ki____en
31. ____agecoach
32. ____essure
33. ____imney
34. ____alkboard
35. ____eeze
36. ri____
37. far____er
38. ____emble
39. ____ore
40. ex____ore
41. some____at
42. ____ustworthy
43. belo____
44. dia____am
45. ____ief
46. ____iendship
47. ____ampion
48. again____
49. ____adow
50. ____ighten

51. ____unk
52. ____ance
53. ari____metic
54. ____ough
55. ____enever
56. ____ind
57. ____ould
58. ____omise
59. ____otection
60. ____ouble
61. ano____er
62. ____ere
63. ____oom
64. ____action
65. ____owball
66. fooli____
67. con____ol
68. ____own
69. ____oomy
70. nor____
71. ____eathe
72. com____ete
73. ____ecial
74. waiti____
75. ____ider

76. lea____
77. ____eedom
78. ____omise
79. ex____ain
80. ____eedy
81. ____actice
82. sur____ise
83. a____eep
84. ____aight
85. ____ee
86. ____ousers
87. ____elling
88. por____
89. ____iveway
90. heal____
91. ____ation
92. dis____arge
93. bewi____
94. ____upid
95. ____orough
96. ex____essed
97. ____under
98. ____equently
99. sou____ern
100. ____illing

Spelling the "sh" and "ch" Sounds

Look at the words "shake," "chef," "lotion," and "sure." All four words contain the "sh" sound, but the "sh" sound is spelled differently in each word. There is no rule to help you spell words with the "sh" sound. You must remember how such words are spelled.

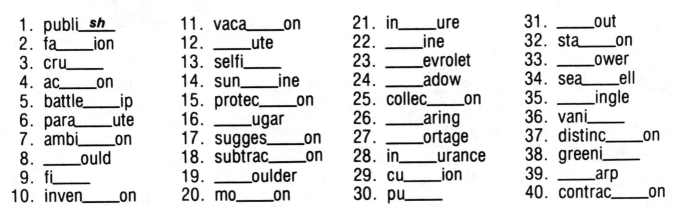

EXAMPLES: a. bushel   c. machine
          b. notion   d. surely

A Complete each word by adding "sh," "ch," "ti," or "s."

1. publi_**sh**_	11. vaca____on	21. in____ure	31. ____out
2. fa____ion	12. ____ute	22. ____ine	32. sta____on
3. cru____	13. selfi____	23. ____evrolet	33. ____ower
4. ac____on	14. sun____ine	24. ____adow	34. sea____ell
5. battle____ip	15. protec____on	25. collec____on	35. ____ingle
6. para____ute	16. ____ugar	26. ____aring	36. vani____
7. ambi____on	17. sugges____on	27. ____ortage	37. distinc____on
8. ____ould	18. subtrac____on	28. in____urance	38. greeni____
9. fi____	19. ____oulder	29. cu____ion	39. ____arp
10. inven____on	20. mo____on	30. pu____	40. contrac____on

Look at the words "punch," "kitchen," and "future." All three words contain the "ch" sound, but the "ch" sound is spelled differently in each word. There is no rule to help you spell words with the "ch" sound. You must remember how such words are spelled.

EXAMPLES: a. catch   c. future
          b. speech   d. chapter

B Complete each word by adding "ch," "tch," or "t."

1. _**ch**_oose	11. na____ural	21. mix____ure	31. ea____
2. pi____er	12. ____ance	22. pea____es	32. na____ure
3. ____estnut	13. pic____ure	23. ex____ange	33. di____
4. ____oice	14. bu____er	24. bun____	34. ____eese
5. ____alkboard	15. tea____er	25. ____ildren	35. rea____
6. for____une	16. bran____es	26. ____arcoal	36. fix____ure
7. signa____ure	17. ma____ure	27. ____allenge	37. wren____
8. ____erish	18. ran____er	28. por____	38. ____eckers
9. mu____	19. tou____	29. wi____es	39. ri____
10. ____arging	20. ____eek	30. ca____er	40. na____urally

Unit 7 cont'd →

The "ər" Sound

Look at the words "offer," "doctor," and "burglar." All three words end with the "ər" sound, but the end of each word is spelled differently. There is no rule to help you spell words with the "ər" sound. You must remember how each word is spelled.

EXAMPLES: **a. labor**   **c. forever**   **e. grammar**
                b. error   **d. differ**   **f. father**

 Complete the spelling of each word by adding "er," "or," or "ar." Each word ends with the "ər" sound.

1. deliv_er_
2. dang____
3. cov____
4. riv____
5. rememb____
6. moth____
7. transf____
8. mirr____
9. fav____
10. thund____
11. bett____
12. weath____
13. maj____
14. sweat____
15. und____
16. lumb____
17. murd____
18. spons____
19. radiat____
20. messeng____
21. irregul____
22. easi____
23. wat____
24. pol____
25. rad____

26. hum____
27. daught____
28. eith____
29. barb____
30. nect____
31. numb____
32. laught____
33. own____
34. slend____
35. rum____
36. timb____
37. whisp____
38. col____
39. lawy____
40. neith____
41. silv____
42. debt____
43. sculpt____
44. emper____
45. ancest____
46. caterpill____
47. lett____
48. prosp____
49. charact____
50. count____

51. cent____
52. cell____
53. broth____
54. newspap____
55. aft____
56. flav____
57. should____
58. flow____
59. copp____
60. disast____
61. act____
62. schol____
63. neighb____
64. fing____
65. oth____
66. butch____
67. answ____
68. plund____
69. cucumb____
70. edit____
71. togeth____
72. sist____
73. wint____
74. ref____
75. reconsid____

76. regul____
77. mot____
78. coll____
79. ord____
80. ang____
81. terr____
82. liv____
83. bewild____
84. passeng____
85. prop____
86. paint____
87. od____
88. min____
89. surrend____
90. sug____
91. val____
92. ov____
93. clatt____
94. calend____
95. wherev____
96. singul____
97. teach____
98. summ____
99. burg____
100. vap____

The "ər" Ending

The "ər" ending may be spelled three ways.

-er	writer	stranger	winter
-ar	cellar	collar	regular
-or	doctor	tractor	humor

A Supply the correct spellings of the "ər" endings.

1. whisp _er_
2. arm ____
3. particul ____
4. rath ____
5. flav ____
6. daught ____
7. maj ____
8. surrend ____
9. cent ____
10. edit ____

11. prison ____
12. terr ____
13. alt ____
14. forev ____
15. deliv ____
16. od ____
17. bewild ____
18. vig ____
19. newspap ____
20. chatt ____

21. summ ____
22. err ____
23. discov ____
24. ord ____
25. popul ____
26. famili ____
27. remaind ____
28. laught ____
29. may ____
30. publish ____

31. horr ____
32. prosp ____
33. eag ____
34. simil ____
35. unfamili ____
36. hunt ____
37. partn ____
38. protect ____
39. togeth ____
40. mirr ____

B Complete each sentence with a word from part A.

1. Every ___summer___ my family and I go to Florida.
2. Dianna is very _____ with everyone at school.
3. The _____ will try to escape at midnight tonight.
4. When did Christopher Columbus _____ America?
5. Mr. Samson has one _____ and three sons.
6. After dinner my parents relax and read the _____.
7. _____ the secret in my ear.
8. Anthony is my _____ for the science project.
9. Mike's uncle works for a magazine _____.
10. Will you _____ this package to Dr. Robinson?
11. We will work _____ as a team.
12. Parts of John's story sound _____.
13. Chocolate is my favorite _____ of ice cream.
14. Allen looked in the _____ while he combed his hair.
15. The _____ of the money will be donated to charity.

Unit 8 cont'd

The "əl" Sound

Look at the words "turtle," "camel," and "total." All three words end with the "əl" sound, but the end of each word is spelled differently. There is no rule to help you spell words with the "əl" sound. You must remember how each word is spelled.

EXAMPLES: a. candle   c. metal   e. final
             b. tickle   d. bushel   f. pickle

 Complete the spelling of each word by adding "le," "el," or "al." Each word ends with the "əl" sound.

1. troub _le_	26. post____	51. humb____	76. tunn____
2. gener____	27. eag____	52. tab____	77. festiv____
3. simp____	28. kett____	53. vow____	78. examp____
4. hospit____	29. jew____	54. possib____	79. doub____
5. magic____	30. norm____	55. med____	80. ped____
6. flexib____	31. enjoyab____	56. brut____	81. cru____
7. cab____	32. obstac____	57. interv____	82. catt____
8. batt____	33. anim____	58. app____	83. pudd____
9. freck____	34. ang____	59. nov____	84. hand____
10. speci____	35. samp____	60. tremb____	85. jung____
11. bott____	36. sing____	61. mod____	86. rif____
12. ridd____	37. sadd____	62. puzz____	87. strugg____
13. funn____	38. vess____	63. ank____	88. gent____
14. need____	39. loy____	64. barr____	89. crumb____
15. sprink____	40. ment____	65. chann____	90. cobb____
16. loc____	41. kenn____	66. music____	91. amp____
17. ratt____	42. stab____	67. smugg____	92. gridd____
18. fab____	43. babb____	68. map____	93. marb____
19. purp____	44. mort____	69. wrigg____	94. punctu____
20. grav____	45. centr____	70. trav____	95. sand____
21. capit____	46. princip____	71. carniv____	96. numer____
22. horrib____	47. plur____	72. fragi____	97. rur____
23. squirr____	48. musc____	73. beag____	98. usu____
24. peop____	49. coup____	74. movab____	99. grumb____
25. equ____	50. shov____	75. pan____	100. tow____

The " əl" Ending

There are six ways to spell the "əl" ending.

"el" as in "bushel"
"ul" as in "careful"
"le" as in "trouble"
"al" as in "hospital"
"ol" as in "pistol"
"il" as in "pencil"

A Complete each word with the correct spelling.

1. funn __el__
2. nation ____
3. unc ____
4. cast ____
5. purp ____
6. grav ____
7. turt ____
8. riv ____
9. leg ____
10. speci ____
11. anim ____
12. triang ____

13. examp ____
14. ridd ____
15. barr ____
16. app ____
17. surviv ____
18. nick ____
19. cam ____
20. nation ____
21. tab ____
22. dev ____
23. batt ____
24. valuab ____

25. pick ____
26. nov ____
27. pudd ____
28. need ____
29. sprink ____
30. shov ____
31. freck ____
32. kenn ____
33. buck ____
34. trav ____
35. chann ____
36. loc ____

37. eag ____
38. illeg ____
39. eas ____
40. musc ____
41. knuck ____
42. tick ____
43. terrib ____
44. norm ____
45. ment ____
46. commerci ____
47. tunn ____
48. tit ____

B Complete each sentence with a word from part A.

1. A ___triangle___ has three sides.
2. My _____ is a rancher.
3. I'll help you _____ the snow.
4. I'm reading a _____ about war.
5. He fell in a mud _____.
6. Bring me a _____ and thread.
7. _____ is my favorite color.
8. I made a _____ dessert for you.
9. Put the bag on the _____.
10. What is the _____ of the book?

11. A _____ needs little water.
12. I want a dill _____.
13. Stealing is _____.
14. Gene was eating an _____.
15. _____ his feet with a feather.
16. Our team's _____ is the Lions.
17. A _____ is five cents.
18. The jewel is very _____.
19. Henry plans to _____ to Europe.
20. Turn the television to _____ two.

Unit 9 cont'd

Beginning and Ending Sounds

Vowel sounds may be either long or short. Sometimes it takes two vowels to make one sound.

Most consonants make their own sounds. However, some consonants may have more than one sound. Sometimes two consonants work together to make one sound.

✱ Write the beginning and ending sounds of each word.

1. laugh _l_ _f_	26. none ___ ___	51. speak ___ ___	76. voice ___ ___
2. smart ___ ___	27. check ___ ___	52. thought ___ ___	77. tomato ___ ___
3. catch ___ ___	28. vine ___ ___	53. zero ___ ___	78. eagle ___ ___
4. giant ___ ___	29. cute ___ ___	54. habit ___ ___	79. break ___ ___
5. sound ___ ___	30. number ___ ___	55. nurse ___ ___	80. health ___ ___
6. heart ___ ___	31. green ___ ___	56. drink ___ ___	81. wheel ___ ___
7. climb ___ ___	32. find ___ ___	57. match ___ ___	82. glove ___ ___
8. church ___ ___	33. differ ___ ___	58. funny ___ ___	83. think ___ ___
9. mouse ___ ___	34. write ___ ___	59. because ___ ___	84. rude ___ ___
10. trip ___ ___	35. value ___ ___	60. polite ___ ___	85. foolish ___ ___
11. garden ___ ___	36. dress ___ ___	61. spoon ___ ___	86. cartoon ___ ___
12. locate ___ ___	37. quit ___ ___	62. flag ___ ___	87. stop ___ ___
13. light ___ ___	38. wash ___ ___	63. three ___ ___	88. large ___ ___
14. gave ___ ___	39. coat ___ ___	64. then ___ ___	89. would ___ ___
15. does ___ ___	40. train ___ ___	65. horse ___ ___	90. work ___ ___
16. start ___ ___	41. talent ___ ___	66. branch ___ ___	91. breeze ___ ___
17. perfect ___ ___	42. stupid ___ ___	67. silent ___ ___	92. village ___ ___
18. birth ___ ___	43. teeth ___ ___	68. please ___ ___	93. strong ___ ___
19. friend ___ ___	44. magnet ___ ___	69. unit ___ ___	94. confess ___ ___
20. state ___ ___	45. equip ___ ___	70. delay ___ ___	95. motto ___ ___
21. gain ___ ___	46. fierce ___ ___	71. lose ___ ___	96. ghost ___ ___
22. borrow ___ ___	47. safe ___ ___	72. change ___ ___	97. grape ___ ___
23. phone ___ ___	48. honest ___ ___	73. prefix ___ ___	98. count ___ ___
24. greed ___ ___	49. free ___ ___	74. job ___ ___	99. later ___ ___
25. magic ___ ___	50. prize ___ ___	75. visit ___ ___	100. potato ___ ___

COMPOSITION EXERCISE

Write 10 words not listed in the exercise above. Write the beginning and ending sounds of each word.

1. _____ ___ ___   6. _____ ___ ___
2. _____ ___ ___   7. _____ ___ ___
3. _____ ___ ___   8. _____ ___ ___
4. _____ ___ ___   9. _____ ___ ___
5. _____ ___ ___   10. _____ ___ ___

The Final Silent "e"

When a one-syllable word ends in a silent "e," the vowel sound of that word is usually long. For example, look at the word "cut." The "u" in "cut" is short. Now add a final silent "e" to "cut." The "u" in the word "cute" is long.

 Underline the word in each pair which contains the final silent "e." Then complete each sentence with the correct word.

1. hug huge
   a. The elephant is a ___huge___ animal.
   b. The child gave the dog a big ___hug___ .

2. us use
   a. Learn to _____ your time wisely.
   b. Tell _____ about your trip to Italy.

3. hope hop
   a. I _____ you can come with us.
   b. _____ like a frog.

4. pin pine
   a. That is a _____ tree.
   b. _____ the tail on the donkey.

5. not note
   a. I am _____ going to the party.
   b. I will write Mother a _____ .

6. here her
   a. Can you be _____ by noon?
   b. Did anyone tell _____ to come in?

7. ate at
   a. The bell will ring _____ two o'clock.
   b. Sally _____ all of the cake.

8. rang range
   a. Who _____ the bell?
   b. The mountain _____ lay before us.

9. stare star
   a. Don't _____ at me.
   b. The _____ sparkled.

10. quite quit
    a. Gerald has _____ his job.
    b. The play was _____ a success.

11. pan pane
    a. Fill the _____ with water.
    b. The window _____ was cracked.

12. rate rat
    a. Now determine the _____ of speed.
    b. Charles has a pet _____ .

13. robe rob
    a. The queen wore a purple _____ .
    b. The man tried to _____ a bank.

14. glob globe
    a. The teacher showed the class a _____ .
    b. A _____ of ink fell on the floor.

15. hate hat
    a. Quincy wore a feather in his _____ .
    b. We _____ spinach and liver.

16. car care
    a. The _____ skidded into the truck.
    b. They _____ about you too.

17. tone ton
    a. A _____ weighs 2000 pounds.
    b. The _____ of her voice scared me.

18. cap cape
    a. Dracula always wears a black _____ .
    b. The wind blew the boy's _____ .

Unit 10 cont'd

The Final "y"

When the letter "y" comes at the end of a word, it may have a vowel sound; or it may be silent.

In these words you can hear the sound of the "y."

rainy   nobody   envy   usually   any

In these words you cannot hear the sound of the "y."

bray   prey   way   okay

 Underline the words in which you can hear the sound of the final "y."

1. sky
2. may
3. jelly
4. cherry
5. canary
6. highway
7. healthy
8. dry
9. railway
10. pry
11. stay
12. gateway
13. angry
14. beauty
15. honesty
16. funny
17. repay
18. hay
19. ready
20. really
21. society
22. comedy
23. rosy
24. shy
25. activity

26. lucky
27. pay
28. probably
29. remedy
30. suddenly
31. fry
32. twenty
33. portray
34. ally
35. grey
36. supply
37. flabby
38. say
39. country
40. tasty
41. nay
42. somebody
43. victory
44. tidy
45. tray
46. pottery
47. deny
48. many
49. day
50. lady

51. play
52. ability
53. obey
54. baby
55. early
56. destiny
57. plenty
58. safety
59. thereby
60. lay
61. try
62. today
63. sorry
64. pray
65. shiny
66. thirsty
67. blueberry
68. courtesy
69. sway
70. tardy
71. economy
72. wordy
73. gray
74. hazy
75. gypsy

76. frequently
77. academy
78. delay
79. century
80. county
81. lazy
82. gravity
83. ugly
84. finally
85. study
86. holiday
87. hungry
88. fly
89. wealthy
90. happy
91. summary
92. necessary
93. fray
94. dictionary
95. easy
96. sanity
97. vocabulary
98. rowdy
99. strawberry
100. story

Comprehension Check

A **Add the consonants. Then rewrite each word.**

1. __b__ ug _____bug_____
2. __ oney _____
3. __ irds _____
4. __ atch _____
5. __ orld _____
6. __ asket _____
7. __ errible _____
8. __ isten _____
9. __ eated _____
10. e __ ery _____

11. __ indow _____
12. __ imer _____
13. u __ efu __ _____
14. __ ount _____
15. __ ollow _____
16. __ alad _____
17. __ ation _____
18. __ aint _____
19. __ e __ urn _____
20. be __ ow _____

21. e __ tra _____
22. o __ ange _____
23. __ ember _____
24. i __ ea _____
25. __ appen _____
26. __ ero _____
27. __ ozen _____
28. pla __ e _____
29. __ ourney _____
30. __ a __ ation _____

B **Add the consonant blends. Then rewrite each word.**

1. __br__ ead _____bread_____
2. ____ ance _____
3. ____ oothly _____
4. seven ____ _____
5. ____ ose _____
6. ____ ive _____
7. ____ under _____
8. ____ anket _____
9. en ____ ose _____
10. ____ ayground _____

11. sur ____ ise _____
12. ex ____ ain _____
13. ma ____ ine _____
14. ____ esent _____
15. ____ ampoo _____
16. ____ ought _____
17. ____ eedom _____
18. ____ aduate _____
19. hun ____ ed _____
20. re ____ esh _____

C **Add either a "ər" or "əl" ending to each word.**

1. wat __er__
2. ab ____
3. nev ____
4. turt ____
5. pudd ____
6. trav ____
7. drizz ____
8. britt ____
9. blund ____
10. midd ____
11. teach ____
12. anim ____

13. nov ____
14. doct ____
15. cast ____
16. edit ____
17. writ ____
18. nozz ____
19. litt ____
20. jing ____
21. mirr ____
22. capit ____
23. shov ____
24. whist ____

D **Underline the words which begin with consonants.**

1. <u>moment</u>
2. energy
3. peace
4. radio
5. goose
6. itself
7. value
8. fiction
9. anyone
10. liquid
11. object
12. ticket

13. human
14. movie
15. usually
16. ownership
17. building
18. addition
19. complete
20. surprise
21. insect
22. dangerous
23. understand
24. newspaper

Test 2 cont'd →

Comprehension Check (continued)

(E) Underline the words in each row which begin with the same consonant sound as the first word in the row.

1. party .... <u>puzzle</u>	pretty	praise	<u>push</u>	plum	<u>person</u>
2. tooth .... tumble	stand	truth	touch	time	tunnel
3. break ...... brave	brown	brush	blue	breath	busy
4. cone .... cover	kitten	crew	circus	curl	keep
5. easy .... eat	even	east	earth	erase	else
6. zone .... zoo	sunny	zebra	zoom	sure	zag
7. raw .... rich	rest	rose	ranch	rule	right
8. still........ she	stop	stump	silly	scream	stay
9. desk .... dream	dear	do	deep	dry	dare
10. hazy ...... heir	high	hear	help	honey	hurry
11. green ...... gem	grow	glass	gum	great	grade
12. ace .... acre	a	above	am	auto	ate
13. think ...... toast	thus	there	three	thin	thief
14. excuse ..... exit	explain	expert	extend	escape	energy
15. icing .... is	idea	if	island	item	ivory
16. lead........ lose	love	left	less	log	light
17. freeze ...... foot	phone	friend	free	fish	first
18. juice .... jump	gate	general	joy	give	judge
19. open ...... over	one	oats	out	other	old
20. change ..... cheese	choose	clay	cattle	cheap	cry
21. find .... food	flea	photo	fix	froze	face
22. up .... use	under	us	usual	ugly	utility
23. mess .... mix	me	move	mud	mark	more
24. bad .... bend	better	blue	bunk	brown	brat
25. glue....... globe	grass	giant	glove	gray	glow

COMPOSITION EXERCISE

Write a paragraph about your favorite meal. Explain why it is your favorite. Underline all words which do <u>not</u> begin with consonants.

_____

_____

_____

_____

_____

_____

_____

_____

Silent Letters

Silent letters are written but not spoken. The following rules frequently apply to words which contain silent letters.

1. The "b" is silent after "m."
EXAMPLE: comb   lamb
2. The "k" is silent before "n."
EXAMPLE: know   knight
3. The "t" is silent in words like "rustle."
EXAMPLE: castle   whistle
4. The "n" is silent in words ending in "mn."
EXAMPLE: autumn   condemn
5. The "d" is silent in words like "edge."
EXAMPLE: ledge   badge

6. The "t" is silent in words like "ditch."
EXAMPLE: match   stitch
7. The "w" is silent before "r."
EXAMPLE: wrong   write
8. The "l" is silent in words like "talk."
EXAMPLE: walk   stalk
9. The "gh" is silent in words like "light."
EXAMPLE: night   bright

Remember that there are other words which contain silent letters for which there are no rules.

 Add the silent letters.

1. dau _gh_ ter
2. fo____ks
3. si____n
4. ____nee
5. glob____
6. dou____t
7. g____est
8. cas____le
9. ____onest
10. sta____k
11. sof____en
12. bri____ge
13. ____reck
14. assi____n
15. ____rong
16. ____night
17. pa____m
18. ____onor
19. ta____king
20. i____ch
21. escap____
22. ____nat
23. ca____cher
24. strang____
25. ____ritten

26. ____nob
27. i____land
28. ans____er
29. ____onesty
30. hi____
31. desi____n
32. of____en
33. ____now
34. ple____ge
35. hym____
36. thi____
37. ti____t
38. ____our
39. deli____t
40. ____riter
41. cas____le
42. nau____ty
43. ya____t
44. shou____d
45. wa____ked
46. bris____le
47. ____eir
48. ____nu
49. ta____ker
50. ____nitted

51. de____t
52. g____ost
53. s____ord
54. ha____f
55. cou____d
56. thum____
57. ____rote
58. priz____
59. ca____m
60. ____new
61. ____rap
62. cha____k
63. dis____onest
64. ____nown
65. ____onorable
66. condem____
67. fas____en
68. lov____
69. clim____
70. unfas____en
71. ____nowledge
72. hors____
73. sunli____t
74. ai____le
75. practic____

76. trib____
77. lis____en
78. strai____t
79. dis____onor
80. ____nock
81. bri____ge
82. fli____t
83. wei____
84. autum____
85. midni____t
86. whis____le
87. ca____f
88. wou____d
89. glis____en
90. cut____
91. rei____n
92. ____ring
93. ali____n
94. pi____ch
95. chang____
96. ju____gment
97. g____etto
98. refus____
99. ____nome
100. throu____

Unit 11 cont'd

Vowels and Consonants

A Add the missing vowels.

1. ch__a__nce
2. w____ndow
3. prom____se
4. t____me

5. f____nny
6. m____p
7. f____nce
8. c____lor

9. mus____c
10. ch____ck
11. pot____to
12. sp____der

13. st____rm
14. p____rson
15. seld____m
16. isl____nd

17. p____cket
18. h____tel
19. f____nger
20. c____stle

B Add the missing consonants.

1. __t__omorrow
2. a____art
3. ____alley
4. be____ieve

5. ____uppy
6. welco____e
7. ____uture
8. ____ozen

9. gu____
10. ____iddle
11. surpri____e
12. hi____e

13. ____ews
14. ____icture
15. ca____e
16. ____ear

17. ____ountain
18. ____ungle
19. ____evil
20. a____venture

C What is the sound of the vowel in each word?

__ā__ 1. race
____ 2. stove
____ 3. coal
____ 4. sob
____ 5. free

____ 6. bell
____ 7. pick
____ 8. big
____ 9. taste
____ 10. trap

____ 11. hump
____ 12. drop
____ 13. wet
____ 14. line
____ 15. suit

____ 16. key
____ 17. rule
____ 18. bright
____ 19. bat
____ 20. rug

D What are the beginning and ending sounds of each word?

__ch__ __z__ 1. cheese
____ ____ 2. carrot
____ ____ 3. voyage
____ ____ 4. south
____ ____ 5. good
____ ____ 6. quick
____ ____ 7. fast
____ ____ 8. kitten
____ ____ 9. jump
____ 10. note

____ ____ 11. train
____ ____ 12. box
____ ____ 13. wait
____ ____ 14. furious
____ ____ 15. tough
____ ____ 16. sleep
____ ____ 17. house
____ ____ 18. moon
____ ____ 19. top
____ ____ 20. freeze

____ ____ 21. dream
____ ____ 22. teach
____ ____ 23. cabin
____ ____ 24. giant
____ ____ 25. friend
____ ____ 26. stage
____ ____ 27. garden
____ ____ 28. plane
____ ____ 29. light
____ ____ 30. push

____ ____ 31. pocket
____ ____ 32. circus
____ ____ 33. phase
____ 34. lone
____ ____ 35. surprise
____ ____ 36. music
____ ____ 37. tooth
____ ____ 38. because
____ ____ 39. happen
____ 40. nag

E List the five letters which are always vowels.

_____

F List the 21 consonants.

_____

Recognizing a Noun

A noun names a person, a place, or a thing.

EXAMPLES:

person	place	thing
a. president	a. Texas	a. subway
b. woman	b. home	b. luxury

 Underline the nouns.

1. <u>dictionary</u>	26. silly	51. shall	76. zone
2. attorney	27. deadline	52. chilly	77. skeleton
3. Phoenix	28. gossip	53. fake	78. signature
4. inside	29. question	54. drowsy	79. more
5. driver	30. doctor	55. parachute	80. obligation
6. motto	31. bitter	56. carefully	81. wisdom
7. aardvark	32. drenched	57. tornado	82. Oklahoma
8. yellow	33. appearance	58. first	83. country
9. beast	34. Fairway Drive	59. statement	84. tomorrow
10. freedom	35. tennis	60. pledge	85. finally
11. pushed	36. generally	61. Dr. Weston	86. guests
12. almanac	37. penalty	62. roam	87. Janice
13. attorney	38. mermaid	63. imagine	88. secret
14. rude	39. obedience	64. Ginger	89. bleach
15. Jackson	40. suggest	65. password	90. lately
16. wicked	41. underneath	66. nurse	91. frown
17. taxes	42. ambition	67. fluffy	92. missing
18. threat	43. whistle	68. clue	93. beach
19. proceed	44. today	69. nightmare	94. truth
20. United States	45. different	70. expected	95. explode
21. journey	46. amendment	71. lower	96. license
22. war	47. replace	72. King Kong	97. forgetful
23. important	48. Ken Davis	73. soldier	98. disaster
24. verse	49. again	74. newspaper	99. confidence
25. decision	50. remedy	75. ordinary	100. career

COMPOSITION EXERCISE

List 20 nouns not used in today's exercise.

1. _____	6. _____	11. _____	16. _____
2. _____	7. _____	12. _____	17. _____
3. _____	8. _____	13. _____	18. _____
4. _____	9. _____	14. _____	19. _____
5. _____	10. _____	15. _____	20. _____

31

Unit 12 cont'd

Noun Positions

Nouns hold certain positions in sentences. They may be subjects, direct objects, indirect objects, objects of prepositions, and linking-verb complements. Nouns may follow noun markers, such as "a," "an," and "the."

EXAMPLES:
  a. *The girl raised her hand.*   *"Girl" is a noun used as a subject.*
  b. *That dog bit Jimmy.*   *"Jimmy" is a noun used as a direct object.*
  c. *Give Sharon the answer.*   *"Sharon" is a noun used as an indirect object.*
  d. *Alex plays in the band.*   *"Band" is a noun used as the subject of a preposition.*
  e. *Ms. Hardy is our teacher.*   *"Teacher" is a noun used as a linking-verb complement.*
  f. *The cat is a tabby.*   *"The" and "a" are noun markers. They show that "cat" and "tabby" are nouns.*

A Identify the position of each underlined noun. Use "s" for subject, "do" for direct object, "io" for indirect object, "op" for the object of a preposition, and "lvc" for linking-verb complement. Underline each noun marker twice.

_s_ 1. One student was late.

____ 2. My dog is a collie.

____ 3. Donna asked for a newspaper.

____ 4. Please sing me a song.

____ 5. Several girls made the team.

____ 6. Who gave Brenda the fudge?

____ 7. Elise set the table.

____ 8. Did you change the channel?

____ 9. The soldier is my brother.

____ 10. My wish was granted.

____ 11. Our dessert is chocolate cake.

____ 12. Ted is an artist.

____ 13. Tell your teacher the news.

____ 14. Noel's expression was a frown .

____ 15. The old man was a war hero.

____ 16. Jan walked home from school.

____ 17. We bought ten tickets.

____ 18. Is the book torn?

____ 19. Amy's parents gave a donation.

____ 20. I saw Tami at the dance.

____ 21. Look in the cabinet for the spices.

____ 22. Chain the dog to the post.

____ 23. Larry's message was lost.

____ 24. The glass is empty.

B There are two nouns in each sentence. Underline the nouns and give their positions. Use the abbreviations given in the instructions to part A.

1. The papers are on the shelf.   _s_ _op_

2. Two students are speakers.   ____ ____

3. Tell Alison your story.   ____ ____

4. Our prize was a vacation.   ____ ____

5. Can you hand Julie the keys?   ____ ____

6. Into the fire went the papers.   ____ ____

7. My arm will be in a cast.   ____ ____

8. Mel washed his motorcycle.   ____ ____

9. With your luck you'll win the prize. ____ ____

10. Allen shook my hand.   ____ ____

11. The children played games.   ____ ____

12. We met Jill after school.   ____ ____

13. I'll give Sara the directions.   ____ ____

14. His question was a surprise.   ____ ____

15. Her name is Wanda.   ____ ____

16. His car slid into the ditch.   ____ ____

Common Nouns

Unit 13

A common noun names any person, place, or thing.

EXAMPLES:

person	place	thing
a. daughter	a. home	a. machine
b. man	b. city	b. money
c. lieutenant	c. school	c. sign

 Underline the common nouns.

1. <u>giant</u>
2. interesting
3. opinion
4. protection
5. country
6. difficult
7. lonesome
8. sailor
9. suddenly
10. business
11. laughter
12. own
13. potato
14. driver
15. dangerous
16. music
17. possible
18. house
19. prisoner
20. anxiously
21. glue
22. education
23. favorite
24. quit
25. valley
26. giraffe
27. thief
28. hermit
29. usually
30. dinner

31. rumor
32. helpless
33. carpet
34. better
35. before
36. vocabulary
37. sofa
38. water
39. cowardly
40. snowman
41. dictionary
42. learn
43. syllable
44. program
45. notebook
46. frequently
47. used
48. race
49. spring
50. intelligent
51. chain
52. wordy
53. story
54. glance
55. important
56. over
57. become
58. because
59. treasure
60. definitions

61. At night the ghosts danced on the tables.
62. The airport was closed because of the snow.
63. Breakfast is the most important meal of the day.
64. The captain of the ship gives the orders.
65. The deadline is next week.
66. My teacher has lived in six countries.
67. The elephant is the largest animal on land.
68. The information is interesting but worthless.
69. The officer repeated the question.
70. His family owns the property.
71. The men pulled the piano up the stairs.
72. My sister works at the newspaper office.
73. The voice on the telephone sounded muffled.
74. Don't forget your umbrella today.
75. The money was hidden in the tree.
76. The children watched the clowns perform tricks.
77. The assignment covered four chapters.
78. The boy lacks confidence.
79. The glass fell off the table and shattered.
80. My mother bought three tickets to the game.
81. Grapes grow on a vine.
82. The hostess greeted her guests at the door.
83. In autumn the leaves fall to the ground.
84. The castle was built on a mountain.
85. My favorite story is about a dog.
86. The jewel is very valuable.
87. The basketball rolled under the parked truck.
88. The zoo is closed for the winter.
89. The police are looking for the owner of the car.
90. The city condemned the building.

Unit 13 cont'd

Identifying Common Nouns

A common noun names any person, place, or thing.

EXAMPLES: a. The <u>building</u> collapsed.
b. My <u>brother</u> bought a car.
c. A <u>plane</u> flew over the <u>sea</u>.
d. That <u>fish</u> is a <u>shark</u>.

 Underline the common nouns. Each sentence contains at least one.

1. My <u>book</u> fell on the <u>floor</u>.
2. That girl is in my class.
3. The trip was tiring.
4. A skeleton fell out of the closet.
5. An almanac is an interesting book.
6. The deadline has passed.
7. The call came too late.
8. Ignorance is forbidden.
9. The battle is over.
10. Jewels are a luxury.
11. The school was rebuilt.
12. The baby ate his food.
13. The doctor stood by the door.
14. A decision was made.
15. The men found a raft.
16. The swallows built a nest.
17. The amendment passed.
18. My dad talked to the owner.
19. The crown broke.
20. The teacher gave her opinion.
21. The obstacle was removed.
22. The flowers bloomed.
23. Her class sang the song.
24. The circus is in town.
25. The password is ''contest.''

26. Your goal is to be a pilot.
27. That man is our guest.
28. The wind is strong.
29. The parachute did not open.
30. Your suggestions are good.
31. The team painted the fences.
32. My mother made our lunch.
33. The rooms were empty.
34. The man shot the lion.
35. This clue solved the puzzle.
36. The prisoner is in the dungeon.
37. The farmer sold his land.
38. The boy answered my questions.
39. The damages were great.
40. The man lacked wisdom.
41. Bleach will ruin this shirt.
42. The plants died.
43. That woman is his attorney.
44. Cowboys ride horses.
45. The people voted.
46. The bees stung the children.
47. The kite blew away.
48. The family moved.
49. Elephants love peanuts.
50. The thief stole my license.

COMPOSITION EXERCISE

List 20 common nouns not used in today's exercise.

1. _____   6. _____   11. _____   16. _____
2. _____   7. _____   12. _____   17. _____
3. _____   8. _____   13. _____   18. _____
4. _____   9. _____   14. _____   19. _____
5. _____   10. _____   15. _____   20. _____

Singular Nouns

A singular noun refers to one person, place, or thing.

EXAMPLES: one person: a. dancer   one place: a. home   one thing: a. word
                      b. woman   b. school   b. ship
                      c. writer   c. beach   c. dessert

A Underline the singular nouns.

1. <u>sky</u>	36. chicken
2. ghosts	37. prize
3. numbers	38. deadline
4. holiday	39. pennies
5. eye	40. echo
6. eagles	41. sun
7. orange	42. dimes
8. blankets	43. breeze
9. mouth	44. nurses
10. airport	45. branches
11. children	46. streets
12. zoo	47. clown
13. markets	48. flowers
14. person	49. comedian
15. vacation	50. gifts
16. piano	51. journey
17. owners	52. exercise
18. tunnels	53. captains
19. wolves	54. calves
20. promise	55. rule
21. leaf	56. jewels
22. offices	57. ideas
23. minute	58. men
24. nights	59. habit
25. mistake	60. snack
26. classes	61. cartoons
27. sign	62. balloons
28. secrets	63. garden
29. list	64. feet
30. doctor	65. fruit
31. crowns	66. bricks
32. knives	67. half
33. pencil	68. lady
34. animal	69. sentence
35. smiles	70. banana

B In each blank write the singular form of the noun in the parentheses.

(umbrellas) 1. Don't forget your ___umbrella___.

(loaves) 2. I need a _____ of bread.

(opinions) 3. What's your _____?

(packages) 4. Will you mail this _____?

(bees) 5. Greg was stung by a _____.

(guests) 6. Mrs. Phillips is our _____.

(days) 7. It is a beautiful _____!

(apples) 8. The _____ tasted sour.

(sisters) 9. My _____ is at school.

(friends) 10. David is my best _____.

(lights) 11. Turn on the _____.

(melons) 12. The _____ was not ripe.

(mice) 13. The _____ ran under the sofa.

(squares) 14. Draw a small _____.

(contests) 15. James won the _____.

(jokes) 16. I know a funny _____.

(decisions) 17. Have you made a _____?

(rooms) 18. Your _____ is a mess!

(teeth) 19. The dentist pulled my _____.

(tables) 20. The _____ was cluttered.

(windows) 21. Open the _____.

(cities) 22. Los Angeles is a big _____.

(islands) 23. I want to live on an _____.

(horses) 24. The _____ jumped the fence.

(women) 25. The _____ was an actress.

(licenses) 26. Show me your _____.

(reasons) 27. Your _____ sounds logical.

(families) 28. The _____ moved to Utah.

(bicycles) 29. Louis has a new _____.

(spoons) 30. The _____ fell on the floor.

(buttons) 31. Push the red _____.

(stores) 32. The _____ is closed today.

(results) 33. The _____ was surprising.

(endings) 34. The _____ was sad.

(stories) 35. I like the _____.

Unit 14 cont'd ⟹

Plural Nouns

A plural noun refers to more than one person, place, or thing.

EXAMPLES: *more than one person:*
a. *men*
b. *students*

more than one place:
a. *villages*
b. *homes*

more than one thing:
a. *branches*
b. *bicycles*

A Underline the plural nouns.

1. stars	36. fence
2. picture	37. numbers
3. amendment	38. newspapers
4. birds	39. penalties
5. mornings	40. war
6. skeletons	41. clocks
7. school	42. zebra
8. knife	43. dollars
9. baskets	44. room
10. fact	45. businesses
11. habit	46. accident
12. excuses	47. chance
13. ideas	48. vines
14. children	49. nickel
15. letter	50. hands
16. adjective	51. box
17. dictionary	52. words
18. steps	53. watermelons
19. kitchen	54. clue
20. baby	55. floor
21. address	56. uncles
22. problems	57. curtain
23. goose	58. stones
24. sun	59. island
25. storm	60. reports
26. women	61. moon
27. heroes	62. year
28. aunt	63. notebooks
29. straws	64. sky
30. valley	65. bodies
31. baths	66. owls
32. minute	67. louse
33. lights	68. trees
34. wings	69. title
35. board	70. heads

B In each blank write the plural form of the noun in the parentheses.

(eye) 1. Close your ___eyes___ .

(bench) 2. We painted the _____ green.

(tooth) 3. The dentist checked my _____ .

(game) 4. What _____ can we play?

(country) 5. I have lived in two _____ .

(jewel) 6. The thief stole the _____ .

(plate) 7. Put the _____ on the table.

(foot) 8. Gerald has big _____ .

(house) 9. Both _____ look alike.

(ghost) 10. Do you believe in _____ ?

(castle) 11. _____ are haunted.

(error) 12. Recheck for _____ .

(exercise) 13. Let's do _____ .

(penny) 14. I have sixty-five _____ .

(banana) 15. Monkeys eat _____ .

(book) 16. Kelly dropped her _____ .

(fox) 17. The _____ chased the rabbit.

(lunch) 18. Mom fixed our _____ .

(frown) 19. _____ get you nowhere.

(sentence) 20. Write four _____ .

(month) 21. Twelve _____ make one year.

(snake) 22. Betsy is afraid of _____ .

(mouse) 23. I have two pet _____ .

(story) 24. He wrote many great _____ .

(day) 25. We stayed there for six _____ .

(jacket) 26. Don't forget your _____ .

(city) 27. Name five big _____ .

(flower) 28. Don't pick the _____ .

(bee) 29. _____ make honey.

(glass) 30. Fill the _____ with ice.

(cat) 31. Mr. Pearson has thirty _____ .

(monkey) 32. I like to watch the _____ .

(car) 33. The two _____ collided.

(cave) 34. Let's explore the _____ .

(teacher) 35. The _____ are absent.

Singular and Plural Nouns

"Singular" means "one."
"Plural" means "more than one."
Nouns may be either singular or plural.

EXAMPLES: a. window   windows
           b. license   licenses
           c. promise   promises

A Underline the singular nouns.

1. My sister claims she saw a ghost.
2. I dropped my key in the sink.
3. She is my best friend.
4. The man drives a jeep.
5. A good breakfast is important.
6. My dog brought me the newspaper.
7. His daughter is a teacher.
8. This is my favorite hat.
9. The woman is a guest in our home.
10. The library is closed.
11. What color was the truck?
12. Give us a clue.
13. My partner wrote a poem.
14. The pan burned my hand.
15. First prize is a new car.
16. You need a license to drive.
17. Take an umbrella.
18. The boy listened to the radio.
19. The prisoner dug a tunnel.
20. My cat caught a mouse.
21. The old man lives in a cabin.
22. The telephone rang twice.
23. The deadline is today.
24. I'll see you at the airport.

B Underline the plural nouns.

1. The flowers are beautiful.
2. Elephants love peanuts.
3. Sixty minutes make an hour.
4. My friends and I like to ski.
5. Are these things yours?
6. We must pay taxes by April 15.
7. Our team won six games.
8. Declarative sentences end with periods.
9. Put the words in alphabetical order.
10. Light the candles.
11. I need ten pennies.
12. These books are about adventures on the seas.
13. The students sold 100 tickets.
14. These men are jewel thieves.
15. Cowboys ride horses.
16. The farmers protested the new laws.
17. Will you water the plants?
18. Answer my questions.
19. The titles are listed on the back.
20. I like to watch cartoons.
21. My parents are doctors.
22. We raked leaves all day Saturday.
23. Move the desks into the hall.
24. He wrote many short stories.

Unit 15 cont'd →

Singular and Plural

A singular noun names one person, place, or thing.

EXAMPLES: mother   school   car

A plural noun names more than one person, place, or thing.

EXAMPLES: mothers   schools   cars

A Write "s" for singular and "p" for plural.

_p_	1. facts	___	16. offices	___	31. mice	___	46. minutes
___	2. newspaper	___	17. piano	___	32. opinion	___	47. voice
___	3. promises	___	18. reward	___	33. secrets	___	48. halves
___	4. adventures	___	19. vacations	___	34. ponies	___	49. matches
___	5. potato	___	20. boxes	___	35. books	___	50. vines
___	6. question	___	21. adult	___	36. market	___	51. tooth
___	7. reasons	___	22. ghosts	___	37. telephone	___	52. daughter
___	8. thought	___	23. umbrella	___	38. fence	___	53. juice
___	9. cacti	___	24. television	___	39. knives	___	54. owner
___	10. necklace	___	25. examples	___	40. candle	___	55. fears
___	11. key	___	26. stories	___	41. blankets	___	56. ideas
___	12. giant	___	27. favorite	___	42. eagle	___	57. jewel
___	13. parachute	___	28. habits	___	43. jobs	___	58. signatures
___	14. holiday	___	29. chances	___	44. sandwiches	___	59. deadlines
___	15. castle	___	30. crowd	___	45. contests	___	60. excuse

B Write the plural of each word.

1. captain	_captains_	14. family	_____	27. ox	_____
2. country	_____	15. change	_____	28. cabin	_____
3. grade	_____	16. joke	_____	29. guest	_____
4. sheep	_____	17. leaf	_____	30. mistake	_____
5. library	_____	18. laugh	_____	31. tomato	_____
6. tunnel	_____	19. machine	_____	32. day	_____
7. highway	_____	20. wrench	_____	33. password	_____
8. boss	_____	21. sky	_____	34. zoo	_____
9. monkey	_____	22. man	_____	35. chief	_____
10. word	_____	23. answer	_____	36. lady	_____
11. watch	_____	24. child	_____	37. picture	_____
12. life	_____	25. branch	_____	38. breeze	_____
13. spoon	_____	26. number	_____	39. tax	_____

Comprehension Check

(A) Add the silent letters.

1. cha _l_ k
2. throu ___
3. ___ now
4. ple ___ ge
5. ___ nat
6. ta ___ ker
7. yo ___ k
8. ___ nit
9. rei ___ n
10. whis ___ le
11. i ___ land
12. fli ___ t
13. ___ not
14. shou ___ d
15. ___ onor
16. com ___
17. autum ___
18. e ___ ge
19. ___ rite
20. wi ___ ch

(B) Write the beginning and ending sounds of each word.

1. _dr_ _m_ dream
2. ___ ___ friend
3. ___ ___ push
4. ___ ___ tooth
5. ___ ___ house
6. ___ ___ moon
7. ___ ___ tell
8. ___ ___ talk
9. ___ ___ desk
10. ___ ___ pen
11. ___ ___ name
12. ___ ___ live
13. ___ ___ loan
14. ___ ___ music
15. ___ ___ joke
16. ___ ___ meal
17. ___ ___ tend
18. ___ ___ like
19. ___ ___ mean
20. ___ ___ guys

(C) Tell whether the underlined letter in each word is a vowel or a consonant. Write "v" for vowel and "c" for consonant.

_v_ 1. drink
___ 2. put
___ 3. salt
___ 4. solo
___ 5. garlic
___ 6. milk
___ 7. rat
___ 8. real
___ 9. chair
___ 10. rent
___ 11. captain
___ 12. like
___ 13. puppy
___ 14. island
___ 15. lean
___ 16. college
___ 17. baby
___ 18. why
___ 19. clerk
___ 20. book
___ 21. picture
___ 22. holiday
___ 23. fire
___ 24. holly
___ 25. pocket
___ 26. luck
___ 27. free
___ 28. sing
___ 29. honey
___ 30. dog
___ 31. write
___ 32. lot
___ 33. fruit
___ 34. cola
___ 35. bake
___ 36. owner
___ 37. evade
___ 38. dream
___ 39. piano
___ 40. clock

(D) Underline each noun.

1. lawyer
2. lint
3. see
4. sea
5. sing
6. leap
7. write
8. penny
9. money
10. like
11. boy
12. it
13. neat
14. lullaby
15. music
16. at
17. rug
18. for
19. wood
20. here
21. read
22. finger
23. cup
24. branch

(E) Write either the singular or plural of each noun.

1. _baby_ babies
2. puppy _____
3. morning _____
4. _____ pledges
5. tale _____
6. country _____
7. license _____
8. ox _____
9. _____ houses
10. _____ taxes
11. _____ sheep
12. _____ tomatoes
13. _____ halves
14. deer _____
15. _____ laughs
16. hero _____
17. mouse _____
18. _____ monkeys
19. _____ men
20. child _____
21. _____ leaves
22. rodeo _____
23. sky _____
24. _____ families

Test 3 cont'd

Comprehension Check (continued)

F **Complete each sentence with either the singular or the plural form of the word in parentheses.**

(star)   1. The _____*stars*_____ are bright tonght.

(family)   2. Three _____ were invited.

(parties) 3. Sheila gave a birthday _____ .

(ox)   4. The _____ are tired.

(wolf)   5. Are those animals _____ ?

(cities)   6. Denver is a large _____ .

(thief)   7. The _____ were arrested.

(turkey)   8. All the _____ were gobbling.

(lice)   9. Have you ever seen a _____ ?

(daisy)   10. _____ make a pretty bouquet.

(fly)   11. I hate _____ !

(bus)   12. Four _____ were stranded.

(bosses) 13. Is your _____ working late?

(match)   14. _____ can be dangerous.

(gas)   15. The _____ were mixed.

(coughs) 16. Her _____ sounded serious.

(decoy)   17. We bought duck _____ .

(foot)   18. Walk several _____ .

(shelf)   19. Mike built three _____ .

(leaf)   20. All the _____ have fallen.

G **Identify the position of each underlined noun. Write "s" for subject, "o" for object, and "lv" for each noun which follows a linking verb.**

_s_ 1. The girls are on the squad.

___ 2. Shut the door.

___ 3. Tell me a story.

___ 4. My parents are on vacation.

___ 5. I understand your problem.

___ 6. Sharon is her sister.

___ 7. The trees were cut down.

___ 8. He found a stray dog.

___ 9. The boys are best friends.

___ 10. An ice cream cone is delicious.

___ 11. Please inform Terry of your plans.

___ 12. Is the report on time?

___ 13. She wants a new car this year.

___ 14. Carrie wrote her theme early.

___ 15. Several bought motorcycle helmets.

___ 16. Michelle is the award winner.

___ 17. Is school closed for the holiday?

___ 18. Alison is the president of our class.

___ 19. Connect the Christmas tree lights.

___ 20. Rachel is a mechanic at Firestone.

___ 21. The animals were restless.

___ 22. We like the beat of the music.

___ 23. Earl is a good writer.

___ 24. Give Rhonda your phone nummber.

Write a paragraph describing one room of your home. Underline each noun which is used as a subject.

_____

_____

_____

_____

_____

_____

_____

_____

_____

_____

Recognizing Singular and Plural Forms

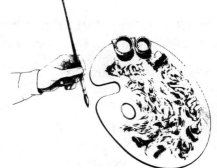

Singular refers to one person, place, or thing. Plural refers to more than one person, place, or thing.

EXAMPLES:
	singular	plural
a.	child	children
b.	minute	minutes
c.	ticket	tickets
d.	yard	yards

A Underline each singular form once and each plural form twice.

1. secret	secrets	21. nights	night	41. umbrella	umbrellas
2. men	man	22. tunnel	tunnels	42. leaf	leaves
3. match	matches	23. country	countries	43. holiday	holidays
4. ghosts	ghost	24. change	changes	44. business	businesses
5. fact	facts	25. artists	artist	45. excuse	excuses
6. home	homes	26. journey	journeys	46. life	lives
7. accidents	accident	27. jewel	jewels	47. prices	price
8. penny	pennies	28. cacti	cactus	48. idea	ideas
9. wolves	wolf	29. zoos	zoo	49. echoes	echo
10. reasons	reason	30. potato	potatoes	50. cabin	cabins
11. dessert	desserts	31. goose	geese	51. students	student
12. wife	wives	32. flowers	flower	52. comedy	comedies
13. radios	radio	33. key	keys	53. opinions	opinion
14. army	armies	34. dollars	dollar	54. boxes	box
15. deadlines	deadline	35. puppy	puppies	55. name	names
16. shelf	shelves	36. woman	women	56. sky	skies
17. donkeys	donkey	37. mouse	mice	57. eyes	eye
18. lesson	lessons	38. habit	habits	58. color	colors
19. branches	branch	39. circles	circle	59. peaches	peach
20. line	lines	40. glass	glasses	60. oxen	ox

B Write "s" for singular and "p" for plural.

_s_ 1. telephone	___ 9. newspapers	___ 17. hour	___ 25. cameras
___ 2. breakfasts	___ 10. dozen	___ 18. contests	___ 26. license
___ 3. teeth	___ 11. promise	___ 19. zero	___ 27. period
___ 4. numbers	___ 12. automobile	___ 20. calves	___ 28. roof
___ 5. family	___ 13. birthday	___ 21. fly	___ 29. bonus
___ 6. foxes	___ 14. parachute	___ 22. skeletons	___ 30. fences
___ 7. half	___ 15. attorney	___ 23. knife	___ 31. library
___ 8. sidewalks	___ 16. grounds	___ 24. foot	___ 32. boards

Unit 16 cont'd →

Noun Number

A singular noun refers to one person, place, or thing. A plural noun refers to more than one person, place, or thing.

EXAMPLES: *singular*
a. sheriff   c. world
b. war   d. color

plural
a. doctors   c. houses
b. parents   d. sandwiches

 Underline the singular nouns. (The nouns you do not underline are plural.)

1. <u>motto</u>	26. suggestions	51. magnet	76. income
2. delays	27. ambition	52. habit	77. frowns
3. almanac	28. deadlines	53. disaster	78. verses
4. accounts	29. effort	54. dungeons	79. license
5. skeletons	30. career	55. clue	80. sections
6. site	31. amendments	56. festivals	81. ability
7. spoon	32. obstacle	57. wink	82. echo
8. cartoons	33. zones	58. shortage	83. earnings
9. breezes	34. penalties	59. appearances	84. ghost
10. budget	35. parachute	60. sentences	85. automobile
11. tragedy	36. tornado	61. ocean	86. hippopotamus
12. threat	37. statements	62. garden	87. comedies
13. exercises	38. exclamation	63. sleighs	88. century
14. bomb	39. questions	64. kangaroo	89. mirror
15. guests	40. commands	65. hotel	90. radios
16. remedy	41. liberties	66. chimney	91. television
17. luxury	42. gem	67. corporation	92. company
18. battles	43. junction	68. calfskin	93. decisions
19. escort	44. library	69. titles	94. interjection
20. triumph	45. mall	70. alphabet	95. moccasin
21. voyages	46. storms	71. fences	96. password
22. clearing	47. fork	72. depot	97. wrenches
23. mermaids	48. family	73. candles	98. branch
24. signature	49. pronouns	74. seat	99. comedian
25. hike	50. thumbs	75. pictures	100. attorneys

COMPOSITION EXERCISE

List 8 singular nouns and 8 plural nouns.

singular

1. _____   5. _____
2. _____   6. _____
3. _____   7. _____
4. _____   8. _____

plural

1. _____   5. _____
2. _____   6. _____
3. _____   7. _____
4. _____   8. _____

Adding "s" to Form Plurals

Most nouns form the plural by adding "s."

EXAMPLES:
- a. **tunnel**   **tunnels**
- b. **ghost**   **ghosts**
- c. **airport**   **airports**

A Write the plural of each noun.

1. secret	*secrets*	13. fact _____	25. minute _____
2. movie _____		14. budget _____	26. list _____
3. jeep _____		15. idea _____	27. stranger _____
4. owner _____		16. job _____	28. opinion _____
5. reason _____		17. error _____	29. vacation _____
6. machine _____		18. crowd _____	30. reward _____
7. office _____		19. prize _____	31. question _____
8. friend _____		20. ocean _____	32. weapon _____
9. ticket _____		21. insect _____	33. skeleton _____
10. grade _____		22. cabin _____	34. career _____
11. desk _____		23. chair _____	35. jacket _____
12. book _____		24. paper _____	36. boot _____

B Complete each sentence with the plural form of the noun in the parentheses.

(robin) 1. The _____ *robins* _____ built a nest.

(sheet) 2. I need two _____ of paper.

(dog) 3. My cousin has six _____ .

(month) 4. Twelve _____ make a year.

(hole) 5. The _____ were deep.

(store) 6. The _____ closed early.

(yolk) 7. The egg had two _____ .

(star) 8. The _____ are bright tonight.

(word) 9. Say the _____ slowly.

(owner) 10. Who are the _____ ?

(smile) 11. _____ are contagious.

(hour) 12. A day has twenty-four _____ .

(plant) 13. Water the _____ .

(room) 14. The house has fourteen _____ .

(grade) 15. Sue always makes good _____ .

(pen) 16. Sharon dropped the _____ .

(wheel) 17. The table has _____ .

(sleeve) 18. Are the _____ too short?

(signature) 19. Do you recognize the _____ ?

(daughter) 20. Mr. West has two _____ .

(contest) 21. Angie loves to enter _____ .

(doctor) 22. These women are _____ .

(license) 23. These _____ have expired.

(language) 24. How many _____ do you speak?

(cracker) 25. Wes ordered soup and _____ .

(blanket) 26. We need more _____ .

(decision) 27. I hate to make _____ .

(window) 28. All the _____ were open.

(captain) 29. They are _____ in the army.

(jewel) 30. The _____ were stolen yesterday.

(promise) 31. He never keeps his _____ .

(answer) 32. What are the _____ ?

(suggestion) 33. Do you have any _____ ?

(basket) 34. We bought three _____ .

(tape) 35. Did the cassette _____ break?

(diamond) 36. The ring has four _____ .

Unit 17 cont'd

Adding "es" to Form Plurals

**When a noun ends in "ch," "sh," "z," "s," "ss,"
or "x," the plural is formed by adding "es."**

EXAMPLES: a. branch   branches
              b. glass   glasses
              c. ax   axes

A Underline the correct plural forms.

1. peach	peachs	<u>peaches</u>	11. buzz	buzzs	buzzes
2. box	boxs	boxes	12. boss	bosses	bosss
3. business	businesses	business	13. bonus	bonuses	bonus
4. bush	bushs	bushes	14. finch	finchs	finches
5. wrench	wrenches	wrenchs	15. inch	inches	inchs
6. dress	dresss	dresses	16. sketch	sketchs	sketches
7. church	churches	churchs	17. fox	foxes	foxs
8. lunch	lunches	lunchs	18. clash	clashes	clashs
9. bench	benchs	benches	19. ax	axes	axs
10. touch	touchs	touches	20. bunch	bunches	bunchs

B Complete each sentence with the plural form of the noun in the parentheses.

(guess) 1. You have three _____ *guesses* _____ .

(watch) 2. The man wore two _____ .

(ranch) 3. She owns two _____ in Texas.

(bench) 4. The _____ were painted yellow.

(brush) 5. Clean these _____ .

(match) 6. Don't play with _____ .

(wish) 7. He granted me three _____ .

(wax) 8. I bought two different _____ .

(cross) 9. The _____ were made of gold.

(fox) 10. The _____ hid in the log.

(patch) 11. Sew the _____ on your jeans.

(box) 12. Put the _____ on the table.

(finch) 13. _____ are small birds.

(glass) 14. I broke five _____ .

(porch) 15. The _____ need painting.

(stitch) 16. The cut required ten _____ .

(toss) 17. It took three _____ to make it.

(beach) 18. The _____ were crowded.

(tax) 19. I hate to pay _____ .

(gas) 20. These _____ are dangerous.

(pouch) 21. Kangaroos have _____ .

(loss) 22. Our team has had four _____ .

(touch) 23. I'll add the finishing _____ .

(press) 24. The _____ are running.

(batch) 25. She made two _____ of cookies.

(bunch) 26. Bring several _____ of carrots.

(torch) 27. Light the _____ .

(peach) 28. The _____ are ripe.

(inch) 29. It measured ten _____ .

(trench) 30. Ken and I dug the _____ .

(starch) 31. These foods contain _____ .

(sandwich) 32. Lee ate two _____ .

(dish) 33. The _____ are blue and white.

(latch) 34. The gates _____ are broken.

If a Noun Ends in "y" — Plurals

If a noun ends in a vowel plus "y," add "s" to form the plural.
EXAMPLES: kidney   kidneys

If a noun ends in a consonant plus "y," change the "y" to "i" and add "es."
EXAMPLES: berry   berries

Proper nouns ending in "y" form the plural by adding "s."
EXAMPLES: Tony   Tonys

✳ Write the plural form of each singular noun.

1.	city	*cities*	26.	navy
2.	toy		27.	key
3.	Betsy		28.	treaty
4.	alley		29.	baby
5.	copy		30.	comedy
6.	lady		31.	spy
7.	monkey		32.	birthday
8.	Jerry		33.	daisy
9.	lullaby		34.	cowboy
10.	candy		35.	Christy
11.	fly		36.	delay
12.	puppy		37.	mystery
13.	highway		38.	Danny
14.	army		39.	party
15.	day		40.	bay
16.	activity		41.	century
17.	Harry		42.	yesterday
18.	victory		43.	Billy
19.	country		44.	memory
20.	Tommy		45.	loyalty
21.	ray		46.	Sally
22.	liberty		47.	Judy
23.	tragedy		48.	luxury
24.	sky		49.	library
25.	family		50.	decoy

COMPOSITION EXERCISE

List 10 nouns which end in "y." Then list the plural form of each word.

1. _____ _____   6. _____ _____
2. _____ _____   7. _____ _____
3. _____ _____   8. _____ _____
4. _____ _____   9. _____ _____
5. _____ _____   10. _____ _____

Unit 18 cont'd →

Plurals of Nouns Ending in "y"

When a noun ends in a vowel plus "y," add an "s" to form the plural.

EXAMPLES: a. toy   toys
          b. turkey turkeys

When a noun ends in a consonant plus "y," change the "y" to "i" and add "es."

EXAMPLES: a. pony   ponies
          b. berry   berries

A Write the number of the rule used to make each plural noun.

_1_ 1. monkeys	___ 7. birthdays	___ 13. libraries	___ 19. spies
___ 2. ladies	___ 8. luxuries	___ 14. parties	___ 20. alleys
___ 3. holidays	___ 9. countries	___ 15. cities	___ 21. families
___ 4. puppies	___ 10. keys	___ 16. kidneys	___ 22. babies
___ 5. delays	___ 11. delays	___ 17. boys	___ 23. rays
___ 6. daisies	___ 12. penalties	___ 18. memories	___ 24. highways

B Write the plural of each noun.

1. copy _copies_	13. day _____	25. army _____
2. fly _____	14. journey _____	26. daisy _____
3. play _____	15. story _____	27. holiday _____
4. county _____	16. alley _____	28. family _____
5. toy _____	17. cowboy _____	29. turkey _____
6. treaty _____	18. victory _____	30. spy _____
7. way _____	19. century _____	31. kidney _____
8. navy _____	20. sky _____	32. berry _____
9. loyalty _____	21. bunny _____	33. puppy _____
10. decoy _____	22. strawberry _____	34. try _____
11. lady _____	23. activity _____	35. mystery _____
12. penny _____	24. yesterday _____	36. cry _____

COMPOSITION EXERCISE

Choose 6 plural words from part A or B. Write a sentence with each word.

1. _____   4. _____
2. _____   5. _____
3. _____   6. _____

Plurals of Nouns Ending in "f" or "fe"

Most nouns which end in "f" or "fe" form the plural by changing the "f" or "fe" to "v" and adding "es."

EXAMPLE: loaf   loaves

A Write the plural of each word.

1. scarf _scarves_	5. calf _____	9. life _____
2. half _____	6. thief _____	10. self _____
3. knife _____	7. leaf _____	11. elf _____
4. wife _____	8. loaf _____	12. wharf _____

Some nouns which end in "f" or "ff" form the plural by adding "s."

B Write the plural of each word.

1. roof _roofs_	5. chief _____	9. Smurf _____
2. belief _____	6. sheriff _____	10. puff _____
3. cuff _____	7. huff _____	11. riff _____
4. tariff _____	8. reef _____	12. staff _____

C Complete each sentence with the plural form of the word in the parentheses.

(thief) 1. The ____thieves____ have been captured.

(cuff) 2. Button your _____ .

(chief) 3. The _____ signed the treaty.

(calf) 4. We saw two _____ .

(wife) 5. Their _____ are attorneys.

(belief) 6. We have different _____ .

(life) 7. Our _____ are important.

(reef) 8. The _____ were just off the shore.

(scarf) 9. Betsy bought two _____ .

(tariff) 10. These _____ are too high.

(leaf) 11. The _____ are turning brown.

(myself) 12. We did it _____ .

(puff) 13. It took three _____ to blow the house down.

(Smurf) 14. The _____ are blue.

(half) 15. Two _____ make a whole.

(staff) 16. The _____ are meeting together.

(loaf) 17. Bring two _____ of bread.

(roof) 18. The _____ need repair.

(knife) 19. Sharpen the _____ .

(sheriff) 20. This town has two _____ .

Unit 19 cont'd →

Plurals of Nouns Ending in "o"

Rule 1. When a noun ends in a vowel plus "o," form the plural by adding "s."

EXAMPLES: a. radio   radios
b. Cheerio   Cheerios

Rule 2. When a noun ends in a consonant plus "o," form the plural by adding "es."

EXAMPLES: a. tomato   tomatoes
b. hero   heroes

A Write the plural of each word. In the blank write the number of the rule you used to form the plural.

_1_	1. rodeo	_rodeos_	___	11. tomato	_____
___	2. potato	_____	___	12. radio	_____
___	3. mosquito	_____	___	13. cameo	_____
___	4. domino	_____	___	14. hero	_____
___	5. Oreo	_____	___	15. trio	_____
___	6. echo	_____	___	16. cacao	_____
___	7. zero	_____	___	17. buffalo	_____
___	8. hobo	_____	___	18. folio	_____
___	9. volcano	_____	___	19. duo	_____
___	10. zoo	_____	___	20. dingo	_____

B Complete each sentence with the plural form of the word in the parentheses.

(rodeo)   1. He is king of the ___ _rodeos_ ___.

(echo)   2. We listened to the _____.

(zoo)   3. The _____ are closed Mondays.

(mosquito) 4. I hate _____!

(potato)   5. They ate roast and _____.

(hobo)   6. The _____ told many stories.

(volcano)   7. We saw two big _____.

(Cheerio)   8. I had _____ for breakfast.

(tomato)   9. Red _____ are ripe.

(domino) 10. Let's play _____.

(buffalo) 11. They hunted _____.

(radio) 12. Turn the _____ off.

(hero) 13. You are _____!

(Oreo) 14. _____ are good to eat.

(zero) 15. Four students made _____.

(dingo) 16. _____ are dogs.

Unusual Plurals

Many nouns change their spellings to form the plural.

    EXAMPLE: goose   geese

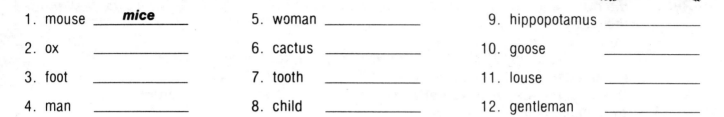

A Write the plural of each noun.

1. mouse ____*mice*____
2. ox _____
3. foot _____
4. man _____

5. woman _____
6. cactus _____
7. tooth _____
8. child _____

9. hippopotamus _____
10. goose _____
11. louse _____
12. gentleman _____

Many nouns stay the same in both the singular and plural forms.

    EXAMPLE: 1 fish   2 fish

B Underline the nouns which stay the same in both the singular and plural forms.

1. <u>sheep</u>
2. decisions
3. athletics
4. careers
5. deer
6. guests
7. food

8. scissors
9. swine
10. pilots
11. markets
12. contests
13. fish
14. people

15. bonuses
16. trousers
17. moose
18. exercises
19. politics
20. persons
21. mathematics

22. news
23. jeans
24. corps
25. journeys
26. hospitals
27. pants
28. outlines

C Complete each sentence with the plural form of the word in the parentheses.

(sheep)   1. We get wool from ____*sheep*____.

(foot)   2. My _____ hurt.

(news)   3. Have you heard all the _____?

(trousers) 4. All the men wore black _____.

(child)   5. The _____ look happy.

(deer)   6. Two _____ crossed the road.

(goose)   7. The _____ flew away.

(fish)   8. I caught five big _____.

(scissors) 9. Our _____ are sharp.

(moose) 10. We saw many _____.

(tooth) 11. The dentist checked my _____.

(mouse) 12. Ann is afraid of _____.

(jeans) 13. The students wore _____.

(woman) 14. These _____ want to see you.

Unit 20 cont'd ⟹

Rules for Forming the Plural

Rule 1 Most nouns form the plural by adding "s."
    EXAMPLES: tree   trees

Rule 2 If a noun ends in "ch," "sh," "x," "z," "s," or "ss," form the plural by adding "es."
    EXAMPLES: box   boxes

Rule 3 If a noun ends with a vowel plus "y," add "s" to form the plural.
    EXAMPLES: day   days

Rule 4 If a noun ends with a consonant plus "y," change the "y" to "i" and add "es" to form the plural.
    EXAMPLES: pony   ponies

Rule 5 If a noun ends in "f" or "fe," change the "f" or "fe" to "e" and add "s" to form the plural.
    EXAMPLES: wolf   wolves

Rule 6 If a noun ends in a vowel plus "o," add "s" to form the plural.
    EXAMPLES: radio   radios

Rule 7 If a noun ends in a consonant plus "o," add "es" to form the plural.
    EXAMPLES: echo   echoes

Rule 8 Some nouns change their spellings to form the plural.
    EXAMPLES: mouse   mice

✳ Write the number of the rule which was used to form the plural of each noun.

_8_	1. children	___	26. zoos	___	51. sketches	___	76. highways
___	2. kittens	___	27. women	___	52. dresses	___	77. boys
___	3. rodeos	___	28. secrets	___	53. eyes	___	78. branches
___	4. plays	___	29. kidneys	___	54. cacti	___	79. puppies
___	5. bushes	___	30. decisions	___	55. potatoes	___	80. selves
___	6. tomatoes	___	31. memories	___	56. flowers	___	81. accidents
___	7. families	___	32. trios	___	57. toys	___	82. men
___	8. wives	___	33. zeroes	___	58. calves	___	83. volcanoes
___	9. chances	___	34. peaches	___	59. glasses	___	84. businesses
___	10. examples	___	35. libraries	___	60. knives	___	85. centuries
___	11. cameos	___	36. lives	___	61. cities	___	86. voices
___	12. holidays	___	37. daughters	___	62. adventures	___	87. buses
___	13. countries	___	38. opinions	___	63. keys	___	88. copies
___	14. geese	___	39. guests	___	64. inches	___	89. reasons
___	15. mistakes	___	40. skies	___	65. treaties	___	90. finches
___	16. monkeys	___	41. attorneys	___	66. mosquitoes	___	91. flies
___	17. leaves	___	42. lice	___	67. berries	___	92. halves
___	18. watches	___	43. buffaloes	___	68. taxes	___	93. birthdays
___	19. beaches	___	44. axes	___	69. foxes	___	94. careers
___	20. ideas	___	45. scarves	___	70. thieves	___	95. folios
___	21. teeth	___	46. promises	___	71. cabins	___	96. fields
___	22. echoes	___	47. dishes	___	72. oxen	___	97. crosses
___	23. loaves	___	48. feet	___	73. sandwiches	___	98. parties
___	24. churches	___	49. mice	___	74. ghosts	___	99. turkeys
___	25. ladies	___	50. journeys	___	75. babies	___	100. losses

Comprehension Check

Ⓐ Identify the singular (s) and plural (p) forms.

_s_ 1. hour	____ 16. lives	____ 31. box
____ 2. rooms	____ 17. numbers	____ 32. hopes
____ 3. foot	____ 18. dancers	____ 33. dinner
____ 4. game	____ 19. movie	____ 34. oxen
____ 5. calves	____ 20. cross	____ 35. drawer
____ 6. ribbon	____ 21. home	____ 36. doctor
____ 7. cars	____ 22. boxes	____ 37. shows
____ 8. exercises	____ 23. person	____ 38. flies
____ 9. men	____ 24. sheets	____ 39. limo
____ 10. zero	____ 25. chicken	____ 40. soup
____ 11. winners	____ 26. kisses	____ 41. loaves
____ 12. child	____ 27. minute	____ 42. hands
____ 13. words	____ 28. store	____ 43. star
____ 14. team	____ 29. volcanoes	____ 44. knives
____ 15. sky	____ 30. libraries	____ 45. window

____ 46. circus
____ 47. laughs
____ 48. war
____ 49. branches
____ 50. page

Ⓑ Write the plural form of each word.

1. tree _trees_	21. match _____	41. foot _____
2. city _____	22. pocket _____	42. circle _____
3. peach _____	23. street _____	43. dime _____
4. bird _____	24. stitch _____	44. boss _____
5. pencil _____	25. half _____	45. lunch _____
6. night _____	26. wind _____	46. dish _____
7. cook _____	27. inch _____	47. baby _____
8. day _____	28. jail _____	48. play _____
9. apple _____	29. tomato _____	49. school _____
10. louse _____	30. ring _____	50. country _____
11. plan _____	31. parent _____	51. writer _____
12. glass _____	32. animal _____	52. porch _____
13. owner _____	33. thorn _____	53. brush _____
14. crown _____	34. tooth _____	54. cry _____
15. line _____	35. uncle _____	55. guest _____
16. house _____	36. needle _____	56. bunch _____
17. toss _____	37. ruler _____	57. family _____
18. glove _____	38. fox _____	58. world _____
19. card _____	39. bag _____	59. student _____
20. price _____	40. visit _____	60. journey _____

Test 4 cont'd

Comprehension Check (continued)

C Fill in the blanks.

1. _____*"Singular"*_____ means "one."
2. _____ means "more than one."
3. Most nouns simply add _____ to form the plural.
4. Nouns which end in "ch," "sh," "s," "ss," "x," or "z" usually form the plural by adding _____ .
5. If a noun ends in a vowel plus "y," form the plural by adding _____ .
6. If a noun ends in a consonant plus "y," form the plural by changing the _____ to _____ and adding _____ .
7. If a noun ends in "f" or "fe," form the plural by changing the "f" or "fe" to _____ and adding _____ .
8. If a noun ends in a vowel plus "o," form the plural by adding _____ .
9. If a noun ends in a consonant plus "o," form the plural by adding _____ .
10. Some nouns change their _____ completely to form the plural.

D Identify the rule from part C which was used to form the plural of each of these nouns.

_3_ 1. words	____ 11. cacti	____ 21. birthdays	____ 31. heroes
____ 2. wolves	____ 12. ladies	____ 22. tomatoes	____ 32. children
____ 3. pennies	____ 13. potatoes	____ 23. women	____ 33. turkeys
____ 4. mice	____ 14. highways	____ 24. shelves	____ 34. berries
____ 5. echoes	____ 15. cameos	____ 25. rodeos	____ 35. patios
____ 6. ranches	____ 16. songs	____ 26. wives	____ 36. teeth
____ 7. radios	____ 17. elves	____ 27. tests	____ 37. teachers
____ 8. monkeys	____ 18. puppies	____ 28. companies	____ 38. leaves
____ 9. watches	____ 19. duos	____ 29. keys	____ 39. buses
____ 10. friends	____ 20. wishes	____ 30. taxes	____ 40. buffaloes

Write a paragraph about the advantages or disadvantages of having brothers and sisters. Underline the plural nouns.

_____

_____

_____

_____

_____

_____

_____

_____

Plural Forms of Nouns

The form of a noun that shows more than one person, place, or thing is the plural form.

A Underline the plural form in each pair of words:

1. parent—<u>parents</u>　　3. cats—cat　　　5. babies—baby　　7. child—children

2. sister—sisters　　4. roofs—roof　　6. marsh—marshes　8. house—houses

The most common plural form is "-s." Some nouns add "-es." These nouns end in the letters "s," "x," "ch," or "sh" in their singular form.

B After each word below, write the correct plural form.

1. number　*numbers*　　3. moss _____　　5. turkey _____

2. kiss _____　　4. fox _____　　6. wrench _____

Many nouns form the plural by changing the last letter "y" to the letter "i" before adding the letters "es." These are nouns with a consonant preceding the final "y" when they are singular.

C Write "yes" in the blank if the plural form of each pair is spelled correctly. Write "no" if it is not.

yes 1. boy — boys　　_____ 3. daily — dailies　　_____ 5. robbery — robberies

_____ 2. party — parties　　_____ 4. spy — spys　　_____ 6. alley — allies

Nouns ending in "f" or "fe" often form the plural by changing the "f" to "v" and adding "-es."

D Write the correct plural for the following words.

1. knife　*knives*　　3. wife_____　　5. thief _____

2. loaf _____　　4. half _____　　6. shelf _____

To other nouns ending in "f" or "fe," simply add an "-s" to form the plural.

E In each of the following trios of words, underline the correct plural form:

1. roof — roofs — rooves　　　　3. safe — safes — saves

2. cliff — clives -- cliffs　　　　4. belief — believes — beliefs

Some nouns form plurals by changing letters within the words.

F Write the correct plural form for each of the following nouns:

1. goose _____　　3. tooth _____　　5. louse _____

2. woman _____　　4. foot _____

Some nouns are the same in both singular and plural forms. Other nouns appear in the plural form only.

G Write "yes" in the blank if the noun is the same in both singular and plural forms.

yes 1. deer　　_____ 3. English　　_____ 5. sheep　　_____ 7. scissors

_____ 2. moose　　_____ 4. thanks　　_____ 6. measles　　_____ 8. trousers

Unit 21 cont'd

Rules for Forming Plurals

1. **Most nouns add "s."**
   EXAMPLES: desk   desks
2. **Nouns ending in "ch," "sh," "z," "s," "ss," or "x" add "es."**
   EXAMPLES: dress   dresses
3. **Nouns ending in a vowel plus "y" add "s."**
   EXAMPLES: monkey   monkeys
4. **Nouns ending in a consonant plus "y" change "y" to "i" and add "es."**
   EXAMPLES: cherry   cherries
5. **Nouns ending in "f" or "fe" change the "f" or "fe" to "v" and add "es."**
   EXAMPLES: life   lives
6. **Some nouns ending in "f" or "ff" add "s."**
   EXAMPLES: cuff   cuffs
7. **Nouns ending in a vowel plus "o" add "s."**
   EXAMPLES: rodeo   rodeos
8. **Nouns ending in a consonant plus "o" add "es."**
   EXAMPLES: hero   heroes
9. **Some nouns change their spellings completely.**
   EXAMPLES: cactus   cacti
10. **Some nouns stay the same in both the singular and plural forms.**
    EXAMPLES: sheep   sheep

A Write the plural of each noun.

1. child   _children_
2. victory   _____
3. tomato   _____
4. bush   _____
5. rodeo   _____
6. highway   _____
7. grade   _____
8. knife   _____
9. berry   _____
10. reef   _____

11. wolf   _____
12. foot   _____
13. castle   _____
14. sheriff _____
15. decoy   _____
16. cactus   _____
17. hobo   _____
18. box   _____
19. folio   _____
20. penny   _____

21. wish   _____
22. fish   _____
23. turkey   _____
24. trousers _____
25. half   _____
26. volcano _____
27. idea   _____
28. radio   _____
29. cuff   _____
30. man   _____

B Write the number of the rule used to make each plural noun.

_10_ 1. jeans
____ 2. oxen
____ 3. ambitions
____ 4. holidays
____ 5. deer
____ 6. cameos
____ 7. peaches
____ 8. zeroes
____ 9. zoos
____ 10. teeth

____ 11. pants
____ 12. wives
____ 13. branches
____ 14. ponies
____ 15. potatoes
____ 16. tariffs
____ 17. toys
____ 18. scissors
____ 19. partners
____ 20. skeletons

____ 21. deadlines
____ 22. women
____ 23. monkeys
____ 24. heroes
____ 25. loaves
____ 26. calves
____ 27. dishes
____ 28. buzzes
____ 29. muffs
____ 30. news

____ 31. buses
____ 32. geese
____ 33. lives
____ 34. leaves
____ 35. owners
____ 36. beefs
____ 37. buffaloes
____ 38. alleys
____ 39. chiefs
____ 40. mice

Recognizing Proper Nouns

A proper noun is a noun that names a specific person, place, or thing. A proper noun begins with a capital letter.

EXAMPLES: a. The <u>girl</u> is the winner.   *"Girl" is a common noun.*

b. <u>Sharon</u> is the winner.   *"Sharon" names a specific person and is a proper noun.*

A Write "c" beside each common noun. Write "p" beside each proper noun.

__c__	1. bridge	_____	6. teacher	_____	11. Ms. Shaw	_____	16. car
_____	2. Yankees	_____	7. London Bridge	_____	12. Saturn	_____	17. student
_____	3. Monopoly	_____	8. game	_____	13. Tuesday	_____	18. idea
_____	4. Cindy	_____	9. day	_____	14. school	_____	19. Chevy
_____	5. English	_____	10. book	_____	15. team	_____	20. planet

B Underline each noun which should be capitalized.

1. The <u>white house</u> is in <u>washington</u>.
2. We poured the cement.
3. We ate some white grapes.
4. I visited chicago last spring.
5. Her house is white and blue.
6. Have you seen the golden gate bridge?
7. Tony and jan got married friday.
8. We watched our team play softball.
9. Jim's new car is a ford.
10. The inventor was thomas edison.
11. My sister, anne, works at J. C. penney.
12. I think the grand canyon is amazing.
13. Bob climbed the large staircase.
14. He was in the empire state building.
15. The sears tower is higher.
16. Marcy lives on barnes road.
17. We visited sun valley in november.
18. I could see the statue of liberty.
19. I like to watch robins and blue jays.
20. We saw them at busch gardens.
21. Ryan's birthday is either in july or in august.
22. Abe lincoln was an outstanding president.
23. We swam in mallard lake on our vacation.
24. The team captain is james martin.

C Write a proper noun(s) in each blank. Remember to capitalize proper nouns.

1. We ate lunch at ___*Sardi's*___ .
2. We went to _____ and _____ last year.
3. My dad's favorite car is a _____ .
4. We watched _____ on television.
5. _____ is my favorite board game.
6. Last night we ordered from _____ .
7. My best friend, _____ , has a date.
8. _____ and _____ won the round.
9. London is the home of _____ Bridge.
10. Mom always buys _____ chips.
11. She also uses _____ baking soda.
12. We named our new puppy _____ .
13. Our favorite station is in _____ .
14. Our family buys groceries at _____ .
15. I want to attend _____ College.
16. James attends _____ Tech.
17. Four people from the _____ Company arrived.
18. They named their new baby _____
19. His last name is _____ .
20. My grandmother lives in _____ .
21. She was born in _____ .
22. The summer months are _____ , _____ , and _____ .
23. His dentist is _____ .
24. We live on _____ Street.
25. I like to study about the country of _____ .
26. Carol has a dress from _____ .

Unit 22 cont'd ⟶

Proper Nouns

A proper noun names a particular person, place, or thing. It is capitalized.

EXAMPLES: a. This is <u>Eric Davison</u>. c. <u>France</u> is my home.
b. <u>Paul</u> drives a <u>Pontiac</u>. d. We visited <u>Ohio</u> and <u>Utah</u>.

 Underline the proper nouns. Each sentence contains at least one.

1. My house is on <u>Pennsylvania</u> <u>Avenue</u>.
2. The man ordered a Pepsi.
3. Dr. Wesley is my neighbor.
4. Napoleon lived in France.
5. Our club watched Superman.
6. John bought a new book.
7. Kathy will bring the Fritos.
8. Where is Charlie Brown?
9. The girl bought Cracker Jacks.
10. Chicago is a big city.
11. The Dr. Pepper is too sweet.
12. The cartoon is about Donald Duck.
13. This bus goes to Jackson Street.
14. We shopped at Macy's.
15. Dan lives in Senath, Missouri.
16. Tomorrow will be Saturday.
17. Today we'll read about England.
18. Linda is Bob's sister.
19. The house on Kate Street burned.
20. Karen is in St. Joseph's Hospital.
21. Tomorrow we are going to Central Park.
22. Mrs. Denson moved to New York.
23. We ate lunch at Wendy's.
24. My mom was born in Australia.
25. Snoopy is everyone's favorite.
26. Jill is a good friend.
27. That pen is a Bic.
28. Capt. King is our pilot.
29. The lady lives in Denver.
30. Look in Webster's store.
31. Our school is on Woodward Avenue.
32. Let's read Robinson's novel.
33. The monkey likes Dennis.
34. Texas is a big state.
35. Mrs. Johnson was angry with us.
36. Daniel and Kay were chosen.
37. The next street is Camden Avenue.
38. The train left Boston on time.
39. He robbed Second National Bank.
40. The store is on Horace Street.
41. Aunt Dee is from Hawaii.
42. We studied World War II.
43. Jerry is Don's brother.
44. My grandmother lives in Alabama.
45. Let's go to Winslow Park Zoo.
46. He attends West High School.
47. Mattel makes good toys.
48. Our class will visit Reeve's Donut Shop.
49. May I introduce Capt. Jay Turney?
50. Tuesday is the last day in April.

COMPOSITION EXERCISE

List 20 proper nouns.

1. _____ 6. _____ 11. _____ 16. _____
2. _____ 7. _____ 12. _____ 17. _____
3. _____ 8. _____ 13. _____ 18. _____
4. _____ 9. _____ 14. _____ 19. _____
5. _____ 10. _____ 15. _____ 20. _____

Plurals of Proper Nouns

Most proper nouns form the plural by adding "s."

EXAMPLES: a. Ann   Anns
          b. Smith   Smiths
          c. Ford   Fords

If a proper noun ends in "s," add "es" to form the plural.

EXAMPLES: Thomas Thomases

A Write the plural of each proper noun.

1. Mary   **Marys**
2. George
3. Chevrolet
4. Houston
5. Jones
6. Weston
7. Denver

8. Ross
9. Jean
10. Kate
11. Baker
12. New York
13. American
14. James

15. Betsy
16. Roy
17. Pontiac
18. Chicago
19. November
20. Cadillac
21. Monday

B Rewrite each sentence changing the proper noun to plural.

1. There are three boys in my class named Frank.

_____

2. There are two girls in the choir named Jill.

_____

3. There are fifty-two days named Monday in a year.

_____

4. I met four boys named Edward today.

_____

5. There are four cities in the United States named Jonesboro.

_____

Unit 23 cont'd

Distinguishing Between Common and Proper Nouns

A common noun is the name of a person, place, or thing. A proper noun names a specific person, place, or thing. A proper noun begins with a capital letter.

EXAMPLES: The car crossed the bridge.   "Bridge" is a common noun.
The car crossed Tower Bridge.   "Bridge" is part of the name of a specific bridge; it is a proper noun in this sentence.

A Underline each noun that should be capitalized as a proper noun.

1. This is the Hudson river.
2. We live on east Street.
3. He's a member of the atlanta Braves.
4. The potomac river is in washington, D.C.
5. The tour went to rome, london, and paris.
6. Those cities are in Italy, england, and france.
7. They'll play in Chicago stadium.
8. The business is in albany, new york.
9. Have you seen the liberty bell?
10. Was our country discovered by columbus?
11. He drives a buick.
12. My favorite holiday is christmas.
13. We work out on tuesday.
14. My uncle writes a column for *newsweek*.
15. The united nations building is closed on holidays.
16. Have you seen niagara falls in autumn?
17. The most beautiful scenery is in hawaii.
18. We studied the bill of rights.
19. Turn left at elm street.
20. He is president of the lions club.

B After each common noun, write a proper noun which is a more specific form.

1. city   *Denver*   13. country
2. girl   14. holiday
3. baby   15. island
4. dog   16. magazine
5. book   17. river
6. language   18. mountain
7. car   19. newspaper
8. lake   20. park
9. month   21. club
10. friend   22. school
11. president   23. team
12. neighbor   24. monument

COMPOSITION EXERCISE

Select 12 common and proper nouns from part B. Write a sentence with each one.

1. _____
2. _____
3. _____
4. _____
5. _____
6. _____
7. _____
8. _____
9. _____
10. _____
11. _____
12. _____

Compound Words

A compound word is two words combined to make one word.

EXAMPLES: a. paintbrush
           b. bedroom
           c. football

A Which two words make up each compound word?

1. airport	*air*	*port*
2. downtown		
3. fingerprint		
4. strawberry		
5. suitcase		
6. playmate		
7. become		
8. nearby		
9. without		
10. rowboat		
11. classroom		
12. buttermilk		
13. crossword		
14. goldfish		
15. woodland		
16. houseboat		
17. daylight		
18. toothpick		
19. fireplace		
20. nevermore		

21. slowpoke		
22. upstairs		
23. grapevine		
24. sidewalk		
25. homesick		
26. landslide		
27. chalkboard		
28. deadline		
29. highway		
30. yardstick		
31. wishbone		
32. sunset		
33. driveway		
34. fairground		
35. reindeer		
36. hardware		
37. birthday		
38. seaweed		
39. meanwhile		
40. flashlight		

B Write the plural of each word.

1. toothbrush	*toothbrushes*
2. strawberry	
3. airport	
4. birthday	
5. warehouse	
6. sidewalk	
7. grapevine	
8. highway	
9. doorbell	
10. storybook	

11. firefly	
12. classroom	
13. baseball	
14. horseshoe	
15. housewife	
16. fireplace	
17. battleship	
18. cupcake	
19. songbird	
20. handcuff	

Unit 24 cont'd

Using Compound Words

A compound word is two words combined to make one word.

EXAMPLES: a. catfish   d. notebook
           b. into   e. housecoat
           c. pancake   f. cowboy

 In each row combine two words to make a compound word that will complete the sentence.

1. (a) light   (b) dark   (c) flash   (d) stop   Hand me the ___*flashlight*___.
2. (a) side   (b) over   (c) walk   (d) run   She's sweeping the _____.
3. (a) draw   (b) out   (c) paint   (d) with   I _____ my objection.
4. (a) pop   (b) core   (c) corn   (d) hop   We ate _____ and candy.
5. (a) what   (b) some   (c) why   (d) where   Are you going _____ ?
6. (a) over   (b) stand   (c) under   (d) sit   He didn't _____ the question.
7. (a) in   (b) line   (c) out   (d) circle _____ the next chapter.
8. (a) wall   (b) door   (c) knob   (d) bell   Ring the _____ again.
9. (a) word   (b) phrase (c) cross   (d) letter Dale likes to work _____ puzzles.
10. (a) up   (b) stairs (c) steps   (d) over   Your room is _____.
11. (a) night (b) star   (c) day   (d) light   We still have two hours of _____.
12. (a) teeth (b) tooth   (c) brush   (d) cloth   I can't find my _____.
13. (a) yellow (b) gold   (c) bronze (d) fish   My cat ate my _____.
14. (a) rail   (b) street (c) road   (d) path   We should stop at _____ crossings.
15. (a) skillet (b) pan   (c) pot   (d) cakes   Jill likes _____ for breakfast.
16. (a) novel (b) store   (c) shop   (d) book   Sam works at the _____.
17. (a) pass   (b) past   (c) word   (d) passed Do you know the _____?
18. (a) snow   (b) coat   (c) rain   (d) sun   Don't forget your _____.
19. (a) die   (b) died   (c) dead   (d) line   The _____ is Wednesday.
20. (a) him   (b) self   (c) selves (d) he   James _____ said so.
21. (a) board (b) drive   (c) plank   (d) way   The truck blocked the _____.
22. (a) eraser (b) board   (c) chalk   (d) blue   Write the answer on the _____.
23. (a) short (b) stop   (c) long   (d) go   Dianne will play _____.
24. (a) side   (b) below   (c) inner   (d) in   Please come _____.
25. (a) butter (b) cheese (c) milk   (d) sour   Do you like _____?
26. (a) sky   (b) plane   (c) air   (d) cloud   I have never ridden an _____.
27. (a) ball   (b) base   (c) bat   (d) glove   Let's play _____.
28. (a) class (b) desk   (c) room   (d) book   The _____ was locked.
29. (a) rain   (b) flower (c) sun   (d) heat   I brought you a _____.
30. (a) ill   (b) sick   (c) house   (d) home   Pete is _____ for Texas.
31. (a) born   (b) birth   (c) week   (d) day   Joe's _____ is June 23.
32. (a) high   (b) low   (c) lane   (d) way   The dog ran across the _____.
33. (a) throat (b) tie   (c) neck   (d) arm   I bought Dad a _____.
34. (a) cup   (b) cake   (c) cookie (d) loaf   Have another _____.
35. (a) place (b) stick   (c) fire   (d) match   All of us sat around the _____.

Changing Compound to Plurals

When a compound noun is changed to plural, only the last part of the word undergoes the change.

EXAMPLES:
a. football   footballs   c. mailman   mailmen
b. yourself   yourselves   d. ballgown   ballgowns

 Write the plural of each word.

1. cowboy   *cowboys*
2. railroad
3. cornstalk
4. nightgown
5. crossword
6. storybook
7. grapevine
8. yardstick
9. flagship
10. raincoat
11. doorknob
12. birthday
13. bathroom
14. milkmaid
15. hallway
16. gentleman
17. footprint
18. necktie
19. postman
20. sunset
21. driveway
22. spaceman
23. wishbone
24. housecoat
25. chalkboard

26. sandman
27. sidewalk
28. broomstick
29. toothbrush
30. password
31. classroom
32. deadline
33. toothpick
34. playground
35. pancake
36. housecoat
37. policeman
38. spaceship
39. baseball
40. blackbird
41. highway
42. steamship
43. cupcake
44. bookstore
45. girlfriend
46. battleship
47. busboy
48. calfskin
49. songbird
50. firefly

COMPOSITION EXERCISE

List 10 compound words not used in today's exercise. Then write the plural of each word.

1. _____ _____
2. _____ _____
3. _____ _____
4. _____ _____
5. _____ _____

6. _____ _____
7. _____ _____
8. _____ _____
9. _____ _____
10. _____ _____

Unit 25 cont'd

Plurals of Compound Words

When a compound word is changed to plural, only the second part of the word undergoes the change.

EXAMPLES: a. hallway   hallways
b. gentleman   gentlemen

A Underline the correct plural form of each compound word. Then write it in the blank to complete the sentence.

1. a. feetprint   b. <u>footprints</u>   c. We followed the ___*footprints*___ to the cave.
2. a. Birthdays   b. Birthsday   c. _____ are fun.
3. a. crossesword   b. crosswords   c. I like to work _____.
4. a. raincoats   b. rainscoat   c. Jason has three yellow _____.
5. a. butterflies   b. buttersfly   c. Sue caught two big _____.
6. a. wishesbone   b. wishbones   c. Some people believe _____ bring luck.
7. a. neckstie   b. neckties   c. My dad received four _____.
8. a. sideswalk   b. sidewalks   c. The _____ need sweeping.
9. a. toothbrushes   b. teethbrush   c. Did you bring your _____?
10. a. watersmelon   b. watermelons   c. We picked _____.
11. a. baseballs   b. basesball   c. Our class is selling _____.
12. a. highsway   b. highways   c. The _____ intersect here.
13. a. cupcakes   b. cupscake   c. Who made the _____?
14. a. playgrounds   b. playsground   c. Keep our _____ clean.
15. a. deadsline   b. deadlines   c. What are the contests' _____?
16. a. newspapers   b. newsspaper   c. I deliver _____.
17. a. grapesfruit   b. grapefruits   c. Mary bought six _____.
18. a. horsesshoe   b. horseshoes   c. These are _____.
19. a. doorbells   b. doorsbell   c. My uncle makes _____.
20. a. handcuffs   b. handscuff   c. The officer dropped the _____.

Some compound words are hyphenated. Such words change the first parts of the words to form the plural.

B Write the plural of the compound word to complete each sentence.

(brother-in-law)   1. Sandra has four _____.

(sister-in-law)   2. Both his _____ are attorneys.

(father-in-law)   3. We invited our _____ to play golf.

(mother-in-law)   4. Their _____ are good friends.

Comprehension Check

(A) Complete each rule by writing "a," "b," "c," or "d" in the blanks.

a. add "es."   b. add "s."   c. completely.   d. singular and plural forms.

_b_ 1. Nouns ending in a vowel plus "y"
___ 2. Nouns ending in "ch," "sh," "z," "s," "ss," or "x"
___ 3. Some nouns ending in "f" or "ff"
___ 4. Nouns ending in a consonant plus "o"
___ 5. Nouns ending in "f" or "fe" change the "f" or "fe" to "v" and
___ 6. Some nouns change their spellings
___ 7. Most nouns
___ 8. Nouns ending in a consonant plus "y" change "y" to "i" and
___ 9. Some nouns stay the same in both the
___ 10. Nouns ending in a vowel plus "o"

(B) Write the plural of each noun.

1. desk	_desks_	13. party	___	25. deer	___
2. wife	___	14. pizza	___	26. cookie	___
3. tooth	___	15. group	___	27. buzz	___
4. dress	___	16. cola	___	28. dream	___
5. ox	___	17. scissors	___	29. mouse	___
6. jeans	___	18. roof	___	30. hero	___
7. bus	___	19. moose	___	31. jewel	___
8. buffalo	___	20. cuff	___	32. church	___
9. chief	___	21. monkey	___	33. singer	___
10. partner	___	22. spy	___	34. candy	___
11. goose	___	23. alley	___	35. giraffe	___
12. English	___	24. fox	___	36. wolf	___

(C) Underline each proper noun. Some sentences do not contain proper nouns.

1. I saw dr. greeley.
2. This is first united bank.
3. We bought a cadillac.
4. The painting is by willis rogers.
5. Did they visit france?
6. Is beth giving a birthday party?
7. Jeannette lives in chicago, illinois.
8. The house on benton avenue is for sale.
9. Our math teacher is mrs. hart.
10. The swallows returned to the island.
11. We shopped in denver.
12. I told ben the secret.
13. Place the order with the watkins company.
14. Do you play tennis?
15. Happy birthday, lora!
16. Reverend kenney is speaking.
17. Alicia moved from kentucky to virginia.
18. Read about george washington carver.
19. I enjoy watching rich little perform.
20. Can you see mercury tonight?
21. His middle name is lee.
22. Go to the discount store.
23. We'll ski at vail, colorado in january.
24. Susan watches reruns of *The waltons.*

Test 5 cont'd

Comprehension Check (continued)

D Write the plural of each proper noun.

1. Kim	*Kims*	11. Tuesday	_____
2. Ford	_____	12. Jones	_____
3. Dad	_____	13. Mary	_____
4. Fred	_____	14. Liberty Bell	_____
5. James	_____	15. *Time*	_____
6. April	_____	16. Easter	_____
7. Paris	_____	17. Blue Lake	_____
8. Russ	_____	18. Chicago	_____
9. Cheryl	_____	19. Christmas	_____
10. Oak Street	_____	20. Wallace	_____

E Connect the words to make a compound word.

1. fire	a. stick
2. yard	b. room
3. neck	c. ground
4. class	d. fly
5. fair	e. tie
6. birth	f. deer
7. rein	g. line
8. tooth	h. day
9. dead	i. pick
10. side	j. walk

F Complete the sentences with the plural form of each compound word in part E.

1. We'll use our ____*yardsticks*____ to measure the rooms.
2. We have three _____ to meet in February.
3. All of the _____ on this street are cracked.
4. Sandy dropped the box of colored _____ .
5. Santa Claus' _____ will pull the sleigh.
6. The _____ are lighting the night.
7. All of his _____ are striped.
8. The carnival will travel to several _____ this season.
9. There are four _____ in our family in March.
10. Are the _____ empty by 4:00 p.m.?

G Write the plural of each compound word.

1. brother-in-law _____
2. sister-in-law _____
3. mother-in-law _____
4. father-in-law _____

Write a paragraph about your family. Use the plural form of at least one of the words in part G.

_____
_____
_____
_____
_____
_____
_____
_____

Nouns of Ownership

A singular noun shows ownership by adding an apostrophe plus "s." A plural noun usually shows ownership by adding an apostrophe (').

EXAMPLES: a. *George's dad likes to fish.*   c. *The lawyer's office was large.*
            b. *The toys' colors were bright.*   d. *Tom's grades are terrible.*

✳ If the underlined noun is singular, add an apostrophe plus "s." If the underlined noun is plural, add an apostrophe after the "s."

1. *The dog's name is Theo.*
2. The <u>tables</u> legs were metal.
3. <u>Sam</u> mother is here.
4. The <u>car</u> lights are on.
5. The <u>owners</u> names are here.
6. This is my <u>sister</u> room.
7. The <u>cats</u> house is gone.
8. These <u>programs</u> titles are funny.
9. The <u>table</u> leg is broken.
10. The <u>lawyer</u> office is there.
11. The <u>story</u> ending was happy.
12. The <u>kittens</u> claws are sharp.
13. The <u>coat</u> pocket was torn.
14. These <u>books</u> pages are yellow.
15. All of the <u>stores</u> doors were locked.
16. <u>Danny</u> bike was stolen.
17. The <u>boat</u> motor stalled.
18. The <u>chief</u> hat was stolen.
19. The <u>cat</u> toy is missing.
20. The <u>knives</u> edges are sharp.
21. Our <u>mothers</u> tempers are flaring.
22. The <u>gate</u> lock is broken.
23. Mr. <u>Taylor</u> car is ready.
24. He took the <u>baby</u> chair.
25. The <u>girl</u> brother is waiting.

26. The <u>farmers</u> crops are ready.
27. <u>Katy</u> bus is always late.
28. We saw the <u>lights</u> glow.
29. Phil is <u>Sally</u> neighbor.
30. The <u>road</u> surface is rough.
31. Where is <u>George</u> house?
32. <u>Peter</u> answers were correct.
33. Those <u>clowns</u> faces look real.
34. The <u>book</u> cover is red.
35. Each <u>room</u> floor was waxed.
36. The brick hit the <u>store</u> window.
37. <u>Karen</u> mom is a doctor.
38. I heard the <u>train</u> whistle.
39. The <u>teachers</u> meetings are tomorrow.
40. This is <u>Jay</u> boat.
41. I pulled the <u>monkey</u> tail.
42. The <u>bike</u> tires are flat.
43. The <u>woman</u> money disappeared.
44. The <u>tests</u> questions were difficult.
45. <u>Sandy</u> paper was the best.
46. This is my <u>friend</u> house.
47. Those <u>curtains</u> hems are torn.
48. <u>Barry</u> coat is blue and yellow.
49. The <u>elephant</u> home is in India.
50. Did you hear the <u>man</u> warning?

COMPOSITION EXERCISE

List 10 singular nouns which show ownership and 10 plural nouns which show ownership.

singular		plural	
1. _____	6. _____	1. _____	6. _____
2. _____	7. _____	2. _____	7. _____
3. _____	8. _____	3. _____	8. _____
4. _____	9. _____	4. _____	9. _____
5. _____	10. _____	5. _____	10. _____

Unit 26 cont'd →

Possessives

A singular noun shows ownership by adding an apostrophe plus "s."

EXAMPLE: Karen   Karen's

A plural noun shows ownership by adding an apostrophe after the "s."

EXAMPLE: farmers   farmers'

A Choose the correct possessive form to complete each sentence.

1. The _____ c _____ room is a mess.
  a. childs   b. childs'   c. child's   d. child

2. There is the _____ mask.
  a. thief's   b. thieves   c. thieves'   d. thiefs

3. Have you seen the _____ purse?
  a. ladies   b. lady's   c. ladies'   d. ladys'

4. _____ tail is too long.
  a. It's   b. It   c. Its   d. Its'

5. The _____ shoes are tiny.
  a. baby's   b. babies   c. babys'   d. babie's

6. The _____ badges are missing.
  a. officers'   b. officers   c. officers's   d. officer'

7. Did you take _____ books?
  a. Ann   b. Anns'   c. Ann's   d. Anns's

8. I saw the _____ pictures.
  a. students   b. students's   c. student's'   d. students'

9. No one remembered _____ birthday.
  a. Julies's   b. Julie's   c. Julies'   d. Julie

10. _____ car is beautiful.
  a. Hank's   b. Hank   c. Hanks'   d. Hanks's

B Complete each sentence with a noun that shows ownership.

1. _____ *Steve's* _____ hair is brown.
2. _____ shoes are expensive.
3. The _____ team beat the boys' team.
4. We like to listen to _____ records.
5. My _____ friend is a cheerleader.
6. The _____ tractor is in the field.
7. The _____ laughter was amusing.
8. How long is the _____ trunk?
9. I enjoyed the _____ half-time performance.
10. The _____ concert is set for Sunday afternoon.
11. The _____ voice kept fading.
12. We like _____ house.
13. The _____ trucks are green.
14. His _____ job involves traveling.
15. The _____ feathers flew all over the place.
16. Look at the _____ crown.
17. Our _____ desk is covered with test papers.
18. The _____ drawings are good.
19. Where are the _____ uniforms?
20. She broke the _____ arm.
21. The _____ tire is flat.
22. The _____ fur is shedding.

Possessive Forms of Nouns Unit 27

Nouns that show ownership take the possessive form. Singular nouns form the possessive by adding an apostrophe and an "s."

A Copy each of the word groups below, adding an apostrophe and an "s."

1. girl notebook _____
2. lady hat _____
3. calf collar _____
4. car engine _____

Plural nouns ending in "s" form the possessive by adding only an apostrophe. Plural nouns not ending in "s" add both an apostrophe and an "s."

B Fill in the blank with the correct possessive form for the plural noun before it.

1. girls__'__ notebooks
2. ladies____ hats
3. calves____ collars

4. children____ toys
5. mice____ tails
6. men____ shoes

When the singular form of a noun ends in "s," we may show the possessive by adding only an apostrophe or by adding an apostrophe and an "s."

C Copy each example to form the possessive twice, as described above.

1. Miss Jones ___*Miss Jones'*___ OR_____
2. Thomas _____ OR_____
3. Mr. Matthews _____ OR_____
4. Mrs. Fields _____ OR_____

D After each sentence below, write the noun that shows ownership and the object owned. Use the possessive form.

EXAMPLE: The tails of rabbits are short.   rabbits' tails

1. The car of my cousin is new. ____*cousin's car*_____
2. A friend of Mary is here. _____
3. These pencils belong to Bill. _____
4. This book is owned by Charles. _____
5. Those coats belong to the boys. _____
6. The radio is owned by two men. _____

Unit 27 cont'd →

Plurals and Possessives

A singular noun shows possession by adding an apostrophe plus "s."

EXAMPLES: woman   woman's

Most plural nouns show possession by adding only an apostrophe.

EXAMPLES: houses   houses'

Some plural nouns show possession by adding an apostrophe plus "s."

EXAMPLES: children   children's

A Write the plural of each word.

1. banana *bananas*	26. mouse _____	51. cactus _____
2. business _____	27. child _____	52. life _____
3. author _____	28. mosquito _____	53. cuff _____
4. wolf _____	29. radio _____	54. enemy _____
5. copy _____	30. company _____	55. chimney _____
6. sandwich _____	31. visitor _____	56. city _____
7. scissors _____	32. sign _____	57. spoon _____
8. library _____	33. delay _____	58. house _____
9. envelope _____	34. pants _____	59. half _____
10. circle _____	35. skeleton _____	60. trousers _____
11. knife _____	36. wife _____	61. echo _____
12. witch _____	37. sketch _____	62. lunch _____
13. victory _____	38. zoo _____	63. shelf _____
14. berry _____	39. breeze _____	64. book _____
15. attorney _____	40. fox _____	65. lamp _____
16. leaf _____	41. branch _____	66. watch _____
17. magazine _____	42. ox _____	67. animal _____
18. ghost _____	43. tomato _____	68. bus _____
19. theory _____	44. insect _____	69. window _____
20. buffalo _____	45. problem _____	70. day _____
21. class _____	46. volunteer _____	71. luxury _____
22. news _____	47. thief _____	72. box _____
23. museum _____	48. table _____	73. loaf _____
24. deadline _____	49. pencil _____	74. highway _____
25. sky _____	50. potato _____	75. chair _____

B Write the possessive form of each word.

1. he *his*	9. Tony _____	17. chimney _____
2. children _____	10. citizen _____	18. river _____
3. Cathi _____	11. you _____	19. puppy _____
4. we _____	12. George _____	20. ant _____
5. baby _____	13. wind _____	21. Mark _____
6. car _____	14. monkeys _____	22. Jones _____
7. Mr. Kent _____	15. tree _____	23. hero _____
8. fox _____	16. mother _____	24. mouse _____
		25. I _____

Articles

"The" *is a definite article.* **"A"** *is an indefinite article. It is used in front of a noun that begins with a consonant sound.* **"An"** *is an indefinite article. It is used in front of a noun that begins with a vowel sound.*

EXAMPLES: *a. The room was empty.*   *c. I need an ink pen.*
           b. Did you hear a scream?   *d. This is the best one.*

 Write either "a," "an," or "the" in the blanks.

1. Alex is ___*a*___ shrewd man.
2. This book is _____ almanac.
3. Did you see _____ explosion?
4. _____ mystery was solved.
5. _____ deed has been signed.
6. I saw _____ mermaid.
7. When is _____ deadline?
8. ____ aardvark is ____ animal.
9. _____ statement is not true.
10. Diane is _____ nurse.
11. Who made _____ decision?
12. He is _____ bitter person.
13. I heard _____ echo.
14. Mr. Jackson is _____ owner.
15. _____ people will rebel.
16. Connie is _____ guest.
17. I voted for _____ amendment.
18. George is _____ unhappy boy.
19. It was _____ long journey.
20. I disapprove of _____ plan.
21. We found _____ empty box.
22. _____ magician is ____ fake.
23. _____ monster was enormous.
24. Mother sang _____ lullaby.
25. I will explain _____ problem.

26. That is _____ old automobile.
27. _____ river is wide and deep.
28. I need _____ spoon.
29. Did you take _____ money?
30. I love to watch _____ monkeys.
31. _____ angry bull chased us.
32. Let's have _____ snack.
33. It was _____ important meeting.
34. _____ trip was cancelled.
35. He is _____ famous poet.
36. We need _____ clue.
37. Where was _____ treasure?
38. I forgot _____ combination.
39. You must choose _____ career.
40. _____ bottle has ____ green cap.
41. Do you have _____ opinion?
42. It's _____ ordinary house.
43. That was _____ stupid joke.
44. I know _____ way.
45. We are _____ family.
46. Give me _____ answer.
47. _____ cartoon was nonsense.
48. Bring your father _____ wrench.
49. I don't know _____ password.
50. ____ dungeon was cold and dark.

COMPOSITION EXERCISE

Write 10 sentences which contain "the," "a," or "an."

1. _____
2. _____
3. _____
4. _____
5. _____

6. _____
7. _____
8. _____
9. _____
10. _____

Unit 28 cont'd ➡

Using "A" and "An"

"A" *is used before nouns which begin with consonant sounds.*
"An" *is used before nouns which begin with vowel sounds.*

EXAMPLES: a. a book   c. an article
               b. a vacancy   d. an elephant

 Write "a" or "an" in each blank.

1. _an_ invitation
2. ____ leather belt
3. ____ amusement park
4. ____ occupation
5. ____ magazine
6. ____ diamond necklace
7. ____ banana
8. ____ parachute
9. ____ kitchen
10. ____ strange pattern
11. ____ elevator
12. ____ anniversary
13. ____ worm
14. ____ mountain
15. ____ inspection
16. ____ hot sidewalk
17. ____ beautiful day
18. ____ escort
19. ____ bridge
20. ____ escaped convict
21. ____ victory
22. ____ dirty window
23. ____ outstanding citizen
24. ____ ditch
25. ____ insect
26. ____ wizard
27. ____ empty jar
28. ____ newspaper
29. ____ handkerchief
30. ____ exercise
31. ____ owner
32. ____ luxury
33. ____ expensive gift

34. ____ cafeteria
35. ____ headache
36. ____ agreement
37. ____ movie
38. ____ journey
39. ____ tall man
40. ____ announcement
41. ____ museum
42. ____ business
43. ____ author
44. ____ sandwich
45. ____ taxi
46. ____ lawyer
47. ____ problem
48. ____ office
49. ____ camera
50. ____ wet sponge
51. ____ jewelry store
52. ____ afternoon
53. ____ odd person
54. ____ volunteer
55. ____ envelope
56. ____ owl
57. ____ dictionary
58. ____ assignment
59. ____ feather
60. ____ opinion
61. ____ ghost
62. ____ spy
63. ____ amendment
64. ____ world map
65. ____ orchestra
66. ____ acorn

67. ____ uninvited guest
68. ____ solution
69. ____ mirror
70. ____ instrument
71. ____ opportunity
72. ____ circle
73. ____ unkind remark
74. ____ weather report
75. ____ idea
76. ____ citizen
77. ____ palace
78. ____ objective answer
79. ____ reason
80. ____ active member
81. ____ coach
82. ____ guitar
83. ____ symbol
84. ____ almanac
85. ____ needle
86. ____ long tunnel
87. ____ explosion
88. ____ costume
89. ____ excellent choice
90. ____ garage
91. ____ sign
92. ____ good book
93. ____ old friend
94. ____ adult
95. ____ cousin
96. ____ officer
97. ____ even number
98. ____ accident
99. ____ easy test

Noun Substitutes

Words used instead of nouns in a sentence are called noun substitutes. The most commonly used noun substitute is the pronoun. Unlike nouns, pronouns often change form when used in different parts of a sentence.

PRONOUN USED AS THE FOLLOWING:

SINGULAR FORM

Subject I	you	he	she	it
Direct Object .me	you	him	her	it
Possessive (with object) . . . . .my	your	his	her	its
Possessive (without object) . . . . . . .mine	yours	his	hers	(none)

PLURAL FORM

Subject . . . . .we	you	they	they	they
Direct Object .us	you	them	them	them
Possessive (with object) . . . . .our	your	their	their	their
Possessive (without object) . . . . . . .ours	yours	theirs	theirs	theirs

A Fill in the blank after each sentence by listing the form of pronoun used.

1. Harry borrowed my skates. ___*possessive*___
2. We saw Mrs. Flynn. _____
3. Don't tell him. _____
4. That book is mine._____

5. You are not to go. _____
6. Its fur was yellow. _____
7. Anne knows her. _____
8. They waved good-bye. _____

Other words may function as noun substitutes. Unlike pronouns their form does not change in use except for the possessive when " 's " is added.

EXAMPLES

each	anyone	nobody	someone	either	everybody	both	many
one	anybody	somebody	no one	neither	everyone	several	few

B Underline the noun substitutes.

1. Both came to my party.
2. Everybody is here.
3. Bill saw nobody.
4. One's word should be kept.

5. Many rode the bus.
6. Either makes a good dinner.
7. Safety is everyone's business.
8. Has anyone seen Harold?

Except for the words "both," "several," "many," and "few" the noun substitutes listed just above are regarded as singular in form.

C Underline the pronoun which agrees with the noun substitute preceding it.

1. No one believed (he, they) would fail the test.
2. Everybody will go if (she, they) can.
3. One cannot always tell when (he, they) will win a prize.
4. Several claimed that the coat was (his, theirs).
5. Both said (he, they) would go.

Unit 29 cont'd

Using Pronouns

When a pronoun functions as the subject or as the linking-verb complement of a sentence, the subject form "I," "you," "he," "she," "it," "we," or "they" is used.

A Identify the use of the pronoun in each of the following sentences. Write "sub" in the blank if it functions as a subject; write "lv-c" in the blank if it functions as a linking-verb complement.

_____ 1. She is the winner.

_____ 2. The winners are they.

_____ 3. Mr. Jones and he went fishing.

_____ 4. The soloists are Karen and I.

B Correct the following sentences by drawing a line through each misused pronoun. Write the correct form above the error. EXAMPLE: She
                                                                                                ~~Her~~ played the part well.

1. Them have won the game.

2. The losing catcher was me.

3. Joe and him are absent.

4. The two cousins in class are Linda and her.

Only in a compound subject should more than one subject word appear. The signal is a connecting word, such as the conjunction "and" or the conjunction "or."

C Identify the use of the pronoun in each sentence below. If it is part of a compound subject, write "c-s" in the blank. If it is mistakenly used to repeat the function of the subject noun, write "error" in the blank.

_____ 1. Tom and she are here.

_____ 2. Bill he is a good swimmer.

_____ 3. Either Carol or you is my partner.

_____ 4. My mother she went home.

Pronouns functioning as direct objects or objects of prepositions use the object form "me," "you," "him," "her," "it," "us," or "them."

D Complete each sentence below by underlining the correct form of the pronoun in parentheses.

1. Mother said she would take me with (she, her).

2. Louise knows (they, them) well.

3. Bring the letter to Joe and (he, him).

4. The candy is for (we, us).

It is customary to refer to "I," "me," "we," or "us" last in a compound subject or compound object.

E Using the words in parentheses, write the customary compound form in the blank space for each sentence.

1. (I, the boys) _____ were dismissed early.

2. (I, Mary, Gail) _____ will make the costumes.

3. (me, Ted, Curly) The newspapers were delivered by _____ .

4. (us, Jim) Mr. Baker congratulated _____ for rescuing the kitten.

Pronouns

Pronouns are noun substitutes. They can take the place of nouns.

EXAMPLES: a. Mrs. Rogers is our neighbor.   b. I love to watch the planes.
                She is our neighbor.   I love to watch them.

 Rewrite each sentence using a pronoun to substitute for the underlined noun or nouns.

1. <u>That girl</u> is my sister.
   She is my sister.

2. <u>The machine</u> works perfectly.

3. <u>Joshua</u> is our best player.

4. I like <u>John, Thomas, and George</u>.

5. Our class bought <u>the stove</u>.

6. <u>Sarah</u> wants to be a pilot.

7. <u>The night</u> was cold and dark.

8. The bike belongs to <u>Jim and me</u>.

9. <u>Mr. Larson</u> was my first teacher.

10. <u>A fierce wind</u> destroyed the house.

11. <u>Janice</u> moved to Boston.

12. <u>The zone</u> ends here.

13. <u>Janice and I</u> have decided to go.

14. <u>Eddie, Joe, and Bob</u> surrendered.

15. Everyone knows <u>Mr. Johnson</u>.

16. <u>The war</u> finally ended.

17. <u>Karen and I</u> are confused.

18. Mother forbids <u>gossip</u>.

19. Did anyone tell <u>Charlotte</u>?

20. <u>Your advice</u> is welcomed.

21. <u>Our guests</u> are leaving.

22. <u>The almanac</u> is missing.

23. <u>Sam and Eric</u> are greedy.

24. Who wrote <u>the motto</u>?

COMPOSITION EXERCISE

Write 12 sentences which contain pronouns.

1. _____
2. _____
3. _____
4. _____
5. _____
6. _____

7. _____
8. _____
9. _____
10. _____
11. _____
12. _____

Unit 30 cont'd →

Pronouns and Number

Pronouns may be singular (referring to one person) or plural (referring to more than one person).

EXAMPLES: *singular*

      I   your   my   he   it

    plural

      we   theirs   our   them

A Write "s" for each singular pronoun or "p" for each plural pronoun.

s	
_____ s _____	1. I
_____	2. they
_____	3. he
_____	4. her
_____	5. we
_____	6. ours
_____	7. my
_____	8. its
_____	9. him
_____	10. you
_____	11. me
_____	12. she
_____	13. it
_____	14. your
_____	15. their
_____	16. them
_____	17. us
_____	18. his
_____	19. mine
_____	20. our
_____	21. theirs
_____	22. yours
_____	23. hers
_____	24. one

B Write a pronoun in each blank. Try to use as many different pronouns as possible.

1. ____*You*____ were talking to Ben.
2. _____ mom and dad are pilots.
3. Why didn't _____ answer me?
4. _____ have been trying to call _____ .
5. All the money is now _____ .
6. _____ decided to come to the party.
7. Have you seen _____ ?
8. Didn't you see _____ ?
9. _____ sounded like a bomb to _____ .
10. _____ don't like _____ attitude.
11. _____ is _____ oldest brother.
12. These toys belong to _____ .
13. _____ wants her share.
14. _____ class is having a picnic.
15. Who told _____ to go home?
16. _____ tail is three feet long.
17. Joshua broke _____ arm.
18. _____ are my friends.
19. This room is _____ .
20. _____ names are the same.
21. _____ must stop Sam immediately.
22. Who said the present was _____ ?
23. _____ bus is always late.
24. _____ must always do his best.

COMPOSITION EXERCISE

List 10 singular pronouns and 10 plural pronouns.

singular

1. _____
2. _____
3. _____
4. _____
5. _____

6. _____
7. _____
8. _____
9. _____
10. _____

plural

1. _____
2. _____
3. _____
4. _____
5. _____

6. _____
7. _____
8. _____
9. _____
10. _____

Comprehension Check

(A) Complete each sentence with the possessive form of the word in parentheses.

(train)   1. The _____*train's*_____ whistle was loud.

(boy)   2. One _____ car was stolen.

(store)   3. The _____ windows are pretty.

(Lara)   4. Give the money to _____ dad.

(friend)   5. My _____ house is on Oak.

(TV)   6. The _____ color control broke.

(dog)   7. We have the _____ collar.

(highway)   8. Check the _____ surface.

(chair)   9. That _____ arm is broken.

(man)   10. The _____ insurance was cancelled.

(B) Write the singular and the plural possessive of each word. Then use the correct possessive form in the sentence following each word.

1. artist	*artist's*	artists	*artists'*	Four ___*artists'*___ brushes are missing.
2. cat	_____	cats	_____	That _____ food is smelly.
3. child	_____	children	_____	The _____ playground is closed.
4. guitar	_____	guitars	_____	All the _____ strings are tuned.
5. room	_____	rooms	_____	Sweep the _____ floor.
6. squad	_____	squads	_____	Five _____ scores were posted.
7. clown	_____	clowns	_____	The _____ face is funny.
8. hat	_____	hats	_____	Several _____ bands are striped.
9. church	_____	churches	_____	Do you see the _____ steeple?
10. eagle	_____	eagles	_____	An _____ eyesight is keen.

(C) Write "a" or "an" before each word.

1. __*an*__ apple
2. _____ feature
3. _____ TV
4. _____ argument
5. _____ drill
6. _____ example
7. _____ headline
8. _____ warehouse
9. _____ apology
10. _____ effort
11. _____ captain
12. _____ journey
13. _____ relative
14. _____ street
15. _____ aunt
16. _____ avenue
17. _____ condition
18. _____ uncle
19. _____ degree
20. _____ shot
21. _____ joke
22. _____ owner
23. _____ scream
24. _____ apartment

(D) Write "a," "an," or "the" in each blank.

1. Please hold ___*the*___ elevator for me.
2. I wrote you _____ letter last week.
3. _____ answer was silly.
4. It's _____ ordinary name.
5. Have you _____ opinion?
6. _____ woman is _____ teacher.
7. Carol is _____ English major.
8. I can answer _____ question.
9. Did you hear _____ echo?
10. Hand me _____ wrench.
11. I want _____ explanation.
12. It was _____ welcome change.

Test 6 cont'd →

Comprehension Check (continued)

E Underline each pronoun.

1. Karen gave <u>me</u> <u>her</u> coat.
2. Her answer was interesting.
3. They are riding in his car.
4. Trisha and she are her friends.
5. Give the keys to Alex and me.
6. Both were late for our party.
7. They ordered several.
8. No one is here to help you.
9. One will be enough for us.
10. This is ours.
11. It is they.
12. One will be the answer.

F Underline the correct pronoun in the parentheses.

1. Tell (I, <u>me</u>) the story.
2. (Her, She) is Kay's sister.
3. Brian and (we, us) will vote now.
4. Give the money to (he, him).
5. (Them, They) will call soon.
6. We asked for Alice and (her, she).
7. Gail, Neta, and (I, me) will sing.
8. The mail is for (us, we).
9. I know (them, they).
10. Serena and (she, her) rode the bus.
11. Tami and (he, him) are going steady.
12. It is (they, them) who are wrong.

G Rewrite each sentence; replace the underlined word(s) in each sentence with a pronoun.

1. <u>The wind</u> destroyed <u>our flowers</u>.   *It destroyed them.* _____
2. The coach gave <u>the award</u> to <u>Rick</u>. _____
3. <u>That kitten's</u> paw is hurt. _____
4. Give <u>the ticket</u> to <u>Sarah</u>. _____
5. <u>Sandra</u> called <u>Ted</u>. _____
6. <u>Susan and Chris</u> got married. _____
7. Tell <u>Karen and me</u> the story. _____
8. We saw <u>Tammy and Roger</u> arrive. _____
9. <u>This book</u> is <u>Jan's</u>. _____
10. <u>Allen and I</u> were wrong. _____
11. <u>Barry and Tim</u> are working. _____
12. <u>The store</u> is closed today. _____

Write a paragraph describing one of your relatives. Underline each pronoun.

_____
_____
_____
_____
_____
_____
_____
_____

Pronouns as Subjects

A pronoun may be used as the subject of a sentence.

EXAMPLES: Monica walked to school.   "Monica" is a noun and is the subject of the sentence.
She walked to school.   "She" is a pronoun and is the subject of the sentence.

A Use these pronouns as subjects.

I	you	he	she	it	we	they

1. Bob is the president.   _**He**_ is the president.
2. My sister popped the popcorn.   _____ popped the popcorn.
3. The rain poured down all day.   _____ poured down all day.
4. The old house fell down last year. _____ fell down last year.
5. A nice lady took our order.   _____ took our order.
6. Ken and I walked Jenny to the car. _____ walked Jenny to the car.
7. Jill got a new skateboard.   _____ got a new skateboard.
8. James is buying a bike.   _____ is buying a bike.
9. Mary talked to the group.   _____ talked to the group.
10. Steve and Sara were elected.   _____ were elected.

B Read each pair of sentences. Each second sentence has a pronoun as its subject. The pronoun replaces a noun in the first sentence. Underline the nouns they replace.

1. Popeye loves Olive Oyl.   He fights with Bruno.
2. Chris bought cotton candy.   It was so sticky!
3. Please come here, Mary.   You need to see this.
4. The baby kicked off the booties.   He loves to kick his legs.
5. We gave Erin a surprise party.   She was truly surprised.
6. Our family had a picnic.   We enjoy being outdoors.
7. Eggs are good for breakfast.   They provide iron in our diets.
8. Eddie and John shared a sandwich. They shared a sandwich.
9. Martha Washington was a good hostess. She had many guests.
10. We watched the rain fall.   It came down in sheets.
11. My sisters are selfish.   They never share their dessert.
12. Leslie eats an apple each day.   It keeps the doctor away.

COMPOSITION EXERCISE

Write two sentences for each pronoun. Use the pronouns as subjects.

1. we _____   4. it _____

_____   _____

2. they _____   5. you _____

_____   _____

3. I _____   6. she _____

_____   _____

Unit 31 cont'd

Pronouns as Objects

The pronouns "me," "you," "him," "her," "it," "us," and "them" may substitute for nouns used as direct objects. They are the object forms of pronouns.

A **Underline the pronouns used as direct objects in the following sentences:**

1. He told <u>us</u> to wait.
2. His grandfather taught him how to fish.
3. They washed it and repainted the edges.
4. My friend knows her very well.
5. She sent them to the store for her package.
6. Everyone wanted you to be captain.
7. Their nurse brought them to my house.
8. He asked me to go with him.

When a pronoun is part of a compound direct object, the object form is used. If the object form sounds strange, omit the noun in the compound direct object as a test of the pronoun.

B **Fill in the blank after each sentence. Write "yes" if the pronoun is used in the correct form. Write "no" if it is not.**

1. Mrs. Smith drove Carol and me to school. _____*yes*_____
2. The coach asked Jim and him to help. _____
3. Bob directed Louise and I to the bus station. _____
4. The grizzly chased the Indians and us ten miles. _____
5. The policeman wanted Jones and them. _____
6. Sandy invited Kathy and he to the party. _____

The object form of a pronoun is used after the words "with," "for," "by," "between," and "to." Mistakes are most often made when the pronoun is accompanied by a noun for a compound object.

C **In the following sentences fill in the blanks with one of the pronouns in parentheses. Be sure to choose the correct form.**

1. In the school parade Sally marched between Gary and ____*me*____. (I, me)
2. The football belongs to Tom and _____. (he, him)
3. Uncle John sent some rare stamps to Aunt Edna and _____. (we, us)
4. We talked to a movie star, who gave his autograph to Mark and _____. (she, her)
5. That airplane was built by two high school boys and _____. (they, them)
6. Miss Lewis will be riding with Mother and _____. (I, me)

D **Each of the sentences below contains a pronoun used in the object form. Write "do" in the blank if it is a direct object; write "io" if it is an indirect object; write "op" if it is an object after "with," "for," "by," "between," or "to."**

1. _____ Mark went home with Mr. Smith and her.
2. _____ The boys fixed it and rode away singing.
3. _____ Grandma brought my brother and me some fresh cookies.
4. _____ We girls are learning to play basketball with them.
5. _____ Now you owe her a favor.

Possessive Forms of Pronouns   Unit 32

Pronouns, like nouns, may indicate ownership but do not use apostrophes.
Possessive pronouns are recognized by these special forms:

my	your	his	her	our	their
mine	yours	its	hers	ours	theirs

A Underline each possessive pronoun in the following sentences.

1. My dog often hides his bones.
2. Where did you put your umbrella?
3. The green house on the corner is ours.
4. The Johnsons spent their vacation in Florida.
5. That rose has dropped its petals.
6. Their sister brought her new record album.

B Underline the possessive pronouns in the following paragraph.

My grandmother's maiden name was Hannah Hilton. She was born in a small town in Illinois where her father taught school. Because his hearing was bad, Mr. Hilton often asked his pupils to speak louder. Sometimes they spoke so loudly that their voices were heard a block away. Their shouts rattled the windows and frightened the principal. In time Great-grandfather Hilton was asked to quit teaching. He bought a pig farm with no houses nearby. "Your hearing is much worse!" shouted young Hannah. Year by year, her voice grew louder as she talked with her father. One day she went to the county fair and entered a hog-calling contest, in which she won first prize. That is why our family has always called her "Hog-Calling Hannah, the Gal from Havana," although she speaks barely above a whisper now.

An apostrophe used with a pronoun signals the contraction of a verb as follows:

you are = you're   it is = it's   they are = they're

C Read each of the following sentences carefully. Underline each possessive pronoun once and each contraction twice.

1. It's the biggest show on earth.
2. Its curtain rises at 8:30 each night.
3. The club sent me your address.
4. You're my first pen pal.
5. I think they're leaving.
6. Their car is being repaired.
7. Your house is near mine.
8. You're riding in my bus.
9. It's his first puppy.
10. See its little tail wag.
11. Did you see their signal?
12. They're marooned on an island.

A pronoun should agree with its antecedent in number when singular and plural forms differ.

EXAMPLES: girl = her, hers   I = my, mine   everybody = his
                  girls = their, theirs   we = our, ours   anyone   = his

D Write the proper possessive form in the blank space in each sentence.

1. Each boy should bring _____ own lunch.
2. All the men put _____ hats on the table.
3. Every lady believes the baby is _____.
4. Has anyone lost _____ coat?
5. We have just painted _____ house red.

Unit 32 cont'd

Pronouns of Ownership

Possessive pronouns are pronouns that show ownership.

EXAMPLES:
a. I need <u>your</u> help.
b. <u>Its</u> home is in Africa.
c. This is <u>my</u> sister.
d. I found <u>her</u> book.

 In each blank write the possessive form of the pronoun in parentheses.

(I) 1. This is ___*my*___ home.
(you) 2. _____ mother has called.
(he) 3. _____ team is losing.
(she) 4. What is _____ name?
(it) 5. Look at _____ teeth!
(we) 6. _____ class isn't going.
(they) 7. I heard _____ story.
(I) 8. The ring is _____.
(you) 9. That paper isn't _____.
(we) 10. Dave told _____ secret.
(she) 11. Susan lost _____.
(I) 12. I want _____ now.
(we) 13. Tomorrow is _____ last day.
(you) 14. Who cut _____ hair?
(they) 15. _____ name is Bergen.
(you) 16. Does he know _____ brother?
(it) 17. _____ eyes were huge.
(you) 18. Where is _____ home?
(he) 19. _____ nose was broken.
(I) 20. You can't have _____.
(she) 21. _____ plane is leaving.
(he) 22. That boat is _____.
(you) 23. The man called _____ name.
(we) 24. There goes _____ bus.
(I) 25. I left _____ at home.

(It) 26. The house lost _____ charm.
(she) 27. _____ father was furious.
(they) 28. It is _____ decision.
(I) 29. _____ throat is sore today.
(you) 30. _____ ideas are too crazy.
(I) 31. Did you see _____?
(he) 32. Have you tried _____ number?
(It) 33. _____ engine failed.
(I) 34. Someone is at _____ door.
(we) 35. Where are _____ lunches?
(it) 36. Do you like _____ colors?
(he) 37. I borrowed _____ skates.
(we) 38. Everything is _____.
(you) 39. Are _____ parents coming?
(she) 40. Will you buy _____ candy?
(he) 41. I've never seen _____ car.
(they) 42. This is _____ last chance.
(you) 43. Someone took _____.
(I) 44. I ate all of _____.
(he) 45. The hammer hit _____ hand.
(you) 46. _____ story is unbelievable.
(It) 47. _____ ending was sad.
(I) 48. _____ grades are terrible.
(she) 49. I don't want _____ desk.
(I) 50. I'm taking _____ time.

COMPOSITION EXERCISE

Write 12 sentences which contain pronouns that show ownership.

1. _____
2. _____
3. _____
4. _____
5. _____
6. _____

7. _____
8. _____
9. _____
10. _____
11. _____
12. _____

Proper Use of "I" and "Me"

"I" is used as a subject. "Me" is used as an object.

EXAMPLES: a. It was easy for me. c. I ignored the insult.
b. I am not greedy. d. She tried to discourage me.

 Write "I" or "me" in each blank.

1. ___I___ need some advice.
2. The skeleton scares _____.
3. _____ persuaded Jill to go.
4. _____ can't meet the deadline.
5. Is the letter for _____?
6. _____ borrowed the money.
7. _____ am not a mermaid.
8. Tell _____ the password.
9. _____ was not invited.
10. Don't talk to _____.
11. _____ misplaced your address.
12. _____ am very sorry.
13. The dog bit _____.
14. The bullet missed _____.
15. _____ heard an echo.
16. Will you come with _____?
17. Janice is helping _____.
18. The coat fits _____ perfectly.
19. _____ will arrive on time.
20. Do _____ know you?
21. The call was for _____.
22. Read the note to _____.
23. _____ don't remember his number.
24. _____ found an old coin.
25. She invited _____ to stay.

26. Don't spill the bleach on _____.
27. They will surrender to _____.
28. _____ am afraid of it.
29. You will assist _____.
30. Give _____ your promise.
31. May _____ help someone?
32. _____ am sure you'll like it.
33. The noise woke _____.
34. _____ am waiting for a bus.
35. _____ must leave early.
36. The kitten likes _____.
37. Did anyone call _____?
38. _____ introduced them.
39. _____ think it is nonsense.
40. You asked _____.
41. It is important to _____.
42. _____ told you the truth.
43. _____ forbid you to talk.
44. Nothing can hurt _____.
45. _____ choose to stay here.
46. _____ thought you had moved.
47. It is interesting to _____.
48. _____ was elected secretary.
49. Now _____ am confused.
50. _____ understand the assignment.

COMPOSITION EXERCISE

Write 5 sentences using "I" and 5 sentences using "me."

I	me
1. _____	1. _____
2. _____	2. _____
3. _____	3. _____
4. _____	4. _____
5. _____	5. _____

Unit 33 cont'd

Using Pronouns

Pronouns may be used as subjects and as objects. They may also show possession.

        s   io poss   s   do   op
EXAMPLES: I told her my story. She heard it from me.

A Underline each pronoun. Over each pronoun, identify its use.

    s - subject   **io - indirect object**   **poss - possession**
    do - direct object   **op - object of preposition**

        do   *op*
1. Tell <u>us</u> about <u>her</u>.

2. She is my cousin.

3. He told us her secret.

4. Janet asked them for their tickets.

5. The cat licked its paw.

6. Our cat ran away from him.

7. The rock singer played his guitar.

8. We met in our school's lunchroom.

9. You and I passed our tests.

10. Will you please open your locker?

11. I want you to go now.

12. Our friends spent their money on us.

13. Tell them about your vacation.

14. Take the keys to him.

15. We are asking you to speak to her.

16. Their car lost its front wheels.

17. Karen gave her the news.

18. We want to use his car.

19. Allen broke his arm after school.

20. Our basket of apples fell off the shelf.

B Write "s" for subject, "o" for object, and "p" for possession beside each pronoun, according to the position each may hold in a sentence.

<u>o</u> 1. me	____ 4. our	____ 7. we	____ 10. it	____ 13. her	____ 16. them
____ 2. they	____ 5. his	____ 8. you	____ 11. she	____ 14. their	____ 17. him
____ 3. us	____ 6. its	____ 9. my	____ 12. I	____ 15. your	____ 18. he

COMPOSITION EXERCISE

Write two sentences for each pronoun position. Underline the pronouns.

1. subject   _____   _____

2. direct object   _____   _____

3. indirect object   _____   _____

4. object of a preposition _____   _____

5. possession   _____   _____

Action Verbs — Present Tense Unit 34

Present tense refers to what is happening now.

EXAMPLES: a. He <u>drives</u> an '82 Chevrolet.
  b. Mom <u>hears</u> everything.
  c. My brother <u>goes</u> to college.

 Underline the sentences which are written in present tense.

1. <u>Janice reads mysteries</u>.
2. The dog hurt his foot.
3. I will choose the winner.
4. Dane always helps her mother.
5. The puppy follows him everywhere.
6. You will enjoy the show.
7. The coach postponed the game.
8. I advise you to stay.
9. George plans our menus.
10. Monkeys climb trees.
11. The warm weather melted the snow.
12. Mom bakes our bread.
13. I will choose Carl and Barry.
14. My uncle bought the land.
15. Birds fly south in the winter.
16. The fish swam away.
17. The turtle moves slowly but surely.
18. I want a new pair of skates.
19. My dog chases cars.
20. James rode his horse to school.
21. Tim promises to help us.
22. Karen wore my jeans.
23. War threatens our safety.
24. This china breaks easily.
25. We revised our budget.

26. Mr. Kent lives in Houston.
27. The girl looked for you.
28. Dad owns the airplane.
29. The comedian tells jokes.
30. Everyone needs a friend.
31. The river reached flood stage.
32. Bears hibernate.
33. I mailed the letter yesterday.
34. Ghosts frighten me.
35. Alex plays basketball.
36. The teacher will read the schedule.
37. Mona used your books.
38. We ride the bus.
39. The ball rolled under the car.
40. Bonnie works every day.
41. That bird sleeps all day.
42. Our dog steals shoes.
43. Brenda will pay the clerk.
44. I suggest plan ''B.''
45. My cat likes liver and cheese.
46. She will fall on the ice.
47. The poison kills bugs.
48. I bought my own bicycle.
49. Mr. Sims gives tennis lessons.
50. Seth always wears that hat.

COMPOSITION EXERCISE

List 20 present-tense verbs.

1. _____
2. _____
3. _____
4. _____
5. _____

6. _____
7. _____
8. _____
9. _____
10. _____

11. _____
12. _____
13. _____
14. _____
15. _____

16. _____
17. _____
18. _____
19. _____
20. _____

Unit 34 cont'd ➡

Action Verbs — Past Tense

Past tense refers to what has already happened.

EXAMPLES: a. Abe <u>ate</u> my candy bar. c. I <u>called</u> Brenda.
  b. The boy <u>ran</u> away. d. You <u>missed</u> the target.

 In each blank write the past tense of the verb in parentheses.

(burn) 1. Eric ___burned___ his finger.
(move) 2. They _____ here last year.
(like) 3. I _____ the red one best.
(want) 4. She _____ to see you.
(play) 5. We _____ basketball.
(walk) 6. The man _____ to town.
(sing) 7. Our class _____ yesterday.
(talk) 8. Jan _____ to your mom.
(build) 9. We _____ a sand castle.
(fight) 10. They _____ for freedom.
(drink) 11. No one _____ the milk.
(fix) 12. Dad _____ the engine.
(surrender) 13. The army _____.
(run) 14. The children _____ home.
(brush) 15. She _____ her hair.
(arrive) 16. The men _____ safely.
(include) 17. The price _____ tax.
(miss) 18. I _____ you yesterday.
(smear) 19. The paint _____ easily.
(replace) 20. Joe _____ the bulbs.
(list) 21. She _____ the items.
(trust) 22. I _____ you.
(match) 23. It _____ perfectly.
(choose) 24. The teacher _____ Mark.
(expect) 25. We _____ you sooner.

(cook) 26. She _____ the meal.
(sign) 27. I _____ my name.
(eat) 28. The lion _____ quickly.
(grow) 29. The plants _____.
(shout) 30. Mom _____ at the dog.
(break) 31. The cookie _____ in half.
(write) 32. Phil _____ you a letter.
(take) 33. Someone _____ our money.
(notice) 34. No one _____ him.
(press) 35. He _____ the buttons.
(gain) 36. I _____ ten pounds.
(drive) 37. Jay _____ our bus today.
(comb) 38. She _____ her hair back.
(crash) 39. The plane _____ last year.
(earn) 40. Our club _____ $40.00.
(convince) 41. We _____ them to stay.
(confess) 42. The thief _____.
(solve) 43. He _____ the mystery.
(pretend) 44. Bill _____ to sleep.
(forget) 45. I _____ your birthday.
(bake) 46. Who _____ this cake?
(freeze) 47. The water _____.
(reach) 48. Finally we _____ the top.
(carry) 49. Paul _____ the boxes.
(ring) 50. The bell _____ again.

COMPOSITION EXERCISE

List 20 past-tense verbs.

1. _____
2. _____
3. _____
4. _____
5. _____
6. _____
7. _____
8. _____
9. _____
10. _____
11. _____
12. _____
13. _____
14. _____
15. _____
16. _____
17. _____
18. _____
19. _____
20. _____

Action Verbs — Future Tense

Future tense refers to what will happen.
The event has not happened yet.

EXAMPLES: a. Kay <u>will sell</u> her car.   c. Mom <u>will drive</u> the truck.
b. The snow <u>will melt</u> soon.   d. <u>Will</u> you <u>pour</u> the tea?

  In each blank write the future tense of the
verb in parentheses.

(see)   1. I ___will see___ you tomorrow.
(eat)   2. Bruce _____ anything.
(ride)   3. Jason _____ the bus.
(feed)   4. Donna _____ the dog.
(help)   5. I _____ you.
(keep)   6. Eva _____ the puppy.
(go)   7. _____ you ____ with me?
(make)   8. You _____ the team.
(pay)   9. Mom _____ us.
(sink) 10. She _____ in the storm.
(walk) 11. Dave _____ to the corner.
(speak) 12. No one _____ to you.
(sell) 13. I _____ the bike to Tim.
(know) 14. They _____ you did it.
(sing) 15. Sara _____ the song.
(hide) 16. We _____ in the closet.
(spend) 17. Katie _____ our money.
(leave) 18. The train _____ soon.
(freeze) 19. The milk _____ in there.
(hit) 20. That car _____ the sign.
(kill) 21. The poison _____ it.
(stop) 22. The noise _____ soon.
(study) 23. We _____ together.
(try) 24. Abe _____ to escape.
(write) 25. I _____ to you.

(deny) 26. She _____ everything.
(hear) 27. Mom _____ us leave.
(run) 28. He _____ up the hill.
(sit) 29. The cat _____ in my lap.
(drop) 30. You _____ the box.
(show) 31. I _____ you the rooms.
(light) 32. He _____ the candle.
(lock) 33. Ted _____ the doors.
(shut) 34. _____ you _____ the door?
(cut) 35. You _____ your hand.
(have) 36. I _____ the smaller one.
(expect) 37. We _____ you today.
(sleep) 38. He _____ until noon.
(invite) 39. I _____ the guests.
(burn) 40. Fire _____ you.
(escape) 41. We _____ tomorrow.
(question) 42. She _____ Phil.
(surround) 43. They _____ us.
(repay) 44. Kent _____ the favor.
(appear) 45. Then a ghost _____.
(turn) 46. _____ you _____ around?
(laugh) 47. No one _____ at you.
(find) 48. Josh _____ your dog.
(smear) 49. You _____ the paint.
(forgive) 50. I _____ you.

COMPOSITION EXERCISE

List 20 past-tense verbs.

1. _____
2. _____
3. _____
4. _____
5. _____
6. _____
7. _____
8. _____
9. _____
10. _____
11. _____
12. _____
13. _____
14. _____
15. _____
16. _____
17. _____
18. _____
19. _____
20. _____

Unit 35 cont'd

Practice with Action Verbs

An action verb tells what is happening in the sentence. The verb may be in present, past, or future tense.

EXAMPLES: present: *He returns every day at noon.*
   past: *He returned at noon.*
   future: *He will return at noon.*

Underline the verb in each sentence. In the blank write whether the verb is in present, past, or future tense. Use "pr" for present, "pa" for past, and "ft" for future tense.

__pr__ 1. You <u>ignore</u> me.	_____ 26. An aardvark followed me home.
_____ 2. The monster vanished.	_____ 27. I want the answer now.
_____ 3. The bomb will explode.	_____ 28. This book looks interesting.
_____ 4. The limb damaged our car.	_____ 29. He will confess to everything.
_____ 5. The monkey opened his cage.	_____ 30. Dad signed the papers.
_____ 6. I will suggest the idea.	_____ 31. He plays the guitar.
_____ 7. This work confuses me.	_____ 32. No one will understand.
_____ 8. He hesitates too often.	_____ 33. Harry will send flowers.
_____ 9. She will delay the test.	_____ 34. We will take the blue car.
_____ 10. We published a paper.	_____ 35. Sue smiled at the clerk.
_____ 11. Paul will forget the bread.	_____ 36. He builds furniture.
_____ 12. The child will obey me.	_____ 37. I expect him today.
_____ 13. The dog barked at us.	_____ 38. Judy estimated our cost.
_____ 14. We measured the windows.	_____ 39. The team will lose the game.
_____ 15. Don sells insurance.	_____ 40. Phil needs another nail.
_____ 16. The contest will end tomorrow.	_____ 41. I disapprove of the plan.
_____ 17. The horse jumped the fence.	_____ 42. Eva likes camping and fishing.
_____ 18. The soup tastes delicious.	_____ 43. We decided on a motto.
_____ 19. We worked all day.	_____ 44. Carrie will paint my picture.
_____ 20. I will fix the faucet.	_____ 45. The movie will end at noon.
_____ 21. She will read us the story.	_____ 46. The people want a change.
_____ 22. Kate walks to school.	_____ 47. Sam bought the set.
_____ 23. Grandma lives in Mexico.	_____ 48. The bull chased us.
_____ 24. Bob will hang the paintings.	_____ 49. I hate cold weather.
_____ 25. The ice cream melted.	_____ 50. It will destroy our city.

COMPOSITION EXERCISE

List 10 verbs in their present-, past-, and future-tense forms.

1. _____ _____ _____   6. _____ _____ _____
2. _____ _____ _____   7. _____ _____ _____
3. _____ _____ _____   8. _____ _____ _____
4. _____ _____ _____   9. _____ _____ _____
5. _____ _____ _____ 10. _____ _____ _____

Comprehension Check

Ⓐ Underline each pronoun used as the subject of its sentence.

1. She is a new student.
2. Give her the records.
3. They are driving to our house.
4. I want to see you soon.
5. We want you to call us.
6. Will you lend me your pen?
7. Alison called her stepfather.
8. The lady asked me for directions.
9. I don't have your notebook.
10. Students may buy their tickets here.

Ⓑ Underline the pronouns used as objects.

1. Please tell us your story.
2. They went with Jim and me.
3. You can tell us about it.
4. He is a good friend to me.
5. The keys belong to him.
6. Jill bought us some candy.
7. The bear chased us.
8. Mrs. Carr sent her to the office.
9. Please wash it and park it here.
10. She told them to wait.

Ⓒ Underline each possessive pronoun.

1. This is my ruler.
2. Pick up your book.
3. The dog wagged its tail.
4. I can understand your reasons.
5. They found their hamster.
6. Our family ghost haunted us.
7. His friends are loyal.
8. She finished her work.
9. The test is hers.
10. One basket is mine.

Ⓓ Put a check (✓) beside each sentence in which the pronouns are used correctly.

✓ 1. Tell Martha your story.
___ 2. Bob and me will be late.
___ 3. Mr. Barnes told us to study.
___ 4. This is mine lunch.
___ 5. Ashley and she are sisters.
___ 6. Give the paper to he.
___ 7. Here is your next clue.
___ 8. Please sign your name.
___ 9. You and he may leave now.
___ 10. Tara bought Lisa and me the gum.

Ⓔ Each sentence contains a pronoun in the subject, object, or possessive position. Write "s," "o," or "p" beside each sentence.

_s_ 1. He has a new bike.
___ 2. The red bike is mine.
___ 3. They are not going.
___ 4. Tell them the story.
___ 5. It's hard to believe.
___ 6. Sign your name here.
___ 7. The bird built its nest.
___ 8. Show her the instructions.
___ 9. You are going to win!
___ 10. They are eager to begin.
___ 11. Please read the article to me.
___ 12. Did Carl read about it?

___ 13. I'm not worried.
___ 14. My sweater is missing.
___ 15. We'll work on the boat.
___ 16. Did Joe paint it?
___ 17. Use the phone in your room.
___ 18. We published the school paper.
___ 19. He's here!
___ 20. Did Kate hear you?
___ 21. Don't tear it down!
___ 22. Did they win the game?
___ 23. The dog barked at us.
___ 24. We opened the cage.

Test 7 cont'd ⟹

Comprehension Check (continued)

F Identify each present, past, and future tense verb. Write "pr," "pa," or "f" beside each verb.

_pr_ 1. freeze
____ 2. baked
____ 3. will laugh
____ 4. will try
____ 5. sang
____ 6. reached
____ 7. fought
____ 8. will leave
____ 9. looked
____ 10. will sell

____ 11. bake
____ 12. try
____ 13. left
____ 14. froze
____ 15. will reach
____ 16. laughed
____ 17. will fight
____ 18. sing
____ 19. sell
____ 20. reach

____ 21. laugh
____ 22. fight
____ 23. will bake
____ 24. leave
____ 25. look
____ 26. tried
____ 27. will sing
____ 28. sold
____ 29. will freeze
____ 30. will look

G Use the verbs in part F in the blanks. Follow the order given in the parentheses.

(f) 1. We _____*will leave*_____ at 4:00 p.m.

(pa) 2. Amanda _____ last Tuesday.

(pa) 3. Terry _____ ten dozen cookies.

(f) 4. The boxers _____ on Friday.

(pr) 5. Can you _____ popcorn tonight?

(pa) 6. They _____ for their rights.

(pa) 7. Jason _____ us along.

(f) 8. Kara _____ in the chorus.

(pa) 9. We _____ the national anthem.

(pr) 10. You can't _____ yet.

(f) 11. The liquid _____ at 32° F.

(pa) 12. We've _____ everywhere!

(f) 13. Jack _____ the cupcakes.

(pr) 14. _____ at this mess!

(pa) 15. Barry _____ his old car.

(f) 16. Mr. Franks _____ into the matter.

(pr) 17. I can't _____ at that joke.

(pa) 18. They _____ to tell you.

(f) 19. The train _____ Dallas soon.

(pr) 20. Please _____ this chili.

(pa) 21. We _____ at the puppy.

(f) 22. _____ they _____ their house?

(f) 23. I'll _____ the birthday cake.

(f) 24. Aaron _____ anything.

Write a paragraph describing a pet that belongs to you or to someone else. Underline each action verb.

_____
_____
_____
_____
_____
_____
_____
_____
_____
_____

Auxiliary Verbs

Auxiliary verbs are helping verbs. They are used to help other verbs.

EXAMPLES: a. We _are_ moving away.   c. Steve _is_ riding a horse.
                b. The baby _was_ growing.   d. The plane _had_ departed.

A Write "am," "is," or "are" in the blank.

1. I __am__ going to Toledo tomorrow.
2. The girls _____ leaving for school.
3. Karen and I _____ studying history.
4. The army _____ planning an attack.
5. She _____ buying your present.
6. The ice _____ melting quickly.
7. They _____ taking your car.
8. He _____ building a cage.

9. We _____ seeking a solution.
10. George _____ holding a tiger cub.
11. The men _____ asking for more money.
12. She _____ playing the piano.
13. I _____ sending a card.
14. Susan and Dean _____ elected to go.
15. The mission _____ accomplished.
16. I _____ making a wish.

B Write "was" or "were" in the blank.

1. Jerry __was__ writing his speech.
2. We _____ helping with the decorations.
3. Janet _____ bewildered.
4. You _____ dreaming again.
5. He _____ acting strangely.
6. The two classes _____ combined.

7. The book _____ published in 1881.
8. I _____ listening to the radio.
9. The spies _____ caught.
10. Dale _____ breaking the rules.
11. They _____ calling for help.
12. Al and Joe _____ fishing in the pond.

C Write "has," "have," or "had" in the blank.

1. The ship __had__ sunk.
2. The amendment _____ passed.
3. The guests _____ arrived.
4. The water _____ evaporated.
5. The flowers _____ bloomed.
6. He _____ finished the job.

7. We _____ heard that story.
8. The time _____ come to begin.
9. The alarm _____ rung.
10. The leaves _____ turned yellow.
11. It _____ begun to rain.
12. No one _____ lived here.

COMPOSITION EXERCISE

Write 10 sentences which contain auxiliary verbs.

1. _____
2. _____
3. _____
4. _____
5. _____

6. _____
7. _____
8. _____
9. _____
10. _____

Unit 36 cont'd ➡

The Position of Auxiliary Verbs

The auxiliary verb usually appears in front of the verb it is helping.

EXAMPLES:
a. The snake *is* *crawling* away.
b. I *am* *answering* your call.
c. She *is* *watching* television.
d. They *were* *buying* the zoo.

 Underline the auxiliary verb and the verb it is helping.

1. I <u>am</u> <u>confused</u> about it.
2. The train is moving slowly.
3. Our team is winning the game.
4. The calves are following us.
5. Jay and I are invited to the party.
6. The check was signed on the back.
7. Susan and Dale were crying again.
8. Larry has forgotten his homework.
9. I have included the answers.
10. The teacher had explained the method.
11. The mail was delivered on time.
12. The child had swallowed a dime.
13. I have accomplished my goals.
14. Sharon is using my pencil.
15. The building was condemned.
16. We are postponing the trip.
17. The men were painting our house.
18. The car was damaged.
19. The truck is pushing the wagon.
20. I am trying to finish early.
21. They were running across the field.
22. The families are eating together.
23. We are pretending to sing.
24. I am hurrying home.
25. We were adding the numbers.
26. The choir is singing.
27. The woman was screaming.
28. The children are playing hopscotch.
29. Your parents have come home.
30. She had seen me.
31. George has broken the vase.
32. Mom and Dad were watching us.
33. The man is stealing our jewels.
34. Dana has cleaned the house.
35. I have heard the story.
36. Johnny is brushing his teeth.
37. We are writing a play.
38. The cat is climbing the tree.
39. They have found the box.
40. She is thinking about me.
41. I am studying for a test.
42. Mark was laughing.
43. The pain has gone.
44. I have watered the garden.
45. Diane had solved the mystery.
46. The class is taking an exam.
47. I am convinced of it.
48. We were losing the contest.
49. Paula is making a cake.
50. You have remembered my birthday.

COMPOSITION EXERCISE

Write a sentence using each of these verbs as auxiliary verbs.

(am) 1. _____
(is) 2. _____
(are) 3. _____
(was) 4. _____
(were) 5. _____

(has) 6. _____
(did) 7. _____
(will) 8. _____
(can) 9. _____
(have) 10. _____

Auxiliaries

Auxiliaries often help main verbs by showing time and number. Forms of be show past, present, and future times and singular and plural numbers. These forms are used with present participles in the active voice and past forms or past participles in the passive voice.

	PRESENT	**PAST**	**FUTURE**
Singular	am, is	was	shall **be**, will **be**
Plural	are	were	shall **be**, will **be**

A Underline the auxiliary in each sentence. Name the time and number shown by writing them in the blank.

1. I am dancing in the school play. _____

2. The thief was arrested after a long chase. _____

3. That vase will be included in our garage sale. _____

4. All of the girls are helping to make costumes. _____

5. Long before Columbus came, Indians were roaming the plains. _____

Special verbs function either as auxiliaries or as main verbs. These include "be" which functions as a linking verb with the addition of "being" and "been." The special verbs "have," "has," "had," and "having" function only with the past forms or past participles of other verbs as auxiliaries; the verbs "do," "does," "did," "doing," and "done" function only with plain forms of verbs as auxiliaries.

B Identify each word underlined by filling in the blank with verb, linking verb, or auxiliary.

1. I <u>have</u> finished my homework. _____

2. We <u>have</u> a new puppy. _____

3. Marjorie <u>is</u> the prettiest girl in school. _____

4. Bill <u>did</u> play in Saturday's game. _____

5. We have <u>done</u> the dishes. _____

Some auxiliaries other than the word "do" function with the plain forms of verbs. These include "shall" and "will," which show future time. Other auxiliaries in this group used to intensify meaning are "can," "may," "could," "should," "would," "might," "must," and "ought."

C Fill in the blank with the auxiliary that produces the meaning shown in parentheses.

1. I _____ be at home when you call. (in the future)

2. You _____ be ready by 8:00. (if you know what's good for you)

3. Jimmy _____ join us later. (not sure that he will)

4. He _____ have forgotten our plans. (a chance that he forgot)

5. _____ you like a cookie? (Will you take one?)

Unit 37 cont'd

Auxiliaries Puzzle

Auxiliaries are often called helping words. They are used with verbs to help express differences in time, intent, attitude, and condition. The auxiliary verb gives a sense of continuing or continued action. When an auxiliary and a verb are used in a question, the auxiliary comes before the subject or noun substitute.

Some auxiliaries are "am," "are," "can," "could," "did," "does," "get," "go," "had," "has," "have," "is," "keep," "may," "must," "shall," "should," "was," "were," "will," and "would."

1. W	2. A	R	E	S	3. W	4. W
	5. M					6. A
		7. G	8. W			
			9. M			10. S
11. C			12. H		13. I	
	14. K	15. H		16. D		
				17. W		
				18. G		
		19. H	20. D			

✳ **Fill in the blanks. Then complete the puzzle.**

Across
2. <u>a r e</u> used with plural nouns to show present tense

4. _ _ _ _ _ first and third person singular; past indicative of "be"

6. _ _ used with "I" in the present tense

8. _ _ _ _ _ _ the past tense of "will"

9. _ _ _ _ _ be forced to; ought to; obliged to

11. _ _ _ to be able to; to know how to

13. _ _ third person singular, present indicative of "be"

15. _ _ _ _ held in one's hand, in one's keeping

16. _ _ _ _ carried through to the end; performed

17. _ _ _ _ _ am going to; is going to; are going to

18. _ _ _ to reach; to arrive; to become; to come or go

19. _ _ _ same as "15" across

20. _ _ _ _ _ third person singular, present indicative of "do"

Down
1. _ _ _ _ _ plural and second person singular past indicative of "be"

3. _ _ _ _ _ _ _ to express duty or obligation

5. _ _ _ _ to be permitted or allowed to

7. _ _ to move along; to leave; to be in motion

10. _ _ _ _ _ _ used to express future time

11. _ _ _ _ _ _ used to convey a shade of doubt

12. _ _ _ _ _ to hold in one's keeping

14. _ _ _ _ _ to have for a long time, forever

15. _ _ _ _ possesses an absolute quality or right

92

Linking Verbs

Linking verbs include "is," "are," "am," "was," and "were." They come between subjects and predicate adjectives or subjects and predicate nouns.

EXAMPLES: a. Mr. Carson <u>is</u> a lawyer.
b. You <u>are</u> silly.
c. The men <u>were</u> cowards.
d. He <u>was</u> a fighter.

A Write "am," "is," or "are" in the blanks.

1. My name __*is*__ George.
2. I _____ a student.
3. He _____ my brother.
4. She _____ our neighbor.
5. We _____ happy here.
6. They _____ fishermen.
7. You _____ my friend.
8. Sharon _____ the queen.
9. The house _____ too large.
10. The animal _____ a fox.
11. They _____ angry.
12. I _____ ill.

13. The money _____ safe.
14. You _____ greedy.
15. Diamonds _____ a luxury.
16. That woman _____ attractive.
17. He _____ busy.
18. We _____ hungry.
19. I _____ a ghost.
20. The men _____ weak.
21. You _____ a guest.
22. The weather _____ cold.
23. The houses _____ modern.
24. The music _____ beautiful.

B Write "was" or "were" in the blanks.

1. The test __*was*__ difficult.
2. Paul and Al _____ a team.
3. The clue _____ significant.
4. The water _____ hot.
5. Cathi _____ shrewd.
6. The men _____ carpenters.
7. The accident _____ tragic.
8. We _____ restless.
9. The dog _____ obedient.
10. The meal _____ delicious.

11. The woman _____ wise.
12. The man _____ famous.
13. They _____ nurses.
14. Josh _____ proud.
15. The cartoons _____ funny.
16. It _____ your signature.
17. Our car _____ a Ford.
18. The moccasins _____ brown.
19. The sentences _____ short.
20. The workers _____ rebels.

COMPOSITION EXERCISE

Write two sentences using each of these verbs as linking verbs.

(am)   1. _____   _____
(is)   2. _____   _____
(are)   3. _____   _____
(was)   4. _____   _____
(were) 5. _____   _____

Unit 38 cont'd

The Position of Linking Verbs

Linking verbs come between subjects and predicate adjectives or between subjects and predicate nouns.

EXAMPLES: a. My name <u>is</u> Poindexter.   c. She <u>is</u> my mother.
                  b. His hair <u>was</u> blonde.   d. The chairs <u>were</u> red.

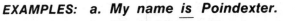

A   Underline the linking verb in each sentence.

1. Mike <u>is</u> bashful.
2. It is a monster.
3. The table was dirty.
4. The man is a farmer.
5. The flowers were red.
6. Alex is a comedian.
7. The ideas are foolish.
8. The glass is empty.
9. This poem is nonsense.
10. The rabbits are white.
11. The man is an artist.
12. The candy was sweet.
13. This knife is sharp.
14. The room was warm.
15. You were rude.
16. The lion is wild.
17. The forest was dark.
18. The frog is fat.
19. The wagon is green.
20. They were funny.
21. The grapes are bitter.
22. The milk is sour.
23. John was our doctor.
24. The breeze is chilly.
25. The children were silent.
26. This song is a lullaby.
27. The lemons are sour.
28. That hammer is useless.
29. He was the thief.
30. You were correct.
31. The letter was open.
32. The coat is too small.
33. The floor is wet.
34. His voice is hoarse.
35. The river is deep.
36. An apple is a fruit.
37. I am happy.
38. My eyes are blue.
39. Karen was the maid.
40. The answer is true.
41. The policemen are busy.
42. I am an actor.
43. You are silly.
44. The movie was good.
45. He is my uncle.
46. Perry is handsome.
47. My sister is smart.
48. You were careless.

B   In each blank write a linking verb.

1. I ___*am*___ a giraffe.
2. You _____ my enemy.
3. Kim _____ the treasurer.
4. My brother _____ a baby.
5. The lot _____ vacant.
6. He _____ a teacher.
7. The liver _____ delicious.
8. Gene _____ an adult.
9. His name _____ Peter.
10. The driver _____ my dad.
11. This flower _____ a rose.
12. We _____ members.
13. It _____ a tornado.
14. Jack _____ the owner.
15. I _____ your friend.
16. She _____ sad.
17. You _____ a devil.
18. He _____ the principal.
19. Tim and Sue _____ late.
20. The locks _____ secure.
21. Omaha _____ a city.
22. The word _____ a noun.
23. Fire _____ dangerous.
24. The problem _____ easy.

COMPOSITION EXERCISE

Write 12 sentences which contain linking verbs.

1. _____
2. _____
3. _____
4. _____
5. _____
6. _____
7. _____
8. _____
9. _____
10. _____
11. _____
12. _____

Distinguishing Between Auxiliary and Linking Verbs

Auxiliary verbs are helping verbs. They are used with other verbs. Linking verbs are used alone. They are followed by adjectives or nouns.

EXAMPLES:

auxiliary verbs	linking verbs
a. I <u>am</u> <u>trying</u> to understand.	a. The dog <u>is</u> a poodle.
b. The paper <u>was</u> <u>burning</u>.	b. Kelsey <u>was</u> upset.

✳ Write "a" if the sentence contains an auxiliary verb.
Write "l" if the sentence contains a linking verb.
Underline the verb in each sentence.

_a_ 1. The sun <u>is shining</u> today.
___ 2. She is a pretty girl.
___ 3. Don is singing our song.
___ 4. I am eleven years old.
___ 5. We are leaving now.
___ 6. That man is my father.
___ 7. You are ruthless.
___ 8. The lights were burning.
___ 9. I have gained ten pounds.
___ 10. I am ignoring you.
___ 11. Eric is a pilot.
___ 12. The dog is sleeping on our sofa.
___ 13. They were cruel to her.
___ 14. Jill and I are friends.
___ 15. I am going to go.
___ 16. The water is freezing.
___ 17. It was an owl.
___ 18. The child is waving good-bye.
___ 19. Your suggestion was great.
___ 20. The amendment was passed.
___ 21. They were helping us.
___ 22. The club is meeting today.
___ 23. The rumor is true.
___ 24. Our team is winning.
___ 25. The stairs are not safe.

___ 26. We are anxious to go.
___ 27. George is always polite.
___ 28. It was important.
___ 29. We are losing money.
___ 30. The jewels are valuable.
___ 31. The family is eating dinner.
___ 32. The damages were estimated today.
___ 33. Mr. Kent is teaching me to swim.
___ 34. Paul and Jack are running the race.
___ 35. We were brave and daring.
___ 36. That dream was a nightmare.
___ 37. A kitten was sitting on our porch.
___ 38. The woman is too fat.
___ 39. I am uncertain.
___ 40. The people were rejoicing.
___ 41. The water has evaporated.
___ 42. Mr. Simon is a famous writer.
___ 43. Gossip is discouraged.
___ 44. You are carefree.
___ 45. This signature is yours.
___ 46. The dungeon was dark.
___ 47. Sandy and I have planned the party.
___ 48. I am wearing a jumpsuit.
___ 49. The password is "carrot."
___ 50. Mother was talking to you.

COMPOSITION EXERCISE

Write 5 sentences which contain auxiliary verbs and 5 which contain linking verbs.

auxiliary	linking
1. _____	1. _____
2. _____	2. _____
3. _____	3. _____
4. _____	4. _____
5. _____	5. _____

Unit 39 cont'd ⟶

Verb Form Shows Voice

Here are the rules for changing active forms to passive forms.

active voice = subject + verb + object
John   rakes   the leaves.
passive voice = object + verb (be + part.) + prep. (by) + subj.
The leaves   are raked   by   John.

✳ Rewrite the following sentences, changing the active form to the passive form. Follow this example:

EXAMPLE: *John rakes the leaves.*
           The leaves are raked by John.

1. The baby sitter watched the children. ___*The*___ *children were watched by the baby sitter.*

2. The students learn grammar. _____

3. Watson studied human behavior. _____

4. Rats and apes solve some simple problems. _____

5. Donna dropped her pencil. _____

6. Dr. Skinner gave a speech. _____

7. The students study French. _____

8. The baby grabs my finger. _____

9. Coach Glenn taught us the play. _____

10. We can find the injured deer. _____

11. Cindy memorized the poem. _____

12. Andy solved the math problems. _____

13. We understand the plan. _____

14. Dad controlled the car. _____

15. Marian made the highest score. _____

16. Tammy used the sewing machine. _____

17. Carol popped the balloon. _____

18. Mrs. Barker added the scores. _____

19. Barry will sign the form. _____

20. Melissa ate the chocolate bunny. _____

Using "Is" and "Are"

"Is" is the singular present-tense form of the verb "be."

EXAMPLES:
  a. Theo is my best friend.
  b. The clock is ticking.

"Are" is the plural present-tense form of the verb "be."

EXAMPLES:
  c. They are students.
  d. The women are working.

Exception: Always use "are" with the pronoun "you."

 Write "is" or "are" in each blank.

1. ___Is___ that all you have done?
2. The lights _____ flickering.
3. You _____ sitting on my coat.
4. These letters _____ yours.
5. The books _____ in order.
6. _____ the door locked?
7. George _____ looking for you.
8. Al _____ sure to win.
9. We _____ planning to leave soon.
10. What _____ wrong with it?
11. The house _____ not for sale.
12. The glasses _____ cracked.
13. It _____ time to go to school.
14. These men _____ pilots.
15. Eddie _____ our secretary.
16. Those words _____ nouns.
17. He _____ my cousin.
18. The wolves _____ hungry.
19. Someone _____ watching us.
20. _____ you going to the party?
21. Where _____ my hat?
22. The crowd _____ gathering.
23. You _____ too tall.
24. That man _____ our principal.
25. We _____ too tired.

26. These shoes _____ comfortable.
27. Liz _____ coming with us.
28. Calvin _____ waiting at the corner.
29. The leaves _____ turning brown.
30. We _____ determined to win.
31. You _____ not the only one.
32. The plane _____ ready for take-off.
33. The winners _____ Kim and Bob.
34. Norman _____ a good friend.
35. It _____ too early.
36. The answers _____ correct.
37. The music _____ too loud.
38. They _____ trying to help us.
39. Everyone _____ welcome.
40. You _____ using the wrong color.
41. We _____ studying math.
42. _____ she your mother?
43. What _____ making that noise?
44. The clowns _____ wearing skates.
45. The ending _____ funny.
46. _____ these pencils yours?
47. Who _____ responsible for this?
48. Ann _____ practicing her part for the play.
49. _____ it raining again?
50. My name _____ Felix.

Unit 40 cont'd

Using "Was" and "Were"

"Was" is the singular past-tense form of the verb "be."

EXAMPLES:
  a. Louis was our captain.
  b. It was snowing again.

"Were" is the plural past-tense form of the verb "be."

EXAMPLES:
  c. Betty and I were late.
  d. They were waiting for us.

Exception: Always use "were" with the pronoun "you."

 Write "was" or "were" in each blank.

1. It __was__ time to leave for school.
2. We _____ hoping to see you.
3. I _____ reading a book.
4. _____ you afraid of the bear?
5. The children _____ eating ice cream.
6. The package _____ delivered today.
7. Mr. Owens _____ busy.
8. The questions _____ easy.
9. He _____ driving a blue car.
10. Mark and Paul _____ absent.
11. _____ you waiting for me?
12. Jana _____ talking to Ms. Cook.
13. No one _____ there.
14. The car _____ sold to Dr. West.
15. I _____ working on my math.
16. The money _____ stolen last night.
17. He _____ at the end of the line.
18. The score _____ tied.
19. The dog _____ chasing a mouse.
20. The books _____ on the top shelf.
21. It _____ our last chance.
22. She _____ thinking about her family.
23. The stores _____ closed.
24. The bus _____ parked in the back.
25. Dave _____ ready to go.

26. The cat _____ asleep in the chair.
27. Nick and I _____ invited.
28. Yesterday _____ my birthday.
29. The windows _____ open.
30. You _____ elected to go.
31. The boys _____ outside.
32. What _____ his answer?
33. _____ the bus on schedule?
34. They _____ taking a test.
35. Chris _____ writing a letter.
36. We _____ sitting behind them.
37. The temperature _____ 33°F.
38. Pete _____ the winner.
39. The pictures _____ ruined.
40. You _____ the best player.
41. The report _____ interesting.
42. The room _____ in a mess.
43. Mindy _____ given the trophy.
44. The trip _____ cancelled.
45. The cards _____ mailed yesterday.
46. We _____ using too much paint.
47. Henry _____ buying a bicycle.
48. The water _____ cold.
49. _____ they happy about the result?
50. Who _____ we supposed to ask?

Comprehension Check

(A) Underline the auxiliary verbs.

1. <u>was</u>	9. can	17. swim
2. has	10. could	18. had
3. drink	11. travel	19. am
4. are	12. will	20. remember
5. should	13. record	21. wave
6. count	14. have	22. would
7. must	15. is	23. were
8. prepare	16. second	24. give

(B) Supply the auxiliary verbs.

1. Mr. Carlson __*will*__ buy the house.
2. Stephen _____ driving me home.
3. The class _____ taking a test.
4. I _____ going to the movies.
5. Kenny _____ writing a note to Dee.
6. We _____ looking for you.
7. Jack _____ visiting his cousins.
8. It _____ addressed to Lester.
9. I _____ help you.
10. You _____ trying too hard.

11. My sister _____ studying art.
12. The water _____ getting cold.
13. Ms. Garner _____ make the cake.
14. The ship _____ been sold to Jack.
15. The teachers _____ backing the students.
16. It _____ make things easier.
17. The people _____ know the truth.
18. They _____ lost their way.
19. Beverly _____ be here on Thursday.
20. The car _____ parked outside.

(C) Underline the auxiliary verb in each verb phrase. Then draw an arrow from the auxiliary verb to the main verb.

1. <u>is</u> working	9. can help	17. were pushing	25. are leaning.
2. will read	10. should know	18. had tried	26. will forget
3. were holding	11. am making	19. are hiring	27. am interested
4. are using	12. has grown	20. could walk	28. would settle
5. have moved	13. are closing	21. will write	29. can swim
6. was owned	14. could talk	22. have needed	30. must protect
7. would buy	15. was fixing	23. is driving	31. may see
8. must visit	16. is listening	24. were eating	32. were singing

Test 8 cont'd

Comprehension Check (continued)

D Underline the linking verb in each sentence.

1. It <u>will be</u> the best one.
2. The soup tasted too salty.
3. I am your only hope.
4. Steven is the star player.
5. Blue cars are most popular.
6. The water was cool.
7. The islands are smaller.
8. Jennifer feels anxious about it.
9. The music was soothing.
10. Robert seemed distracted.
11. He and I will be partners.
12. David and Donald are twins.
13. The noise sounded foreboding.
14. She acted indifferent.
15. You are too kindhearted.
16. Hank is not trustworthy.
17. The lost puppy looked helpless.
18. Benny is a reporter.
19. Nigel became angry.
20. The moon is full tonight.

E Write either "is" or "are" in each blank.

1. Harold __*is*__ the new owner.
2. These books _____ mine.
3. Katherine _____ my cousin.
4. The decorations _____ green.
5. It _____ too late now.
6. Nothing _____ the same.
7. The movie _____ excellent.
8. Six cars _____ behind the gym.
9. You _____ perfect for the part.
10. The weather _____ beautiful.
11. Edna and I _____ the announcers.
12. The breeze _____ refreshing.

F Write either "was" or "were" in each blank.

1. The news __*was*__ a relief.
2. I _____ sure he would do it.
3. They _____ students from India.
4. The streets _____ deserted.
5. The men _____ members of the club.
6. No one _____ willing to wait.
7. Julia _____ nervous about her speech.
8. Mr. Hillston _____ our sponsor.
9. The people _____ for the new laws.
10. Paul and Tom _____ late as usual.
11. Stanley _____ Jackie's neighbor.
12. Three women _____ outside.

Write a paragraph about the advantages or disadvantages of being famous. Use at least two linking verbs. Underline them when you use them.

_____
_____
_____
_____
_____
_____
_____
_____

Adjectives

An adjective is a word describing a noun. In sentences it usually appears before a noun or after a linking verb.

EXAMPLES: The <u>small</u> boy wore a <u>new red</u> coat. *(noun modifiers)*
The boy was <u>small</u>. His coat looked <u>new</u>. *(linking-verb complements)*

A Underline each adjective in the following paragraph.

It was a <u>hot</u>, <u>windy</u> day. Jerry stood alone at the bus stop, wondering if his mother had baked a chocolate cake. He was hungry and tired after two hours of baseball practice. Twice his blue cap was yanked from his head by the hot wind. Bits of old newspaper tumbled along the curb. Jerry felt miserable and lonesome in the sun's bright glare. He stared at a dusty car across the street. It seemed familiar, but fine flecks of dust hid the license plate. Then Jerry noticed a bald head, pink and shiny, behind the steering wheel. "Uncle John!" Jerry shouted at the tall man in the car.

"I just got back from a long boring trip," replied his uncle. Then he asked, "Want a ride home? We'll have a cold drink on the way. You're lucky to be able to play all day," he added.

As modifiers, adjectives may show comparison. Regular adjectives of one or two syllables add "-er" and "-est." Some two-syllable adjectives and all adjectives with three syllables or more use the intensifiers "more" and "most" or "less" and "least." A few adjectives change form for irregular comparison.

POSITIVE	COMPARATIVE	SUPERLATIVE
kind	kinder	kindest
heroic	more heroic	most heroic
good	better	best
bad	worse	worst

B Fill in the blank of each sentence with the comparative or superlative form of the adjective in parentheses.

1. Of all my friends, Mr. Parks is the (kind) _____ .
2. Ginny said that my ice-cream cone was (big) _____ than hers.
3. I believe that is the (good) _____ book I've ever read.
4. Each time I give a report, I feel (confident) _____ than the time before.
5. That was the (bad) _____ game.

Adjectives must not be confused with adverbs which modify verbs, adjectives, and other adverbs. Most people make such mistakes when the modifier appears in the predicate.

C Underline the word in parentheses that should complete each sentence.

1. That milk tastes (<u>sour</u>, sourly).
2. He (sure, surely) tries hard.
3. Lunch tastes (bad, badly) today.
4. Linda always looks (neat, neatly).
5. Dennis sings (good, well).
6. Tom won the race (easy, easily).

Unit 41 cont'd ⟶

The Position of Adjectives

Adjectives usually come in front of the nouns they are describing.

EXAMPLES:
  a. The <u>first</u> person wins.
  b. Karen made a <u>banana</u> pie.
  c. She wore <u>yellow</u> shoes.
  d. I want the <u>softest</u> pillow.

 Underline the adjectives.

1. He always wears <u>purple</u> socks.
2. Two students are absent.
3. I made a lemon cake.
4. She bought a straw hat.
5. Dave is a marvelous cook.
6. He is a friendly ghost.
7. The last boy is Bruce.
8. My brother is in the tenth grade.
9. Ms. Jenks is a retired nurse.
10. I love strawberry ice cream.
11. We need a long rope.
12. Here is the missing piece.
13. He ate a hot pepper.
14. The lost puppy cried.
15. This is an excellent report.
16. Mom made vegetable soup.
17. I enjoy ice skating.
18. Jack is a great artist.
19. The yellow roses have bloomed.
20. He turned on a gravel road.
21. It has been a cold winter.
22. Mr. Norton is a busy man.
23. Do you have a flower garden?
24. Sad movies make me cry.
25. I saw a pink elephant.
26. The teacher read us a silly poem.
27. He comes from a large family.
28. They own valuable property.
29. The football game is tonight.
30. We own a green truck.
31. I saw an enormous monster.
32. The strong wind bent our flowers.
33. Let's take a short walk.
34. Darren is my oldest friend.
35. She gave us an easy test.
36. Mom bought a square table.
37. The lonely man walked away.
38. We watched a spooky movie.
39. Look at that green bike.
40. She needs new shoes.
41. It made a loud noise.
42. A new budget is needed.
43. The family portrait is finished.
44. He leads a carefree life.
45. Phil is a terrible player.
46. The orange balloon popped.
47. May I have a cold drink?
48. That is a useless clue.
49. I dialed the wrong number.
50. You have a big mouth.

COMPOSITION EXERCISE

Write 12 sentences which contain adjectives.

1. _____
2. _____
3. _____
4. _____
5. _____
6. _____
7. _____
8. _____
9. _____
10. _____
11. _____
12. _____

Adding "er" and "est" to Adjectives

To show comparison, an adjective of one or two syllables adds "er." Greatest comparison is shown by adding "est."

EXAMPLES:
  a. fat — fatter — fattest
     c. young — younger — youngest
  b. old — older — oldest
     d. late — later — latest

 Add "er" or "est" to each adjective. Watch out for changes in spelling.

	+ -er	**+ -est**			**+ -er**	**+ -est**
1. cold	*colder*	*coldest*	25. soon			
2. warm			26. fast			
3. large			27. quick			
4. big			28. slow			
5. high			29. long			
6. low			30. weak			
7. soft			31. full			
8. hard			32. new			
9. easy			33. old			
10. pretty			34. sweet			
11. ugly			35. safe			
12. straight			36. strong			
13. green			37. clean			
14. small			38. fresh			
15. happy			39. cheap			
16. sad			40. rich			
17. thick			41. close			
18. thin			42. great			
19. tall			43. sharp			
20. few			44. deep			
21. short			45. simple			
22. near			46. busy			
23. kind			47. bright			
24. nice			48. dark			

COMPOSITION EXERCISE

Choose 5 adjectives from today's exercise. Write a sentence with both the "er" and "est" forms of each adjective.

1. _____ _____
2. _____ _____
3. _____ _____
4. _____ _____
5. _____ _____

Unit 42 cont'd

Adding "More" and "Most" to Adjectives

To show comparison, an adjective of two or more syllables adds "more." Greatest comparison is shown by adding "most."

EXAMPLES: a. important — more important — most important
               b. perfect — more perfect — most perfect

 Add "more" and "most" to each adjective.

1. expensive
   more expensive
   most expensive

2. appropriate

3. helpful

4. significant

5. wicked

6. selfish

7. beautiful

8. confident

9. attractive

10. valuable

11. precise

12. ruthless

13. wonderful

14. horrible

15. terrific

16. awkward

17. ignorant

18. intelligent

19. tragic

20. unimportant

21. recent

22. obedient

23. famous

24. correct

25. difficult

26. carefree

27. modern

28. glamorous

29. bashful

30. forgetful

31. polite

32. foolish

COMPOSITION EXERCISE

Choose 4 adjectives from today's exercise. Write a sentence with both the "more" and "most" forms of each adjective.

1. _____

2. _____

3. _____

4. _____

Identifying Adjectives

Adjectives describe nouns and pronouns.

EXAMPLES: *Janie gave an excellent report.*   *"Excellent" describes the report.*
                                                       "Report" is a noun.

              Her report was the best one.   *"Best" describes "one."*
                                                       "One" is a pronoun.

A Underline the adjectives. Draw an arrow to the noun or pronoun that each one describes.

1. The <u>note</u> paper was used by Tony.

2. The rock singer has green hair.

3. He plays loud music.

4. I love cloudy days!

5. We'll have rainy weather today.

6. Our old car finally gave out.

7. Kathy has a sunburned nose.

8. Watch out for the reckless driver!

9. The sweater is pale blue.

10. This is such a small piece of pie.

11. She lost five pounds.

12. The gold rings are the prettiest ones.

13. Lee has a sore shin.

14. He hit it on a heavy steel beam.

15. The baby weighs ten pounds.

16. Jean bought high heels.

17. She ate green apples.

18. I have a better idea.

19. We've had a busy day.

20. She has a beautiful voice.

B Use three adjectives to describe each noun.

1. flag	*red*	*foreign*	*new*
2. show			
3. shoes			
4. TV			
5. chair			
6. school			
7. light			
8. student			
9. driver			
10. cars			

11. leaves			
12. sea			
13. paper			
14. package			
15. treasure			
16. watch			
17. puppy			
18. star			
19. girl			
20. game			

C Choose from your adjectives in part B to fill in the blanks.

1. We found _____*buried*_____ treasure.

2. I fell out of a _____ chair.

3. Sherry bought _____ shoes.

4. We have a _____ puppy.

5. The _____ cage broke.

6. They flew the _____ flag.

7. We watched a _____ show.

8. The ship sailed the _____ sea.

9. You should use _____ paper.

10. Marla is a _____ girl.

11. Are you a _____ student?

12. _____ cars are on sale.

13. The _____ package was mine.

14. Tom is a _____ driver.

Unit 43 cont'd

Adding Adjectives

Adjectives are words that describe. They may tell how many, what color, what kind, or which one.

EXAMPLES: a. **An _old_ man bought the _sports_ car.**
b. **The _two_ boys wanted a _ten-speed_ bicycle.**
c. **Collier is reading a _thick_ book.**

 Fill in each blank with an adjective.

1. Your ___ _big_ ___ brother took my ___ _math_ ___ book.
    ___ _math_ ___   ___ _English_ ___

2. The _____ owner built a _____ store.
    _____   _____

3. _____ students visited the _____ museum.
    _____

4. I gave the _____ boy a _____ toy.
    _____   _____

5. A _____ car hit the _____ sign.
    _____   _____

6. _____ men pushed the _____ truck.
    _____   _____

7. The _____ policeman helped the _____ child.
    _____   _____

8. The _____ doctor cured the _____ girl.
    _____   _____

9. My _____ neighbor is my _____ friend.
    _____   _____

10. _____ horses jumped the _____ fence.
    _____   _____

11. Our _____ team won the _____ game.
    _____   _____

12. The _____ winner received a _____ trophy.
    _____   _____

13. The _____ club discovered a _____ treasure.
    _____   _____

14. Her _____ class postponed the _____ trip.
    _____   _____

COMPOSITION EXERCISE

List 20 adjectives.

1. _____   6. _____   11. _____   16. _____
2. _____   7. _____   12. _____   17. _____
3. _____   8. _____   13. _____   18. _____
4. _____   9. _____   14. _____   19. _____
5. _____   10. _____   15. _____   20. _____

Adverbs

An adverb is a modifier that tells how, when, or where.

A Fill in the blank with the question that each underlined adverb answers.

1. Please walk <u>slowly</u>. _____*how*_____   5. My aunt visits us <u>often</u>. _____

2. We'll leave <u>tomorrow</u>. _____   6. Turn <u>on</u> the radio, please. _____

3. Please bring the book <u>here</u>. _____   7. The car is rolling <u>backward</u>. _____

4. We found a store <u>nearby</u>. _____   8. I have <u>never</u> visited Chicago. _____

Many adverbs are formed by adding "-ly" to a noun or an adjective.

B Underline the adverb in each sentence below.

1. George stared <u>woodenly</u> at the door.   4. She spoke softly to the growling bear.

2. He tugged quickly on the rope.   5. The door hung loosely on its hinges.

3. Our newspaper is delivered daily.   6. Patty sang loudly to hide her fright.

C In each sentence below, underline the adverb; fill in the blank with "f"
if the position is fixed. Write "m" if the position is movable.

1. I ran quickly to the bus stop. _____*m*_____   5. Dad drove south of Memphis. _____

2. Louise ice-skates well. _____   6. The thief crept quietly to the door. _____

3. Mother is shopping today. _____   7. That family will be moving soon. _____

4. We walked off the curb. _____

Some adverbs show comparison by adding "-er" and "-est." Other adverbs change form or
are preceded by such modifiers as "more," "most," "less," and "least."

D In each sentence below, underline the adverb. Fill in the blank with the correct
form of the adverb in the comparative and superlative degrees.

1. Please handle the package carefully. _____

2. I dress fast in the morning. _____

3. Joe plays the piano well. _____

4. We thought little of it. _____

5. It rains often near the beach. _____

Unit 44 cont'd

Defining an Adverb

An adverb is a word that tells when, where, or how.

EXAMPLES: a. *When will we meet again? We will meet <u>tomorrow</u>.*
b. *Where is my new bike? Your new bike is <u>outside</u>.*
c. *How does Joe work? He works <u>quickly</u>.*

 Write an adverb in the blank to make the answer to the question complete. You may choose from the list below or use your own word.

1. When will you come home? I will come home _____*later*_____.
2. When does the plane leave? The plane is leaving _____.
3. When does the show begin? The show will begin _____.
4. When did Sam arrive? Sam arrived _____.
5. When may I have it? You may have it _____.
6. When will you be sure? I'll _____ be sure.
7. When did you buy that table? I bought the table _____.
8. When is her appointment? Her appointment is _____.
9. When will we eat? We will eat _____.
10. Where did you put your hat? I put my hat _____.
11. Where did Mike go? Mike went _____.
12. Where did you park the car? I parked the car _____.
13. Where is the monkey? The monkey is _____.
14. Where are the horses running? The horses are running _____.
15. Where does Kate live? Kate lives _____.
16. Where are we going? We are going _____.
17. Where is your mother? My mother is _____.
18. How did the turtle move? The turtle moved _____.
19. How did they sing? They sang _____.
20. How did George run? George ran _____.

wisely	yesterday	here	there	outside	quickly
truthfully	never	slowly	tomorrow	beautifully	immediately
out	inside	well	home	later	easily
early	carefully	nearby	away	now	today

COMPOSITION EXERCISE

Choose 10 adverbs from the box. Write a sentence with each.

1. _____
2. _____
3. _____
4. _____
5. _____

6. _____
7. _____
8. _____
9. _____
10. _____

Where to Find Adverbs

Adverbs are words that tell when, where, or how. They usually come close to verbs.

EXAMPLES:
a. *Carrie went downstairs.*
b. *Come here immediately.*
c. *Mr. Carson waited patiently.*
d. *Suddenly it was dark.*

Underline the adverbs.

1. I always eat slowly.
2. The mail will come soon.
3. The puppy ran outside.
4. The plane landed safely.
5. The paper comes daily.
6. The spider moved closer.
7. You acted foolishly.
8. Bring your paper here.
9. Lisa cried quietly.
10. The class finally ended.
11. It occurred recently.
12. The circus leaves tonight.
13. He quickly hid the evidence.
14. I locked the doors securely.
15. He planned his attack wisely.
16. Mother came immediately.
17. The people shouted angrily.
18. Lately you've been rude.
19. My aunt left yesterday.
20. I will be there.
21. You must come quickly.
22. Thomas ran upstairs.
23. Come inside.
24. The hospital is nearby.
25. Chris works carelessly.
26. She seldom visits us.
27. The accident happened suddenly.
28. Why were you late?
29. I usually bring my own.
30. The lion roared loudly.
31. Luckily we arrived safely.
32. The choir sang beautifully.
33. Can you come sooner?
34. Generally we take checks.
35. Read the book now.
36. The coins rolled everywhere.
37. Sometimes you bother me.
38. The ship sailed smoothly.
39. School begins tomorrow.
40. Stack the books neatly.
41. She swims gracefully.
42. I had called her earlier.
43. The colors match perfectly.
44. Peter has never seen a parade.
45. They are here.
46. Dean sat quietly and waited.
47. Why did you run away?
48. The man was badly hurt.
49. Are you always this happy?
50. The dog ate greedily.

COMPOSITION EXERCISE

List 20 adverbs.

1. _____
2. _____
3. _____
4. _____
5. _____
6. _____
7. _____
8. _____
9. _____
10. _____
11. _____
12. _____
13. _____
14. _____
15. _____
16. _____
17. _____
18. _____
19. _____
20. _____

Unit 45 cont'd

When, Where, and How

Adverbs answer the questions when, where, and how.

EXAMPLES:
 a. The bus will come <u>soon</u>. *"Soon" tells <u>when</u> the bus will come.*
 b. The bus goes <u>there</u>.   *"There" tells <u>where</u> the bus goes.*
 c. The bus travels <u>fast</u>.   *"Fast" tells <u>how</u> the bus travels.*

A Underline the adverb in each sentence. Then answer the question following each sentence.

1. Sara arrived <u>yesterday</u>. When did Sara arrive?   *yesterday*
2. She frowned unhappily. How did she frown?   _____
3. Larry laughed crazily at the movie. How did Larry laugh? _____
4. Terra promptly answered the letter. When did Terra answer the letter? _____
5. Margo laughed silently at her sister. How did Margo laugh at her sister? _____
6. Put the glasses here. Where should you put the glasses? _____
7. I am going home. Where am I going? _____
8. He turned the cap slowly. How did he turn the cap? _____
9. We will then dismiss class. When will we dismiss class? _____
10. Mom planted the bulbs today. When did Mom plant the bulbs? _____
11. Alex glanced nervously at the baby. How did Alex glance at the baby? _____
12. He opened the door noisily. How did he open the door? _____
13. They traveled abroad last summer. Where did they travel last summer? _____
14. Richard shook his head sadly. How did Richard shake his head? _____
15. Steve walked rapidly into the store. How did Steve walk into the store? _____

B Underline the adverb in each sentence and then tell which question the adverb answers.

1. He can <u>easily</u> solve the problem. *How?* 11. He often calls his grandmother. _____
2. She plays the trumpet poorly. _____ 12. Hal worriedly paid the bill. _____
3. I'm seriously considering leaving. _____ 13. They hurriedly left the scene. _____
4. Then we'll read the directions. _____ 14. The crowd cheered wildly. _____
5. The band arrived late. _____ 15. The hunters walked far into the woods. _____
6. The monster came near. _____ 16. Bill got a haircut yesterday. _____
7. We proudly sang the anthem. _____ 17. The pilot flew up into the clouds. _____
8. My best friend lives here. _____ 18. I've seen this movie before. _____
9. I'll answer you soon. _____ 19. The batter swung fast. _____
10. Put the candy close to me. _____ 20. She looked down into the well. _____

COMPOSITION EXERCISE

Write 10 sentences which contain adverbs. Underline the adverbs.

1. _____ 6. _____
2. _____ 7. _____
3. _____ 8. _____
4. _____ 9. _____
5. _____ 10. _____

Comprehension Check

(A) Underline the adjectives.

1. <u>short</u>	11. burst	21. could
2. red	12. cold	22. good
3. like	13. winter	23. yell
4. run	14. green	24. happy
5. sad	15. large	25. turn
6. thick	16. season	26. new
7. jump	17. dive	27. bounce
8. fell	18. man	28. thin
9. play	19. deep	29. gym
10. narrow	20. kind	30. busy

(B) Underline each adjective once. Underline the word each adjective modifies twice.

1. Sherry is a <u>new</u> <u>student</u>.
2. I can't draw a straight line.
3. Use a thick, strong rope.
4. We have a new teacher.
5. The room is too warm.
6. Anna has a friendly smile.
7. Greg is a fast sprinter.
8. We have a secret plan.
9. The pie is too rich.
10. Keep the answers simple.

(C) Write the positive, comparative, or superlative form of each adjective.

	positive	comparative	superlative
1.	short	shorter	*shortest*
2.		easier	easiest
3.	blue		bluest
4.		happier	happiest
5.	good		best
6.	kind	kinder	
7.	beautiful		most beautiful
8.	dark	darker	
9.	sweet		sweetest
10.		harder	hardest

(D) Complete each sentence with either the comparative or the superlative form of the adjective in parentheses.

(pretty)   1. The spruce tree is _____ *prettier* _____ than the fir tree.

(peaceful)   2. That meadow is the _____ place I know.

(thin)   3. The white spaghetti noodle is _____ than the yellow strand.

(silly)   4. You're _____ than ever!

(clean)   5. My room is _____ than it was last week.

(fresh)   6. This room spray has the _____ scent.

(low)   7. Put the volume on the _____ setting.

(confident)   8. Angela is _____ now about speaking in public.

(polite)   9. The little girl is _____ than her sister.

(difficult)   10. This is our _____ test.

(valuable)   11. Gold is _____ than silver.

(foolish)   12. You are even _____ than I thought.

Test 9 cont'd →

Comprehension Check (continued)

E Underline each adverb.

1. <u>loudly</u>
2. left
3. nearby
4. move
5. early
6. slowly
7. sang
8. cry
9. outside
10. more
11. live
12. now
13. hat
14. well
15. yesterday
16. river
17. never
18. run
19. away
20. begin

F Complete each sentence with an adverb from part D.

1. Can you hear _____ *well* _____ ?
2. The fire is _____ .
3. Put the garbage _____ .
4. We will _____ eat lunch.
5. We're _____ for the concert.
6. Alex left _____ .
7. We _____ have spinach.
8. She played the guitar _____ .
9. Put your books _____ .
10. Chew your food _____ .

G Underline each adverb.

1. The baby cried <u>sadly</u>.
2. We quickly ran home.
3. I'll never agree to that!
4. Tim hurriedly ran upstairs.
5. There are the car keys.
6. We will then hear the new song.
7. Luckily we weren't late.
8. It happened so suddenly.
9. We tossed the frisbee up.
10. Don't let the spider get near.
11. Sharla will then make her plans.
12. Clean your room completely.
13. Jim proudly accepted the award.
14. The crippled jet landed safely.
15. I'm terribly sorry about it.
16. Bring the test here.
17. Janice wisely stayed home.
18. Trudy left early today.
19. The lion roared loudly.
20. He drove wildly around the corner.
21. I'll see you around.
22. Shut the door carefully.
23. I'm usually better at this.
24. Ivan rarely joins us.

Write a paragraph describing a storm. Underline each adjective and each adverb.

_____
_____
_____
_____
_____
_____
_____
_____
_____

Prepositions   Unit 46

Prepositions introduce word-group modifiers that end in nouns or pronouns.

EXAMPLES:

a. We walked <u>through the woods</u>.

b. I have a letter <u>for you</u>.

c. The man <u>behind the window</u> waved.

d. <u>After the game</u> they went <u>to the dance</u>.

e. The ride <u>down the mountain</u> was exciting.

f. The argument was <u>between him and her</u>.

g. Joe walked <u>with John</u> <u>along the river</u>.

h. Your napkin is <u>under the table</u>.

A In the sentences below, underline the word-group modifiers.

1. This book is <u>for us</u>.

2. Many houses by the river were flooded.

3. Put the broom behind the door.

4. Do you see the closet below the stairs?

5. Millie sits between us in class.

6. From this window we can see above the trees.

Word-group modifiers introduced by prepositions are called prepositional phrases. The concluding nouns or pronouns are called objects of prepositions. Pronouns must take the object forms "me," "him," "her," "it," "you," "us," and "them."

B Write the correct forms of the pronouns in parentheses in the blanks below. Underline the prepositions twice and the nouns used as objects of prepositions once.

1. (you, I)   Jim is going to the game with _____ .

2. (we)   Mrs. Simms, our math teacher, lives in the apartment over _____ .

3. (she)   Although she disagreed, we should not go over the hill without _____ .

4. (he)   The ball slammed against the fence and then rolled toward _____ .

5. (they, she)   During recess the window near _____ broke into little pieces.

Prepositional phrases may be placed anywhere in a sentence. However, we must be watchful of misplaced phrases like the following underlined ones:

EXAMPLES: a. The man ⬇ fell overboard <u>in the boat</u>.

              b. The player ⬇ was taken to a doctor <u>with a broken leg</u>.

C Underline the prepositional phrase in each sentence below; then draw an arrow where it should appear, as illustrated above.

1. We went and had dinner into the house.

2. The house is haunted by the gas station.

3. Jill saw a man wave good-bye with her father.

4. A picture on the floor fell down.

5. Some houses were flooded by the hill.

Unit 46 cont'd ➡

Adding Prepositions

Prepositions are words that show what relationship one word has to another.

EXAMPLES:
a. in   d. over
b. for   e. with
c. to   f. among

A Underline the prepositions.

1. <u>of</u>
2. under
3. words
4. in
5. are
6. from
7. by
8. at
9. crash
10. storm
11. around
12. for
13. Mike
14. into
15. number
16. over
17. to
18. toward
19. head
20. across
21. after
22. paper
23. on
24. ring
25. with
26. nest
27. through
28. behind
29. ice
30. between
31. down
32. up
33. floor
34. within
35. above
36. is
37. except
38. ten
39. inside
40. table
41. without
42. flower
43. music
44. outside
45. bank
46. out of
47. in front of
48. George
49. until
50. against

B Write a preposition in each blank.

1. ____in____ the morning
2. _____ Alex
3. _____ an hour
4. _____ the fence
5. _____ the street
6. _____ the house
7. _____ class
8. _____ the book
9. _____ the car
10. _____ my head
11. _____ the window
12. _____ a friend
13. _____ the chair
14. _____ the meeting
15. _____ January
16. _____ our home
17. _____ the corner
18. _____ Sam's house
19. _____ the hall
20. _____ the center
21. _____ the door
22. _____ his father
23. _____ the train
24. _____ his nose
25. _____ help
26. _____ us
27. _____ the clouds
28. _____ her mother
29. _____ the road
30. _____ the tree
31. _____ my room
32. _____ me
33. _____ the box
34. _____ Janice
35. _____ the sofa
36. _____ the table
37. _____ the hill
38. _____ noon
39. _____ time
40. _____ the edge
41. _____ the river
42. _____ the store
43. _____ a doubt
44. _____ the pages
45. _____ tomorrow
46. _____ the rainbow
47. _____ your eye
48. _____ a pencil
49. _____ Mark Twain
50. _____ television

COMPOSITION EXERCISE

Choose 10 prepositional phrases from part B. Write a sentence with each.

1. _____
2. _____
3. _____
4. _____
5. _____
6. _____
7. _____
8. _____
9. _____
10. _____

Identifying Prepositions   Unit 47

A preposition is a connective word that joins a word group to the rest of a sentence. The preposition plus the word group is called a prepositional phrase and may come at the beginning, in the middle, or at the end of a sentence.

A In the following sentences underline the prepositions once and their objects twice.

1. Karen went shopping <u>with</u> her <u>mother</u>.

2. She lost one of her earrings in the tall grass.

3. The baseball team had to choose between Mike and Eric to be their captain.

4. The old man was asleep during the whole storm.

5. She looked through the files to find the mine deeds.

6. Pressing the inked stone against the paper will create a print.

7. Most of the pictures were taken near the mountain area.

8. The valley lies below the steep mountain.

9. She slipped on the ice and cut her head.

10. He reached under the counter and pulled out the rusty box.

B In these sentences some of the prepositional phrases are placed too far from the words they modify. Rewrite each sentence correctly.

1. The dog was chasing a car with a spot on his nose.

   _____

2. The man wiped his forehead on the ground.

   _____

3. The horse was taken to the veterinarian with a broken leg.

   _____

4. The baby was lying in the car with the measles.

   _____

5. The farm house was purchased by an old lady with red doors.

   _____

COMPOSITION EXERCISE

Write five sentences containing prepositional phrases.

1. _____
2. _____
3. _____
4. _____
5. _____

Unit 47 cont'd

Prepositions Puzzle

A preposition connects a word group to the rest of the sentence.

Other prepositions are as follows:

above	by
across	concerning
against	during
along	except
among	for
around	from
before	in
behind	inside
beside	into
besides	near
between	off
beyond	

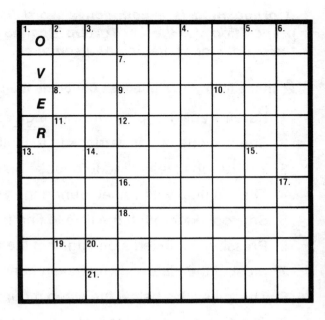

Down

1. _o_ _v_ _e_ _r_ above in place or position

2. _ _ _ _ to a higher place

3. _ _ _ _ _ _ _ _ from one end to the other

4. _ _ _ _ _ _ from a higher to a lower place in a river

5. _ _ _ _ _ forth from; away; not in or at a position

6. _ _ _ _ _ _ place lower than another

8. _ _ _ above or supported by

11. _ _ _ _ _ close to in space, time, condition, or relation

13. _ _ _ _ _ _ below the surface of

15. _ _ _ _ _ _ _ something near or close to; not far from

Fill in the blanks. Then complete the puzzle.

17. _ _ _ _ _ in the company of; in the same direction of; toward

Across

1. _ _ _ _ _ _ _ _ _ beyond the limits of; not inside

7. _ _ _ _ _ _ He stood _ _ _ _ _ the rung of the ladder.

9. _ _ _ made from; containing

10. _ _ _ in, on, by, or near

12. _ _ _ _ _ _ _ from a past time until now; at any time between

14. _ _ _ _ _ _ _ up to the time of

16. _ _ _ _ _ _ farther on than; later than; no longer capable of

18. _ _ _ _ _ _ resembling something or each other

20. _ _ _ _ _ _ _ going or coming in the rear of; behind

21. _ _ _ _ _ _ _ _ _ covered by; in a lower place; below

116

Conjunctions

A conjunction is a connecting word that joins single words, word groups, and sentence patterns.

EXAMPLES:
and	yet	nor	either or
but	for	so	neither nor
or			

A Underline each conjunction in the sentences below.

1. Louise <u>and</u> Fred are playing in the band.
2. The girls worked hard and saved carefully for three months.
3. The man spoke softly but sternly to the boys.
4. Neither John nor Debbie plans to enter the contest.
5. That road will take you across the river and into town.
6. Jim should have won the prize, for he had been carefully preparing all year.
7. Mr. Baker is a fine artist, yet he has never sold a painting.
8. The bus broke down on Fletcher Street, so we had to call home for rides.
9. My uncle says he has never gone to Chicago, nor will he go there.
10. Either we will go to Florida this Christmas or we will visit my grandmother.

A coordinate conjunction connects ideas of equal importance. It is frequently used to join two or more sentence patterns for a compound sentence.

B Fill in each blank with "and," "but," "yet," or "so."

1. A sofa stood along one wall, _____ a table stood along another.
2. We went to the movies, _____ Mother stayed at home.
3. My brother makes a lot of money, _____ he never saves any.
4. Teddie was late for school, _____ he was sent to the principal's office.
5. Jim's grandfather is a good swimmer, _____ he is 72 years old.

Subordinate conjunctions connect ideas that are not of equal importance. If the conjunction is omitted, the meanings of the two parts of the sentence are changed.

EXAMPLES:
if	how	until	where	because
as	when	while	unless	although
since	after	though		

C Write "c" above the conjunction in each sentence below.

1. Julie couldn't sleep bec^cause she was frightened by the strong winds outside.

2. You may join the club if the other members agree to it.

3. We will stay here until the roads are cleared of snow.

4. Did you fall asleep while Mr. Mitchell was talking?

5. Pete will stay since we are having fried chicken for dinner.

6. The pictures should be good unless the camera's batteries are weak.

7. I don't know how you made that bird feeder so neatly.

Unit 48 cont'd

Connectives

A **connective** is a word that holds a sentence together. Some connectives are **and**, **but**, and **or**.

EXAMPLES: *Jean and Joan are twins.*
It rained, but we didn't get wet.
Are you coming or going?

A Use the correct connective in each sentence.

1. Either we go to the party, __*or*__ we stay home alone.
2. He may go with us, _____ I doubt it.
3. The race car crashed _____ burned.
4. We tried to get there, _____ we didn't make it.
5. Susan _____ Tom are having a surprise party tonight.
6. We planted our crops, _____ the rain destroyed them.
7. Could you see the wreck _____ not?
8. You do the shopping, _____ I will clean the house.
9. We looked around the house, _____ I couldn't find the dog.
10. She packed her suitcase _____ left the house.
11. Are your cousins _____ your friends going with you?
12. Mother bought me some shoes _____ a dress.
13. The boys played baseball, _____ they stopped for lunch.
14. Please hurry, _____ we will be late for school.
15. He works _____ goes to school.

B Write three sentences using the word **and**.

_____
_____
_____

Write three sentences using the word **but**.

_____
_____
_____

Write three sentences using the word **or**.

_____
_____
_____

Using Conjunctions

Conjunctions are words which connect words or groups of words. Conjunctions include the words "and," "but," "or," "for," "yet," and "so."

EXAMPLES: conjunctions connecting words:

Rick and Danny went skating.

Sharon washed and ironed her shirt.

conjunctions connecting groups of words: We knew he won, for he was smiling.

Jim wasn't hungry, but he ate our dessert.

A Use "and," "but," and "or" in the blanks. Underline the words being connected.

1. Nick __*and*__ Chris walked home.

2. The dogs _____ cats were on display.

3. The manager _____ the clerk had a meeting.

4. I think that either Karen _____ Sue will sing.

5. Lynn will sing _____ dance for the club.

6. I like to watch basketball _____ football.

7. We will eat now _____ watch television later.

8. They won the game _____ then celebrated.

9. Her favorite foods are yogurt _____ bananas.

10. Steve is tired _____ happy.

11. English _____ history are Greg's best subjects.

12. Tony tried to slow down _____ fell anyway.

13. Jill jumped high _____ broke the ceiling light.

14. I want either a hamburger _____ a hot dog.

15. Alex likes to ski _____ to ice skate.

16. I don't know whether I will stay _____ go.

17. Patty _____ Andy will make the speech.

18. The pitcher _____ the catcher will signal.

19. He raised his hand _____ answered the question.

20. Should I watch cartoons _____ the news?

21. We have a test in math _____ in French today.

22. His new bike is red, white, _____ black.

23. Josh _____ his friends practiced yesterday.

24. He hit his opponent _____ knocked him down.

B Use "and," "but," "or," "nor," "for," "yet," and "so" in the blanks.

1. Lynn tripped on his shoelace, __*and*__ he fell.

2. Ken reached down, _____ he helped him up.

3. Alison didn't want beans, _____ did she want rice.

4. Lana was late, _____ she missed her bus.

5. He made a low grade, _____ he'll try to improve.

6. Beth baked a cake, _____ now she'll frost it.

7. John learned to sew, _____ he can't hem the cuffs.

8. Candy saw the detour, _____ she slowed down.

9. You must go to sleep, _____ you'll be tired tomorrow.

10. Be quiet, _____ you'll wake the baby.

11. She wasn't finished, _____ she closed the book.

12. Watch carefully, _____ you'll see the deer.

13. I didn't shop yesterday, _____ will I shop today.

14. Alex jumped, _____ the parachute opened.

15. He wanted to play, _____ he had practiced.

16. He decided to jump again, _____ he rented a plane.

17. Sandy wants a good grade, _____ she'll study.

18. Chris did well, _____ he was proud of himself.

19. Her parents said "No," _____ Jan stayed home.

20. Jack was tired, _____ he couldn't sleep.

21. My uncle dieted, _____ he couldn't lose weight.

22. Jane went to bed early, _____ she had a game today.

23. Bob uses ketchup, _____ he doesn't like mustard.

24. I felt a draft, _____ the window was broken.

COMPOSITION EXERCISE

Write 8 sentences using conjunctions. Use each conjunction at least once.

1. _____

2. _____

3. _____

4. _____

5. _____

6. _____

7. _____

8. _____

Unit 49 cont'd

Adding Conjunctions

Conjunctions are connecting words. Common conjunctions are "and," "but," and "or."

EXAMPLES: a. The man is rich <u>and</u> famous. c. Is Michael short <u>or</u> tall?

b. Read the book, <u>and</u> write a report. d. He aimed carefully <u>but</u> missed.

 In each blank write a conjunction.

1. Dave __AND__ I will defend you.
2. Take a pen _____ pencil.
3. I ate not one _____ six cakes.
4. Choose Karen _____ Doris.
5. Do you need Paul _____ me?
6. The show is on Tuesday _____ Friday.
7. Go home _____ stay here.
8. Not John _____ Al is responsible.
9. Kay ran away _____ hid.
10. Is the dog a collie _____ a poodle?
11. We had lunch _____ not dinner.
12. The boy pushed _____ pulled.
13. Was that Sue _____ Kate?
14. I can skate _____ swim.
15. Is she calling you _____ me?
16. Are they friends _____ enemies?
17. Will you bring apples _____ bananas?
18. Did she choose red _____ orange?
19. The river was wide _____ deep.
20. Answer yes _____ no.
21. I saw a zebra _____ an elephant.
22. Runners were on first _____ second.
23. You _____ his are pronouns.
24. Mr. James is old _____ wise.
25. Your mom _____ dad must attend.

26. We must fight _____ surrender.
27. Diane _____ Steve are twins.
28. Did you _____ Jan see the accident?
29. Perry _____ Chris were elected.
30. It took Jay _____ Phil to hold him.
31. We had peas _____ carrots.
32. She is cute _____ not pretty.
33. Ms. Kay brought pencils _____ paper.
34. I like math _____ science.
35. Did you invite Jack _____ Pam?
36. Pete _____ Lee tied for first place.
37. The water was cold _____ dirty.
38. We ate sandwiches _____ drank Cokes.
39. The baby yawned _____ fell asleep.
40. Candy is sweet, _____ lemons are sour.
41. Yellow ____ green are my favorite colors.
42. Don _____ I are neighbors.
43. Bring me a hammer _____ a nail.
44. I have a brother _____ two sisters.
45. Am I invited _____ not?
46. Is the answer true _____ false?
47. Tim is small _____ strong.
48. Do you want a fork _____ a spoon?
49. He opened the door _____ walked inside.
50. The advice was helpful _____ unwanted.

COMPOSITION EXERCISE

Write 10 sentences which contain conjunctions.

1. _____
2. _____
3. _____
4. _____
5. _____

6. _____
7. _____
8. _____
9. _____
10. _____

Interjections

An interjection is any word in a statement that shows surprise or strong feeling.

heavens	goodness	my	help	why
good	fine	well	ouch	oh
alas	humbug	gosh	golly	wow
bah	hurrah	hurray	yes	
no	rats			

When an interjection is used to show extreme excitement, it is separated from other words in a sentence by an exclamation mark (!) ; and the first word that follows it begins with a capital letter.

EXAMPLE: Gosh! I knew that all the time.

Interjections used to express milder emotions are set off with commas.

EXAMPLES: **Oh,** we practice every day.
Why, where are you going?

Interjections are signals of emphasis in both writing and speaking. When used with an exclamation mark, they symbolize the unusually high pitch and loudness heard when a speaker is very excited. Used with a comma, interjections may symbolize a sudden drop in pitch, which is another means of oral stress.

A Underline the interjections in each of the following sentences.

1. Heavens! I forgot my lunch.

2. Bah! Humbug! Parties are a waste of time!

3. Golly, when do you think we can go?

4. Wow! That was some game!

5. Ouch! I just stubbed my toe.

6. Well, young man, do you think you can carry all those books by yourself?

7. Oh, my! I'm still in my pajamas!

8. Yes, you are absolutely right.

9. No! I won't do that.

10. "Alas!" moaned the maid, "Now I'll never wed!"

B Punctuate the following sentences to set off the interjections. If the statement suggests strong excitement, use an exclamation mark (!) and capitalize the first word that follows. If less excitement is suggested, use a comma (,).

1. No, I didn't have the right answer.

2. Gee must you always make fun of me?

3. My goodness Charlie, you're wet from head to foot.

4. Hurray we won the game!

5. Help I'm stuck in this dark mine shaft.

6. Rats I'll never do that again.

Unit 50 cont'd

Adding Interjections

Interjections are words that express strong feelings. Exclamation points follow them.

EXAMPLES: a. _Rats!_ *I struck out.*   c. _Hey!_ *Who are you?*
                 b. _Stop!_ *You'll get hurt.*   d. _Wait!_ *I'll help you.*

 In each blank write an interjection. Punctuate each interjection properly.

1. __Ouch!__ That hurts.
2. _____ You forgot me.
3. _____ You can't do that.
4. _____ Did you see that?
5. _____ Who did this?
6. _____ He is strong.
7. _____ How could you?
8. _____ Did you hear that?
9. _____ That was a good meal.
10. _____ We lost.
11. _____ It's 5 o'clock.
12. _____ Now we can begin.
13. _____ I won't help you.
14. _____ You're nice.
15. _____ It's for me.
16. _____ We're late.
17. _____ What a beautiful day this is.
18. _____ That's a silly idea.
19. _____ I'm home.
20. _____ I'd love to go.
21. _____ I hate holidays.
22. _____ It's raining again.
23. _____ I missed it.
24. _____ He deserved it.
25. _____ I can't move.

26. _____ It tastes terrible.
27. _____ What can I do?
28. _____ I made it.
29. _____ Now we can eat.
30. _____ That's a relief.
31. _____ Don't come in here.
32. _____ It's I.
33. _____ Report cards are today.
34. _____ This game is great.
35. _____ You're taking my car.
36. _____ Be careful.
37. _____ You don't mean that.
38. _____ She'll see you.
39. _____ I'm coming.
40. _____ I can't swim.
41. _____ You've worked all day.
42. _____ I'm glad you came.
43. _____ Thanksgiving is a bore.
44. _____ Here comes Terry.
45. _____ You did it perfectly.
46. _____ What will we do?
47. _____ She broke my heart.
48. _____ I can do it.
49. _____ You stop that.
50. _____ It's another home run.

COMPOSITION EXERCISE

Write 10 sentences which begin with interjections.

1. _____
2. _____
3. _____
4. _____
5. _____

6. _____
7. _____
8. _____
9. _____
10. _____

Comprehension Check

Ⓐ Underline each preposition.

1. <u>in</u>	11. have	21. into
2. behind	12. about	22. recent
3. jump	13. before	23. after
4. event	14. around	24. across
5. out	15. if	25. beneath
6. off	16. with	26. upon
7. cover	17. for	27. over
8. at	18. upstairs	28. up
9. thought	19. of	29. from
10. to	20. lonely	30. by

Ⓑ Complete each sentence with a preposition.

1. Karla looked ____*in*____ the window.
2. The horse jumped _____ the fence.
3. Please go _____ me, Andrew.
4. The stones skipped _____ the water.
5. Speak _____ the microphone.
6. Mary stood _____ the porch.
7. Terry paid the money _____ Melvin.
8. May I have a piece _____ candy?
9. Mrs. Bach looked _____ Sandra.
10. Lynn will speak _____ Wilma.

Ⓒ There are no prepositions in these sentences. Rewrite them, putting prepositions where they belong.

1. We jumped the pool. — *We jumped into the pool.*
2. Call me the dance. _____
3. Wrap the band the cap. _____
4. Let me tell you the party. _____
5. Look the sofa the keys. _____
6. I saw Linda the mall. _____
7. I'll vote Harrison. _____
8. Gayle drove school today. _____
9. We'll leave it the door. _____
10. Our dog jumped the deck. _____

Ⓓ Punctuate each interjection and match it with an appropriate sentence.

1. Nonsense!
2. Stop
3. You're wrong
4. Beware
5. Wonderful
6. Yes

7. Yea
8. No
9. Welcome
10. Let me
11. Don't
12. At last

a. Please quit making noise.
b. That's silly.
c. That isn't the answer.
d. There's danger ahead.
e. We agree with you.
f. I'm happy for you.

g. I won't do it.
h. I can do it.
i. Come right in.
j. We won.
k. I've waited so long.
l. You must stop.

Test 10 cont'd →

Comprehension Check (continued)

E Complete the sentences with the conjunctions in the box.

and	but	or	nor	for	yet	so	either . . . or	neither . . . nor

1. Ted ___*and*___ Carol are friends.
2. Dan's voice is soft _____ firm.
3. Our car is gray _____ white.
4. Season it with sugar _____ spices.
5. The wallet was lost _____ stolen.
6. They are poor _____ happy.
7. _____ Wendy _____ Gail will win.
8. _____ Diane _____ Jill called me.
9. Stacie _____ Rhonda are dancers.
10. Roger is tall _____ slim.
11. We'll attend, rain _____ shine.
12. _____ Ken _____ Jack is correct.
13. I tore the page, _____ I taped it.
14. We called Jean, _____ he was gone.
15. Tammy took the test, _____ she passed it.
16. Don't tell anyone, _____ I'll be angry.
17. Kevin is young, _____ he's a fine athlete.
18. I don't want this, _____ will I ever want it.
19. Turn on the lights, _____ you'll stumble.
20. Frank arrived early, _____ we can begin now.
21. Earl drove too fast, _____ he got a ticket.
22. Russ doesn't eat fruit, _____ does he eat bread.
23. Kris was tardy, _____ she got an admit slip.
24. Holly sleeps late, _____ she's always on time.

F Write the subordinate conjunction contained in each sentence in the blank after the sentence.

1. Since you are so interested, I'll give you the details. ___*since*___
2. I'm sleepy because I stayed up too late last night. _____
3. When Roy arrived, he offered to give us a ride. _____
4. Because I failed a semester of math, I have to repeat the class. _____
5. We won't know the results until the returns come in. _____
6. Though the shoes hurt my feet, I'll wear them tonight. _____
7. Kendra can't remember where she put her car keys. _____
8. While the singers are practicing, Eric will build the bleachers. _____
9. Ellen wants to see you before you leave for the game. _____
10. As Laura was answering the phone, the doorbell rang. _____

Write a paragraph about some good luck you have had. Underline each preposition.

_____

_____

_____

_____

_____

_____

_____

Contractions

A contraction is a shortened word made from two or more words. An apostrophe shows where one or more letters have been omitted.

EXAMPLES: a. of the clock ➜ o'clock
             b. what is ➜ what's
             c. are not ➜ aren't

A Write the contraction for each set of words.

1. let us __let's__
2. can not _____
3. do not _____
4. I will _____
5. you are _____
6. where is _____
7. should not _____
8. he has _____
9. we are _____
10. it is _____

11. I am _____
12. could not _____
13. have not _____
14. we will _____
15. what is _____
16. will not _____
17. was not _____
18. is not _____
19. there is _____
20. she is _____

21. you have _____
22. are not _____
23. she will _____
24. I have _____
25. did not _____
26. that is _____
27. they are _____
28. were not _____
29. would not _____
30. you will _____

B Complete each sentence by adding a contraction.

1. The meeting will be at six __o'clock__.
2. _____ arrive at noon.
3. I _____ remember the story.
4. Ken and I _____ invited.
5. _____ the address?
6. _____ my sister.
7. Mr. Woods _____ at home.
8. _____ finished the assignment.
9. You _____ keep your promise.
10. They _____ move.
11. _____ classmates at school.
12. _____ go to the park.
13. _____ my hat?
14. You _____ tell her.
15. _____ too late.
16. He _____ tell me anything.
17. It _____ matter now.
18. _____ your ticket.

19. _____ not enough time.
20. _____ be here soon.
21. We _____ ready yet.
22. Rick _____ called today.
23. _____ already begun.
24. It _____ your fault.
25. _____ waiting for a friend.
26. _____ late again.
27. _____ not true!
28. Brad _____ able to help us.
29. Someone _____ like me.
30. _____ asleep.
31. _____ you come in?
32. _____ coming tomorrow.
33. I _____ recognize her.
34. _____ talk to Dave about it.
35. _____ your room?

Unit 51 cont'd ➜

Writing Contractions

A contraction is a shortened word made from two words written together.

An apostrophe shows where one or more letters have been omitted to make a contraction.

EXAMPLES:
   a. can not → can't
   b. would have → would've
   c. she is → she's
   d. I will → I'll
   e. did not → didn't
   f. you are → you're

A Write the contraction for each set of words.

1. here is ___here's___
2. he is _____
3. let us _____
4. you will _____
5. I am _____
6. there is _____
7. they are _____
8. does not _____
9. they have _____
10. could have _____

11. you have _____
12. what is _____
13. have not _____
14. could not _____
15. is not _____
16. had not _____
17. who is _____
18. it will _____
19. he would _____
20. she is _____

21. it is _____
22. we are _____
23. were not _____
24. is not _____
25. will not _____
26. do not _____
27. we will _____
28. are not _____
29. should have _____
30. where is _____

B Complete each sentence by adding a contraction.

1. ___Let's___ visit my Aunt Martha.
2. Katherine _____ arrived yet.
3. _____ someone help me?
4. _____ already chosen our leader.
5. I _____ told you that.
6. The teacher _____ surprised.
7. _____ my coat ?
8. _____ the owner of the blue car.
9. _____ you remember who he is?
10. _____ going on here!
11. We _____ allowed to go outside.
12. _____ someone in the house!
13. Gilbert _____ finished yet.
14. Why _____ you call me?
15. Surely you _____ believe that!

16. _____ too tired to do anything.
17. They _____ heard the news.
18. _____ that man in the gray suit?
19. Lynn _____ coming to the party.
20. It _____ anyone's fault.
21. _____ discuss the matter further.
22. I _____ understand the assignment.
23. Mr. Johns _____ like sports.
24. _____ you give him the message?
25. _____ too late to stop her.
26. _____ a letter for you, Mark.
27. It _____ hurt you.
28. You _____ been here at noon.
29. _____ waiting in the hallway.
30. _____ predicted snow for tomorrow.

COMPOSITION EXERCISE

List 12 contractions.

1. _____
2. _____
3. _____

4. _____
5. _____
6. _____

7. _____
8. _____
9. _____

10. _____
11. _____
12. _____

The Parts of Speech

The dictionary shows the part of speech of the entry word. The part of speech is written before the definition or definitions. The part of speech is abbreviated.

n. — noun	adv. — adverb
v. — verb	conj.—conjunction
pron. — pronoun	prep. — preposition
adj. — adjective	

 Use the following dictionary entries to answer the questions.

---

au/tumn (ô′təm) *n., adj.* —n. the season of the year between summer and winter. —adj. coming in autumn.

ba/nan/a (bə năn′ə) *n.,* a yellow fruit with firm, creamy flesh.

cap/ture (kăp′chər) *n., v.* —n. the act of taking by force. —v. make a prisoner of.

har/bor (här′bər) *n., v.* —n. 1 place of shelter for ships. 2 any place of shelter. —v. 1 give shelter. 2 keep in the mind.

prob/a/bly (prŏb′ə blē) *adv.,* more likely than not.

we (wē) *pron.,* the speaker and another person.

---

1. Which of the entries may be used as an adjective? _____ *autumn* _____

2. Which of the entries may be used as an adverb? _____

3. Which of the entries may be used as a pronoun? _____

4. Which of the entries may be used as verbs? _____

5. Which of the entries may be used as nouns? _____

6. What is the adjective definition of "autumn"? _____

7. What is the verb definition of "capture"? _____

8. How many noun definitions are given for "harbor"? _____

9. How many verb definitions are given for "harbor"? _____

10. Could "banana" be used as a verb? _____

11. What is the definition of "probably"? _____

12. What is the definition of "we"? _____

13. What part of speech is "banana"? _____

14. What part of speech is "we"? _____

15. What parts of speech is "capture"? _____

Unit 52 cont'd

Identifying Parts of Speech

1. **noun** — names a person, place, or thing
   EXAMPLES: farmer   home   tractor
2. **pronoun** — takes place of a noun
   EXAMPLES: I   you   it
3. **verb** — shows action or state of being
   EXAMPLES: run   work   is
4. **adjective** — describes a noun
   EXAMPLES: green   big   chocolate

5. **adverb** — tells when, where, or how
   EXAMPLES: now   here   easily
6. **conjunction** — connects
   EXAMPLES: and   or   but
7. **interjection** — shows strong feelings
   EXAMPLES: Ouch!   Hey!   Eek!
8. **preposition** — shows word relationships
   EXAMPLES: in   with   under

✳ Identify the part of speech of each underlined word.   n — noun   p — pronoun   v — verb
adj — adjective   adv — adverb   con — conjunction   int — interjection   pr — preposition

___n___ 1. The <u>house</u> was built in 1901.
_____ 2. <u>He</u> is the star player.
_____ 3. Dave <u>smashed</u> the vase.
_____ 4. I bought a <u>yellow</u> hat.
_____ 5. Come <u>now</u>.
_____ 6. You <u>and</u> I are going.
_____ 7. <u>Wow</u>! What a game that was.
_____ 8. Run <u>to</u> the house.
_____ 9. Josh is an <u>astronaut</u>.
_____ 10. This is a <u>good</u> book.
_____ 11. <u>It</u> has stopped raining.
_____ 12. Put the box <u>on</u> the floor.
_____ 13. I ate not one <u>but</u> six pies.
_____ 14. <u>Hurray</u>! We won.
_____ 15. <u>You</u> are in trouble.
_____ 16. Paul <u>and</u> Isaac raced.
_____ 17. He <u>always</u> finishes first.
_____ 18. The <u>second</u> car is on fire.
_____ 19. I <u>love</u> it.
_____ 20. These <u>vegetables</u> are fresh.
_____ 21. Don <u>pushed</u> the car.
_____ 22. I <u>am</u> Stephen.
_____ 23. They were blue <u>and</u> white.

_____ 24. The dog is <u>under</u> the porch.
_____ 25. Choose Barry <u>or</u> me.
_____ 26. The <u>swing</u> is broken.
_____ 27. <u>I</u> need $30.00.
_____ 28. Where did <u>she</u> go?
_____ 29. <u>Bill</u> works for my dad.
_____ 30. Eve <u>fell</u> on the ice.
_____ 31. That is a <u>dangerous</u> animal.
_____ 32. <u>Is</u> this yours?
_____ 33. <u>Ouch</u>! You stuck me.
_____ 34. Lee <u>and</u> George will help.
_____ 35. We found an <u>old</u> trunk.
_____ 36. <u>Sometimes</u> I can't sleep.
_____ 37. The child is <u>crying</u> again.
_____ 38. Have <u>they</u> called yet?
_____ 39. The <u>trip</u> is postponed.
_____ 40. <u>Well</u>! You could warn me.
_____ 41. <u>My</u> sister has already gone.
_____ 42. Take Gina <u>into</u> the kitchen.
_____ 43. I <u>will see</u> him Thursday.
_____ 44. <u>James</u> filled the box.
_____ 45. She sings <u>and</u> dances.
_____ 46. Everyone must leave <u>now</u>.

COMPOSITION EXERCISE

Write a sentence illustrating each part of speech.

(n) 1. _____

(p) 2. _____

(v) 3. _____

(adj) 4. _____

(adv) 5. _____

(con) 6. _____

(int) 7. _____

(pr) 8. _____

The Sentence

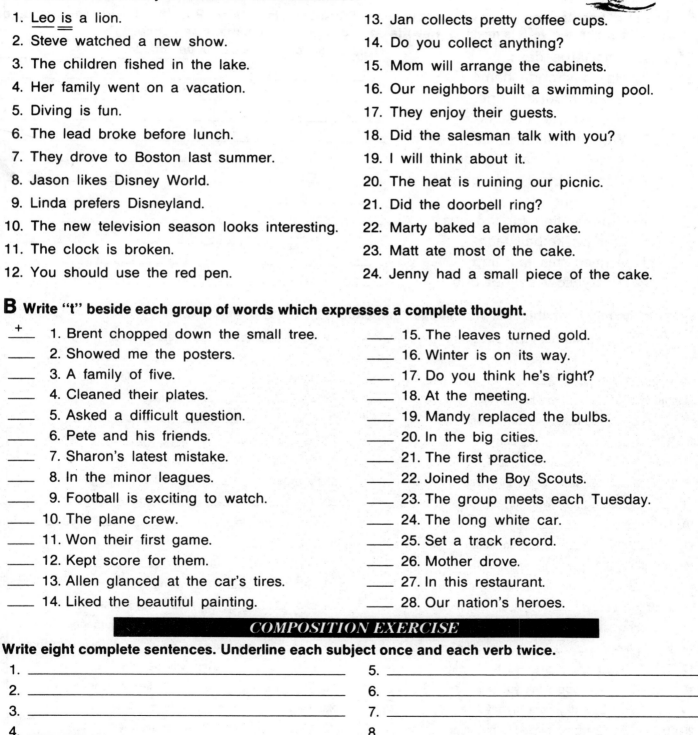

Unit 53

A sentence is a group of words containing a subject and a verb and expressing a complete thought.

EXAMPLE: Chris paid his dues.
            ˢ   ᵛ

A Underline each subject once and each verb twice.

1. Leo is a lion.
2. Steve watched a new show.
3. The children fished in the lake.
4. Her family went on a vacation.
5. Diving is fun.
6. The lead broke before lunch.
7. They drove to Boston last summer.
8. Jason likes Disney World.
9. Linda prefers Disneyland.
10. The new television season looks interesting.
11. The clock is broken.
12. You should use the red pen.

13. Jan collects pretty coffee cups.
14. Do you collect anything?
15. Mom will arrange the cabinets.
16. Our neighbors built a swimming pool.
17. They enjoy their guests.
18. Did the salesman talk with you?
19. I will think about it.
20. The heat is ruining our picnic.
21. Did the doorbell ring?
22. Marty baked a lemon cake.
23. Matt ate most of the cake.
24. Jenny had a small piece of the cake.

B Write "t" beside each group of words which expresses a complete thought.

+ 1. Brent chopped down the small tree.
___ 2. Showed me the posters.
___ 3. A family of five.
___ 4. Cleaned their plates.
___ 5. Asked a difficult question.
___ 6. Pete and his friends.
___ 7. Sharon's latest mistake.
___ 8. In the minor leagues.
___ 9. Football is exciting to watch.
___ 10. The plane crew.
___ 11. Won their first game.
___ 12. Kept score for them.
___ 13. Allen glanced at the car's tires.
___ 14. Liked the beautiful painting.

___ 15. The leaves turned gold.
___ 16. Winter is on its way.
___ 17. Do you think he's right?
___ 18. At the meeting.
___ 19. Mandy replaced the bulbs.
___ 20. In the big cities.
___ 21. The first practice.
___ 22. Joined the Boy Scouts.
___ 23. The group meets each Tuesday.
___ 24. The long white car.
___ 25. Set a track record.
___ 26. Mother drove.
___ 27. In this restaurant.
___ 28. Our nation's heroes.

COMPOSITION EXERCISE

Write eight complete sentences. Underline each subject once and each verb twice.

1. _____
2. _____
3. _____
4. _____

5. _____
6. _____
7. _____
8. _____

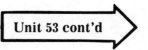

Unit 53 cont'd

Is This A Sentence?

A sentence has a subject and a verb and expresses a complete thought.

EXAMPLE: Richard walked to the grocery store.
(s above Richard, v above walked)

A Put an "s" beside each group of words in which the subject is missing. Put a "v" beside each group of words in which the verb is missing. Rewrite each group into a complete sentence.

___v___ 1. This large desk. *This large desk needs to be moved.* _____

_____ 2. Has a strange name. _____

_____ 3. Is an important one. _____

_____ 4. Her favorite pastime. _____

_____ 5. Won a million dollars. _____

_____ 6. Asked the leader a question. _____

_____ 7. Ronnie and Rick's parents. _____

_____ 8. That song. _____

_____ 9. Was waiting for the bus. _____

_____ 10. Our basketball team. _____

_____ 11. Arrived this morning. _____

_____ 12. The yellow school bus. _____

B Write the missing subject or verb in each sentence.

1. __*Alison*___ wanted more pizza.

2. _____ don't care!

3. The postman _____ the mail.

4. Will _____ be next in line?

5. _____ asked a silly question.

6. Rob _____ a big party.

7. Good _____ do their homework.

8. _____ want to be the best.

9. _____ may want to attend.

10. The map _____ .

11. Susan _____ the car today.

12. Will the _____ attack?

13. _____ told me to clean the garage.

14. Jack _____ to get up this morning.

15. The chocolate fudge _____ the best.

16. Which flavor _____ you like?

17. The _____ are beautiful today.

18. _____ you think you will go?

19. _____ days are my favorite.

20. The _____ mailed a package.

21. Her _____ is getting tired.

22. _____ you _____ this steak?

23. James _____ at his little brother.

24. He _____ to be last.

25. The wind _____ and _____ .

26. _____ you _____ it?

27. Her _____ had a big fight.

28. They _____ happy with his grades.

29. The _____ was red and orange.

30. The alarm clock _____ me up today.

31. My _____ left me a note.

32. _____ the injury _____ ?

33. Susan _____ sorry for the delay.

34. Did _____ read today's paper?

35. The _____ is filled with garbage.

36. _____ and _____ were my presents.

37. I _____ Jim will be late.

38. The _____ was a terrible one.

39. They _____ very carefully.

40. I _____ so much money.

Conveying Ideas

We use sentences to convey ideas. A sentence is a group of words arranged to convey an idea in grammatically correct language.

In order for a group of words to be a sentence, it must contain a subject and a predicate. The subject tells what or whom the sentence is about. The predicate tells us something about the subject.

EXAMPLE: *Billy ran. The subject is Billy. The predicate is ran.*

   The subject tells who — Billy. The predicate tells what Billy did — ran.

A Write "y" in the blank if each of the following groups of words is a sentence. Write "n" if it is not a sentence.

__y__ 1. Sue went swimming.

_____ 2. Got wet.

_____ 3. Swimming is fun.

_____ 4. Sue is a good swimmer.

_____ 5. Has fun sometimes doesn't.

_____ 6. Good swimmers are careful.

_____ 7. Right after eating.

_____ 8. Too tight and she couldn't.

_____ 9. Sue won a medal for swimming.

_____ 10. Always a good time.

_____ 11. Take your medicine.

_____ 12. Swimming is a good exercise.

_____ 13. Dick does not like to swim.

_____ 14. Do like to swim?

_____ 15. A swimming pool.

_____ 16. Her suit is red.

_____ 17. Can dog-paddle yet?

_____ 18. No, I can float.

_____ 19. Can you do a swan dive?

_____ 20. The ducks gracefully.

_____ 21. The swans are more graceful.

_____ 22. The student on the left.

B Rewrite these fragments as complete sentences.

1. at the same time _____ *We spoke at the same time.* _____

2. asked a silly question _____

3. is never on time _____

4. the kittens playfully _____

5. wrote in his book _____

6. a new house _____

7. is too bright _____

8. a red pen _____

9. tore the pages _____

10. a solar calculator _____

11. in the rain _____

12. when you run _____

Unit 54 cont'd →

Importance of Word Order

a. *A big fish ate Dad!*   *These two sentences use the same words, but they do not say the same thing. The order of the words in the sentences was changed. When the word order was changed, the meaning was changed.*

b. *Dad ate a big fish.*

A Here are some sentences for you to change. Make each sentence below say something different by changing the word order.

1. Jeff saw a bird.   *A bird saw Jeff.*

2. The snowman ran away and melted. _____

3. Johnny spoke to the little girl. _____

4. The dog caught the cat. _____

5. Carol fell on the stairs. _____

6. The car hit the tree. _____

7. John likes my little dog. _____

8. The ghost frightened the boy. _____

9. Summer always changes to winter. _____

10. The boat slid into the water. _____

11. The hunter chased the bear. _____

12. Mother burned the trash pile. _____

13. Tammy took a train. _____

14. Mother made Jeff angry. _____

Remember, when the word order of a sentence is changed, the meaning changes.

B Unscramble the words to make a sentence. Be sure to capitalize the first word of each sentence and to use end punctuation.

1. cried the puppy sadly   *The puppy cried sadly.*

2. cake bought we a yesterday _____

3. karate sport my favorite is _____

4. of you eat did doughnuts all the _____

5. shoes worn-out are these _____

6. workbook locker in is the my _____

7. decorated we tree our Christmas _____

8. bone dog its the hid _____

9. sentences wrote the James _____

10. story she us to read a _____

11. took Tami test a today _____

12. pencil your drop you did _____

Fragments

A sentence contains a subject and a verb and expresses a complete thought. A group of words without these elements is a fragment.

EXAMPLES:

a.	Bob and Bill.	This is a fragment. It does not contain a verb.
b.	Went fishing.	This is a fragment. It does not contain a subject.
c.	Bob and Bill went fishing.	This is a complete sentence. It contains both a subject and a verb.

A Underline the groups of words which are fragments.

1. Yesterday I watched television. Some good shows. Friday is a good day to watch.
2. The boat belongs to my uncle. He uses it as a fishing boat. Painted it blue.
3. Chris needs to feed the dog. He's hungry. Hasn't had any food today.
4. I think the curtains are torn. At the hem. They're our best ones.
5. A friend of mine. She told me she'd call later. Wait and see.
6. Steve missed school Tuesday. Was sick. Watched television all day.
7. She found her presents. Hidden in the closet. Not a good hiding place.
8. The students studied until midnight. Were very tired. Couldn't remember the answers.
9. Go to the picnic today. We'll take the bread and colas. Will also take paper plates.
10. Brad likes to play baseball. His favorite sport. Wants to play on the senior team next year.
11. Which was a surprise. I don't like surprises. Make me nervous.
12. Judy types very fast. Learned when she was in junior high. A good skill to have.
13. Her win was lucky. May never happen again. She was very excited.
14. Kenny wants to learn how to fly an airplane. His dream. Would love to own a plane.
15. Anne thought she saw a sea monster. Must have been her imagination. No such thing.

B Use each group of words to write a complete sentence.

1. Richard	Rick	gave	*Rick gave Richard a birthday present.*
2. swam	Ruth	home	
3. typing	paper	he	
4. friends	have	good	
5. examine	food	cooks	
6. afraid	is	sister	
7. movie	popcorn	will	
8. fan	buy	will	
9. bicycle	race	did	
10. read	this	paper	
11. like	people	music	
12. pies	baked	Tom	
13. doughnuts	Jan	frosted	
14. dialed	Bert	number	
15. Randy	books	dropped	
16. talent	has	Tim	
17. grass	cut	Gene	

Unit 55 cont'd

Correcting Fragments

A fragment is only part of a sentence. It doesn't express a complete thought.

EXAMPLES: *We write complete sentences.*   *This is a complete sentence.*
                To make our meaning clear.   *This is a fragment.*

A Write "s" beside each sentence. Write "f" beside each fragment.

_s_ 1. Tim told us a funny story.

____ 2. About his dog.

____ 3. It was funny.

____ 4. We laughed until we cried.

____ 5. Had to make some money.

____ 6. When I needed to buy Christmas gifts.

____ 7. I couldn't afford anything.

____ 8. After I worked seven hours.

____ 9. I decided to find another job.

____ 10. Not my favorite kind of work.

____ 11. Her singing sounded beautiful.

____ 12. Like a bird.

____ 13. Larry can play the bugle.

____ 14. Practices each day.

____ 15. Took lessons for years.

____ 16. Sandy plays in the marching band.

____ 17. The band performs at each home game.

____ 18. When the team plays at home.

____ 19. Practice after school.

____ 20. The band plays better than the team does.

B Write "s" beside each sentence in which the subject is missing. Write "v" beside each sentence in which the verb is missing. Write "i" beside each sentence which is an incomplete thought. Rewrite the sentences correctly.

_s_ 1. Watched television last night.   *Carol watched television last night.*

____ 2. The most interesting shows.

____ 3. When I had to go to bed.

____ 4. Brent and his sister.

____ 5. The lawn mower and the edger.

____ 6. When they bought the gas.

____ 7. Where to borrow more.

____ 8. A complete list.

____ 9. How the book disappeared.

____ 10. Should be made.

____ 11. Hates to go to the dentist.

____ 12. Cries and screams.

____ 13. Where to turn.

____ 14. How much money.

____ 15. Drinks a glass of milk.

____ 16. With each meal.

____ 17. Just as I reached the counter.

____ 18. His turn at bat.

____ 19. Jerry and his dad.

____ 20. Had a great time.

Comprehension Check

(A) Write the contraction for the words.

1. I am _____*I'm*_____
2. you are _____
3. we are _____
4. he is _____
5. they are _____
6. do not _____
7. will not _____
8. we will _____
9. you will _____
10. does not _____

11. we have _____
12. they would_____
13. you have _____
14. it is _____
15. she had _____
16. was not _____
17. it will _____
18. did not _____
19. he has _____
20. have not _____

21. I have _____
23. we would _____
23. what is _____
24. were not _____
25. can not _____
26. where is _____
27. are not _____
28. would not _____
29. let us _____
30. should not_____

(B) Identify the part of speech of each underlined word.

n-noun	p-pronoun	v-verb	adj-adjective
adv-adverb	con-conjunction	int-interjection	pr-preposition

_**p**_ 1. <u>She</u> is the actress.
____ 2. My <u>sister</u> is visiting us.
____ 3. The <u>black</u> dog is Erin's.
____ 4. I <u>enjoy</u> the opera.
____ 5. He drove <u>recklessly</u>.
____ 6. <u>Halt</u>! Who goes there!
____ 7. Tracy <u>and</u> Walt are the speakers.
____ 8. Jackie and <u>he</u> guided the boat.
____ 9. Store it <u>in</u> the closet.
____ 10. Paulette <u>bought</u> a teddy bear.
____ 11. Bring the money <u>here</u>.
____ 12. Samuel has a large <u>desk</u>.

____ 13. The tape player <u>is</u> Rhonda's.
____ 14. We'll shop <u>and</u> go to a movie.
____ 15. I saw Jeremy <u>at</u> the gym.
____ 16. <u>Yes</u>! I heard you!
____ 17. The <u>plaid</u> jacket is an old one.
____ 18. The bears were <u>restless</u>.
____ 19. <u>They</u> are from Africa.
____ 20. Cover the answers <u>completely</u>.
____ 21. The players were tired <u>but</u> happy.
____ 22. Call me <u>at</u> 4:30.
____ 23. The newscaster <u>read</u> the news.
____ 24. Don't chop down this <u>tree</u>!

(C) Underline each subject once and each verb twice.

1. The chocolate <u>candy</u> <u>is</u> Leslie's.
2. Lisa won the award.
3. Football is my favorite sport.
4. Roger's homework is lost.
5. I have Al's dog.
6. Greg gave me the message.
7. The hospital is around the corner.
8. The trumpet section played.
9. Danny and Craig watched the movie.
10. Ray and Jay are twins.

11. She is very sad.
12. The airplane crashed in the desert.
13. My sunglasses are crooked.
14. One family moved out today.
15. Did you hear the bell?
16. We want steak for dinner.
17. The report is correct.
18. The cook is grumpy today.
19. Don't drink that water!
20. Anne painted that picture.

Test 11 cont'd

Comprehension Check (continued)

(D) Write "f" beside each fragment. Write "c" beside each complete sentence.

_f_ 1. always arrives late.

____ 2. Jim is a good friend.

____ 3. Kate and Sarah.

____ 4. When we close the door.

____ 5. Hole in his sock.

____ 6. Spilled the glue.

____ 7. Tony studied last night.

____ 8. Dropped the pages.

____ 9. The brown dog.

____ 10. Everyone in our class.

____ 11. The door slammed.

____ 12. Julia and her mother.

____ 13. The beautiful wedding music.

____ 14. When Stan passed.

____ 15. Called his stepmother.

____ 16. Dawn talks too much.

____ 17. We'll use red ink pens.

____ 18. Until we meet again.

____ 19. Albert and his motorcycle.

____ 20. Since you're ready.

(E) Rewrite these fragments as complete sentences.

1. Ran a mile yesterday.   _Ron ran a mile yesterday._____

2. The white kitten.   _____

3. Won the game.   _____

4. Until 4:00 p.m.   _____

5. Yesterday's paper.   _____

6. Bill's room.   _____

7. When you called.   _____

8. Hoping to hear from you.   _____

9. Gave me the list.   _____

10. In the park.   _____

11. While waiting for Sue.   _____

12. Wearing my new jeans.   _____

Write a paragraph describing your plans for your next birthday. Circle each contraction.

_____

_____

_____

_____

_____

_____

_____

_____

Run-Ons

Run-on sentences are often two sentences separated by a comma instead of a period. Divide them into separate sentences.

EXAMPLES: *The bell rang, the students left the room.*   *This is a run-on sentence.*
     The bell rang. The students left the room.   *These sentences are correctly divided.*

A Rewrite the run-on sentences into two separate sentences.

1. The light turned green, all the cars raced. *The light turned green. All the cars raced.*

2. I had to turn in my homework, I didn't have it. _____

3. The dog was hungry, I had to feed him. _____

4. We were late for school, the teacher didn't notice. _____

5. My dad was angry, he grounded me. _____

6. You need to practice, you can't play the music. _____

7. Marie has the money, she plans to buy a TV. _____

8. Go to bed early, you'll be too sleepy tomorrow. _____

9. I didn't see the end of the movie, I can predict the outcome. _____

10. Chris fell off his bike, he hurt his ankle. _____

B Rewrite the first five sentences from part A. Use "and" or "but" to connect them.

1.   *The light turned green, and all the cars raced.*

2. _____

3. _____

4. _____

5. _____

C Underline the run-on sentences.

 Amy and Judy decided to have a party. <u>They bought ice cream and cake, they also bought balloons and streamers.</u> The two girls couldn't agree on the guest list, they each wanted to invite ten people. The house wouldn't hold that many people, they had to revise their list.

 Amy brought her stereo to Judy's house. Judy had a great collection of records and tapes, they decided to borrow some more records from James. All the guests would like rock music better than any other kind. They made sure there would be music to please everyone.

 Amy and Judy almost forgot to order pizzas and cola, they called in a last-minute order at the nearest pizza parlor. They ordered several cheese pizzas. They knew most of their friends would like cheese. They decided that seven large pizzas would be enough.

 On the night of the party, they waited for their guests to arrive. Everyone was late, Amy and Judy began to worry. Suddenly, Judy remembered something they'd forgotten to do: they hadn't sent out any invitations.

Unit 56 cont'd

Correcting Run-Ons

Using a comma or failing to use a period between sentences results in a run-on sentence.

EXAMPLES: *Here comes Bill, he's my best friend.* *This is a run-on sentence.*
Here comes Bill he's my best friend. *This is a run-on sentence.*
Here comes Bill. He's my best friend. *These sentences are punctuated correctly.*

A Write "r" beside each run-on sentence. Write "c" beside each correctly punctuated sentence.

_r_ 1. Marie is a clever person she knew the answers.

_____ 2. Our dog is lost he ran away yesterday.

_____ 3. Television can be a teacher, there are many good shows.

_____ 4. Her mom picked her up, they were going shopping.

_____ 5. Credit is easy to get. It is sometimes too tempting.

_____ 6. The awards program is tonight. I can't wait to see it!

_____ 7. We studied about WWII it was a terrible time.

_____ 8. The cat's dish is empty, she lets us know about it.

_____ 9. Pete loves baseball he wants to join a team.

_____ 10. The nominations are in I think I'm on the list.

_____ 11. Alex will be late today. He has to take a test.

_____ 12. Miriam studied until midnight, she's sleepy today.

_____ 13. Her answers were wrong. She was embarrassed.

_____ 14. Terra saves coupons, this means she saves money.

_____ 15. The dog's collar broke, he escaped.

_____ 16. I went to the fair I wanted some cotton candy.

_____ 17. My album is missing, I think Janey borrowed it.

_____ 18. Lynn is a fast reader. She read three books last week.

_____ 19. I love weekends, we usually go out of town.

_____ 20. Tim lost his billfold, it had ten dollars in it.

B Underline each run-on sentence.

Sarah had a great deal of homework she couldn't seem to get started. She ate a snack after school. She watched three television shows. Her mother asked her to go to the grocery store. Sarah walked home very slowly, she didn't want to get home too quickly. The homework was waiting for her when she got home. She opened her English book, the assignment wasn't too hard. The history work was easy to understand it didn't take too long to complete. Sarah worked on her math homework last. She finished everything before 9:00 p.m.

C Rewrite these run-on sentences correctly.

1. Green apples are sometimes sour they're tart.

2. I like this movie, it has a good plot.

3. The children ran outside they were eager to play.

4. Bonnie is the winner, she'll make a good president.

5. Gwen was early for class she needed to speak to the teacher.

6. The music is too loud it'll damage your eardrums.

7. This kitchen needs more sunlight, open the curtains.

8. The car won't start it must have a dead battery.

9. Have you read this article, it's an interesting one.

10. The pages are torn, you'll have to pay a fine.

11. The fire was out of control, thousands of acres burned.

12. The leaves are falling it's time to get out the rake.

Green apples are sometimes sour. They're tart.

_____

_____

_____

_____

_____

_____

_____

_____

_____

_____

_____

Subjects That Tell Who

The subject performs the action of an action verb and may answer the question "Who?"

EXAMPLE: *The doctor examined the patient.*   *"Doctor" tells <u>who</u> examined the patient.*

A Write the subject of each sentence by telling who performed the action of each verb.

1. The baby crawled across the floor.	Who crawled across the floor?	*baby*
2. The garbageman made too much noise.	Who made too much noise?	_____
3. My cousin saw the news story.	Who saw the news story?	_____
4. His driver missed his turn.	Who missed his turn?	_____
5. Jeff wanted to borrow the car.	Who wanted to borrow the car?	_____
6. The star of the movie argued too much.	Who argued too much?	_____
7. Jimmy fell out of the walnut tree.	Who fell out of the walnut tree?	_____
8. Sharon demanded a refund.	Who demanded a refund?	_____
9. The audience wept at the sad ending.	Who wept at the sad ending?	_____
10. The announcer yelled into the microphone.	Who yelled into the microphone?	_____
11. Anna looked in the kitchen for the book.	Who looked in the kitchen?	_____
12. Steve worked late last night.	Who worked late last night?	_____

B Fill in the blanks with a word which answers the question "Who?"

1. _____ *Rosalind* _____ asked for a raise.
2. The _____ examined my teeth.
3. The _____ welcomed us to the party.
4. Will the _____ of the ring claim it?
5. _____ will receive a free prize.
6. _____ caught a huge trout.
7. The _____ hopped, skipped, and jumped.
8. Have _____ shown the teacher your test?
9. _____ wondered why I came home late.
10. _____ made a wish.
11. His _____ planned a surprise party.
12. Do _____ think you can attend?
13. The _____ helped her raise money.
14. My _____ hopes it'll rain today.
15. _____ pulled the drapes.
16. Did _____ close the door?
17. _____ pushed the baby buggy.
18. _____ will skip stones across the water.
19. The _____ allowed us to be late.
20. The entire _____ will attend the play.
21. The _____ will speak on Sunday.
22. _____ worked on the problem.

23. Did _____ take the children home?
24. _____ wants us to help him.
25. The _____ dreamed he could fly.
26. My _____ wrote me a letter.
27. The _____ will clean the oven.
28. The dog's _____ demanded his obedience.
29. The train _____ looked out the window.
30. A new _____ sliced the meat.
31. The _____ has written a new book.
32. The _____ served our food.
33. Ten _____ chose the winner.
34. The _____ built us some cabinets.
35. My _____ owns several apartments.
36. Can _____ connect the wires?
37. A _____ threatened him in the park.
38. Did the _____ record the sale?
39. The _____ concealed his surprise.
40. _____ of the audience applauded.
41. Did _____ accept his apology?
42. The _____ harvested his corn.
43. My _____ collected the rent.
44. His little _____ believed the story.

139

Unit 57 cont'd →

Subjects That Tell What

The subject tells what a sentence is about.

EXAMPLES: a. The chair is broken. "Chair" tells what is broken.
           b. My bicycle goes fast. "Bicycle" tells what goes fast.

A Underline the subject of each sentence.

1. The trees swayed in the strong wind.
2. My dog barked at the stranger.
3. The chickens clucked at one another.
4. Our television blared.
5. The red car spun in the gravel.
6. The drainage ditch overflowed.
7. Her telephone rang earlier.
8. The water dripped from the faucet.
9. The tablecloth fell off the table.
10. Fish swim in schools.
11. The bank closed early today.
12. That coffee spilled on the counter.
13. Birds chirp in the morning.
14. Paper can be folded.
15. The city was jolted by an earthquake.
16. Rae's kitten ran away yesterday.
17. Our clocks stopped at noon.
18. The rabbit hopped into the field.
19. His refrigerator worked until yesterday.
20. Our clothes were thrown out the window.
21. The new puppy slept through the night.
22. The tiles fell off the roof.
23. An otter swam downstream.
24. Elephants eat at night.

B Fill in each blank with a subject that tells "what."

1. _____Canaries_____ sing beautifully.
2. The _____ worked well.
3. The _____ skipped over the water.
4. Do _____ cook well on the grill?
5. The _____ turned rapidly.
6. _____ told of the disaster.
7. _____ sleep during the day.
8. _____ perched on the wire.
9. The _____ drifted off course.
10. _____ dissolved in the water.
11. The _____ spun crazily.
12. _____ bounced off the wall.
13. The _____ were dressed for the sale.
14. Has _____ disappeared recently?
15. The guitar _____ popped loose.
16. Do _____ dream?
17. The _____ were burned by the fire.
18. _____ were hanging in the closet.
19. Are my _____ being washed now?
20. The _____ stops here.

C Underline the subject of each sentence.

New television shows are fun to watch. New shows are usually telecast in September. Comedies entertain us and make us laugh. Dramas keep us in suspense. News shows tell us what is going on in our world. Even new commercials are fun to see..

The new television season will arrive soon. Networks will try to win audiences over to their programs. Different types of shows will be broadcast. Television tries to appeal to millions of people.

Finding the Subject

The subject is what the sentence is all about.
Usually it will come before the verb.

EXAMPLES: a. The <u>weather</u> is terrible.   c. The <u>picture</u> looks beautiful.
            b. <u>Mike</u> called his sister.   d. His <u>actions</u> were rude.

✱   **Underline the subject of each sentence.**

1. Your <u>brother</u> broke the window.
2. The train will be here soon.
3. Jane sat on the steps.
4. This house scares me.
5. Penny finished the story.
6. My favorite movie is ''King Kong.''
7. The money belongs to Kathy.
8. Mrs. Benton lives next door.
9. This plant needs special care.
10. The fish is a shark.
11. His answer is no.
12. Laura knows the secret.
13. Our club meets on Thursday.
14. Jane copied the sentences.
15. You have finished too early.
16. This pen doesn't write.
17. The book was interesting.
18. A monkey followed me home.
19. The trip must be postponed.
20. That building is very old.
21. The account is closed.
22. Donna stepped on the bug.
23. The money is safe now.
24. The dog is a collie.
25. Mark is ill.

26. The skeleton fell out of the closet.
27. We repeated the pledge.
28. The suggestion was rejected.
29. Dan announced the winners.
30. The penalty is too harsh.
31. The remedy is working.
32. Connie will stay here.
33. The class worked together.
34. He raised his hand.
35. Onions made me cry.
36. Susan decorated the room.
37. They asked for you.
38. His speech was excellent.
39. The question was difficult.
40. The game is over.
41. I made the mess.
42. The ghosts vanished.
43. Jill forgot her shoes.
44. The grass needs cutting.
45. The frog chased me.
46. The paint was spilled on the rug.
47. We followed the footprints.
48. Cathi arrived at noon.
49. Two men argued.
50. That man is a coward.

COMPOSITION EXERCISE

Write a sentence using each of these words as subjects.

(boat)   1. _____
(man)   2. _____
(farm)   3. _____
(we)   4. _____
(book)   5. _____

(lake)   6. _____
(trip)   7. _____
(it)   8. _____
(sister) 9. _____
(Jason) 10. _____

Unit 58 cont'd

The Predicate

The predicate tells what the subject does.

s   v
EXAMPLE: *The store opened.*
            "Opened" tells what the store did.

A Underline each subject once and each verb twice.

1. The <u>play</u> <u><u>began</u></u>.
2. Bill will drive.
3. The teacher spoke.
4. Alison can swim well.
5. We looked in the window.
6. The top spun rapidly.
7. They kissed in the dark.
8. We ate at noon.
9. Phyllis hurriedly asked for the answer.
10. Several children rushed into the shelter.
11. William asked for the pepper.
12. The women walked around the track.
13. The bulb burned out.
14. Some thieves ran into the bank.
15. Life is running smoothly.
16. Leaves fell into the pool.
17. Sherry dreamed about the lottery.
18. Alex's jeans shrank in the dryer.
19. The plane banked to the left.
20. The contestant spoke rapidly.
21. The noise began suddenly.
22. Our team lost last Friday.
23. The dress was taken off the rack.
24. The forest fire burned in this area.
25. The puppy shivered.
26. Alan sang at the seminar.
27. Have you heard of the plan?
28. The bird is flying high.
29. Mr. Barker knew.
30. The apple was peeled for Tommy.
31. Jennifer sat on the sofa.
32. Chris asked for his allowance.
33. The plants are growing along the driveway.
34. The pajamas dried in twenty minutes.
35. The play will begin soon.
36. Lea is playing in the last quarter.
37. Our family will fly to Disney World.
38. We will eat at the new restaurant.
39. Megan's mom will drive.
40. Your attitude is showing.

B Fill in each blank with a verb that tells what the subject does.

1. The baby ____*yawned*____ sleepily.
2. My dad _____ .
3. Steve _____ at 9:00 p.m.
4. We _____ to the lake.
5. The car _____ .
6. The dog _____ .
7. The lamp _____ off the table.
8. Which chair _____ over?
9. He _____ at his dog.
10. Did the students _____?
11. Nancy _____ her answers.
12. You _____ after me.
13. The television _____ too loudly.
14. Matt _____ on the paper.
15. The little boy _____ away from home.
16. The ball _____ into the street.
17. The dog _____ from his dish.
18. Susan _____ after lunch.
19. She _____ through the disguise.
20. His stereo _____ .
21. Barbara _____ very well.
22. Frank _____ the truck.

142

Subject-Verb Agreement

Unit 59

In every sentence the subject and verb work together to show number. This relationship is called agreement. For all verbs except the verb "to be," agreement is necessary only in the present tense.

Plural nouns end in "-s" and agree with the plain form of the verb, while singular nouns agree with the singular form of the verb, which ends in "-s."

GENERALIZATION

NOUN	VERB
-s	no -s
no -s	-s

Subject pronouns must also agree with the verb. I, you, we, and they agree with the plain form of the verb. He, she, and it agree with the singular form of the verb.

GENERALIZATION

PRONOUN	VERB
I, you, we, they, he, she, it	no -s, -s

A Underline the correct verb form in parentheses for each sentence below.

1. I (<u>do</u>, does) like candy.
2. Lucy (say, says) she is in the play.
3. Birds usually (fly, flies) south in the fall.
4. They (go, goes) to bed at nine.
5. That rose (look, looks) wilted.
6. Joe often (run, runs) to school.

The verb "to be" has special forms to show agreement in past time as well as present time as shown below.

SUBJECT	PRESENT	PAST	SUBJECT	PRESENT	PAST
I	am	was	you	are	were
he, she, it	is	was	we, they	are	were
singular nouns	is	was	plural nouns	are	were

B Copy the correct verb form in parentheses for each sentence below.

1. (Are, Is) __*are*__ you in the school chorus?
2. (am, is) I _____ joining the band.
3. (Was, Were) _____ that Jim Brown?
4. (are, is) Those plums _____ nice.
5. (was, were) I _____ at home.
6. (was, were) It _____ a good movie.

Word groups separating the subject and verb do not affect agreement.

C Underline the subject of each sentence, and put two lines under the correct verb form in parentheses.

1. The apples in the orchard (is, are) ripe.
2. That stack of records (is, are) mine.
3. People named Johnson (live, lives) next door.
4. The cap belonging to you (is, are) the green one.
5. The clocks on the wall (is, are) new.

143

Unit 59 cont'd

Subject-Verb Agreement Practice

The subject must agree with the verb in number. A singular subject refers to one person or thing and needs a singular verb. A plural subject refers to two or more persons or things and needs a plural verb.

EXAMPLES: a. *She takes piano lessons.* "She" is a singular subject; "takes" is a singular verb.
  b. *They take piano lessons.* "They" is a plural subject; "take" is a plural verb.

A Underline the correct verbs.

1. Bob (is, are) going to the dance.
2. Good talkers (is, are) needed for the meeting.
3. This road (have, has) no signs.
4. My aunt (like, likes) soap operas.
5. My uncle also (like, likes) them.
6. History books (tell, tells) us about our past.
7. They (was, were) whispering in the corner.
8. Angie (need, needs) some new shoes.
9. He (make, makes) me angry.
10. I (know, knows) what you mean.
11. Real friends (forgive, forgives) you.
12. Rick (tell, tells) stories sometimes.
13. Your fingers (is, are) dirty.
14. Banks (pay, pays) interest.
15. Our bank (pay, pays) high interest.
16. He (do, does) whatever must be done.
17. His parents (are, is) understanding.
18. They (miss, misses) their puppy.
19. Schools (close, closes) early today.
20. The boy (like, likes) my sister.
21. Cokes and chips (are, is) on my list.
22. The vitamins (was, were) misplaced.
23. This (complete, completes) our research.
24. John and Lee (is, are) my friends.
25. Wrinkles (tell, tells) your age.
26. She (doesn't, don't) like cold pizza.
27. The directions (say, says) to go left.
28. Which flavor (do, does) you want?
29. She (weeds, weed) the garden daily.
30. He (wish, wishes) them a good day.

B Write "s" beside each singular word. Write "p" beside each plural word.

_s_ 1. sits
____ 2. sleep (verb)
____ 3. gets
____ 4. sell
____ 5. were
____ 6. they
____ 7. drive (verb)
____ 8. it
____ 9. teacher
____ 10. eat

____ 11. sells
____ 12. was
____ 13. she
____ 14. sleeps
____ 15. enjoy
____ 16. get
____ 17. I
____ 18. do
____ 19. break (verb)
____ 20. drives (verb)

____ 21. are
____ 22. is
____ 23. carry
____ 24. students
____ 25. closes
____ 26. girl
____ 27. have
____ 28. does
____ 29. he
____ 30. breaks (verb)

____ 31. close
____ 32. sit
____ 33. lady
____ 34. eats
____ 35. makes
____ 36. has
____ 37. carries
____ 38. make
____ 39. we
____ 40. get

C Write a sentence with each word.

1. look (v) _____ *They look great!* _____
2. waters (v) _____
3. walk (v) _____
4. jar (s) _____
5. save (v) _____
6. ladies (s) _____
7. salute (v) _____
8. they (s) _____

The Simplest Sentence

A simple sentence has a subject and a verb.

EXAMPLE: *Jane drove to the store. "Jane" is the subject. "Drove" is the verb.*

A Underline each subject once and each verb twice.

1. Chris ran into the back yard.
2. She danced in the aisle.
3. The students cheered at the game.
4. My lazy cat slept all day.
5. He smiled at his reflection.
6. We traveled last summer.
7. Have you helped with dinner?
8. We ate breakfast.
9. Larry laughed at his friends.
10. They were jumping around the room.
11. I can dance very well.
12. You are failing!

13. Jim wondered about his grades.
14. A green snake hissed at me.
15. Gail thought quickly.
16. The dog barked all night.
17. Can you pitch well?
18. Rhonda worked until morning.
19. Mom shopped at my favorite store.
20. You should study.
21. We swam with our group.
22. They will sing at the concert.
23. Steve rapidly recovered from his shock.
24. Will you look at that!

B Underline each subject once and each verb twice.

1. Jimmy and Gail went to school.
2. They laughed and talked on the way.
3. Are you passing or failing?
4. Brad and Donna danced and skated.
5. Mom and Dad are going on a vacation.
6. They will ski and sightsee.
7. Melissa and I will stay home.
8. We will stay up late and talk.
9. Ben and Brad will drive by.
10. They will honk and wave.

11. The neighbors will yell and scream.
12. We will turn and push now.
13. Ben and Barbie are going to the movie.
14. The book slid and fell off the table.
15. The children hopped and skipped down the street.
16. Mandy and Candy can sing and play.
17. My brother begged and pleaded for the car.
18. Susan and Beth are paying for the dinner.
19. Ice cream and cake will be served.
20. The TV and radio are broken.

C Write either a subject or a verb in each sentence.

1. The book _____*is*_____ on the table.
2. Marsha and Alice _____ .
3. They _____ going to the concert.
4. The two _____ in the morning.
5. He _____ in our place.
6. Jenny _____ at the bus stop.
7. Robert _____ for the bus.
8. The children _____ in their treehouse.
9. We _____ to the radio.
10. Paul _____ on the door.

11. The teacher _____ to the office.
12. We _____ to another channel.
13. They _____ in the winter.
14. Tim _____ for a refund.
15. Andy _____ on the whistle.
16. Our _____ barked all night.
17. She will _____ for us now.
18. The _____ was in the car.
19. Marie and Margie _____ to the restaurant.
20. _____ and _____ are leaving.

Unit 60 cont'd ⟹

Subjects and Verbs

The subject answers the questions "Who?" or "What?" The verb answers the question "What did the subject do?"

EXAMPLE: Marion played well.
Who played well?   "Marion" is the subject.
What did Marion do?   "Played" is the verb.

A Read each sentence and answer the questions.

1. Mom baked yesterday.   Who? _____ **Mom** _____   Did what? _____ **baked** _____
2. The bulbs burned out.   What? _____   Did what? _____
3. Jan ate in the kitchen.   Who? _____   Did what? _____
4. We ordered yesterday.   Who? _____   Did what? _____
5. I traveled today.   Who? _____   Did what? _____
6. Ben and Bill swim well.   Who? _____   Did what? _____
7. Dad frowned at us.   Who? _____   Did what? _____
8. Karen and Angie shopped after school.   Who? _____   Did what? _____
9. We left after the dinner.   Who? _____   Did what? _____
10. Jim asked for his pen.   Who? _____   Did what? _____
11. The brown dog yelped angrily.   What? _____   Did what? _____
12. A white shark swam nearby.   What? _____   Did what? _____
13. A few students waited nervously.   Who? _____   Did what? _____
14. She quickly answered.   Who? _____   Did what? _____
15. Jenkins drove dangerously.   Who? _____   Did what? _____

B Write either a subject or a verb in each sentence.

1. _____ **Janet** _____ cried at the movie.
2. The _____ fell from his crib.
3. My family _____ well.
4. The _____ experimented.
5. _____ played outside.
6. The _____ lasted forever.
7. A tiny _____ cried at the door.
8. Her sister _____ yesterday.
9. We _____ for a new sled.
10. She _____ late.
11. _____ giggled at the clown.
12. He _____ for one-half hour.
13. _____ applauded loudly.
14. The audience _____ .
15. They _____ late for the movie.
16. _____ questioned stubbornly.
17. The _____ were early.

18. The _____ rose early today.
19. The team _____ easily.
20. They _____ after the concert.
21. Marla _____ well.
22. Mr. Watkins _____ crazily.
23. Fred _____ at the store window.
24. He _____ into the lake.
25. Jill _____ in the band.
26. We _____ daily.
27. She _____ beautifully.
28. The wheel _____ to the left.
29. Puppies _____ for their mother.
30. The clock _____ hourly.
31. The _____ shines brightly.
32. The sound _____ in the distance.
33. Her sister _____ to Florida.
34. The _____ rings downstairs.

Comprehension Check

(A) Put a check (✓) beside each run-on sentence.

✓ 1. The baby cried she was hungry.
___ 2. Save some money you'll be sorry.
___ 3. We were late, but the movie hadn't begun yet.
___ 4. John and Jim are twins. They look alike.
___ 5. The dog barked loudly he wanted in the house.
___ 6. Marie gave a speech she was nervous.
___ 7. We will go skiing we'll have a great time.
___ 8. Watch out for that car! It's moving too fast.
___ 9. Lisa is sad I think she failed the test.
___ 10. Lester walked slowly, and he missed his bus.

(B) Rewrite the run-on sentences. Use "and," "but," or "or" to connect them.

1. The winners will be announced today, I can't wait to hear the results!
   The winners will be announced today, and I can't wait to hear the results!

2. Gwen is a good friend my best friend is Doris.
   _____

3. You need to climb carefully you'll fall off the ladder.
   _____

4. Listen closely you'll miss the bell.
   _____

5. Doug went to bed early he couldn't go to sleep.
   _____

6. Leslie bought three cake mixes she baked only two cakes.
   _____

7. Elizabeth ate two green apples, her stomach began to hurt.
   _____

8. We saved our money for a month, we used it to buy Hannukah presents.
   _____

9. Pete is a good wrestler he didn't make the team.
   _____

10. Bert intended to come to the party he couldn't find his keys.
   _____

11. Mix in the eggs now your batter will get too thick.
   _____

12. The forest fire is several miles away, it's getting closer every minute.
   _____

13. We have to tell Elise now she won't be able to make plans.
   _____

14. Just freeze the juice for two hours you'll have a tasty treat.
   _____

Test 12 cont'd ➡

Comprehension Check (continued)

C **Underline each subject once and each verb twice.**

1. The car is green and white.
2. Her friends gave her a party.
3. The gym is open today.
4. Did you see the chipmunk?
5. My parents are not at home.
6. Rose got a TV for Christmas.
7. Jill took her math exam.
8. The mechanic repaired our van.
9. Can you bring me the paper?
10. That jewelry store is closed.
11. The waiter was somewhat rude.
12. Patrick is Irish.
13. That chair broke during our move.
14. Is the carpet soiled?
15. You must not laugh at Sam!
16. Many lights are out.
17. Could you wash the windows today?
18. I don't understand the problem.
19. Two students are tardy.
20. Firemen have dangerous jobs.

D **Underline the correct verbs.**

1. The boxes (is, are) made of cardboard.
2. Schools (closes, close) when it snows.
3. They (waters, water) their yard daily.
4. This bank (pays, pay) high interest.
5. Edgar (tells, tell) jokes very well.
6. I (is, am) learning to drive.
7. People (is, are) always in a hurry.
8. (Is, Are) your records scratched?
9. That group (is, are) late.
10. You (is, are) a good friend.
11. (Is, Are) the tapes missing?
12. Some people (makes, make) me angry.
13. The jackets (was, were) misplaced.
14. My uncle (likes, like) Corvettes.
15. Good friends (helps, help) you.
16. Those printers (does, do) good work.
17. Mrs. Henry (sells, sell) real estate.
18. The chocolates (looks, look) delicious.
19. Several ladies (was, were) members.
20. Al and Joe (drives, drive) recklessly.
21. Two pictures (was, were) excellent.
22. My aunt (saves, save) too much junk.
23. The weather (gets, get) colder in November.
24. The first days (is, are) the hardest.

Write a paragraph describing a building in your city. Use "and" to connect two of the sentences.

_____

_____

_____

_____

_____

_____

_____

_____

N-V Diagramming

The N-V sentence consists of a simple subject and its verb. It is diagrammed as follows:

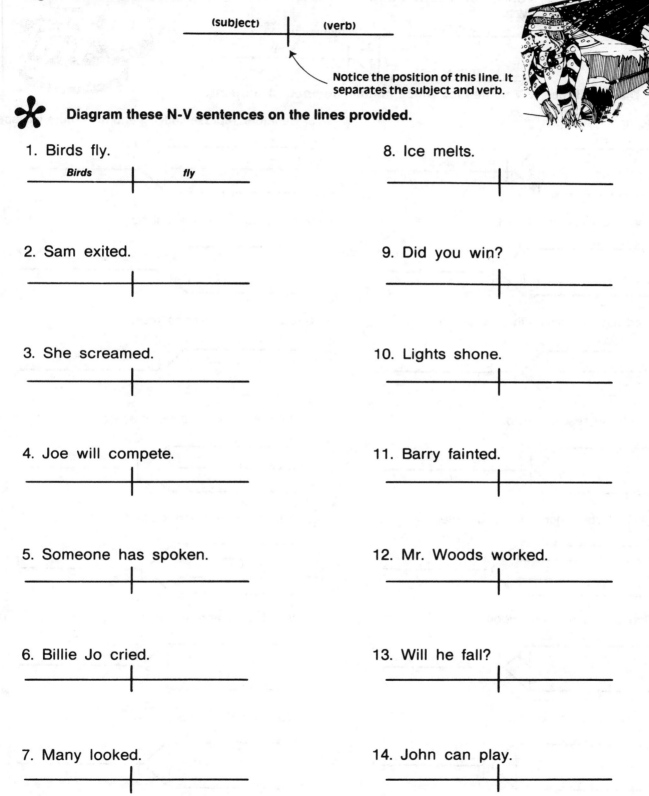

(subject) | (verb)

Notice the position of this line. It separates the subject and verb.

Diagram these N-V sentences on the lines provided.

1. Birds fly.

Birds | *fly*

2. Sam exited.

3. She screamed.

4. Joe will compete.

5. Someone has spoken.

6. Billie Jo cried.

7. Many looked.

8. Ice melts.

9. Did you win?

10. Lights shone.

11. Barry fainted.

12. Mr. Woods worked.

13. Will he fall?

14. John can play.

Unit 61 cont'd

Diagramming N-V Sentences with Compound Subjects

The N-V sentence may consist of a compound subject and its verb. It is diagrammed as follows:

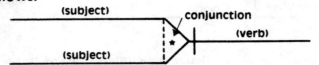

 Diagram these N-V sentences which contain compound subjects.

1. He and I struggled.

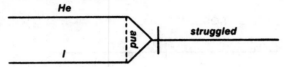

2. Lisa and Debbie finished.

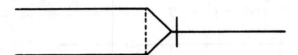

3. Brad, David, and Keith may watch.

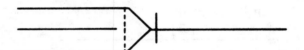

4. Food and rest will help.

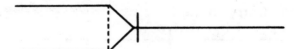

5. Neither Steve nor Chris succeeded.

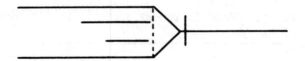

6. Bob and Gene understood.

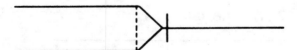

7. Gary and Diane enrolled.

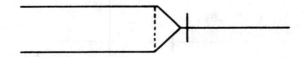

8. Senators, representatives, and governors will speak.

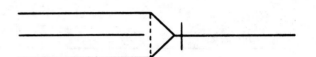

9. Food and exercise will help.

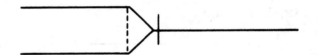

10. Either you or Donna must try.

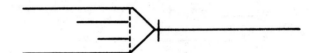

11. John, Eric, and Jarrod practiced.

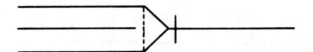

12. Neither he nor she studied.

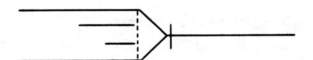

13. Will Daniel and Tim rise?

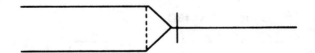

14. Ted and Sue dated.

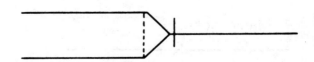

Diagramming N-V Sentences with Compound Verbs

The N-V sentence may consist of a simple subject and its compound verb. It is diagrammed as follows:

 Diagram these N-V sentences which contain compound verbs.

1. They sang and danced.

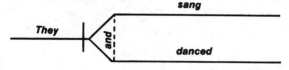

2. Shea rose and left.

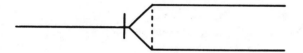

3. Did he win or lose?

4. Lanny fell but continued.

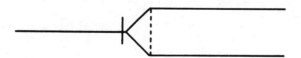

5. Sheila sews, knits, and crochets.

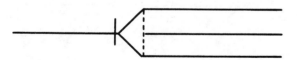

6. Mrs. Wright paints and draws.

7. He ran and jumped.

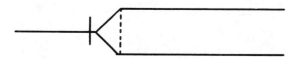

8. Can Karen practice and audition?

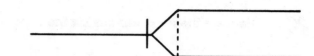

9. Linda looked but trembled.

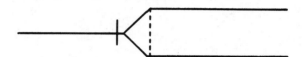

10. Kyle ate and ran.

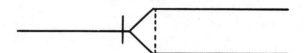

11. We laughed and talked.

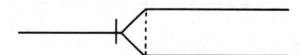

12. Did he drive or fly?

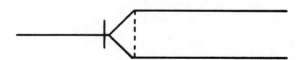

13. Greg tried but failed.

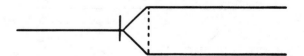

14. Stan was tried and sentenced.

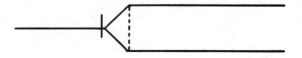

Unit 62 cont'd

Diagramming Articles and N-V Sentences

"A," "an," and "the" are articles. They may modify the subject of the N-V sentence. An article is diagrammed as follows:

(subject) | (verb)

(article)

← The article is placed directly under the noun (subject) it modifies.

 Diagram these sentences on the lines provided.

1. The buzzer sounded.

buzzer | sounded

The

2. A car backfired.

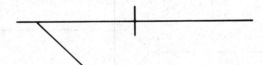

3. The child dozed.

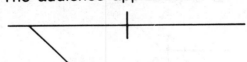

4. The audience applauded.

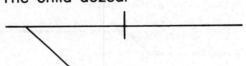

5. Did the President speak?

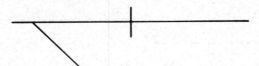

6. The engine roared.

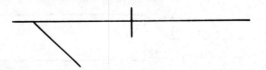

7. An animal growled.

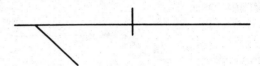

8. A ship sank.

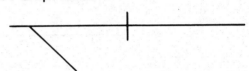

9. The monkey chattered.

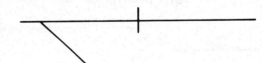

10. Can a horse swim?

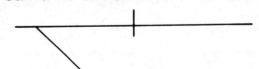

11. An aunt visited.

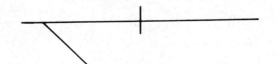

12. The soldier fired.

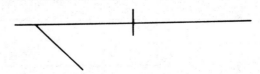

Diagramming Adjectives and N-V Sentences

An adjective is a word that tells which one, what color, what kind, or how many. An adjective may modify the noun (subject) in a N-V sentence. An adjective is diagrammed as follows:

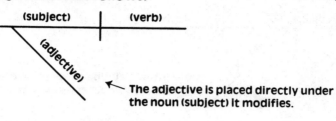

(subject) | (verb)

(adjective)

← The adjective is placed directly under the noun (subject) it modifies.

❋ **Diagram these sentences on the lines provided.**

1. Five minutes remain.

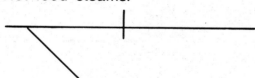

2. Snake bites hurt.

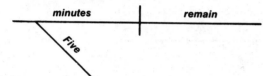

3. Bright lightning flashed.

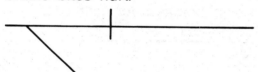

4. Hot food steams.

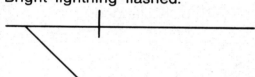

5. Foolish men stumble.

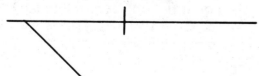

6. Football players tackle.

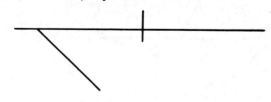

7. Twenty people stood.

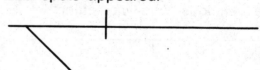

8. Have four bells rung?

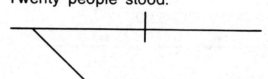

9. Mountain streams flow.

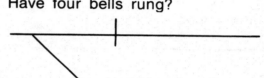

10. Red spots appeared.

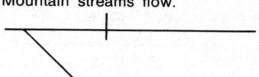

11. Good players will win.

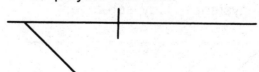

12. Some individuals gossip.

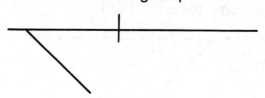

Unit 63 cont'd →

Diagramming Articles, Adjectives, and N-V Sentences

The subject of a N-V sentence may be modified by both an article and an adjective. Such a sentence is diagrammed as follows:

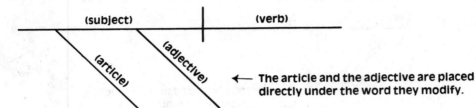

← The article and the adjective are placed directly under the word they modify.

 Diagram these N-V sentences with adjectives and articles.

1. The pretty girl sang.

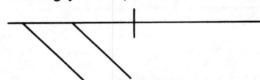

2. An angry mob protested.

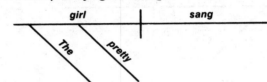

3. The happy couple entered.

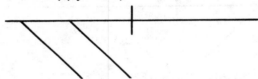

4. The delicious food was eaten.

5. The hysterical lady screamed.

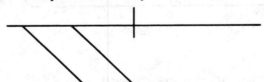

6. The huge tower swayed.

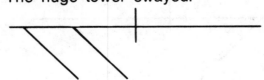

7. The poor man begged.

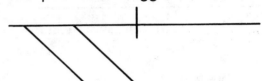

8. A foreign ambassador visited.

9. The awful noise clanged.

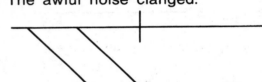

10. The old man slept.

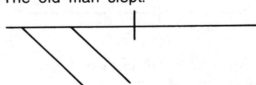

11. Did the construction workers finish?

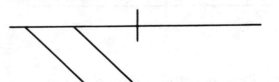

12. The older child competed.

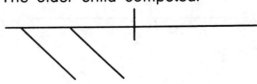

154

Diagramming Compound Adjectives

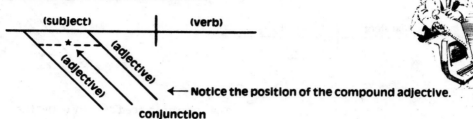

Unit 64

A compound adjective may modify the subject of a N-V sentence.
A compound adjective is diagrammed as follows:

← Notice the position of the compound adjective.

 Diagram these sentences on the lines provided.

1. Red and white flags flew.

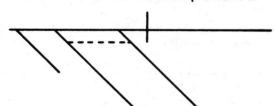

2. The small but complex component shattered.

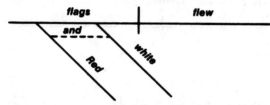

3. The quick and easy recipe worked.

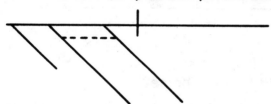

4. The third and fourth attempts failed.

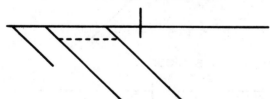

5. The track and field coach shouted.

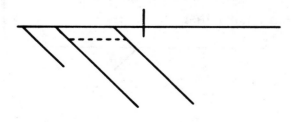

6. Blue and purple flowers blossomed.

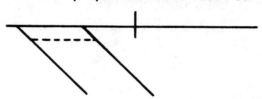

7. The cool and clear water glistened.

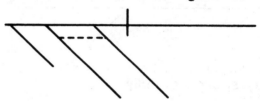

8. The tired and disturbed victim wept.

9. Ten or twelve tickets remain.

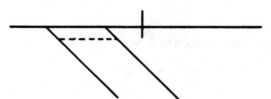

10. Old but sturdy gates stood.

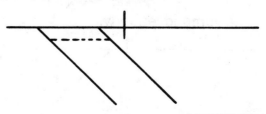

Unit 64 cont'd

Diagramming N-V Sentences
with Adverbs

An adverb is a word that tells when, where, why, or how. An adverb may modify the verb in a N-V sentence. An adverb is diagrammed as follows:

(subject) | (verb)

(adverb)

← The adverb is placed directly under the verb it modifies.

 Diagram these sentences on the lines provided.

1. Donna talks continuously.

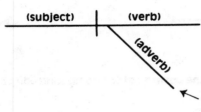
Donna | talks

continuously

2. Larry worked hard.

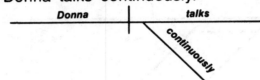

3. They spoke carefully.

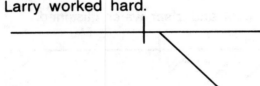

4. Jonathan seldom loses.

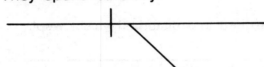

5. Mr. Dyer departed yesterday.

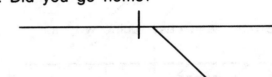

6. Roberta jumped eagerly.

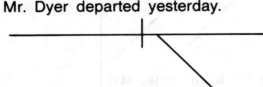

7. Randy never quits.

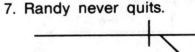

8. Boris moved cautiously.

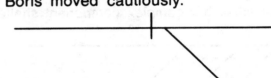

9. Did you go home?

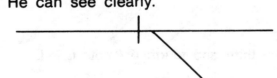

10. He can see clearly.

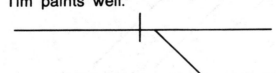

11. Tim paints well.

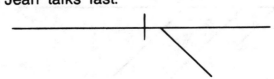

12. Jean talks fast.

Diagramming Double Adverbs

Unit 65

A N-V sentence may contain more than one adverb. It is diagrammed as follows:

Diagram these sentences on the lines provided.

(subject) | (verb)

(adverb) (adverb)

← Notice the position of the adverbs.

1. You can go there later.

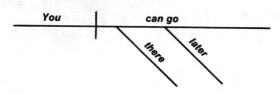

2. They'll arrive here soon.

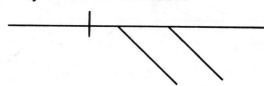

3. Joan stood up quietly.

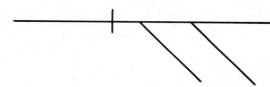

4. Corbit waited outside shyly.

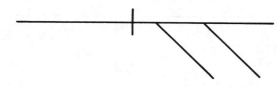

5. Pat and Donnie always come here.

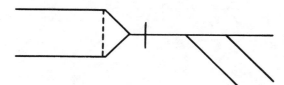

6. The boat ran aground again.

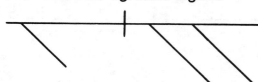

7. Come here now.

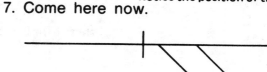

8. Tammy moved inside slowly.

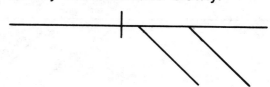

9. John spoke up sarcastically.

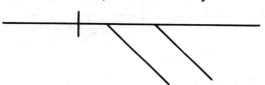

10. Did she waltz in gracefully?

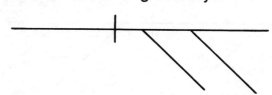

11. Mrs. Harris taught here before.

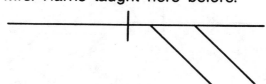

12. You never answer truthfully.

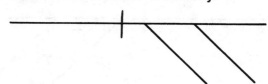

Unit 65 cont'd →

Diagramming Compound Adverbs

A N-V sentence may contain a compound adverb. It is diagrammed as follows:

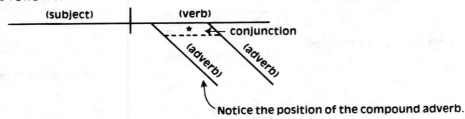

Notice the position of the compound adverb.

 Diagram these sentences on the lines provided.

1. He followed slowly and unwillingly.

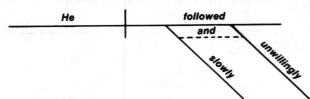

2. Bells rang loudly and clearly.

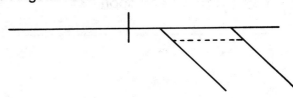

3. The waves tossed to and fro.

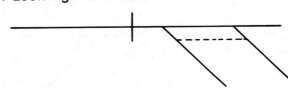

4. Do we travel east or west?

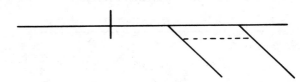

5. Adam worked hurriedly but carefully.

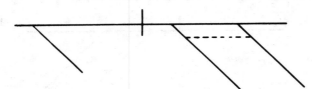

6. Angela rambled on and on.

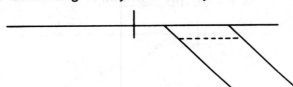

7. Look right and left.

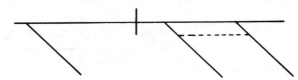

8. Should we walk fast or slow?

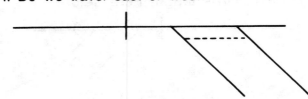

9. The students sang loudly and cheerfully.

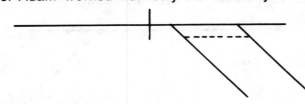

10. Eric fished lazily and halfheartedly.

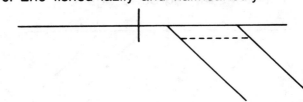

Comprehension Check

Ⓐ Identify each part of these N-V sentences.

       N   **V**

1. Katherine smiled.
2. He will arrive soon.
3. The two men disagreed.
4. The soldiers marched on.
5. Brooks babble.
6. I sat down and listened.
7. No one objected.
8. The team practiced.
9. Harriet and Ted tied.
10. The sale ends tomorrow.
11. Nelson answered truthfully.
12. The ice cream melted slowly.
13. I never shop there.
14. Jennifer worked slowly and carefully.
15. The yellow motorcycle won.
16. Dr. Minton always frowns.
17. Theresa sat down and cried.
18. The last train had already left.
19. Samantha winced.
20. It works!

Ⓑ Add the missing subjects.

1. __*Frank*__ reads every day.
2. The _____ shines brightly.
3. _____ swam across.
4. The _____ applauded.
5. _____ stayed home.
6. _____ watched impatiently.
7. The old _____ backfired.
8. The _____ melted.
9. The _____ sold quickly.
10. _____ paced nervously.
11. _____ and _____ ski.
12. _____ stopped and rested.
13. The _____ grew.
14. _____ never studies.
15. _____ and _____ agree.
16. _____ ran outside.

Ⓒ Add the missing verbs.

1. Eagles __*soar*__ .
2. It _____ Tuesday.
3. The lights _____ out.
4. Mr. Larson _____ .
5. The baby _____ all night.
6. The bells _____ loudly.
7. The fire _____ .
8. The frogs _____ .
9. The plane _____ safely.
10. Dogs and cats _____ .
11. The meeting _____ today.
12. It _____ too much.
13. Casey already _____ .
14. Dr. Baker _____ daily.
15. The cereal _____ .
16. My uncle _____ .
17. The thief _____ .
18. No one _____ .
19. I _____ and _____ .
20. Ms. Walters _____ early.
21. The man's family _____ .
22. We _____ twice.
23. Our team _____ .
24. Blake _____ forward.

Test 13 cont'd

Comprehension Check (continued)

D **Diagram these N-V sentences.**

1. Amos and Carl will not leave.

2. Serena moved away last year.

3. Ben and Kate were married.

4. The yellow truck sold first.

5. The sheriff lives there.

6. The ladder slipped.

7. Bradley drives defensively.

8. I usually sit here.

9. You played beautifully.

10. The principal went home early.

11. The tired old man sat down.

12. Rex turned away and sighed.

Write a paragraph about your favorite holiday. Use at least three N-V sentences.

_____

_____

_____

_____

_____

_____

_____

Diagramming Adverbs
Modifying Adverbs

A N-V sentence may contain an adverb which modifies another adverb. It is diagrammed as follows:

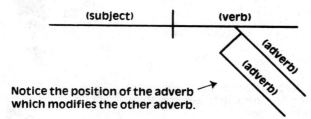

Notice the position of the adverb which modifies the other adverb.

* **Diagram these sentences on the lines provided.**

1. It looks too easy.

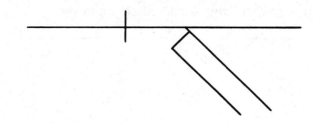

6. Mr. Neely worked very carefully.

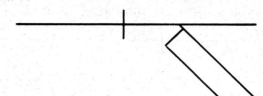

2. He seldom practices very hard.

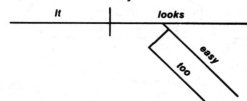

7. She continued more cautiously.

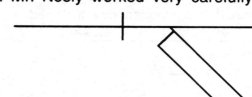

3. Lionel sings really well.

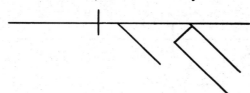

8. Rhonda dances most gracefully.

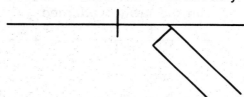

4. Answer very quickly.

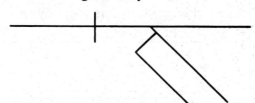

9. Practice more quietly.

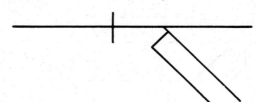

5. Dennis spoke rather well.

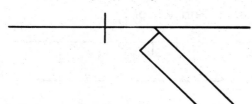

10. I have arrived too soon.

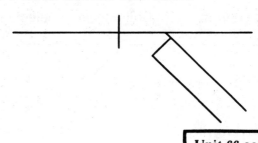

Unit 66 cont'd

Diagramming Prepositional Phrases
Used as Adjectives

A N-V sentence may contain a prepositional phrase which functions as an adjective. It is diagrammed as follows:

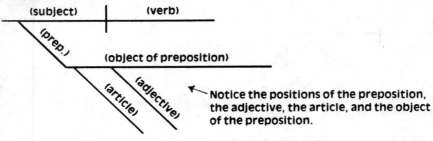

Notice the positions of the preposition, the adjective, the article, and the object of the preposition.

 Diagram these sentences on the lines provided.

1. The cat in the wooden box meowed.

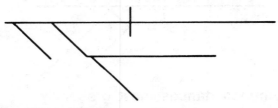

6. The students from Alma won.

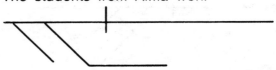

2. The chair on the lawn overturned.

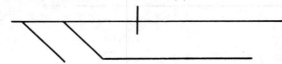

7. Is oil from Alaska expensive?

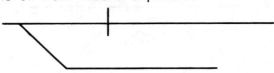

3. The notes of music stopped.

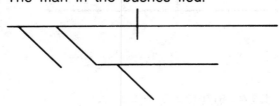

8. The car in the garage was destroyed.

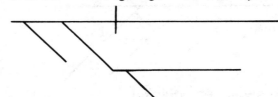

4. The man in the bushes fled.

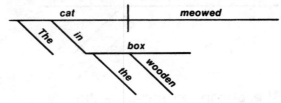

9. Songs by Prince won.

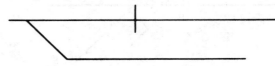

5. Players from South Chicago were selected first.

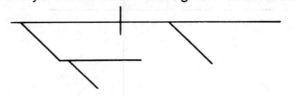

10. A man in the back office bellowed.

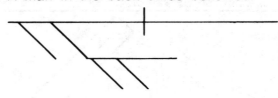

Diagramming Prepositional Phrases Used as Adverbs

A N-V sentence may contain a prepositional phrase which functions as an adverb. It is diagrammed as follows:

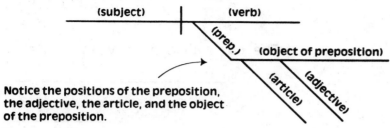

Notice the positions of the preposition, the adjective, the article, and the object of the preposition.

* **Diagram these sentences on the lines provided.**

1. I am at the office.

2. He talked of peace.

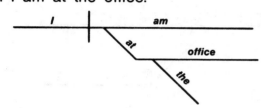

3. The emigrant departs from his homeland.

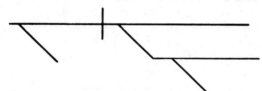

4. The members will meet on Friday.

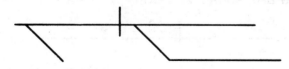

5. Stop at the drugstore.

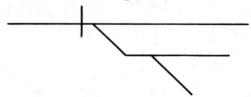

6. The cow jumped over the fence.

7. We sent for an officer.

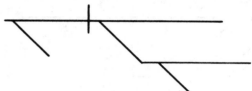

8. Wait in the back room.

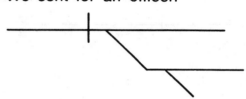

9. Lawrence studies before each exam.

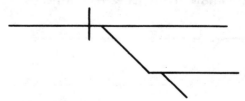

10. I'll come back on the bus.

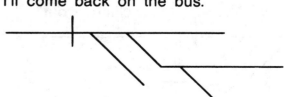

Unit 67 cont'd

Diagramming Prepositional Phrases

 Diagram these sentences on the lines provided.

1. The picture hung on one wall.

picture | *hung*
The *on* *wall* *one*

7. The car stalled near Martin Street.

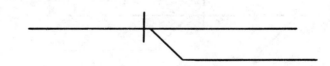

2. The man behind us shoved.

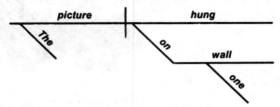

8. Mark went for a ride.

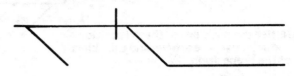

3. The hose beside the pool always leaks.

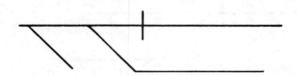

9. Candy moved to the front.

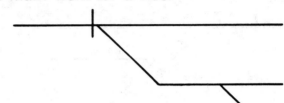

4. Get off the table.

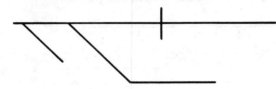

10. The store in town closed.

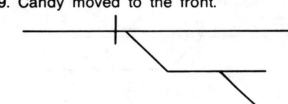

5. The salesman from Ecenro came.

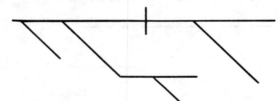

11. Gerard spoke at noon.

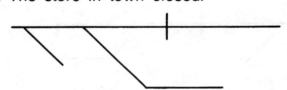

6. Four men with tools climbed out.

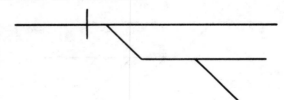

12. Don't go to that movie.

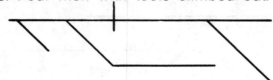

164

Diagramming N-V Sentences

 Diagram these sentences on the lines provided.

1. Crawl under the desk.

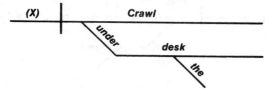

2. Manuel sat and read.

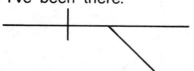

3. I've been there.

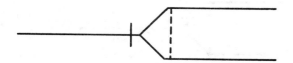

4. Ten firemen arrived.

5. Do you mind?

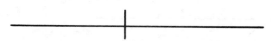

6. Sit straight and still.

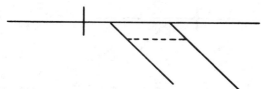

7. He sings every day.

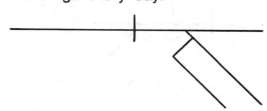

8. The pilot flew home yesterday.

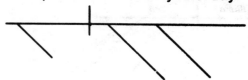

9. The sounds stopped.

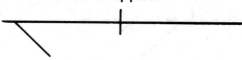

10. The waiter in the restaurant laughed.

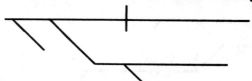

11. Chris and Eric finished.

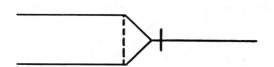

12. Move quickly.

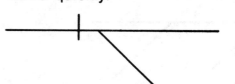

13. The old car died.

14. The green and gold banner waved.

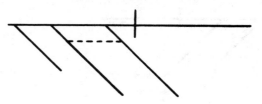

Unit 68 cont'd

Diagram Practice

 Diagram these sentences.

1. William ran home today.

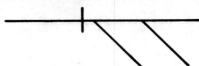

2. Donna talks too much.

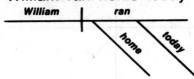

3. Get out or get in.

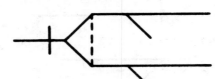

4. Time flies.

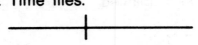

5. That car goes fast.

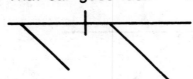

6. The players waited patiently.

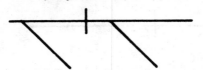

7. The former president resigned.

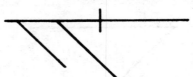

8. Both boys ran through the mud.

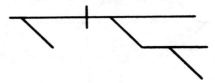

9. He and I will compete.

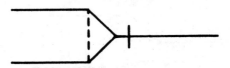

10. Who lives here?

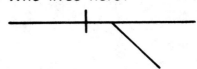

11. My right leg aches.

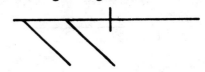

12. The entire population voted.

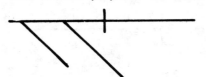

13. Move along.

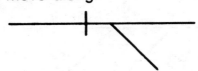

14. Are you shopping today or tomorrow?

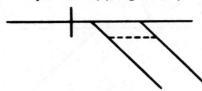

The Direct Object

The direct object receives the action of an action verb. The subject performs the action of an action verb.

```
          subj  av      do
```
EXAMPLES: Chris rode his bike.

The subject performs the action.
The action verb tells what the subject does.
The direct object receives the action.

A Underline each subject once. Underline each action verb twice. Put parentheses around the direct object.

1. My brother fed his (dog).
2. Steve prepared dinner.
3. Janie popped the balloon.
4. The driver started the engine.
5. Our coach blew his whistle.
6. The lightning hit the tree branch.
7. Wayne memorized his spelling list.
8. Jimmy bought flowers for Jill.
9. We made some spaghetti.
10. Bill painted the blue house.
11. Cliff lost his new billford.
12. Rick burned his hand on the stove.
13. We toasted marshmallows last night.
14. The clerk broke my record.
15. The shark attacked the boat.
16. Barbara colored the poster.
17. Margie measured the material.
18. Judy typed the paper.
19. Sam spent too much money.
20. I bought a catalog.

B Underline each action verb. Tell who or what performed the action. Then tell who or what received the action.

1. The puppy chewed my socks.   Performed action: ____*puppy*____   Received action: ____*socks*____
2. A thief stole my stereo.   Performed action: _____   Received action: _____
3. Laura answered my question.   Performed action: _____   Received action: _____
4. Donna made a correction.   Performed action: _____   Received action: _____
5. Lee drew a pretty picture.   Performed action: _____   Received action: _____
6. Myra moved the clock back.   Performed action: _____   Received action: _____
7. Dad arranged furniture last Saturday.   Performed action: _____   Received action: _____
8. He answered the letter.   Performed action: _____   Received action: _____
9. My sister placed the order.   Performed action: _____   Received action: _____
10. The teacher called my parents.   Performed action: _____   Received action: _____
11. A tattletale told my secret.   Performed action: _____   Received action: _____
12. Dan plays video games.   Performed action: _____   Received action: _____
13. He flew the plane.   Performed action: _____   Received action: _____
14. We saw the new show.   Performed action: _____   Received action: _____
15. My cousin sent a message.   Performed action: _____   Received action: _____
16. Kevin earned enough money.   Performed action: _____   Received action: _____
17. Alan bought a new car.   Performed action: _____   Received action: _____
18. I have a plan.   Performed action: _____   Received action: _____
19. The children built a snowman.   Performed action: _____   Received action: _____
20. They gave a surprise party.   Performed action: _____   Received action: _____

Unit 69 cont'd

Direct Objects

A sentence arranged in the **noun-verb-noun** pattern contains a direct object. In this pattern the direct object is always a noun following the verb.

A Write "yes" in the blank at the left if the sentence contains a direct object. Write "no" if it does not.

_____1. The squirrel hid the nuts.

_____2. Bill felt dizzy.

_____3. Our team won the game.

_____4. The day was hot.

_____5. Mother brought two cakes to the church social.

Nouns as direct objects complete the thought of a sentence by answering the question "What?"

B Complete each sentence below by underlining the words in parentheses that include a direct object.

1. Lightning struck (<u>the house</u>, twice in two weeks).

2. The sailors rowed (very quickly, the boat).

3. Our class visited (a bakery, last Saturday).

4. Throw (to Mary, the ball).

5. We would like to eat (French fries, every noon).

6. Mark Twain wrote (several stories, while living in Nevada).

7. Mother picked (in her garden, some roses).

8. Jill reads (many books, because she enjoys it).

A compound direct object is formed of two or more connected direct objects. However, a name consisting of more than one word makes only one direct object.

C Write "true" in the blank if the sentence contains a compound direct object. Write "false" if the sentence does not.

_____1. We ate hot dogs and hamburgers at the picnic.

_____2. Lewis Carrol wrote <u>Alice in Wonderland</u>.

_____3. George invited Betty, Elmer, Kate, and Ronnie.

_____4. My grandfather always watches "All in the Family" and "Wild Kingdom."

_____5. Steve bought five candy bars.

Nouns as Direct Objects

The direct object receives the action of the verb. Nouns may receive the action of the verb.

EXAMPLE: Our dog bit the <u>postman</u>. "Postman" is a noun which receives the action of the verb "bit."

A Underline the subject once, the verb twice, and the direct object once.

1. Marie accepted the watch.
2. The children sang a song.
3. Please wake your brother.
4. Did he bother the students?
5. The big stick will protect the joggers.
6. Alison cleaned her room yesterday.
7. You should connect the wires.
8. Janey collects gold butterflies.
9. The store rejected our request.
10. Bobby wrecked his dad's car.
11. The dog snatched the steak from the grill.
12. We ate cheesecake and angel food cake.
13. My parents danced the twist.
14. Can we surprise our guests?
15. Who built this house?
16. Steve can't find his skis.
17. Please slice this bacon.
18. Do you want these eggs?
19. The ladies planned a Christmas bazaar.
20. Did you guess the answer?

B Underline each verb. Fill in the blanks after each sentence.

1. Larry dropped the ladder. Performed action: _____*Larry*_____ Received action: _____*ladder*_____
2. We collected the money. Performed action: _____ Received action: _____
3. Darrin had a nightmare. Performed action: _____ Received action: _____
4. The old hermit built a fire. Performed action: _____ Received action: _____
5. Suzy bought a pink prom dress. Performed action: _____ Received action: _____
6. The mechanic repaired our truck. Performed action: _____ Received action: _____
7. Chad answered the test questions. Performed action: _____ Received action: _____
8. The baby threw his rattle at me. Performed action: _____ Received action: _____
9. The school's clubs chose their officers. Performed action: _____ Received action: _____
10. The travel agency collected Marie's money. Performed action: _____ Received action: _____
11. Dad bought maps at the service station. Performed action: _____ Received action: _____
12. Five students raised their hands. Performed action: _____ Received action: _____
13. His mom and dad gave a lecture. Performed action: _____ Received action: _____
14. Have you ever met a real cowboy? Performed action: _____ Received action: _____
15. We watched the movie closely. Performed action: _____ Received action: _____
16. Anne gave a choice to us. Performed action: _____ Received action: _____
17. We bought a cordless phone. Performed action: _____ Received action: _____
18. Gum usually annoys teachers. Performed action: _____ Received action: _____

COMPOSITION EXERCISE

Write four sentences which contain nouns as direct objects. Underline the direct objects.

1. _____
2. _____
3. _____
4. _____

Unit 70 cont'd

Pronouns as Direct Objects

Pronouns may be direct objects. They receive the action of an action verb.

EXAMPLE: *The class chose her as the president.*
"Her" is a pronoun receiving the action of the verb "chose."

A Underline the pronouns which are used as direct objects.

1. Marilyn asked me to the dinner.
2. Mother took them to the zoo.
3. Dad sent me in late.
4. The news took me by surprise.
5. Lynn's parents advised her about college.
6. Can we return them now?
7. The members thanked me for the donation.
8. I will show you in a minute.
9. Who named you?
10. Please catch her for me.
11. Did you tell him about the change?
12. Molly informed us of the change.
13. Jenna answered one of the questions.
14. Katy hit her by accident.
15. We saw him too late today.
16. Bob lost them in the crowd.
17. Millie answered me with a smile.
18. We heard it on the radio.
19. The teacher kept him after class.
20. He held it under the light.

B Replace the nouns used as direct objects with pronouns.

1. Sarah cooked dinner last night.   Sarah cooked _____*it*_____ last night.
2. Bill barbecued the chickens.   Bill barbecued _____ .
3. Marie asked Judy for the paper.   Marie asked _____ for the paper.
4. Chris heard the news on television.   Chris heard _____ on television.
5. We asked Dad for the car.   We asked _____ for the car.
6. They named their new dog yesterday.   They named _____ yesterday.
7. Sherry drove Mary to work.   Sherry drove _____ to work.
8. Did he tell Janice and you about the party?   Did he tell _____ about the party?
9. We saw Barb and Tom at the fair.   We saw _____ at the fair.
10. Rhoda kept Allen and me late.   Rhoda kept _____ late.
11. Eric met Al after the concert.   Eric met _____ after the concert.
12. Jason answered a question correctly.   Jason answered _____ correctly.
13. Pat likes hamburgers for breakfast.   Pat likes _____ for breakfast.
14. The little girl answers the phone like an adult.   She answers _____ like an adult.
15. Joe saw a movie at this theater.   Joe saw _____ at this theater.

COMPOSITION EXERCISE

Write 10 sentences; use a pronoun as a direct object in each one.

1. _____
2. _____
3. _____
4. _____
5. _____
6. _____
7. _____
8. _____
9. _____
10. _____

Comprehension Check

Ⓐ **Identify each part of these N-V sentences.**

    N   *V*

1. Harry sneered at the suggestion.
2. The people laughed.
3. Isaac drove away slowly.
4. She sat by the window for hours.
5. Something in the box moved!

6. Jetta volunteered cheerfully.
7. The story ended abruptly.
8. It fell on my toe.
9. David lives in Cleveland.
10. He always argues with me.

Ⓑ **Identify the underlined parts of these sentences.**

1. <u>Deborah</u> will easily win.   *noun as subject*
2. I spoke to no one <u>at the party</u>.   _____
3. The <u>new</u> one doesn't work.   _____
4. My parents arrived <u>early</u>.   _____
5. Kenny <u>should have called</u> today.   _____
6. The woman <u>sat</u> here.   _____
7. We went <u>to the mall</u>.   _____
8. Leslie ran <u>home</u> and cried.   _____
9. Are <u>you</u>?   _____
10. The <u>fire</u> alarm sounded twice.   _____
11. Ginger walked <u>across the stage</u>.   _____
12. Chris <u>looked</u> directly at Tom.   _____
13. <u>Three</u> boys applied for the job.   _____
14. <u>Martha</u> laughs at my jokes.   _____
15. <u>I</u> wished for a new camera.   _____

Ⓒ **Underline the direct objects. Then identify if they are nouns (1) or pronouns (2).**

_1_   1. Melanie is fixing your <u>car</u>.
____ 2. Do you like it?
____ 3. Terry caught the snake.
____ 4. They need our support.
____ 5. Roger checked the plugs.
____ 6. I can't see the boat now.
____ 7. Cameron won't do it.
____ 8. The puppy chased Ashley.

____ 9. I rode the bus to Dallas.
____ 10. My brother plays basketball.
____ 11. The man watched the film.
____ 12. Do you know him?
____ 13. The clock struck twelve.
____ 14. Thunder scares me.
____ 15. Sylvia chose Karen.
____ 16. Put the package on the sofa.

Test 14 cont'd ➡

Comprehension Check (continued)

(D) Diagram these N-V sentences.

1. The chain caught on my shirt.

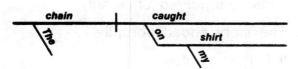

2. Something has happened to it.

3. The students left early today.

4. Jasper called about the ad.

5. The stack of books fell to the floor.

6. Several people gathered around.

7. The truck always comes at four.

8. Juanita traveled to Spain.

9. I waited for you at Conrad's.

10. No one asked about the trial.

Look at the picture on the right. Write a paragraph describing what you see. Use at least two N-V sentences. Underline them.

_____

_____

_____

_____

_____

_____

_____

_____

_____

_____

The N-V-N Sentence

The N-V-N pattern consists of a subject, a verb, and a direct object. The subject and the direct object will be a noun or a noun substitute.

EXAMPLES:
           N   V   N
   a. Marty flew the plane.
           N   V   N
   b. He flew it.

A Label each subject, verb, and direct object by writing "N" or "V" over them.

     N   V   N
1. My brother hit me.

2. I saw the forest.

3. The children played Monopoly.

4. The ants built the hill.

5. The doctor examined his patient.

6. The golfer bent her clubs.

7. We shut the cage door quickly.

8. Bob blamed himself for the loss.

9. We understand the object of the game.

10. Honey bees build honeycombs.

11. Alison read three books last week.

12. The salesman sold the camp trailer.

13. Band members stored their instruments.

14. Brad has been eating onions again.

15. Skipper brought the paper to us.

16. The crowd watched the game closely.

17. We examined the record for defects.

18. Mr. Moore planted watermelons in his field.

19. We wrote our names in the wet cement.

20. Did you see the latest video?

B Write "x" beside each sentence which has the N-V-N pattern.

__x__ 1. Dad missed last week's game.

____ 2. Mona is swimming today.

____ 3. Ted is running around the track.

____ 4. Alice slipped away from camp.

____ 5. Someone stole my lunch.

____ 6. They asked for my student number.

____ 7. Tad is late.

____ 8. Bev asked a very silly question.

____ 9. Chris took the dog for a walk.

____ 10. Gene has walked out the door.

____ 11. Steve and Wayne dropped the table.

____ 12. Tony dusted the furniture.

____ 13. Lara invited Tammy and Jenny to the party.

____ 14. The nurse took Anne's temperature.

____ 15. We ate dinner at the restaurant.

____ 16. The birds called loudly.

COMPOSITION EXERCISE

Write 8 sentences which follow the N-V-N pattern.

1. _____
2. _____
3. _____
4. _____

5. _____
6. _____
7. _____
8. _____

Unit 71 cont'd

The N-V-N Pattern

The N-V-N sentence consists of a subject, a verb, and a direct object.

EXAMPLE:
      s   v   do
    The cat ate the canary.

A Underline each subject once, each verb twice, and each direct object once.

1. We visited the zoo.
2. I corrected the answers.
3. Some dinosaurs ate plants.
4. Bill repaired the raft.
5. The baby untied his shoes.
6. Kathy brushed her teeth.
7. We counted the votes.
8. She won the election.
9. The scientist made a discovery.
10. My sister told my secret.
11. Mel drove Dad's car.
12. Shirley broke my favorite mug.
13. The wind tossed the kites.
14. Sharks circled the boat.
15. I called the discount store.
16. Students must close their books.
17. Barry covered his answers.
18. Lee gave the command.
19. The collie wagged his tail happily.
20. Gail made a mistake.
21. Susie planned a trip.
22. Mabel cooked dinner for us.
23. My favorite author wrote another book.
24. Melanie likes romantic movies.
25. The rain is hitting the skylight.
26. She is washing the towels now.
27. I'll read a chapter now.
28. A hunter shot those ducks.
29. The officer flashed her badge.
30. We will eat fried fish.

B Complete each sentence with a subject, a verb, or a direct object.

1. _____ *Larry* _____ wrote a story.
2. Chris _____ dinner.
3. Americans _____ their presidents.
4. The workers built our _____ .
5. Sarah attends _____ .
6. Ms. Baxter _____ the class.
7. Marian collected the _____ .
8. _____ drives a red truck.
9. We _____ television last night.
10. Our _____ gave the directions.
11. We had _____ for lunch.
12. Milton crushed the _____ .
13. We made up our _____ .
14. _____ has a new pair of jeans.
15. We _____ the topic.
16. Alice _____ the kitchen floor.
17. Jessica explained the _____ .
18. Our class visited a _____ .
19. The _____ ate my ham sandwich.
20. We _____ the news.
21. We _____ a new schedule.
22. Abby _____ the telescope first.
23. A guard _____ the door.
24. The pilot _____ the small plane.
25. Martha chews _____ in class.
26. Eddy passed the _____ .

COMPOSITION EXERCISE

Write 8 sentences which follow the N-V-N pattern.

1. _____
2. _____
3. _____
4. _____
5. _____
6. _____
7. _____
8. _____

Diagramming N-V-N Sentences

The **N-V-N** sentence consists of a subject, a transitive verb, and a direct object. It is diagrammed as follows:

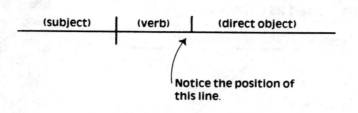

| (subject) | (verb) | (direct object) |

Notice the position of this line.

 Diagram these sentences on the lines provided.

1. Biff likes pizza.

| Biff | likes | pizza |

9. Phil stole the pen.

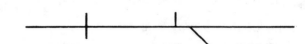

2. I rode the horse.

10. I bought a car.

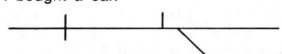

3. The family ate the dinner.

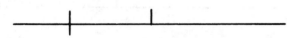

11. Felix answered the questions.

4. Mrs. Carr made tea.

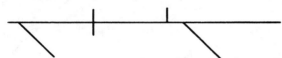

12. The Suttons sold their camper.

5. He loves the Orient.

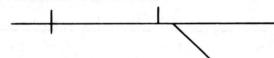

13. The committee appointed Sarah.

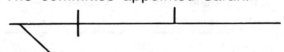

6. We caught a bus.

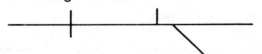

14. Albert wears suspenders.

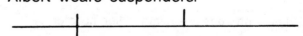

7. James hates sentences.

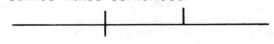

15. Patricia kept the house.

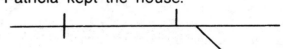

8. Terri saved the day.

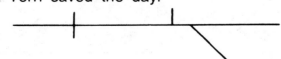

16. Joe committed the crime.

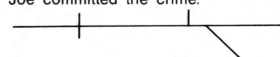

Unit 72 cont'd ⟶

Diagramming Adjectives and N-V-N Sentences

An adjective may modify the subject or the direct object of the N-V-N sentence. It is diagrammed as follows:

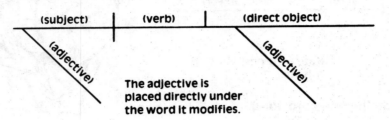

The adjective is placed directly under the word it modifies.

 Diagram these sentences on the lines provided.

1. Laurie bought a gray sweater.

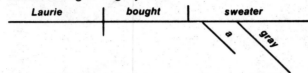

2. An orange wall surrounded the palace.

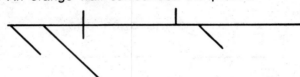

3. I carried the huge box.

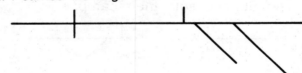

4. The train rounded the long curve.

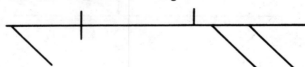

5. Lee Ann rode the giant roller coaster.

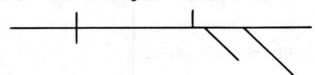

6. Several women petitioned the mayor.

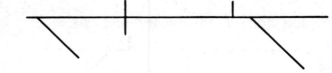

7. My English teacher speaks Spanish.

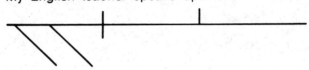

8. Sharon shook the rug.

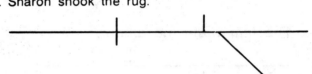

9. Teresa helped the puppy.

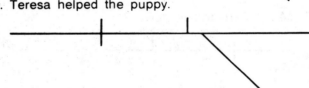

10. The woman applied more greasy lipstick.

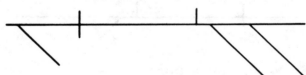

11. Did they like the party?

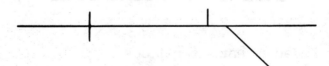

12. The students completed the entire test.

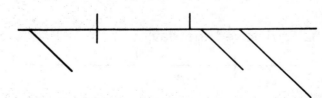

Diagramming Adverbs and N-V-N Sentences

An adverb may modify the transitive verb in the N-V-N sentence. It is diagrammed as follows:

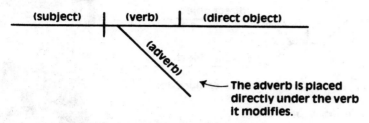

(subject) | (verb) | (direct object)

(adverb)

← The adverb is placed directly under the verb it modifies.

✳ **Diagram these sentences on the lines provided.**

1. His cat won't eat bones.

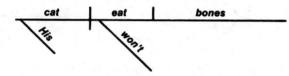

cat | eat | bones

His   won't

2. Hank never buys fresh fish.

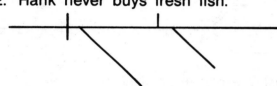

3. I'll take the chair downstairs.

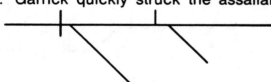

4. Garrick quickly struck the assailant.

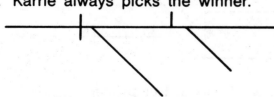

5. Karrie always picks the winner.

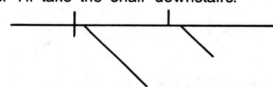

6. I told him once.

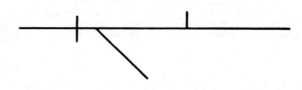

7. Lynn cast her vote twice.

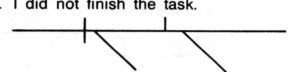

8. I did not finish the task.

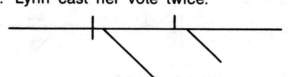

9. Charlie took notes carefully.

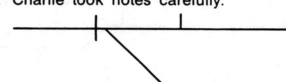

10. He solved the problem quickly.

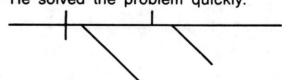

11. Alan admitted guilt reluctantly.

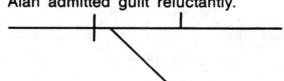

12. I will write the statement now.

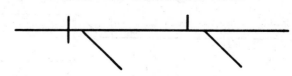

Unit 73 cont'd ➡

Diagramming N-V-N Sentences with Compounds

The subject, verb, or direct object of the N-V-N sentence may be compounded. Compounds are diagrammed as follows:

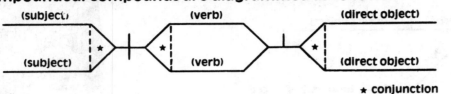

★ conjunction

 Diagram these sentences on the lines provided.

1. Simon and I caught the train.

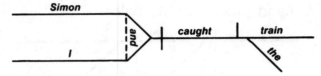

2. Martha builds and repairs foreign motors.

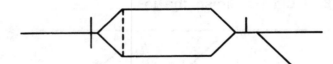

3. Lance ate meat and potatoes.

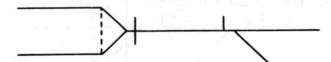

4. Luke and Beau watched the game.

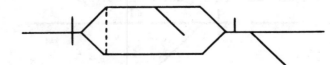

5. I ran out and bought a watch.

6. You may keep Rusty and Dusty.

7. Carol took but failed the examination.

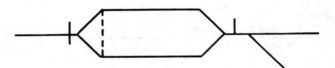

8. Matthew and Steven carried the bundle.

9. Wesley wrote and revised his report.

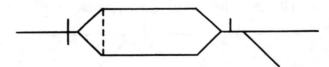

10. Mom cooked beans and cornbread.

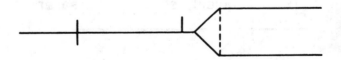

11. Jennifer and Darlene washed clothes.

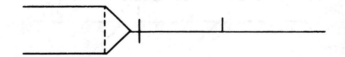

12. We won't use salt or pepper.

Diagramming N-V-N Sentences with Prepositional Phrases

A prepositional phrase may modify the subject, the transitive verb, or the direct object of the N-V-N sentence. It is diagrammed as follows:

```
(subject)  |  (verb)  |  (direct object)
                \ (prep.)
                  _____ (object of preposition)
                          \ (adjective)
```

The prepositional phrase is placed directly under the word it modifies.

✳ Diagram these sentences on the lines provided.

1. The lady behind the desk asked my name.

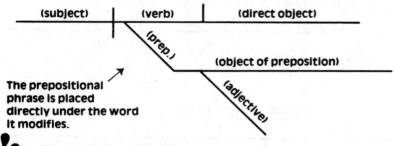

2. My aunt put the meal on the table.

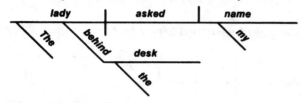

3. The dog placed its head on its paws.

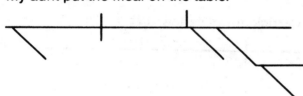

4. Fred gave the gift to Charles.

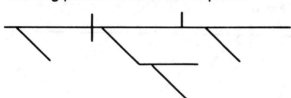

5. Has he borrowed my book from you?

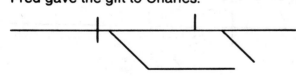

6. I drove Ann to work.

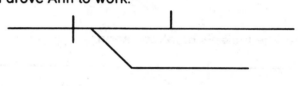

7. Her story about Kim upset us.

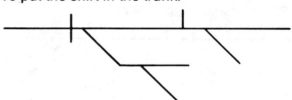

8. We put the shirt in the trunk.

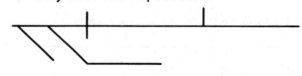

9. Mr. King explained math rules to us.

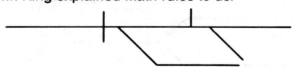

10. Shannon baked the cake for her dad.

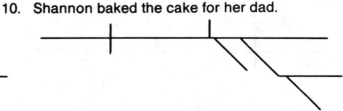

Unit 74 cont'd ➔

N-V-N Sentence Diagramming

Diagram these sentences.

1. Ivan never uses deodorant.

2. Peter rang the bell.

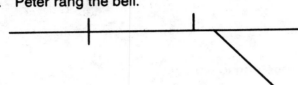

3. Eddie took his break too soon.

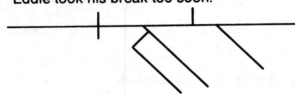

4. The lady on the subway ate candy.

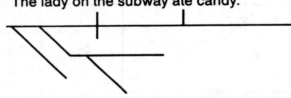

5. Phil customizes antique cars.

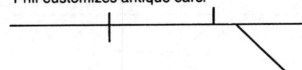

6. Cheryl and I wrote the address twice.

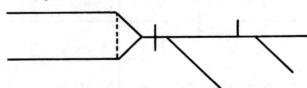

7. Don changed the oil.

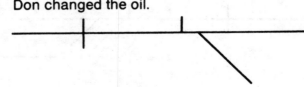

8. Waldo placed the ad today.

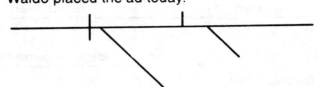

9. She can catch a cab.

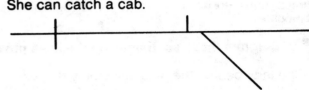

10. The board selected Mr. Johnson and Mr. Diaz.

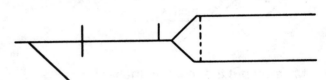

11. Derrick draws cartoons.

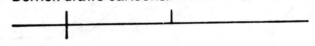

12. Maxwell put the groceries in the cabinet.

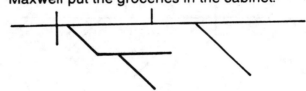

13. He hates me.

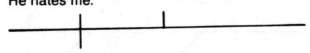

14. I'll bring you here.

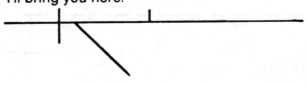

The Predicate Noun

A predicate noun follows a linking verb and renames the subject.

```
            subj.  lv        pn
EXAMPLE:    Shawn is the winner.
            "Winner" follows a linking verb and renames the subject.
```

A Label the subjects with an "s," the linking verbs with "lv," and the predicate nouns with "pn."

```
    s  lv        pn
```
1. Alex is a good student.
2. The boys are drummers.
3. She is a good cook.
4. Tom became a good dancer.
5. The secretary is Ms. Loften.
6. My Uncle Len is an artist.
7. Ben is an excellent driver.
8. I am your new teacher.
9. The carpenter is a craftsman.
10. Mr. Barker is a baker.
11. Sally will be a ghost on Halloween.
12. The old car is an antique.
13. Children are the future of America.
14. Ice cream is a delicious treat.
15. Her hobby is needlecraft.
16. Most dogs are friendly creatures.
17. Julia is a dreamer.
18. Steak is my dad's favorite food.
19. An emergency exit can be a lifesaver.
20. Her older sister is an actress.
21. Jean is usually a clown.
22. Our pet turkey became Thanksgiving dinner.
23. Baked apples were part of our menu.
24. The astronauts were brave pioneers.

B Supply the missing subject, linking verb, or predicate noun for each sentence.

1. Potatoes are ___*vegetables*___ .
2. The table _____ our desk.
3. _____ is my birthday.
4. The Liberty Bell _____ a national monument.
5. Wheat is a necessary _____ .
6. My cousin is a basketball _____ .
7. The eagle is our national _____ .
8. The old trail became a _____ .
9. Today is _____ .
10. The bride _____ a happy lady.
11. We are the _____ .
12. The bridge _____ became winners.
13. This _____ is a puzzle.
14. Marie is the _____ .
15. You are a good _____ .
16. This is my best _____ .
17. Mrs. Jenkins _____ our hostess.
18. This place is a _____ .
19. Her sisters are _____ .
20. Your room is a _____ .
21. The _____ became a riot.
22. That concert was a _____ .

Unit 75 cont'd

Predicate Nouns

A predicate noun is a noun which follows a linking verb and renames the subject.

EXAMPLES:
a. The book is a classic.   "Classic" follows a linking verb and renames "book."

b. Marty is my friend.   "Friend" follows a linking verb and renames "Marty."

A Underline each subject once, each linking verb twice, and each predicate noun once.

1. Jane is a new bride.
2. My favorite room is the library.
3. Marie's lunch was a peanut butter sandwich.
4. The big tree is an oak.
5. Jenny's favorite season is summer.
6. A school bus will be our transportation.
7. The broken dish was my best china.
8. The race will be a fifty-yard dash.
9. Bob and Sara are newscasters.
10. My dream is a Hawaiian vacation.
11. Golf is Ron's favorite sport.
12. Is wrestling a sport?
13. Speeding is a hazard.
14. Judith is a cheerleader.
15. A quarter and a nickel are the necessary coins.
16. The small protest became a riot.
17. An oar is necessary equipment for a rowboat.
18. A small town in Germany is a village.
19. Our only clue was a broken branch.
20. Chris's room is a disaster area.
21. The rescue operation was a great effort.
22. This green tent is our only shelter.
23. Pigs and cows are farm animals.
24. Dr. Matthews is a surgeon.
25. Delaware was the first state.
26. Breakfast is Tom's favorite meal.
27. Dinner will be barbecued chicken.
28. Rhonda is our newest student.
29. My favorite states are Texas and Colorado.
30. A radio is a good source for news reports.

B Put a check (✓) beside each sentence which has a predicate noun.

✓ 1. Movies are my favorite programs.
___ 2. The program is interesting.
___ 3. Her story was scary.
___ 4. Jim's hobby is skiing.
___ 5. The water heater is new.
___ 6. Her least favorite topic is war.
___ 7. This is my decision.
___ 8. Our repairman was Randy.
___ 9. The repaired car was a welcome sight.
___ 10. Barry's song was the best entertainment.
___ 11. Willie's song was a plea for help.
___ 12. Gene is a good auto mechanic.
___ 13. Judy is our typesetter.
___ 14. She does a good job.
___ 15. Tonight's award winner was a disappointment.
___ 16. It is a beautiful day.
___ 17. The insulation in our house is fiberglass.
___ 18. A hurricane is a disaster.
___ 19. Television can be a good teacher.
___ 20. Credit cards can be a problem.
___ 21. Sharon is a policewoman.
___ 22. This is our home gym.
___ 23. Mr. Blake's advice was poor.
___ 24. The rain was a relief from the heat.

COMPOSITION EXERCISE

Write 6 sentences which contain predicate nouns. Underline the predicate nouns.

1. _____
2. _____
3. _____
4. _____
5. _____
6. _____

Comprehension Check

(A) Identify each part of these N-V-N sentences.

      N   **V**   **N**

1. The dog chased the paper boy.

2. Marie collects matchbooks.

3. The thief stole $15,000 from the bank.

4. Tim hit his arm on the desk.

5. Joanne set the alarm for seven.

6. Nancy read the ad again.

7. The rain ruined my new shirt.

8. Donna loves chocolate.

9. Someone called your name.

10. The news shocked everyone.

11. Henry will check the tests.

12. The man put the cat outside.

13. Jim answered the questions easily.

14. Terri practiced her guitar lesson.

15. Ms. Martin rode the bus home.

16. Arnie broke his aunt's vase.

17. Dr. Newton drives a red Porsche.

18. I must call Jetta by Monday.

19. The cook prepared a feast.

20. No one said a word.

(B) Underline the direct objects.

1. He watches the <u>news</u> at six.

2. The old woman predicted snow.

3. Heidi wore yellow plaid pants.

4. We attended the meeting.

5. Jan repeated the message.

6. The boy counted the money again.

7. It cut my hand.

8. Our group painted the fence.

9. Johnathan loves the ballet.

10. Everyone needs guidance.

11. The officer arrested Ted.

12. His uncle builds houses.

13. Barry borrowed my car.

14. Judy made the quilt by hand.

15. The story frightened the children.

16. Cathy read the poem to the class.

(C) Supply the missing parts of these N-V-N sentences.

1. The ___*teacher*___ graded our papers.

2. Edna _____ too much money.

3. Ken eats _____ for breakfast.

4. Do you like _____ ?

5. The _____ stole my shoes.

6. Carl _____ everyone there.

7. Sidney wrote the _____ .

8. Andrew cut the _____ .

9. Gina _____ a new jacket.

10. I wrapped the _____ .

11. _____ danced the polka with me.

12. We celebrated _____ early.

13. _____ hid the money.

14. The blue team _____ the relay.

15. Paul finished his _____ first.

16. Her mother teaches _____ .

Test 15 cont'd

Comprehension Check (continued)

D **Diagram these N-V-N sentences.**

1. I opened the door for him.

```
 ____I____|____opened____|____door____
            \ for            \ the
              \    him
```

6. Rudy reached the top at noon.

2. Liz and Bill sent a telegram.

7. They cleaned and waxed the floors.

3. We ordered a pizza for lunch.

8. You and I will win the debate.

4. Karen needs our help now.

9. The last person in line locked the door.

5. The man gave a boring speech.

10. The dog followed me home.

Write a paragraph describing the person at the right. Use at least three N-V-N sentences.

_____

_____

_____

_____

_____

_____

_____

_____

_____

Nouns as Predicate Nouns

A predicate noun follows a linking verb and renames the subject.

EXAMPLES:
           s   lv   pn
a. Her new dog is a poodle.
      "Poodle" is a noun which follows a linking verb and renames the subject.

            s   lv   pn
b. Ms. Shaw was the writer.
      "Writer" is a noun which follows a linking verb and renames the subject.

A In each sentence, label the subject (s), the linking verb (lv), and the predicate noun (pn).

     s   lv   pn
1. Todd Nixon is a state senator.

2. A general is a leader.

3. Mars and Saturn are satellites of the sun.

4. Frank is a good student in math class.

5. Jennifer was the speaker today.

6. My dad is a hunter and a fisherman.

7. Smoking is a health hazard.

8. The Arctic Ocean is a large body of water.

9. James and Tim are candidates now.

10. The library should be a quiet area.

11. Our school is a good place for the meeting.

12. Snakes and spiders are Jack's pets.

13. My favorite days are Saturday and Sunday.

14. A whistle is a carefree sound.

15. The wind is not a stranger to the desert.

16. The sale of pennants will be our fund-raising project.

17. Today Jill will be the spokesperson.

18. Will Janet be the narrator of the story?

19. Mr. Baily's only expression is a frown.

20. His salary is a joke.

B Supply either a subject or a predicate noun for each blank.

1. The unfair trade was a good ____lesson____ for me.

2. _____ are good entertainment.

3. The young Indian was a _____ .

4. The newsman must be a good _____ .

5. The church bells are a lovely _____ .

6. Our heavy tent is a good _____ .

7. The actors and actresses will be local _____ .

8. The small _____ becomes an oak tree.

9. Jason will become an eagle _____ .

10. The small plants are _____ .

11. The _____ is a healthful fruit.

12. A toupee is false _____ .

13. A noun is a useful _____ .

14. My brother is a good _____ .

15. Columbus was a famous _____ .

16. Early pioneers were brave _____ .

17. This year's best _____ is wheat.

18. The three men were _____ .

19. The beautiful woman is a _____ .

20. Today's special is _____ .

21. The triplets are _____ , _____ , and _____ .

22. _____ is the loudest student in the room.

23. Is she the first _____ ?

24. Jeannie's problem is a small _____ .

25. Tim and Jim are my _____ .

26. My _____ is the girl with red hair.

Unit 76 cont'd

Pronouns as Predicate Nouns

Pronouns are noun substitutes and can be in the predicate noun position.

EXAMPLES: a. The winner is a red car.   *"Car" is a noun in the predicate noun position.*
b. The winner is a red one.   *"One" is a pronoun in the predicate noun position.*

A Underline each subject once, each linking verb twice, and each pronoun used in a predicate noun position once.

1. The speech was a long one.
2. Larry will be "it" in our game.
3. It is he on the phone.
4. The winners are they.
5. It has to be she.
6. It might have been he.
7. It certainly wasn't I.
8. Was it she?
9. My best friend is she.
10. The two doctors are they.

11. The cast members are we.
12. Our piano player will be you.
13. Brenda and Cathy are the ones in blue shoes.
14. Dog lovers are we.
15. This train is it.
16. The new students in school are they.
17. The loudest screamers are we in the north bleachers.
18. Their latest contest winner is he.
19. One earlier winner was I.
20. Yearbook staff members are they.

B Put a check (✓) beside each sentence which contains a predicate pronoun.

___✓___ 1. She is the one in the black car.
_____ 2. My brother is happy with his grades.
_____ 3. The students are going today.
_____ 4. It is I at the door.
_____ 5. Jonathon will be the boss.
_____ 6. Her birthday present is a new car.
_____ 7. It had to be you.
_____ 8. The red pen is lost.
_____ 9. The winner is she.
_____ 10. The baby is hers.
_____ 11. Their fire was hot.
_____ 12. It was they in the store.
_____ 13. The artist could be he.
_____ 14. Many people are absent.
_____ 15. The clowns in disguise are we.

_____ 16. Harriet was eager to begin.
_____ 17. It must have been she.
_____ 18. The farmers in the protest were they.
_____ 19. The biggest children are they.
_____ 20. The earthquake was terrible.
_____ 21. The readers will be we.
_____ 22. This flavor is the one in the first carton.
_____ 23. The contest winner is you.
_____ 24. Karen is a good reader.
_____ 25. The city is in the distance.
_____ 26. This puppy is his.
_____ 27. This choice will be it.
_____ 28. The postage is missing.
_____ 29. A candy bar is his favorite snack.
_____ 30. The new mother is she.

COMPOSITION EXERCISE

Write 12 sentences which each contain a predicate pronoun. Underline the predicate pronouns.

1. _____
2. _____
3. _____
4. _____
5. _____
6. _____

7. _____
8. _____
9. _____
10. _____
11. _____
12. _____

Diagramming N-LV-N Sentences

A N-LV-N sentence consists of a subject, a linking verb, and a predicate noun which renames the subject. It is diagrammed as follows:

(subject) | (linking verb) \ (predicate noun)

└─ Notice how this line slants.

 Diagram these sentences on the lines provided.

1. Rusty is a leader.

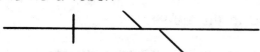

2. They are guerillas.

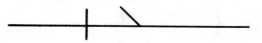

3. He is the governor.

4. Barney was captain.

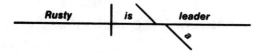

5. Is he a rebel?

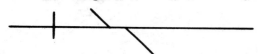

6. The boy is Kevin.

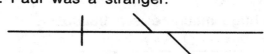

7. Joe became a pilot.

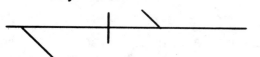

8. Christy will be president.

9. I am Christopher.

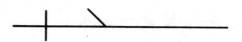

10. We are capitalists.

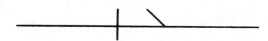

11. The spy is a communist.

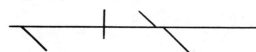

12. You are the culprit.

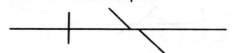

13. Paul was a stranger.

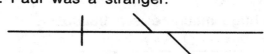

14. She was Miss Crawford County.

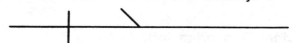

15. The coat was a gift.

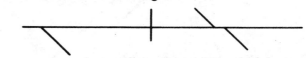

16. Is this the finish?

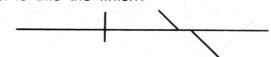

Unit 77 cont'd

Diagramming Adjectives and N-LV-N Sentences

An adjective may modify the subject or the predicate noun of a N-LV-N sentence. It is diagrammed as follows:

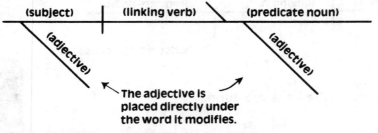

(subject) | (linking verb) | (predicate noun)

(adjective)   (adjective)

The adjective is placed directly under the word it modifies.

* **Diagram these sentences on the lines provided.**

1. The blue truck is a Chevrolet.

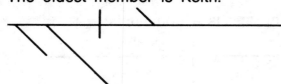

truck | is | Chevrolet
The blue a

2. The oldest member is Keith.

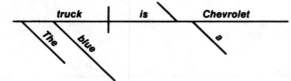

3. Harry's kitten was a Persian one.

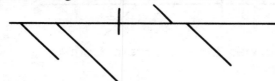

4. The huge machine is a bulldozer.

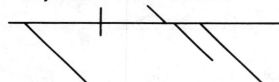

5. Mom is a great lady.

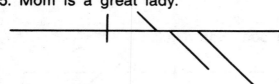

6. The entire trip was confusion.

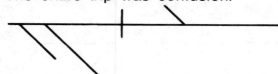

7. Several teachers were firefighters.

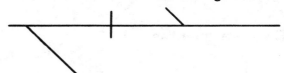

8. Poe was a sinister poet.

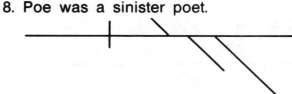

9. The chocolate cake is my breakfast.

10. Debra is the queen.

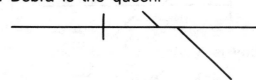

11. My sister is a strange person.

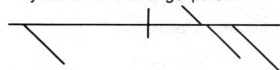

12. The largest mammal is a whale.

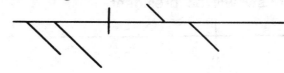

Diagramming Adverbs and N-LV-N Sentences

An adverb may modify the linking verb of a N-LV-N sentence. It is diagrammed as follows:

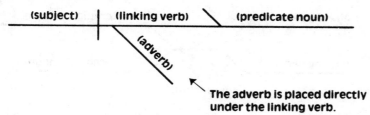

(subject) | (linking verb) \ (predicate noun)

(adverb)

The adverb is placed directly under the linking verb.

❋ Diagram these sentences on the lines provided.

1. He never was king.

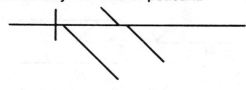

He | was \ king

never

2. I've always been an artist.

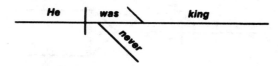

3. Carl is seldom a winner.

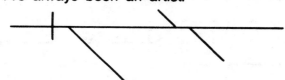

4. Yesterday he was a peasant.

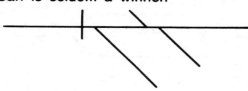

5. The girls have always been our cheerleaders.

6. Jeff is usually the craziest guy.

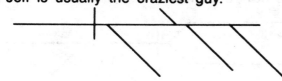

7. Lanita is still a waitress.

8. Occasionally I play a role.

9. Janet was never an engineer.

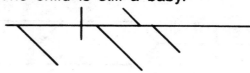

10. The child is still a baby.

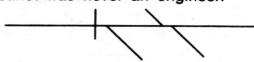

11. The painting will always be a classic.

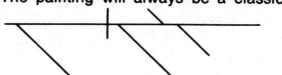

12. Today she will be the teacher.

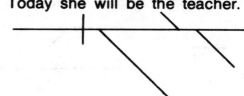

Unit 78 cont'd →

Diagramming N-LV-N Sentences with Compounds

The subject, verb, or predicate noun of a N-LV-N sentence may be compounded. Compounds are diagrammed as follows:

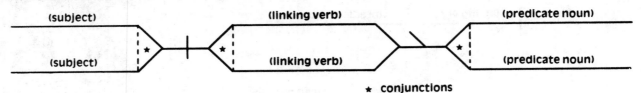

★ conjunctions

 Diagram these sentences on the lines provided.

1. Mike and Larry are brothers.

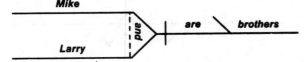

2. The mechanics were Scott and Bill.

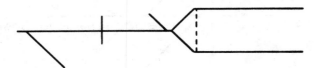

3. You were and still are a great guy.

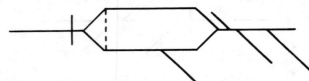

4. Is it a Siamese or a Persian?

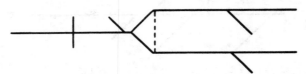

5. Beth and Derinda are characters.

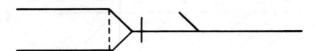

6. My wife is a mother and a spouse.

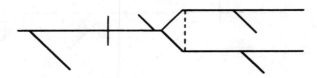

7. The towns are Dyer and Mulberry.

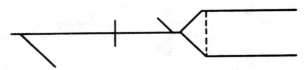

8. Cedric and I are sculptors.

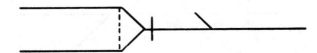

9. Kim was then and is now my friend.

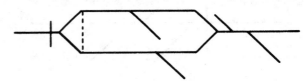

10. The gift was a shirt and tie.

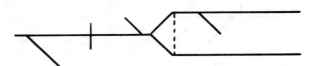

11. Greg and Shawn were volunteers.

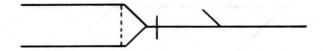

12. Is Jonas or Howard the thief?

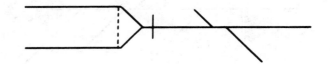

Diagramming N-LV-N Sentences with Prepositional Phrases

A prepositional phrase may modify the subject, the linking verb, or the predicate noun of the N-LV-N sentence. It is diagrammed as follows:

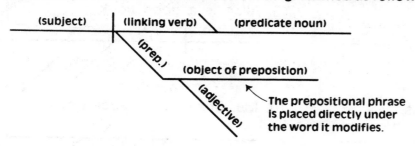

 Diagram these sentences on the lines provided.

1. The man at the desk is Mr. Hathorn.

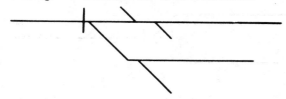

2. I became a writer after graduation.

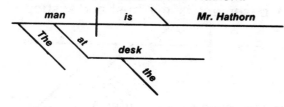

3. They are the diplomats from Grenada.

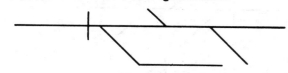

4. The treat on Halloween is candy.

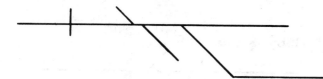

5. During the summer he is a counselor.

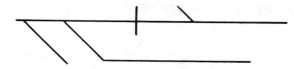

6. Monroe was the Duke of Eddington.

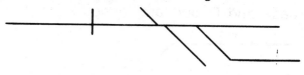

7. The photographer for the newspaper is Mr. Downy.

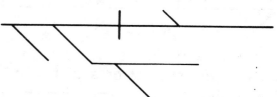

8. The store in Caraway was a success.

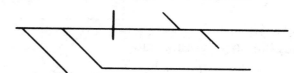

9. The lady in the kitchen is my mom.

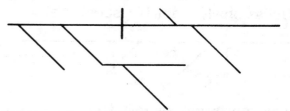

10. Sid is spokesperson for our group.

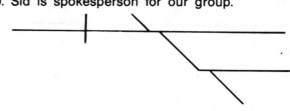

Unit 79 cont'd

N-LV-N Sentence Diagramming

1. Jerry is secretary.

| Jerry | is | secretary |

2. That girl is not the princess.

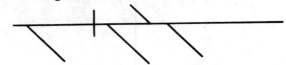

3. Jack and Robert are friends.

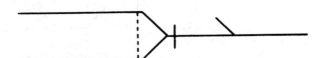

4. The speaker is my professor.

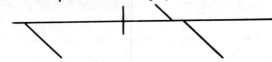

5. Are you an architect or a draftsman?

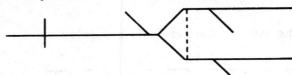

6. Sophia is a young lady.

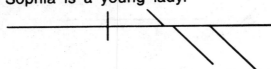

7. Occasionally I am his substitute.

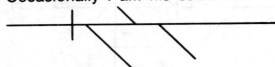

8. Chicken is my favorite food.

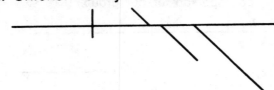

9. Alice is a good cook.

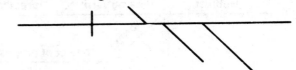

10. Ms. Shaw is my supervisor.

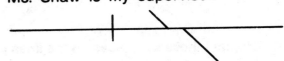

11. The basement is my husband's shop.

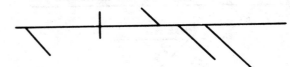

12. You will always be a friend.

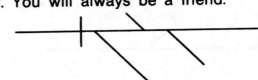

13. The man is a policeman.

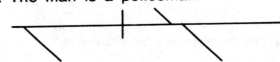

14. Ruby is the winner.

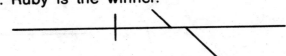

15. James is the loser again.

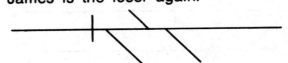

16. He and I are enemies.

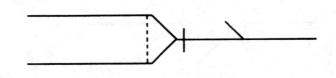

The Predicate Adjective

A predicate adjective follows a linking verb and describes the subject.

EXAMPLES:
        s   lv   pa
        The joke was funny.
        "Funny" follows a linking verb and describes the subject.

         s   lv pa
        My sister is happy.
        "Happy" follows a linking verb and describes the subject.

A Underline each linking verb. Draw an arrow from each predicate adjective to the word it describes.

1. James is very tall.
2. The players are good.
3. Many children were early.
4. Are you tired?
5. The breakfast was delicious.
6. The bell is late today.
7. The water is deep here.
8. Some clouds are fluffy.
9. My uncle's boat is large.
10. The room is too hot.
11. Mary is very nervous.
12. The workers grew weary.
13. Green apples are often sour.
14. Your answers are correct.
15. His face turned red with rage.
16. Drivers should be careful.
17. This plant looks dead.
18. Allen's story sounded silly.
19. The tiny baby became sleepy.
20. The kitchen looks attractive.

B Put a check (✓) beside each sentence which contains a predicate adjective.

✓ 1. This movie is interesting.
___ 2. She is a good singer.
___ 3. Amanda was singing.
___ 4. Her answers are accurate.
___ 5. This new song is great!
___ 6. The patient grew worse.
___ 7. We had a wonderful time!
___ 8. This book is a good one.
___ 9. The teacher's methods are successful.
___ 10. Is this plant poisonous?
___ 11. Arsenic is poison.
___ 12. Stay in the shallow water.
___ 13. Her plans were excellent.
___ 14. You must be good.
___ 15. You are a good person.
___ 16. Our new car is white.
___ 17. The actor is famous.
___ 18. This flavor is tasty.
___ 19. The dog was out in the cold.
___ 20. My motorcycle is fast.
___ 21. We're not happy with the results.
___ 22. Halloween can be exciting.
___ 23. The big dog appears harmless.
___ 24. Terry's voice is pleasant.
___ 25. The sky became deep purple today.
___ 26. The novel is too long.

Unit 80 cont'd

Predicate Adjectives

**Predicate adjectives come after a linking verb and
describe the subject.**

EXAMPLE:
$$\overset{s}{\text{The pie}} \overset{lv}{\text{tasted}} \overset{pa}{\text{good.}}$$
"Good" follows a linking verb and
describes "pie," the subject.

A Underline each subject once, each linking verb twice, and each predicate adjective once.

1. The lemons were sour.
2. Our new teacher seems nice.
3. Her eyes are dark blue.
4. Violets are tiny and purple.
5. The kitten's fur is soft.
6. Our climate is hot and dry.
7. Tuesday or Wednesday will be too late.
8. William's suit is too small.
9. Her friends were happy for her.
10. The jar lid was too tight.
11. The small child seems polite.
12. Her song sounds better.
13. This mask is ancient.
14. You look marvelous!
15. Her purchase was a bargain.
16. The report is too long and boring.
17. Her face looked sad.
18. Lea was hopeful about the cookies.
19. Steve's cassette deck is small.
20. That grizzly bear appears gentle.

B Fill in each blank with a predicate adjective.

1. The lunch was _____awful_____ .
2. She seems _____ .
3. Her pages were _____ .
4. Bill's suggestion sounds _____ .
5. Martin's food tastes _____ .
6. Grilled hamburgers are _____ .
7. Jenny's prom dress looks _____ .
8. Andy suddenly became _____ .
9. The noise grew _____ .
10. Her eyesight is becoming _____ .
11. Alex's answers were _____ .
12. Is the pie too _____ ?
13. My favorite food is _____ .
14. Her teeth are _____ .
15. Our school colors are _____ and
    _____ .
16. Cool water feels _____ .
17. My new shoes are too _____ .
18. Kara's fingernails are _____ .
19. Roses smell so _____ .
20. Our family recipe is _____ .
21. The cars remained _____ .
22. This novel's plot is _____ .
23. Just stay _____ .
24. Ben's story sounded _____ .
25. Your meaning is _____ .
26. Margie's hair style is _____ and
    _____ .
27. This outline is _____ .
28. The package is _____ .
29. Eddie's girlfriend is _____ .
30. Cindy's speech sounded _____ .
31. Danny's directions were _____ .
32. Kittens are _____ .

COMPOSITION EXERCISE

Write 10 sentences, each of which contains a predicate adjective. Underline each predicate adjective.

1. _____
2. _____
3. _____
4. _____
5. _____
6. _____
7. _____
8. _____
9. _____
10. _____

Comprehension Check

Ⓐ Identify each part of these N-LV-N sentences.

      N   **LV**   **N**

1. My cousin became a soldier.
2. The waiter is a student.
3. Hank was Phil's partner.
4. The car is a convertible.
5. His teacher is Ms. Braker.
6. Theodore and Ed were members.
7. Jean is the one.
8. An alligator is a lousy pet.
9. Dr. Cookson is Rick's neighbor.
10. Capone was a gangster.
11. Chicago is a big city.
12. Linda is a news reporter.
13. The prize is two tickets.
14. Kimberly was a sore loser.
15. This house is my home.
16. Her father is the owner.
17. The tree is an oak.
18. I am your guide.
19. The place is a paradise.
20. Football is a sport.

Ⓑ Underline the predicate nouns.

1. Peter is a <u>lawyer</u> from Memphis.
2. Caroll and Joe will be hosts.
3. Her sister is an actress.
4. One of us will be the new king.
5. That boat is a yacht.
6. Jessica is a cheerleader.
7. You are the next president.
8. Penny became my roommate.
9. George is a character.
10. I am a native of Montana.
11. Your dress is an original.
12. The jewels were rubies.
13. We are customers.
14. Your dog is a pest.
15. It is the end of the line.
16. Daisies are pretty flowers.

Ⓒ Supply the missing parts of these N-LV-N sentences.

1. _____ *Wes* _____ is my brother.
2. The machine _____ a metal detector.
3. I am your best _____ .
4. Mr. Kranston is my French _____ .
5. David will be the _____ .
6. The boy _____ a famous chef.
7. This _____ is an opal.
8. _____ was a farmer.
9. _____ will become the captain.
10. His sentence _____ five years.
11. He has been a good _____ .
12. The _____ were family pets.
13. My camera _____ a Canon.
14. _____ acted the villain.
15. "Cosby" is my favorite _____ .
16. You should be a _____ .

Test 16 cont'd

Comprehension Check (continued)

D **Diagram these N-LV-N sentences.**

1. Julia was the leader of the group.

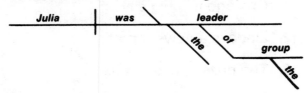

2. They were good friends.

3. I am an only child.

4. The deadline will be Thursday.

5. Kevin and Joel are twins.

6. My aunt is the judge.

7. He is the captain of the ship.

8. The blue vase is an antique.

9. Becky became an artist.

10. Stephanie was our first choice.

Write a paragraph describing the man in the picture. Use at least two N-LV-N sentences.

_____

_____

_____

_____

_____

_____

_____

Diagramming N-LV-Adj. Sentences

A N-LV-Adj. sentence consists of a subject, a linking verb, and a predicate adjective which describes the subject. It is diagrammed as follows:

(subject) | (linking verb) \ (predicate adjective)

Notice how this line slants.

 Diagram these sentences.

1. Miriam smells nice.

Miriam | smells \ nice

2. Tilley became involved.

3. We are interested.

4. It tastes fine.

5. Cynthia is tired.

6. I am ready.

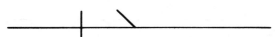

7. It feels funny.

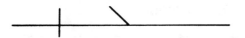

8. Are you prepared?

9. Kelly seems friendly.

10. They are frightened.

11. It looks simple.

12. Ida was exhausted.

13. He is sinister.

14. I will be hungry.

15. Jim Bob is guilty.

16. Reta was upset.

Diagramming Adjectives and N-LV-Adj. Sentences

An adjective may modify the subject of a N-LV-Adj. sentence. It is diagrammed as follows:

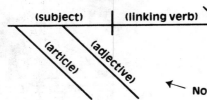

(subject) | (linking verb) \ (predicate adjective)

(article) (adjective)

← Notice the position of the adjective.

 Diagram these sentences on the lines provided.

1. That terrible music sounds sick.

music | sounds \ sick

That   terrible

7. A new car is expensive.

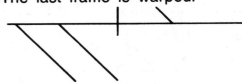

2. A blue tie would look better.

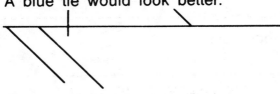

8. The last frame is warped.

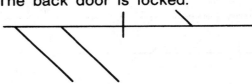

3. The final draft was fine.

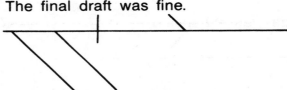

9. The back door is locked.

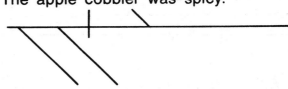

4. Four books were open.

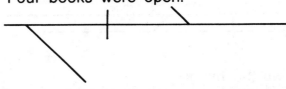

10. The apple cobbler was spicy.

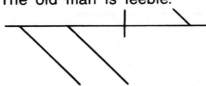

5. The barbecued chicken smells delicious.

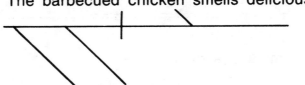

11. The old man is feeble.

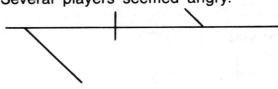

6. The back tires look worn.

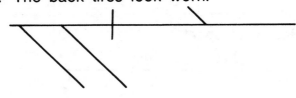

12. Several players seemed angry.

Diagramming Adverbs and N-LV-Adj. Sentences

An adverb may modify the linking verb of a N-LV-Adj. sentence. It is diagrammed as follows:

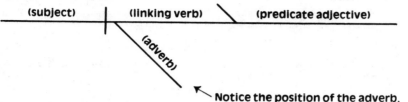

(subject) | (linking verb) \ (predicate adjective)
(adverb)
← Notice the position of the adverb.

* **Diagram these sentences on the lines provided.**

1. Kathleen seldom looks happy.

Kathleen | looks \ happy
seldom

2. Curtis was late again.

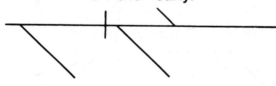

3. The train is never early.

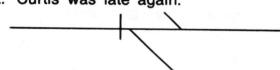

4. Yesterday she was nice.

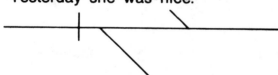

5. Harry is easily fooled.

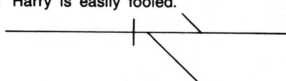

6. The windows are closed now.

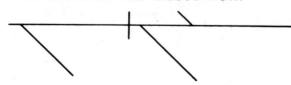

7. Ronald's car is always filthy.

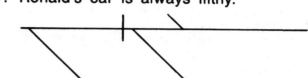

8. Tomorrow I'll be calmer.

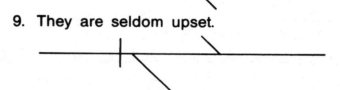

9. They are seldom upset.

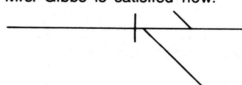

10. Mrs. Gibbs is satisfied now.

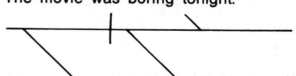

11. The movie was boring tonight.

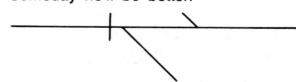

12. Someday he'll be better.

199

Unit 82 cont'd →

Diagramming N-LV-Adj. Sentences with Compounds

The subject, verb, or predicate adjective of a N-LV-Adj. sentence may be compounded. Compounds are diagrammed as follows:

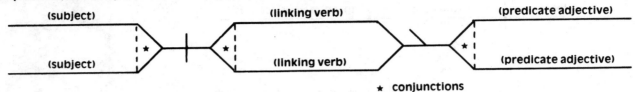

★ conjunctions

 Diagram these sentences on the lines provided.

1. Francis and I are content.

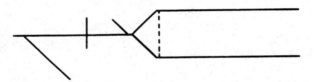

2. Milk and cookies are delicious.

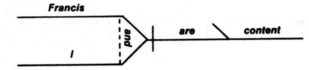

3. His plan is impossible and absurd.

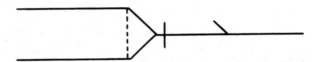

4. Donald and Anthony look rested.

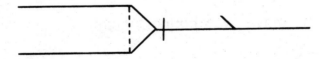

5. Are you better or worse?

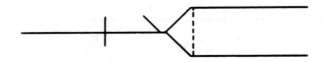

6. The casserole looks and tastes fabulous.

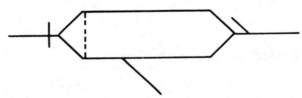

7. The horse was brown and white.

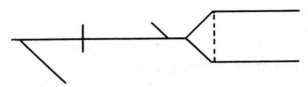

8. They are and always will be unfair.

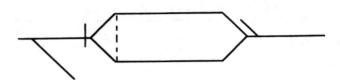

9. Brandon seems strong and intelligent.

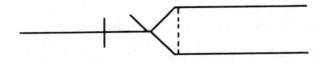

10. Ali looks tired but happy.

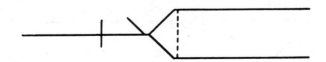

Diagramming N-LV-Adj. Sentences with Prepositional Phrases

A prepositional phrase may modify the subject, the linking verb, or the predicate adjective of the N-LV-Adj. sentence. It is diagrammed as follows:

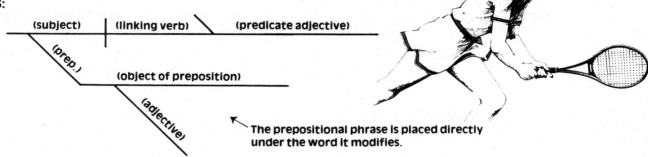

The prepositional phrase is placed directly under the word it modifies.

 Diagram these sentences on the lines provided.

1. She looks better in red.

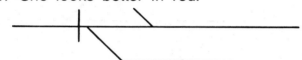

2. The tiger in the jungle was vicious.

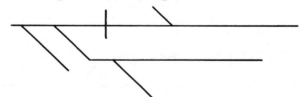

3. The painting by Barry was beautiful.

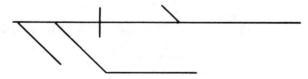

4. Jody is tired of losing.

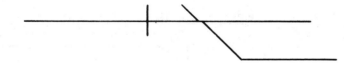

5. The people on the bus were unusual.

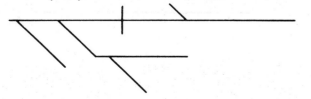

6. The man with the dark glasses looks evil.

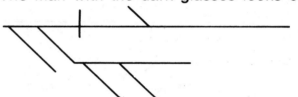

7. The bell at break time sounded heavenly.

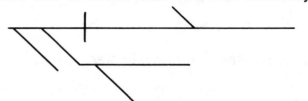

8. The book about Big Foot was interesting.

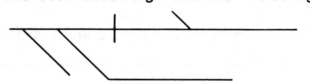

9. The tables at McDonald's are yellow.

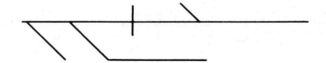

10. I am angry at you.

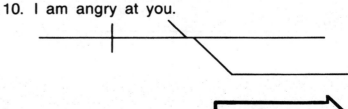

201

Unit 83 cont'd

N-LV-Adj. Sentence Diagramming

 Diagram these sentences.

1. The question was puzzling.

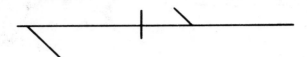

2. The clear water was freezing.

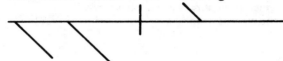

3. The young driver is reckless.

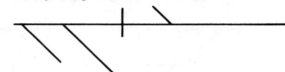

4. Today the lecture was boring.

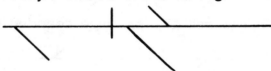

5. Chico sounds hoarse.

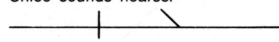

6. The car under the carport is green.

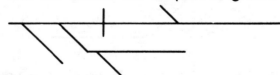

7. The last chapter is best.

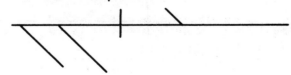

8. The job was complicated.

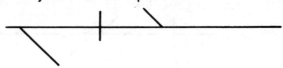

9. The finale was breathtaking.

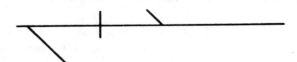

10. The kitten was lost and scared.

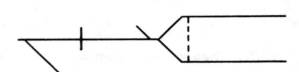

11. The child never looks happy.

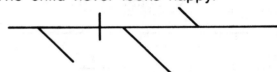

12. Mickey looked disturbed.

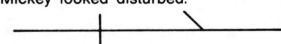

13. Ollie is always late.

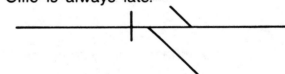

14. The dress was blue with red stripes.

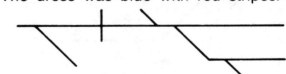

15. Ray and Rachel are trustworthy.

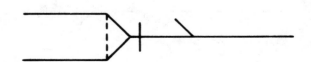

16. Mr. Redding is finished.

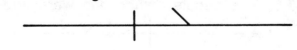

N-LV-N and N-LV-Adj. Sentences

Predicate nouns, or noun substitutes, and predicate adjectives follow a linking verb; they will either rename or describe the subject.

EXAMPLES:
    s   lv   pn
Rob was the speaker. "Speaker" renames the subject.
    s   lv   pa
His speech was interesting. "Interesting" describes the subject.

A Label each subject (s), linking verb (lv), predicate noun (pn), and predicate adjective (pa).

       s   lv pn
1. Allen's bicycle is a racer.

2. He is interested in finance.

3. The teacher became angry.

4. Steve is a good tennis player.

5. The winner is she.

6. Bacon and eggs was our breakfast.

7. Lana is a good cook.

8. The apple pies were hot and delicious.

9. The last bell is late today.

10. Mr. Foster and Ms. Metz are substitutes.

11. The coach became a pumpkin at midnight.

12. Running and jogging are healthful activities.

13. Marie and Margie appear bored with the game.

14. My teacher must be he.

15. Ellen is not too pleased with her brother.

16. Our new car is red and white.

17. The flowers are dead now.

18. The children seem happy about the snow.

19. Martha is the one in the red shoes.

20. The tiny puppy is brown and tan.

B Fill each blank with either a predicate noun or a predicate adjective.

1. The baby was _____*sweet*_____ .

2. The leaves turned _____ , _____ , and _____ .

3. Our teachers are _____ .

4. This television show is _____ .

5. Their new car must be a _____ .

6. The clown's nose is _____ .

7. Daisies, roses, and tulips are pretty _____ .

8. The music is too _____ .

9. Jill's book bag is _____ .

10. Pink and purple are pretty _____ .

11. Summer is a _____ .

12. Mel and Tina were our _____ .

COMPOSITION EXERCISE

Write 4 sentences with the N-LV-N pattern and 4 with the N-LV-Adj. pattern.

N-LV-N

1. _____
2. _____
3. _____
4. _____

N-LV-Adj.

1. _____
2. _____
3. _____
4. _____

Unit 84 cont'd ⟶

Four Sentence Patterns

Four commonly used sentence patterns are N-V, N-V-N, N-LV-N, and N-LV-Adj.

EXAMPLES:
a. N-V
    N   **V**
    The child cried.

b. N-V-N
    N   **V**   **N**
    That dog bit me.

c. N-LV-N
    N   **LV**   **N**
    Mary is my friend.

d. N-LV-Adj.
    N   **LV** **Adj.**
    Rick is tired.

A Label the nouns and verbs in each N-V or N-V-N sentence.

1. Our mom will drive.   (**N** = mom, **V** = will drive)
2. Millie dances well.
3. Lou asked for the money.
4. Sherry and Ann won the contest.
5. Rhoda designed a lovely dress.
6. Ted sold his electric train.
7. Susan had a chance, too.
8. Chris and Alan built a treehouse.
9. Aaron appeared at the door.
10. The new actress asked me for advice.

B Label the nouns, linking verbs, and adjectives in each N-LV-N or N-LV-Adj. sentence.

1. Wayne is a new employee.   (**N** = Wayne, **LV** = is, **N** = employee)
2. The boat is blue now.
3. Skipper's paws are dirty.
4. Rachel was the winner last year.
5. Ellen is sad today.
6. Is Mel the best mechanic?
7. That soup is too salty.
8. Melanie's hair turned green.
9. Our old car was good transportation.
10. Libby will be a doctor in four years.

C Beside each sentence, write "N-V," "N-V-N," "N-LV-N," or "N-LV-Adj."

__N-V__ 1. The canary sang sweetly.	_____ 13. Brenda will dust the furniture.
_____ 2. She knew about the test.	_____ 14. The speakers are they.
_____ 3. Grandfather made a will.	_____ 15. Are the teachers absent today?
_____ 4. Jon is an author.	_____ 16. Joey has a new brother.
_____ 5. You should study math tonight.	_____ 17. Jan expects a good grade in science.
_____ 6. Michael turned the volume down.	_____ 18. Anthony washed a stack of dishes.
_____ 7. Mindy took an aspirin at noon.	_____ 19. Carla mentioned her to me.
_____ 8. Whales are mammals.	_____ 20. Angela arrived late.
_____ 9. The novel is a good one.	_____ 21. Ginger makes the sausage too spicy.
_____ 10. Beth's music is too loud.	_____ 22. They joined us for dessert.
_____ 11. The carpet is very dirty.	_____ 23. The sun was too bright.
_____ 12. A saleslady asked for my credit card.	_____ 24. The hawk was a killer.

Telling Sentences

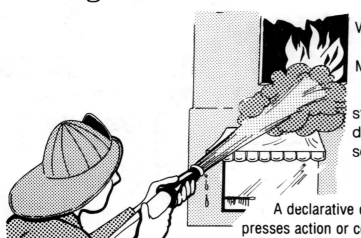

What does the following sentence do?

Many buildings catch fire each year.

The sentence above tells something. It makes a statement. This kind of sentence is also called a declarative sentence because it declares or tells something.

A declarative or "telling" sentence is a sentence in which the verb expresses action or condition. It tells that the subject does something, that it is something, or that something is true about it. It always begins with a capital letter and ends with a period.

A In each of the following sentences, underline the subject once and the verb twice. In the space at the left, write the word "does" if the verb states that the subject does something and "is" if the verb states that the subject is something.

does   1. Firemen help people.

_____ 2. They put out fires.

_____ 3. Firemen must be brave.

_____ 4. Their work is extremely dangerous.

_____ 5. Sometimes firemen rescue animals.

_____ 6. Firetrucks are usually red.

_____ 7. Some firemen fight forest fires.

_____ 8. Firemen have special training.

_____ 9. Dogs are sometimes firemen's mascots.

_____ 10. Most firemen can give first aid.

_____ 11. Their clothing helps protect them.

_____ 12. Firemen are friendly.

_____ 13. Firemen risk their lives to save others.

_____ 14. They are essential to the well-being of a community.

_____ 15. They are a vital part of any community.

B In the following sentences, underline the subject once and the verb twice. Then place a check mark (✓) in the blank beside each declarative sentence.

✓   1. I saw a house burn.

____ 2. Have you ever seen a fire?

____ 3. It made me sad to see it burn.

____ 4. Look, there goes a firetruck!

____ 5. Do you see the lights flashing?

____ 6. I can hear the siren too.

____ 7. Many people follow firetrucks.

____ 8. Do you want to follow this one?

____ 9. Fires are terribly destructive.

____ 10. John exclaimed to the fireman, "Be careful!"

____ 11. Will the firetrucks arrive in time?

____ 12. Jeff wants to be a fireman.

____ 13. His mother, however, is trying to discourage him.

____ 14. Other people are begging him to try it **before** making a final decision.

____ 15. What will John decide to do?

Unit 85 cont'd

Statements

A statement, or declarative sentence, gives you information. It begins with a capital letter and ends with a period.

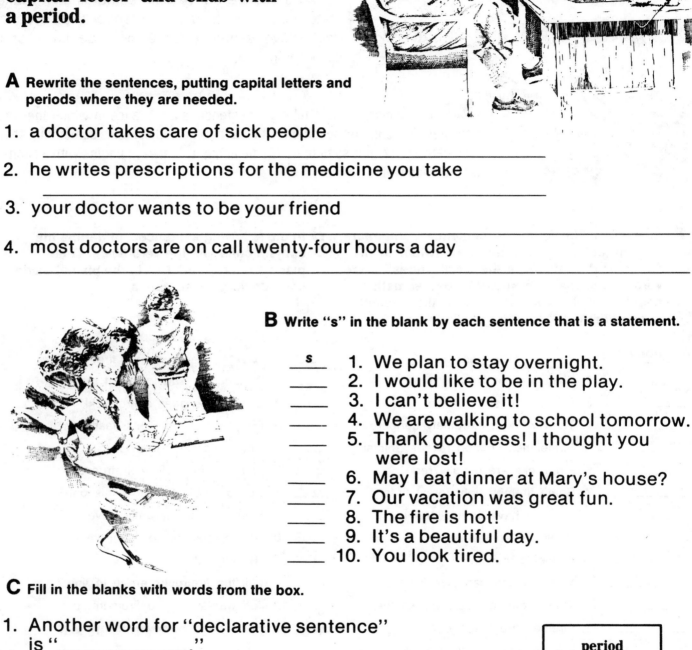

A Rewrite the sentences, putting capital letters and periods where they are needed.

1. a doctor takes care of sick people

   _____

2. he writes prescriptions for the medicine you take

   _____

3. your doctor wants to be your friend

   _____

4. most doctors are on call twenty-four hours a day

   _____

B Write "s" in the blank by each sentence that is a statement.

   __s__ 1. We plan to stay overnight.
   ____   2. I would like to be in the play.
   ____   3. I can't believe it!
   ____   4. We are walking to school tomorrow.
   ____   5. Thank goodness! I thought you
            were lost!
   ____   6. May I eat dinner at Mary's house?
   ____   7. Our vacation was great fun.
   ____   8. The fire is hot!
   ____   9. It's a beautiful day.
   ____ 10. You look tired.

C Fill in the blanks with words from the box.

1. Another word for "declarative sentence" is "_____."

2. A statement gives _____.

3. A statement ends with a _____.

4. Every sentence must have a _____ and a _____.

| period |
| information |
| subject |
| statement |
| verb |

Comprehension Check

(A) Identify each part of these N-LV-Adj. sentences.

       N   *LV*   *Adj.*

1. Suzanna was very upset.
2. The weather is cold and wet.
3. My brother is smart in science.
4. Mrs. West looked angry.
5. His feelings were hurt.
6. No one was late today.
7. The food tasted delicious.
8. Your shoes are muddy.
9. My parents were pleased.
10. A smile is beautiful.

11. The river is too swift for swimming.
12. The breeze felt refreshing.
13. The green one looks awful.
14. His hair is dark brown.
15. The show was entertaining.
16. This rope will be long enough.
17. Bobby is so energetic.
18. Our guide was most helpful.
19. Jennifer's family is poor.
20. School can be educational.

(B) Underline the predicate adjectives.

1. The ribbons were blue.
2. My hands feel numb.
3. The potatoes taste salty.
4. Mr. Hawkins looked friendly.
5. It looks great!
6. Pamela seems very nice.
7. The flowers smell sweet.
8. The woman became very sad.

9. Charlotte looks tired and sleepy.
10. We were hungry for pizza.
11. Oliver seems anxious about the test.
12. The decorations were beautiful.
13. I look terrible in pink!
14. Are you ready for the trip?
15. He acted interested in sports.
16. The news was exciting.

(C) Supply the missing parts of these N-LV-Adj. sentences.

1. Dr. Franklin seems very ____busy____ .
2. This car _____ sportier.
3. His _____ has been supportive.
4. Your dog _____ mean.
5. The _____ were burnt.
6. The _____ smelled sour.
7. _____ was tall and slender.
8. The newspaper _____ wet.

9. _____ was happy.
10. The children _____ sleepy.
11. You _____ very special.
12. The room looked _____ .
13. _____ acted disinterested.
14. The bridge doesn't look _____ .
15. The trip was _____ .
16. It _____ complete.

Test 17 cont'd ➔

Comprehension Check (continued)

(D) Diagram these N-LV-Adj. sentences.

1. You look wonderful today.

```
 You    |  look   \  wonderful
               \ today
```

2. Sonja and Lee act so childish.

3. The soup smells fishy.

4. Tina seems happy about it.

5. The diamond ring is expensive.

6. The new show was funny.

7. I don't feel well today.

8. Corey was too short for the team.

9. The music sounds soothing.

10. It will be fun.

Write a paragraph describing the picture at the right. Use at least three N-LV-Adj. sentences.

_____

_____

_____

_____

_____

_____

_____

_____

Questions

A Add a "question marker" to complete each sentence. Use proper punctuation.

when	did	why	how
what	which	who	whom

1. ____*Did*____ he buy the car?
2. _____ time is it
3. _____ color do you like
4. _____ does the movie start
5. _____ are you scared
6. _____ many do you need
7. _____ moved the desk
8. _____ does she want

B Rewrite the sentences as questions. Use correct capitalization and end punctuation.

EXAMPLE: Mrs. Smith has gone to the grocery store.

Has Mrs. Smith gone to the grocery store?

1. The house keys are missing.
   Where are the house keys?
2. You like to sing.

3. The circus begins in an hour.

4. The bell rings loudly.

5. Someone took my book.

6. The final score was 7-6.

C Matching

__*i*__ 1. A question sometimes begins with a
____ 2. Interrogative sentences are the same as
____ 3. Questions end with
____ 4. A question requires an
____ 5. A question tends to make people
____ 6. Yes or no questions are usually
____ 7. "When," "what," "where," and "why" are all
____ 8. The first word of a question is always
____ 9. A question

a. answer.
b. inverted.
c. "question markers."
d. questions.
e. asks something.
f. capitalized.
g. question marks.
h. respond.
i. "question marker."

Unit 86 cont'd

Question Sentences

? *This is the symbol that we use to mark questions.*

who, whom, whose, what, which, when, where, how, why

These are called question words. Another word for them is "interrogatives." When they begin the sentence, they signal a question.

Questions tend to make the hearer say something in answer to the question:

   Have you seen Harry? *(The hearer answers "yes" or "no.")*
   Who was with you? *(The hearer answers "Angela.")*

The following sentences are all statements. Turn each one into a question in three different ways.

Example: Robert is here.   3. Who is here?
             1. Is Robert here?   Why is Robert here?
             2. Robert is here, isn't he?   When is Robert here?

Notice that questions 1 and 2 are yes-no questions and that the questions in 3 are not.

1. She was sick.
   Is she sick?
   _____
   She is sick, isn't she?
   _____
   Why is she sick?
   _____

2. The children are feeling better.
   _____
   _____
   _____

3. They felt better.
   _____
   _____
   _____

4. Her mother is a good cook.
   _____
   _____
   _____

5. Sandy's mother makes good cakes.
   _____
   _____
   _____

6. There's a doctor in the house.
   _____
   _____
   _____

7. Tom fixed the car himself.
   _____
   _____
   _____

8. Martha knows how to change a tire.
   _____
   _____
   _____

9. She went to see the doctor.
   _____
   _____
   _____

10. The float looks pretty.
   _____
   _____
   _____

Commands and Requests

A request or command sentence tends to make people do something in response to the sentence. This kind of sentence has the understood subject "you." "Please" and "let's" are sometimes signals for this pattern. A request or command ends with a period unless the sentence is also exclamatory.

A Place a check mark (✓) before each request or command.

✓ 1. Please come in.
   2. Sit in the lounge chair.
   3. Is that your dog?
   4. Let's go outside.
   5. What is your dog's name?
   6. He is really polite.
   7. How did you do it?
   8. Teach me to dance.
   9. Please close the door.
  10. This is my purse.

B Some of the sentences illustrate correct end punctuation. Put "s" in the blank before each sentence that is satisfactory. Put "u" in the blank before each sentence that is unsatisfactory.

___s___ 1. Are we going to the party?

_____ 2. Please tell me a story.

_____ 3. How do you think we can seat everybody.

_____ 4. Will you please give me a ride to school?

_____ 5. Turn off the lights when you leave.

_____ 6. What silly person would do that.

_____ 7. Be careful when you start the grill.

_____ 8. Let's buy some popcorn?

_____ 9. Stand in that corner.

_____ 10. You are my best friend.

_____ 11. I like to swim.

_____ 12. Please let me go?

Unit 87 cont'd

The Understood Subject "You"

Most commands contain the understood subject "you." It is not written in the sentence.

EXAMPLES: a. *Write a short sentence.* c. *Kill the spider.*
b. *Draw a straight line.*

 Underline the sentences which contain the understood subject "you."

1. <u>Give me your hand.</u>
2. The film is about glass.
3. Show her your pictures.
4. Come here.
5. I can't find my sweater.
6. Finish your dinner.
7. Kay lives on Reed Street.
8. Persuade him to come.
9. Call your parents.
10. Explain yourself.
11. This hat is too large.
12. The rabbit ate carrots for lunch.
13. Replace the bulb.
14. Decide on the one you want.
15. No one will see you.
16. Forget the idea.
17. This flower is beautiful.
18. Listen to this riddle.
19. There are too many numbers.
20. Measure the room.
21. Surround the house.
22. She is an actress.
23. Your map is torn.
24. Begin now.
25. Tell her I am leaving.

26. We know the answers.
27. Postpone the meeting.
28. Consult a dictionary.
29. Pam will mail the letter.
30. Defend your rights.
31. The tape doesn't stick.
32. He wants to go home.
33. Combine the two numbers.
34. I am not able to come.
35. Climb the ladder.
36. Suggest a new method.
37. Invite Dorothy too.
38. State the problem.
39. Dana is going to England.
40. The show begins at six o'clock.
41. Clear the table.
42. Include a stamp.
43. The painting was done by Keith.
44. The bullet missed the target.
45. Match the pieces.
46. I am mixing the paints.
47. Think about your answer.
48. Leave me alone.
49. My friend lives in Chicago.
50. Sign on the bottom line.

COMPOSITION EXERCISE

Write 12 sentences which contain the understood subject "you."

1. _____
2. _____
3. _____
4. _____
5. _____
6. _____

7. _____
8. _____
9. _____
10. _____
11. _____
12. _____

Exclamations

A Place "x" before each sentence you might use as an exclamation. Punctuate each sentence properly.

_x_ 1. The dog is barking!
___ 2. Please empty the trash
___ 3. Eek The mouse escaped
___ 4. You lost
___ 5. Help I'm drowning
___ 6. Terry is a good sport
___ 7. See that train
___ 8. Don't sit there
___ 9. Listen carefully
___ 10. Hey Wait for me
___ 11. We're leaving
___ 12. I have forgotten
___ 13. Keep off the stairs
___ 14. Please read us a story
___ 15. Well you finally arrived

B Identify each sentence as a statement, question, request or command, or an exclamation. Place the letter of the correct answer in the blank.

a. **statement** c. **request or command**
b. **question** d. **exclamation**

_b_ 1. Who broke the window?
___ 2. Sally is a friendly girl.
___ 3. Go get the mail.
___ 4. Are you quitting?
___ 5. Wait! I forgot my coat!
___ 6. Let's stop here.
___ 7. He broke all of the rules.
___ 8. I'm hurt!
___ 9. My dad is out of town.
___ 10. Where is my pencil?
___ 11. Please answer the telephone.
___ 12. This is it!
___ 13. They aren't at home.
___ 14. Lock the door.

___ 15. Are you her sister?
___ 16. Give me the keys.
___ 17. We have two kittens.
___ 18. The dance is Friday night.
___ 19. Are you going?
___ 20. Fire! Run out the front door!
___ 21. Don't tell me the answer.
___ 22. Quick! Open the door!
___ 23. This is my best friend.
___ 24. Is this your house?
___ 25. You're driving me crazy!
___ 26. She's in the chorus.
___ 27. You're a real pal.
___ 28. Why are we leaving early?

Unit 88 cont'd

End Punctuation Showing Meaning

A As you read the fable of "The Frog and the Ox," listen for the speech patterns that indicate the meaning of a sentence. Then put a question mark, a period, or an exclamation point at the end of each sentence.

The Frog and the Ox

¹"Oh, Father!" cried a little frog to the big one sitting by the side of a pool ²"I have seen such a terrible monster ³It was as big as a mountain with horns on its head and a long tail, and it had hoofs divided in two

⁴"Tush, child, tush," said the old frog ⁵"That was only Farmer White's ox ⁶It isn't so big either ⁷He may be a little bit taller than I, but I could easily make myself quite as broad ⁸Just you see " ⁹So he blew himself out and blew himself out and blew himself out ¹⁰"Was he as big as that " asked he.

¹¹"Oh, much bigger than that " exclaimed the young frog

¹²Again the old one blew himself out and asked the young one, "Was he as big as that "

¹³"Bigger, Father, bigger " shouted the little frog

¹⁴So the frog took a deep breath and blew and blew and blew and swelled and swelled and swelled ¹⁵Then he said, "I'm sure the ox is not as big as … " ¹⁶Then he burst

B Read each of the sentences. Then place the correct punctuation mark at the end of each one.

1. Please tell your parents.
2. Are you on the schedule
3. What a relief
4. Did you answer the question
5. Stop That hurts
6. Are you angry
7. You may join our club
8. I love it
9. What are your reasons
10. The car is on fire
11. Please type your paper
12. James took a picture of Barry

13. Did he smile
14. No, you may not go with us
15. Underline your answers
16. I see a tornado
17. What did you mean by that
18. What a surprise
19. Set the oven for me
20. Can you help us
21. I want to reheat the pizza
22. What kind is it
23. Would you like some
24. Yes I'd love to

The Period

Use a period at the end of a statement or a command.

EXAMPLES: *James has a new brother. This sentence is a statement.*
Shut the door.   This sentence is a command.

A Put a period at the end of each statement or command.

1. Susan is a dentist.
2. I love to eat fast food
3. Turn that music down
4. The horse is a champion runner
5. Our car needs to be washed and waxed
6. Jenny refuses to taste spinach
7. Are you going on the trip
8. Do you eat watermelon
9. Turn on the hot water now
10. The bank robbers fled on foot
11. You should go now
12. We had an exciting camping trip
13. The city elections were held today
14. She likes to write short stories
15. We watched an interesting movie
16. Misty bought a new winter wardrobe
17. Tell me about your accident
18. Do you enjoy watching birds
19. The three white mice escaped
20. Is that your dog in the street
21. Angela, meet me after school
22. Did you write Merrilyn a letter
23. The group met its deadline
24. Do you use your home computer very often
25. Which pizza toppings do you want
26. The street lights are burned out
27. Is your bicycle tire bent
28. Eat your vegetables, Sharon
29. Do you like potato chips
30. Get out of the tree

B Put a check (✓) beside each sentence which needs a period at the end.

✓ 1. Robert is a computer genius
___ 2. Are you ready yet
___ 3. Janice brushes her teeth regularly
___ 4. Do you enjoy science class
___ 5. Alex, stop asking so many questions
___ 6. She's not sure of the outcome
___ 7. Step over the cracks in the sidewalk
___ 8. This water is too cold
___ 9. Have the tomatoes turned red yet
___ 10. We'll plan a vacation to Florida
___ 11. Do you like the beach
___ 12. Lance is a talented athlete
___ 13. Will that big dog bite
___ 14. Look to the left
___ 15. I'm ready for the weather to change
___ 16. I didn't make the team this year
___ 17. Have you met my parents, Jean
___ 18. Take the medicine three times a day
___ 19. I don't believe in UFO's
___ 20. We're expecting a thunderstorm

COMPOSITION EXERCISE

Write 6 sentences which are statements and 6 which are commands.

statements

1. _____
2. _____
3. _____
4. _____
5. _____
6. _____

commands

1. _____
2. _____
3. _____
4. _____
5. _____
6. _____

Unit 89 cont'd

Names in Direct Address

Names in direct address are set off from the rest of the sentence by a comma.

EXAMPLES: a. Marty, are you late?   b. Close the window, Tim.

A Put commas in these sentences to indicate where your voice should make brief pauses.

1. Philip, please shut the door.
2. You carry Kathy George.
3. Pick up those rocks Jeff.
4. Will you be home by four o'clock Jennifer?
5. Please Mr. Rogers let us leave early.
6. Leslie your sister is on the phone.
7. Wait for us Jack.
8. You know Marilyn that I've been sick.
9. Do you always sleep late Steve?
10. It's good for your health Todd.

11. Are you still in the choir Judy?
12. Mrs. Sullivan where is the clock?
13. Go to your room David.
14. Emily is that you?
15. Let Rover in Charlie.
16. No Nancy you may not leave.
17. Heather please turn in your paper.
18. Do you want to read Jason?
19. Yes Mr. Bowen I can help you.
20. Michael did you mow the lawn?

B Underline the words which should be capitalized. Then insert commas and correct end punctuation.

1. what night is the ball game?
2. yes i'm planning to be there
3. turn left at the light
4. unless you're going i'm staying home
5. what is the telephone number rick
6. you are so wrong
7. oh may i have one
8. if i'm late wait for me
9. when you get home call your grandmother
10. because we lost the game we will practice harder tomorrow
11. sit in the swing
12. donna teach me to dance
13. stop i'm tired
14. i would like to go with you
15. please lynn come to the party

16. my mother is mad at me
17. larry go get the mail
18. who closed the window
19. are you sure
20. since he's here you may go
21. which color do you prefer
22. what a darling baby
23. did you know i won karen
24. which dog is yours
25. i hope donna that you're happy
26. yes Ellen i have three sisters
27. what time does the game start
28. mr. allen may i speak to you
29. yes rhonda you are invited
30. yea we won the game

Commas in Series

Use commas to separate words or phrases in a series.

EXAMPLES: *We ate pizza hamburgers and hot dogs at the party. The meaning of this sentence is not clear. We ate pizza, hamburgers, and hot dogs at the party. The commas separate the words in a series, making the meaning of the sentence clear.*

A Insert commas between the words in a series.

1. Dad likes baseball, basketball, and hockey.
2. Sue hopped skipped and jumped down the street.
3. We bought mustard mayonnaise and pickles.
4. Put on your cap coat and scarf.
5. Tonight we'll read draw and study.
6. Paul needs to wash dry and wax the truck.
7. I spoke to Karen John and Richard today.
8. Chris lost his notebook pens and backpack.
9. Kara borrowed my book paper and pen.
10. Bill dropped the nickels dimes and quarters.
11. Yesterday it rained sleeted and snowed.
12. We picked peaches pears and apples.
13. Elaine sneezed coughed and laughed.
14. I voted for Paul James and Melissa.
15. We'll eat cake candy and pie for dessert.

16. We have a new president secretary and treasurer.
17. The team played in Chicago Boston and Tulsa.
18. Ed writes plays novels and short stories.
19. Color the rivers oceans and seas blue.
20. You should stop look and listen at crossings.
21. Jeff took biology algebra and English.
22. We fed the bears seals and giraffes at the zoo.
23. Mary washed dried and styled her hair.
24. Cereal toast and juice make a good breakfast.
25. We'll visit Dallas Fort Worth and Austin.
26. Sarah watched a comedy a drama and a game show.
27. Fans furniture and carpets are on sale.
28. Vanilla pecan and peppermint are popular flavors.
29. Matt washed scrubbed and waxed the floor.
30. We went to the meeting to talk listen and plan.

B Put a check (✓) beside each sentence which is correctly punctuated.

✓ 1. Call him today, tomorrow, or Tuesday.
____ 2. I enjoy ice cream chocolate and marshmallows.
____ 3. Rich Cheryl, and Matt are the members.
____ 4. Selma always eats cottage cheese, pears and toast for lunch.
____ 5. Nails, hammer, and wood are necessary.
____ 6. She played the roles of an angel, a bum, and a bird.
____ 7. Our school colors are red white and black.
____ 8. We sang, cheered, and yelled at the pep rally.
____ 9. Susie dropped her sunglasses, camera and film.

____ 10. I think her birthday is on the 11th, 12th or 13th of July.
____ 11. Sue bought a sofa a chair, and a table.
____ 12. He has a tv, a stereo, and a radio in his room.
____ 13. Eric watched a comedy, a drama and a game show.
____ 14. The scarf is red, green, and white.
____ 15. We'll eat popcorn, drink cola, and munch candy.
____ 16. My favorite sports are tennis, golf and karate.
____ 17. My mother, sister, and cousin spent the night.
____ 18. Alice raked, sacked, and discarded the leaves.

COMPOSITION EXERCISE

Write 10 sentences which use commas to separate words in a series.

1. _____
2. _____
3. _____
4. _____
5. _____

6. _____
7. _____
8. _____
9. _____
10. _____

Unit 90 cont'd

The Series

 Answer the following.

1. One use of the comma is to separate the items in a series. Compare these:
   a. He is tall and dark and handsome.
   b. He is tall, dark, and handsome.
   The first comma is used after "tall" in sentence "b" in place of the word "__*and*__."

2. It takes at least three elements to make a series. Compare these:
   a. He was paid by the hour for delivering packages and for running errands.
   b. You can help by coming early, by serving breakfast, and by cleaning up.
   A series is contained in sentence _____.

3. The elements that make up a series may consist of these:
   WORDS: They traveled by car, bus, and train.
   PHRASES: He came in, sat down, and fell asleep.
   CLAUSES: He said that the facts were clear, that the decision was correct, and that the action was appropriate.
   A series may consist of _____, _____, or _____ and usually contains not less than _____ elements.

4. Punctuate the sentence:
   For lunch we had cheese crackers lemonade and a small bowl of soup.

5. Cross out the commas that should be removed:
   We import, uranium, gold, and diamonds, from Africa.

6. You must not insert a comma after the last item in a series, as in the sentence:
   a. New York, Chicago, and Boston, are large cities.

   You must not insert a comma before the first item in a series, as in this sentence:
   b. It was time for, coffee, tea, or milk.

   In sentence "a" no comma should be placed after _____.
   In sentence "b" no comma should be placed after _____.

7. Sometimes the comma before the connective in a series is omitted in order to make the meaning clear. Compare these:
   a. At Janet's birthday party she served us punch, sandwiches, strawberries, and ice cream.
   b. At Janet's birthday party she served us punch, sandwiches, strawberries and ice cream.
   Which sentence shows that strawberries and ice cream were one refreshment?_____

218

Comprehension Check

(A) Underline the interrogative in each sentence.

1. <u>Who</u> is calling you?
2. Whose cookies are these?
3. Why are you so angry?
4. When are Jim and Jason moving?
5. What is your cousin's name?
6. When is the bus due?
7. Where did Gran go?
8. How cold is the temperature?
9. Which house is Marcia's?
10. Whose music did you borrow?

(B) Write "c" beside each command.

__c__ 1. Tell me why you're late.
____ 2. Did you hear the noise?
____ 3. May I borrow your guitar?
____ 4. It's time to go to the library.
____ 5. Go to the library now.
____ 6. You need to clean your room.
____ 7. Clean your room.
____ 8. Throw the ball to me.
____ 9. All the seats are taken.
____ 10. Let me have your chair.

(C) Put a check (✓) beside each sentence which has the understood subject "you."

__✓__ 1. Suggest a different menu.
____ 2. I'm not kidding you!
____ 3. Erika made an Easter basket.
____ 4. Turn the burner off.
____ 5. Did Chris wreck his bike?
____ 6. Don't watch this show.
____ 7. We'll visit Grandmom soon.
____ 8. Lock the door when you leave.
____ 9. Look at the name tag.
____ 10. Decide which movie we'll see.

(D) Punctuate each exclamation.

1. Stop that!
2. We'll open the back door
3. Hey Stop hitting that dog
4. You're a good friend, Mona
5. Larry plays in our band
6. Help It's falling down
7. Eek There's a gigantic mouse
8. Yes, I understand the answer
9. Fire Use the side door
10. We won a free vacation

(E) Use a period, an exclamation point, or a question mark to punctuate each statement, command, request, exclamation, or question.

1. Jack is Max's friend.
2. I can't believe my eyes
3. We drove to Maine last year
4. This was a good treat
5. Ice cream is my favorite dessert
6. Is Rhoda from New Jersey
7. Let's mail her a gift
8. Stop pretending to be angry
9. Do you like the striped sofa
10. Open the door for me
11. No I won't get a haircut
12. We have new neighbors
13. I'm getting braces Tuesday
14. Will you buy me a cola
15. Are these clothes dirty
16. Please change the channel
17. Ms. Ryan is an editor
18. Are you a good cook
19. This pen ruined my clothes
20. We had a family picture made
21. That song is Angie's favorite
22. Repair the leak under the sink
23. Listen to my speech
24. Ouch That hurts
25. Melanie likes country music
26. Can you read this
27. Quick Crush that spider
28. Could you help Charlie

Test 18 cont'd →

Comprehension Check (continued)

(F) Use commas to separate the words or phrases in a series.

1. Allen, Carla, and Lana are soloists tonight.
2. The movie made us laugh cry and cheer.
3. They visited Las Vegas Los Angeles and Reno.
4. You can learn by listening writing and studying.
5. We bought ice cream cake and candles for the party.
6. I want to buy a red dress a red hat and a black coat.
7. Wilson walked in sat down and listened to the lecture.
8. I've looked in the garage under the bed and in the closets.
9. We've lived in the mountains near the beach and by a river.
10. Sharla will eat lunch go shopping and attend exercise class.
11. Tonight we'll eat dinner wash dishes and go to choir practice.
12. Ms. Austin teaches beginning intermediate and advanced guitar lessons.

(G) Underline the words which should be capitalized. Add commas and end punctuations.

1. you're one of my best teachers.
2. stop hitting me
3. we have hot dogs hamburgers and chips
4. may i speak with you
5. turn right at the crossroads
6. he's our new math teacher
7. who dropped this algebra book
8. will you work this summer
9. have you met jenny hendrix
10. what a blinding light

11. yes margaret you may use the phone
12. i think i'll call you tonight
13. andy mickey and dan are on the list
14. todd please sweep the driveway
15. my grandad moved to miami
16. look out arnold
17. please kris give me the code
18. tell me matt what you think
19. may we leave early mr. james
20. who is planning a vacation

Write a paragraph about gifts you have received. Write at least one sentence containing words or phrases in a series.

_____
_____
_____
_____
_____
_____
_____
_____

Introductory Words

A List six introductory words.

Example: therefore

1. _finally_
2. _____
3. _____
4. _____
5. _____
6. _____

B Add commas where needed.

Examples: Yes, it is raining.
Therefore, the picnic is canceled.

1. Finally, the winner was announced.
2. No the bus was empty.
3. It is four o'clock.
4. The music was too loud.
5. Nevertheless Paul might know.
6. Yes Jill is here.
7. You are right.
8. Yes I will help you.
9. Besides we were told to leave.
10. Louise answered the question.
11. No Mr. Jones lives next door.
12. Arnold trusts you.
13. Besides you look tired.
14. Tomorrow is Saturday.
15. Come here.
16. No you may have mine.
17. Yes he is my brother.
18. Therefore we lost our seats.
19. Finally it began to snow.
20. I like spinach.
21. Otherwise we must wait for her.
22. No Sam has not arrived.
23. The train left for New York.
24. Yes I remember.
25. No it is too cold.
26. The man wore a yellow hat.
27. Nevertheless Sally voted for Ben.
28. No Roy was not invited.
29. Wait for me outside.
30. Yes the book is on the table.
31. Mary plays the piano.
32. Therefore you must not come in.
33. Ted delivers our newspaper.
34. Meanwhile James had gone home.
35. The house was repainted.
36. No I didn't know that.
37. Sign your name here.
38. I have read the book.
39. Yes Jim is a good student.
40. However we must think of the cost.

C Fill in the blanks.

1. Introductory words usually are followed by _____.
2. At the beginning of a sentence, a comma always follows "_____" or "_____."
3. Transitional words "link" one _____ to another.

Unit 91 cont'd

Using Pauses

We use pitch and stress to give meaning to what we say. Another way to give meaning is to pause for natural breaks within sentences and to stop briefly at the ends of sentences.

 While reading the following story silently, place a comma at each place where you pause and a period where you stop briefly. Be sure to put a capital letter at the beginning of each sentence.

This story happened a long time ago when good King Arthur lived a poor man and his wife who lived in Arthur's kingdom wanted a son their happiness would be complete they thought if they only had a son the poor man went to see a magician named Merlin who lived at the court of King Arthur he begged the magician to give him and his wife a son he told Merlin that he and his wife would be happy with any son even if he were no bigger than a thumb realizing that the poor man was sincere Merlin decided to give him what he wanted Merlin did not tell the man that he would get the son he wanted instead he let the poor man go home where he found his wife holding the child the little boy was no bigger than the poor man's thumb that is how Tom Thumb came to be born

As Tom Thumb grew older he was always in danger his mother often lost him because he was so small when his mother took him with her to milk the cow she tied him to a thistle with a piece of thread she did this so that the wind would not blow him away a big red cow however ate the thistle and Tom too poor Tom did not like to be in the cow's mouth so he began to kick and scratch then the cow decided to spit him out

After many escapes from danger Tom found himself at the court of King Arthur tom soon became a favorite of the king and all of his famous knights of the Round Table one day King Arthur dubbed Tom Thumb a knight too because he was such a favorite of everyone

Commas in Conversation

A Write the sentences as a conversation in paragraph form. Be sure to use capital letters and correct punctuation. Remember, a new paragraph starts with each change of speaker.

1. ''did you like the movie'' asked Roger
2. shawn answered ''yes I have been waiting to see it for a long time''
3. ''it had many funny characters'' added Andy
4. ''the animals were my favorites'' Roger exclaimed.
5. ''i wouldn't mind sitting through that movie again'' said Shawn
6. andy replied ''I'll go with you any time''

"Did you like the movie?" asked Roger.

_____

_____

_____

_____

_____

_____

Direct quotations require commas, as in the following:
a. He said, "Nothing doing."
b. "Cross the streets carefully," she warned.
c. "I am happy," he said, "to be here."

B Insert all necessary marks of punctuation. Some of the sentences do not need additional punctuation.

1. "Why are you leaving?" Laura asked.

2. The disappointed boy said "I want to go home"

3. The man exclaimed that the dam had broken.

4. "Come here Randy" requested his mother

5. Did you hear me say "Please call for Nancy"

6. The girl replied, "I've heard all of this before."

7. He said that he had no intention of studying tonight.

8. "If that's what you like you've chosen wisely" he agreed

Unit 92 cont'd →

Quotation Marks in Conversation

Direct—but not indirect—quotations are enclosed by double quotation marks.

EXAMPLES: direct   *Jay ordered, "Give him the money."*
indirect   *Jay ordered me to give him the money.*

A Place "x" by each sentence that is an indirect quotation. Correctly punctuate each sentence that is a direct quotation.

1. ____ a. Bobby promised that he would study harder.
   ____ b. Bobby promised I will study harder.
2. ____ a. He insisted it is not my fault.
   ____ b. He insisted that it was not my fault.
3. ____ a. The man shouted the plane has crashed.
   ____ b. The man shouted that the plane had crashed.

B Write "whether," "when," or "where" in each blank.

1. a. "Do you know the answer?" he asked.
   b. He asked me _____ I knew the answer.

2. a. Bobby asked, "Where is the lesson?"
   b. Bobby asked _____ the lesson was.

3. a. He wondered, "When will school be out?"
   b. He wondered _____ school would be out.

C Beside each sentence, write "s" for "satisfactory" and "u" for "unsatisfactory."

_u_ 1. "Students," our teacher said. "you are to be excused twenty minutes early."

____ 2. Our teacher said, "Omit the third exercise."

____ 3. She shouted, "We'll be late!"

____ 4. "I'm hurrying as fast as I can!" Midge replied.

____ 5. "We'll leave at noon Marion announced."

____ 6. "All you need," the coach said. "is a little self-confidence."

____ 7. "Is that you, George?" I called.

____ 8. Our neighbors kept asking us, "What they could do to help"?

224

The Apostrophe

Use an apostrophe (') in a contraction to show that one or more letters are missing. Use an apostrophe to form the possessive of singular and plural nouns.

EXAMPLES:
  a. **Use an apostrophe in a contraction: We didn't buy the car.**
  b. **Use an apostrophe to form a possessive:**
      This is Janey's homework.
      The dogs' owners are here.

A Place an apostrophe in each contraction.

1. We're happy with our school.
2. Im not studying late.
3. I think its going to rain.
4. Dont drop the eggs.
5. The bacons ready to eat.
6. Theyve gone shopping together.
7. I knew youd understand.
8. Angela thinks theyre pretty.
9. Well buy a new car next year.
10. This ones my favorite color.
11. Shes always wanted a mink coat.
12. The matching hats made of mink.
13. Doesnt Ginger graduate this year?
14. Donna decided shed type the page.
15. Lets switch channels.
16. Theyre too shy to join the group.
17. Allen said hed finish painting the house.
18. Your favorite shows on now.
19. This actors one of the best.
20. Bob and Rob arent twins.
21. William thinks youre wonderful.
22. Theyll call this afternoon.
23. My moms a good speaker.
24. Im getting a haircut today.

B Use an apostrophe to form the possessive of each singular or plural noun.

1. The woman's car was stolen.
2. The childrens parents were relieved.
3. Our cars tires are new.
4. Shellys shoes are in her locker.
5. All the students answers are good.
6. Let's meet at Anitas house.
7. Peoples names are sometimes strange.
8. The birds nests fell out of the tree.
9. One childs desk is broken.
10. Four girls coats are blue.
11. Many workers helmets are missing.
12. All the actors parts are taken.
13. Our principals door is open.
14. Februarys holiday is Valentine's Day.
15. New York Citys celebration is a large one.
16. The officers badge is silver.
17. Kara likes the songs message.
18. Tuesdays special is fried fish.
19. The maps pages were torn.
20. She babysat her two sisters children.
21. Three teachers reports were read.
22. That cloths texture is rough.
23. Rand Streets surface is uneven.
24. We enjoyed the Rocky Mountains beauty.

COMPOSITION EXERCISE

Write 5 sentences using apostrophes in contractions and 5 using apostrophes in possessives.

contractions	possessives
1. _____	1. _____
2. _____	2. _____
3. _____	3. _____
4. _____	4. _____
5. _____	5. _____

Unit 93 cont'd

Capitalization

Capitalize:
  a. *proper nouns*
      EXAMPLE: **United States**
  b. *the word "I"*
      EXAMPLE: *I live here.*
  c. *the first word of a sentence*
      EXAMPLE: *That man is Mr. Graves.*

A Underline the words which should always be spelled with capital letters.

1. <u>dr. morrison</u>
2. organization
3. english
4. question
5. new york
6. school
7. river
8. pepsi
9. sentence
10. washington
11. rocky mountains
12. parrot
13. combination

14. i
15. central park
16. mixture
17. language
18. french
19. detroit zoo
20. mississippi river
21. doctor
22. wheaties
23. karen
24. answer
25. christmas
26. country

27. michael
28. dutch
29. people
30. america
31. newspaper
32. king
33. homework
34. lake ryan
35. miss winston
36. classmate
37. catholic
38. queen anne
39. capt. nelson

40. landscape
41. hawaii
42. donald duck
43. plumber
44. atlantic ocean
45. citizen
46. spanish
47. conjunction
48. alice
49. south america
50. company

B Underline the words which should be capitalized.

1. <u>do</u> you speak <u>german</u>?
2. the window is broken.
3. we visited overton park.
4. i am going to california.
5. anne is talking to you.
6. have you met conrad?
7. the show begins tomorrow.
8. these students have volunteered.
9. you know the answer.
10. my aunt is a judge.
11. the lady bought a magazine.
12. my cousin lives in boston.
13. kathy made us an apple pie.
14. did you eat lunch?
15. what did you tell mrs. stephens?

16. where do you live?
17. the building was built in 1907.
18. today is wednesday.
19. our vacation begins next week.
20. have you ever been to canada?
21. mr. and mrs. martin are here.
22. it's jack's birthday.
23. the house needs repainting.
24. look at these pictures.
25. i saw him at school.
26. tomorrow is thanksgiving.
27. dr. weston came from australia.
28. the people here speak chinese.
29. kim and i live next door.
30. may i introduce donovan?

The Days of the Week

> **The name of each day of the week begins with a capital letter.**
>
> <u>S</u>unday   <u>M</u>onday <u>T</u>uesday <u>W</u>ednesday   <u>T</u>hursday   <u>F</u>riday   <u>S</u>aturday
>
> **Do not capitalize adverbs used instead of the names of days.**
>
> yesterday   today   tomorrow   now   then

 In the following sentences underline each letter that should be capitalized.

1. The annual Rose Parade begins next <u>m</u>onday, the third of <u>j</u>une.
2. Our girls' club usually meets on the first and third tuesday of each month.
3. wednesday's menu features hot dogs and chili.
4. Choir practice is held on thursdays between 7:00 and 8:00 p.m.
5. My father says that friday is his favorite day of the week.
6. Our movie theatre has a saturday matinee featuring children's cartoons.
7. Every sunday, Grandmother visits us for dinner.
8. In the year 2000 christmas day will fall on monday.
9. Did you know that thursday was named after Thor, the Norse god of thunder and war?
10. My grandfather was born on friday, june 29, 1906.
11. We met yesterday to plan the school dance scheduled for friday.
12. Tomorrow we shall go skating, and on thursday we shall watch football practice.
13. My mother is taking a night class on tuesdays.
14. Did you say that we are having a pep rally on friday afternoon?
15. Now and then we go bowling on saturday morning.
16. According to my calendar watch, today is wednesday.
17. In the nineteenth century nearly everyone worked each day but sunday.
18. Every saturday in the summertime, Grandpa used to take me fishing.
19. The ancient Romans named monday after the moon and sunday after the sun.
20. Spring vacation begins friday afternoon at three o'clock.
21. My sister takes piano lessons each tuesday and saturday from Mr. Langford.
22. Uncle Henry is arriving at the airport on wednesday at 10 a.m.
23. I wonder why the Anglo-Saxons named both tuesday and thursday after war gods?
24. We are leaving for the lake on saturday morning and will return on sunday night.
25. Last monday's newspaper contained a picture of our class.
26. Our school play will be presented on thursday and friday of next week.
27. If today is tuesday, what is tomorrow?
28. Old Saxons named wednesday after Woden, their supreme god.
29. Mother says I must clean out the garage next saturday.
30. I forgot that we were having band practice yesterday; I thought it was monday.

Unit 94 cont'd ⟶

Months and Holidays

Capitalize the names of months and holidays.

January	February	March	April	May
June	July	August	September	October
November	December			

Valentine's Day	St. Patrick's Day	Easter	Memorial Day
Flag Day	Fourth of July	Labor Day	Father's Day
Thanksgiving	Christmas	Veterans Day	Mother's Day
New Year's Eve	Yom Kippur	Lent	

✳ In the following sentences underline each letter that should be capitalized.

1. Many states recognize columbus day on october 12, the day Columbus discovered America in 1492.
2. Each year ash wednesday marks the beginning of lent.
3. In april or may most states set aside arbor day for the planting of trees.
4. Last year my birthday fell on easter.
5. Did you know that flag day commemorates the adoption of the Stars and Stripes as our national flag in 1777?
6. In recent years veterans day has replaced armistice day, which celebrated the conclusion of World War I on november 11, 1918.
7. We usually celebrate the fourth of july with a family picnic.
8. When I was very small, I watched for Santa Claus each christmas eve.
9. Each year lent begins 40 weekdays before easter.
10. The most solemn feast day of the Jewish calendar is yom kippur.
11. In many parts of Europe, gifts are exchanged on january sixth, rather than christmas, to celebrate the visit of the Three Wise Men to the child Jesus.
12. Do you exchange valentines on february 14?
13. For many people summer begins on memorial day and ends on labor day, even though the official dates are from june 21 or 22 to september 23.
14. Where I live, january is the coldest month of the year.
15. South of the equator new year's eve is celebrated in early summer.
16. In France august serves as a month-long holiday for many people.
17. Each year people of Irish descent observe st. patrick's day in the middle of march.
18. Our parents are honored on mother's day, the second Sunday in may, and father's day, the third Sunday in june.
19. My brother says he hates roast turkey but enjoys thanksgiving anyway.

Words in Place of Family Names

Capitalize words indicating family relationship when used as names. Such words preceded by a possessive noun or pronoun are not capitalized unless the person's name is used.

EXAMPLES: Mother   my mother   Father   Linda's father   Mom   Dad
Grandmother   his grandmother   Grandfather   her grandfather
Aunt Mae   their aunt   Uncle Joe   Bob's uncle   her Uncle Sam
Brother Ben   Brother   our brother
Sister Sue   Sister   Sis   his sister
Cousin Jim   Cousin   Bill and Roy's cousin

In the following sentences underline each letter that should be capitalized.

1. last week mother drove to Dallas to visit her sister.
2. we frequently get letters from cousin emily, who lives in Chicago.
3. "hurry up, sis!" called joey, who was running to the bus stop.
4. my father has three brothers: uncle harold, uncle lee, and uncle ross.
5. when he was young, grandfather sailed around the world with the U. S. Navy.
6. as we were walking to school, we saw grandma watering her flowers.
7. my oldest brother has joined the Marine Corps.
8. last week we found dad's high school yearbook in the attic.
9. we have always called her aunt helen, although she is really our mother's cousin.
10. uncle bill burst through the door and yelled, "brothers and sisters, I'm home at last!"

11. next month cousin jim and linda's sister will be married.
12. when father is out of town, mother drives us to school.
13. we visited aunt florence and uncle ted in Florida last winter.
14. each year we have christmas dinner with grandma and grandpa.
15. my brother won a bicycle in a recent contest.
16. as soon as the plane landed in Cleveland, dad phoned to tell us that he'd arrived safely.
17. we always give mom a bouquet of red carnations on mother's day.
18. george's aunt and uncle live next door to grandmother hill.
19. as usual, cousin charley was the life of the party.
20. "that was the day brother bill surprised a skunk," said grandma, laughing.

Unit 95 cont'd ⟶

Underlining Titles

Underline the first word and all important words in a title.

A Underline the titles.

1. I haven't read <u>Huckleberry</u> <u>Finn</u>.
2. Our family subscribes to The Wall Street Journal.
3. My favorite television program is Happy Days.
4. We're going to see Jungle Book today.
5. Dad reads the sports section of The Jonesboro Sun.
6. I like to read Boys' Life each month.
7. Our teacher told us to buy a copy of Moby Dick.
8. He's watching Little House on the Prairie in the den.
9. We listen to Sportsworld each afternoon on the radio.
10. We remember when Gunsmoke used to be a radio program.
11. Southern Living is a thick magazine.

B Write these authors' names and book titles as they should appear in bibliographies.

1. Jane Addams, World Neighbor by Miriam Gilbert
   Gilbert, Miriam. <u>*Jane Addams*</u> *,* <u>*World Neighbor*</u>

2. Fun with Magic by Joseph Leeming

3. The First Book of Words by Sam and Beryl Epstein

4. He Heard America Sing by Claire Lee Purdy

5. Horse in the Clouds by Helen Griffiths

6. Eddie and His Big Deals by Carolyn Haywood

7. The Racers by Richard Petty

8. Happy Book of ABC by Helen Fredrico

9. Lincoln's Animal Friends by Carroll Lane Fenton

Comprehension Check

(A) Write "d" beside each direct quotation. Write "i" beside each indirect quotation.

_i_ 1. Ms. Wood said that we should buy a ticket.

____ 2. "I'm sure," said Joe, "that you tried."

____ 3. Aaron was sure he'd go with us.

____ 4. Robin yelled, "You're wrong!"

____ 5. Richard said that you're wrong.

____ 6. "Is Ralph a wrestler?" Lynn asked.

____ 7. Stan said that he bought a new guitar.

____ 8. "That keyboard is mine," stated Cindy.

____ 9. "Heather is on her way," Ann announced.

____ 10. Jenny said that she saw a mouse.

(B) Underline the introductory word in each sentence. Add commas where necessary.

1. Yes, I've practiced the piano.

2. No the band isn't marching.

3. However we don't need red paint.

4. Meanwhile Vera was knitting.

5. Besides Trish has a lovely voice.

6. Therefore you should invite him.

7. Finally the snow stopped falling.

8. Otherwise we can't leave until noon.

9. Nevertheless he's our best forward.

10. Finally Melanie offered to cook.

(C) Add all necessary punctuation. Some sentences are correct.

1. My stepmother said, "Blair is welcome to visit us on Sunday, Dawn."

2. He said that his brother is on an African safari

3. Elise replied, "I have no use for this old coat."

4. Can you phone me asked Elliott

5. I thought I told you to knock first yelled Randy

6. Can you recite a poem for us asked Mrs. Sheldon

7. Ken asked me whether I knew the answer

8. Denise he called Are you ready to leave

9. Bob told me where the fuse box is located.

10. Where are you going inquired Marion

(D) Underline the words which should always be capitalized.

1. capt. finn	11. spanish	21. braces
2. easter	12. hanukkah	22. apple pie
3. i	13. sparrow	23. magazine
4. pictures	14. vanessa	24. february
5. ozark lake	15. princess anne	25. turkey
6. united states	16. citizens	26. month
7. park	17. garden	27. indians
8. palmer lake	18. france	28. pep rally
9. river	19. style	29. boston
10. name	20. dr. moore	30. america

(E) Underline the words which should be capitalized.

1. we gave jane a birthday present.

2. do you think i'm right?

3. claire is my aunt.

4. is your cousin named ted?

5. will grandmother be here on tuesday?

6. my sister is eleven years old.

7. has dad called uncle lee yet?

8. you need to call your grandpa.

9. is lucky your puppy?

10. angela's brother is my teacher.

Test 19 cont'd ➡

Comprehension Check (continued)

(F) Place an apostrophe in each contraction.

1. Let's watch our favorite show.
2. Youre so right, Ashley!
3. Do you think were late?
4. This chairs new, isnt it?
5. Its not my job!
6. That ones my best picture.
7. Thats the bike thats on sale.
8. Isnt that your dogs collar?
9. Doesnt she know shes the winner?
10. Arent they aware of the joke?

(G) Underline the titles.

1. I read <u>Two Sisters</u> when I was twelve.
2. The Stepmother was an interesting book.
3. I saw Three Thieves on the shelf.
4. The Stranger Beside Me was scary!
5. Andersonville is about the Civil War.
6. My First Mistake was about shoplifting.
7. PT-109 was written by John F. Kennedy.
8. Bay of Pigs is a true story.
9. I thought The Pigman was so sad.
10. A Bridge Too Far was set in World War II.

(H) Use an apostrophe to form the possessive of each singular or plural noun.

1. The women's cookies were delicious.
2. That cars paint is scratched.
3. Three actors parts were filled.
4. The teachers meeting is at 3:00.
5. A soldiers gun was stolen.
6. Our trees lowest branch is dead.
7. I'll call you in two weeks time.
8. The gifts paper is ripped.
9. That pictures colors are vivid.
10. Julys holiday is Independence Day.
11. The questions answers are given.
12. Three girls lockers are broken.
13. The lawnmowers blade is broken.
14. All the students tickets were sold.
15. That books pages are torn.
16. Eight gifts boxes were crushed.
17. The heaters noise is loud.
18. A frowns message is obvious.
19. Jessies arguments are good.
20. My aunts children irritate me.
21. The robes belt is missing.
22. I enjoy the breads aroma.
23. Tinas jeep is being repaired.
24. The mountains peak is snow covered.

Write a paragraph describing a country you'd like to visit. Underline each contraction.

_____
_____
_____
_____
_____
_____
_____
_____
_____

Writing Titles Correctly

The first, last, and all important words in a title are capitalized. The second part of a hyphenated word in a title is capitalized if it is a noun, a proper adjective, or of equal importance to the first word.

EXAMPLES:
a. (magazine) <u>Hot</u> <u>Rod</u>
b. (newspaper) <u>New</u> <u>York</u> <u>Times</u>
c. (poem) "<u>Jabberwocky</u>"
d. (book) <u>One-Time</u> <u>Friend</u>
e. (speech) "<u>Are</u> <u>Wars</u> <u>Necessary?</u>"
f. (essay) "<u>Man's</u> <u>Best</u> <u>Friend</u>"
g. (play) <u>Our</u> <u>Town</u>
h. (report) "<u>Indian</u> <u>Legends</u>"
i. (short story) "<u>Paul's</u> <u>Case</u>"
j. (TV show) <u>The</u> <u>Cosby</u> <u>Show</u>
k. (movie) <u>A</u> <u>Long-Ago</u> <u>Dream</u>
l. (article) "<u>My</u> <u>Month</u> with the <u>Natives</u>"

Articles (a, an, the), short prepositions, and conjunctions are not capitalized unless they begin titles.

EXAMPLES:
a. "<u>The</u> <u>Tell-Tale</u> <u>Heart</u>"
b. <u>Reach</u> for a <u>Star</u>

A Underline each word which should be capitalized.

1. "state of the union address"
2. slapshot!
3. "journalism today"
4. a chorus line
5. "know your community"
6. tom swift
7. the dollmaker
8. legends of king arthur
9. love is for sharing
10. old three-legged dog
11. "south america—what next?"
12. "living in the south seas"
13. "on to victory!"
14. wild river
15. the a-team
16. "night shift"
17. sports illustrated
18. a christmas story
19. magnum, p.i.
20. 101 dalmations

B Put a check (✓) beside each sentence in which the title is correctly capitalized.

_✓_ 1. I checked out *The Shining* today.
____ 2. *life with father* was funny.
____ 3. We saw *Miracle on 34th street* again.
____ 4. Mr. Avery read "Father Was a Genius."
____ 5. "The lottery" has an unusual ending.
____ 6. We discussed "snowstorm" in class.
____ 7. *The Denver Post* is a large newspaper.
____ 8. I saw reruns of *Happy Days* last week.
____ 9. Who's starring in *annie* now?
____ 10. What was the meaning of "the silence"?
____ 11. *Miss Susie* is a children's book.
____ 12. Did Lyle see *Ghostbusters*?
____ 13. Poe's "The black Cat" is still read.
____ 14. Mr. Warren discussed "summit at Geneva."
____ 15. "A good, true friend" was sentimental.
____ 16. *Please Don't Eat the Daisies* became a movie.
____ 17. Ada watches *All My Children* daily.
____ 18. *Lassie Come-home* is a children's classic.
____ 19. We watched Michael Jackson's *Thriller* video.
____ 20. Is *War of the Worlds* a movie, too?

Unit 96 cont'd →

Titles

The first word and all other words, with the exception of conjunctions, articles (a, an, the), and short prepositions, in a title are capitalized.

A Rewrite each book title correctly.

1. *the shining*   **The Shining**
2. *flowers in the attic* _____
3. *animal farm* _____
4. *the jungle book* _____
5. *sister carrie* _____
6. *english is fun!* _____
7. *the bell jar* _____
8. *best-loved recipes* _____
9. *the deep* _____
10. *the lemon tree* _____

B Rewrite each poem and song title correctly.

1. annabel lee   **"Annabel Lee"**
2. stairway to heaven _____
3. we are the world _____
4. fire and ice _____
5. pioneers! O pioneers! _____
6. meeting-house hill _____
7. raspberry beret _____
8. joy to the world _____
9. heart of gold _____
10. snow-bound _____

C Punctuate each title. Put a slash (/) through each letter which should be capitalized.

1. We saw the play annie in London.
2. world hunger was the title of the speech.
3. The poem eldorado became a song.
4. Did you read the article our greatest joy?
5. seventeen is one of my favorite magazines.
6. Poe wrote the poem the raven.
7. Our library has the book in cold blood.
8. The gazette telegraph is my favorite newspaper.
9. I enjoy santa claus, the movie each December.
10. Eddy watches reruns of leave it to beaver each day.
11. book report style sheet is a thick pamphlet.
12. the lottery is a short story with an unexpected ending.
13. Sheila read the poem snowstorm to us.
14. Ella saw a chorus line on stage.
15. The article is titled granada: what now?
16. I saw the movie gallipoli on TV last night.
17. Children love the poem the night before Christmas.
18. I liked the old twilight zone series.
19. bridge over troubled water has beautiful harmony.
20. The textbook is titled great english short stories.
21. The essay was titled the death of sadat.
22. My dad reads field and stream magazine.

Writing Abbreviations and Numbers **Unit 97**

An abbreviation is a shortened form of a word. A period often follows an abbreviation.

EXAMPLES: a. November ➜ Nov.
             b. highway ➜ hwy.

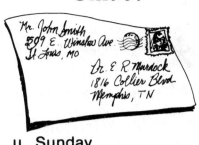

A Match the abbreviations with the words they abbreviate.

_u_	1. Sun.	____	21. st.	a. in care of	u. Sunday
____	2. Mon.	____	22. ave.	b. November	v. Captain
____	3. Tues.	____	23. etc.	c. dozen	w. apartment
____	4. Wed.	____	24. vs.	d. Monday	x. liter
____	5. Thurs.	____	25. Capt.	e. anonymous	y. Saturday
____	6. Fri.	____	26. M.D.	f. millimeter	z. quart
____	7. Sat.	____	27. Lt.	g. January	A. doctor of medicine
____	8. Jan.	____	28. no.	h. mountain	B. March
____	9. Feb.	____	29. mm	i. Tuesday	C. October
____	10. Mar.	____	30. in.	j. weekly	D. Wednesday
____	11. Apr.	____	31. ft.	k. highway	E. feet
____	12. Aug.	____	32. lb.	l. centimeter	F. Lieutenant
____	13. Sept.	____	33. doz.	m. versus	G. afternoon
____	14. Oct.	____	34. l	n. February	H. street
____	15. Nov.	____	35. cm	o. September	I. number
____	16. Dec.	____	36. qt.	p. inch	J. Thursday
____	17. a.m.	____	37. anon.	q. Friday	K. pound
____	18. p.m.	____	38. mt.	r. avenue	L. and so forth
____	19. c/o	____	39. apt.	s. morning	M. April
____	20. hwy.	____	40. wkly.	t. August	N. December

Numbers have both numeral names and word names.

EXAMPLES: a. 3 ➜ three
             b. 21 ➜ twenty-one

B Write out each number.

1 — _one_	11 — _____	21 — _____
2 — _____	12 — _____	22 — _____
3 — _____	13 — _____	23 — _____
4 — _____	14 — _____	24 — _____
5 — _____	15 — _____	25 — _____
6 — _____	16 — _____	26 — _____
7 — _____	17 — _____	27 — _____
8 — _____	18 — _____	28 — _____
9 — _____	19 — _____	29 — _____
10 — _____	20 — _____	30 — _____

Unit 97 cont'd ➜

Abstract Abbreviations and Titles

_23_	a.	gallon
____	b.	foot
____	c.	rural route
____	d.	street
____	e.	pages
____	f.	hour
____	g.	pounds
____	h.	abbreviation
____	i.	ounce
____	j.	New York State
____	k.	Post Office
____	l.	boulevard
____	m.	teaspoon
____	n.	illustration
____	o.	cubic
____	p.	volume
____	q.	miles per hour
____	r.	tablespoon
____	s.	United Nations
____	t.	page
____	u.	revolutions per minute
____	v.	road
____	w.	Mistress
____	x.	quart
____	y.	Reverend
____	z.	Mister
____	A.	apartment
____	B.	cents
____	C.	December
____	D.	height
____	E.	dozen
____	F.	enclosure
____	G.	association
____	H.	horsepower
____	I.	management
____	J.	cash on delivery
____	K.	week
____	L.	Saturday
____	M.	treasurer
____	N.	package

1. m.p.h.
2. lbs.
3. Mr.
4. tsp.
5. p.
6. R.R.
7. vol.
8. Mrs.
9. ft.
10. ill.
11. abbr.
12. rd.
13. NY
14. pp.
15. r.p.m.
16. qt.
17. P.O.
18. cu.
19. UN
20. hr.
21. Rev.
22. blvd.
23. gal.
24. tbs.
25. oz.
26. st.
27. COD
28. hgt.
29. treas.
30. apt.
31. encl.
32. mgt.
33. cts.
34. Sat.
35. Dec.
36. pkg.
37. hp
38. wk.
39. doz.
40. assn.

SUN	MON	TUE	WED	THU	FRI	SAT
		1	2	3	4	5
6	7	8	9	10	11	12
13	14	15	16	17	18	19
20	21	22	23	24	25	26
27	28	29	30	31		

The Dictionary

Words in a dictionary are arranged in alphabetical order.

Words arranged according to the letters of the alphabet are in alphabetical order. If two words begin with the same letter, the second letter determines order. If two words begin with the same two letters, the third letter determines order.

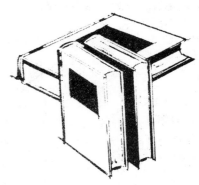

A Arrange each list of words into alphabetical order.

1. advice _____absent_____
2. crowd _____
3. career _____
4. battle _____
5. allow _____
6. adult _____
7. business _____
8. absent _____
9. bowl _____
10. airport _____

11. joke _____
12. magic _____
13. normal _____
14. laugh _____
15. job _____
16. jewel _____
17. key _____
18. noise _____
19. license _____
20. modern _____

21. terrible _____
22. television _____
23. thought _____
24. tunnel _____
25. tune _____
26. through _____
27. trouble _____
28. together _____
29. ticket _____
30. telephone _____

✳ A dictionary is arranged according to the alphabet. If your dictionary were divided into three parts, in which part would each word appear?

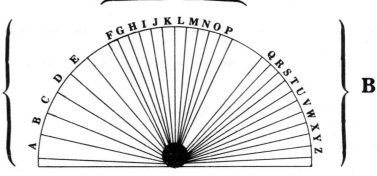

B Write "f" for front, "m" for middle, and "b" for back.

_m_ 1. peace
___ 2. accident
___ 3. zero
___ 4. minute
___ 5. freedom
___ 6. excuse
___ 7. strange
___ 8. visitor
___ 9. rush
___ 10. waist

___ 11. use
___ 12. interest
___ 13. wisdom
___ 14. fame
___ 15. business
___ 16. adventure
___ 17. knee
___ 18. dozen
___ 19. weigh
___ 20. double

___ 21. cabin
___ 22. quiet
___ 23. decision
___ 24. sleep
___ 25. secret
___ 26. umbrella
___ 27. example
___ 28. honesty
___ 29. greed
___ 30. extra

___ 31. habit
___ 32. leaf
___ 33. tomato
___ 34. youth
___ 35. time
___ 36. education
___ 37. vacation
___ 38. reason
___ 39. none
___ 40. you

Unit 99 cont'd

Dictionary Entries

Each entry word is divided into syllables.

The pronunciation follows the entry word. It is always in parentheses. It shows how to say the entry word.

The dictionary shows the part of speech of the entry word.

Some words have more than one meaning. Each of the meanings is numbered.

ar/ti/cle (är′tə kəl), *n*, 1 a literary composition: *This magazine has an interesting article on snakes.* 2 a particular thing: *an article of clothing.* 3 one of the words "a," "an," or "the."

Some definitions use examples to show the meanings of entry words.

---

change (chānj), *v., n.* —*v.* 1 put in place of another: *I will change the dime for two nickels.* 2 make different. —*n.* small coins.

har/vest (här′vĭst), *v., n.* —*v.* 1 reaping and gathering in grain. 2 gather in: *to harvest rice.* —*n.* 1 time of harvest. 2 a season's crop.

in/crease (in′krēs), *n., v.* —*n.* the amount added. —*v.* 1 make greater. 2 gain in size.

per/haps (pər hăps′), *adv.,* It may be.

sharp (shärp), *adj.,* 1 having a pointed or thin cutting edge. 2 a sudden change of direction: *a sharp turn.*

 Use the dictionary entries to answer the questions.

1. Which entry words have only one syllable? _____*change, sharp*_____
2. Which entry words have two syllables? _____
3. What is the vowel sound of "change"? _____
4. What is the sound of the "g" in "change"? _____
5. Which syllable in "harvest" is stressed? _____
6. Which syllable in "increase" is unstressed? _____
7. What is the sound of the "a" in "perhaps"? _____
8. Can "change" be used as a verb? _____
9. Which part of speech is "perhaps"? _____
10. Which part of speech is "sharp"? _____
11. What is the example for "harvest"? _____
12. How many definitions are given for "change" as a verb? _____
13. Could "perhaps" be used as a noun? _____
14. What is the noun definition for "increase"? _____
15. What is the noun definition for "change"? _____

Alphabetical Order

Words are put into alphabetical order
by their first letters.

EXAMPLE: airport
baggage
passenger

When two words begin with the same letter,
order is determined by the second letter.

EXAMPLE: gain
general
globe

✳ **Arrange each set of words into alphabetical order.**

1. decision	_adventure_	21. practice	_____
2. adventure	_business_	22. postpone	_____
3. education	_condition_	23. penalty	_____
4. condition	_decision_	24. purpose	_____
5. business	_education_	25. partner	_____
6. flexible	_____	26. luxury	_____
7. protection	_____	27. understand	_____
8. lonesome	_____	28. nuisance	_____
9. newspaper	_____	29. truth	_____
10. nonsense	_____	30. occupation	_____
11. opinion	_____	31. intelligent	_____
12. jewelry	_____	32. itself	_____
13. honesty	_____	33. idea	_____
14. order	_____	34. ignorant	_____
15. question	_____	35. impossible	_____
16. yesterday	_____	36. surprise	_____
17. television	_____	37. freedom	_____
18. wisdom	_____	38. reasoning	_____
19. ambition	_____	39. budget	_____
20. exercise	_____	40. information	_____

Unit 100 cont'd ➡

Using Alphabetical Order

Words are put into alphabetical order by their first letters. When two words begin with the same letter, order is determined by the second letter.

EXAMPLES:
silver	copper
gold	gold
uranium	silver
copper	uranium

✳ **Arrange each list of words in alphabetical order.**

1. aardwolf _____ *aardvark*
2. above _____
3. abandon _____
4. about _____
5. ability _____
6. aardvark _____
7. abolish _____
8. abbreviate _____
9. absent _____
10. able _____

11. demonstrate _____
12. democratic _____
13. department _____
14. dentist _____
15. demand _____
16. deny _____
17. den _____
18. democracy _____
19. depart _____
20. demolish _____

21. grade _____
22. grammar _____
23. grain _____
24. gravel _____
25. grab _____
26. grasp _____
27. gray _____
28. grand _____
29. gravy _____
30. grace _____
31. grass _____
32. grant _____
33. grave _____
34. graceful _____
35. grape _____

36. smoke _____
37. snatch _____
38. small _____
39. smear _____
40. smile _____
41. snack _____
42. smart _____
43. smog _____
44. snake _____
45. smash _____
46. sneak _____
47. smooth _____
48. smell _____
49. snag _____
50. smudge _____

COMPOSITION EXERCISE

List the names of 10 things in your classroom. Then put your list in alphabetical order.

1. _____   6. _____   1. _____   6. _____
2. _____   7. _____   2. _____   7. _____
3. _____   8. _____   3. _____   8. _____
4. _____   9. _____   4. _____   9. _____
5. _____   10. _____   5. _____   10. _____

Comprehension Check

A Match each word with its abbreviation.

_f_ 1. highway
___ 2. Monday
___ 3. avenue
___ 4. Mister
___ 5. street
___ 6. morning
___ 7. horsepower
___ 8. feet
___ 9. enclosure
___ 10. week
___ 11. anonymous
___ 12. in care of

___ 13. millimeter
___ 14. pound
___ 15. quart
___ 16. inch
___ 17. teaspoon
___ 18. cash on delivery
___ 19. dozen
___ 20. package
___ 21. cubic
___ 22. pages
___ 23. abbreviation
___ 24. number

a. abbr.
b. Mon.
c. no.
d. wk.
e. lb.
f. hwy.
g. cu.
h. Mr.
i. doz.
j. ft.
k. in.
l. hp

m. a.m.
n. mm
o. pp.
p. st.
q. qt.
r. encl.
s. tsp.
t. pkg.
u. ave.
v. c/o
w. COD
x. anon.

B Match each abbreviation with the word it abbreviates.

_c_ 1. hgt.
___ 2. Dec.
___ 3. treas.
___ 4. apt.
___ 5. m.p.h.
___ 6. oz.
___ 7. blvd.
___ 8. R.R.
___ 9. gal.
___ 10. ill.

___ 11. UN
___ 12. r.p.m.
___ 13. etc.
___ 14. vs.
___ 15. cm
___ 16. wkly.
___ 17. l
___ 18. p.
___ 19. p.m.
___ 20. Capt.

a. gallon
b. versus
c. height
d. and so forth
e. December
f. weekly
g. apartment
h. miles per hour
i. centimeter
j. Rural Route

k. treasurer
l. page
m. revolutions per minute
n. liter
o. ounce
p. afternoon
q. United Nations
r. boulevard
s. illustration
t. Captain

C Punctuate each sentence. Underline each word which should be capitalized.

1. "are you ready?" asked kris.
2. ken and andy bought chips and colas
3. yes replied ellen i understand
4. the statue of liberty looks better
5. i bought pants sweaters and socks
6. stop it screamed alison
7. is the game over asked doug
8. do you celebrate valentine's day
9. i know that you are wrong
10. please answer me called mom

11. we watched the super bowl
12. angie's birthday is march 14
13. tell me coach said bill do we play
14. we bought a new ford sedan
15. the book is titled *friends forever*
16. jan moved to salt lake city utah
17. i bought it on carmel road
18. i think ms. burns lives in ohio
19. we drove to new england last summer
20. texas is a large state

Test 20 cont'd ⟶

Comprehension Check (continued)

(D) Answer the questions about the dictionary entry.

contact (kŏr´ tăkt) *n.* 1. A coming together or touching of objects or surfaces. 2. A relationship; association. 3. Connection. 4. A conducting connection between two electric conductors. —*v.* 1. To come or put into contact. 2. To get in touch with: *contact another person.* —*adj.* (kŏn´ tăkt´). 1. Of or making contact. 2. Caused by touching: *The contact wires burned.*

1. What parts of speech may "contact" be? _____
   noun, verb, adjective

2. Write the respellings of "contact." _____

3. How many syllables are in "contact"? _____

4. Which syllable receives more stress? _____

5. What is the vowel sound for the two vowels in "contact"?
   _____

6. Write the definitions for "contact" as a verb. _____
   _____

7. Write the example for "contact" as an adjective. _____
   _____

(E) Write each list of words in alphabetical order.

1. movie	a. _make_	11. grass	k. _____	21. call	u. _____
2. make	b. _____	12. grasp	l. _____	22. cart	v. _____
3. super	c. _____	13. grand	m. _____	23. cake	w. _____
4. seven	d. _____	14. grape	n. _____	24. cane	x. _____
5. tune	e. _____	15. grade	o. _____	25. calf	y. _____
6. bail	f. _____	16. smell	p. _____	26. heal	z. _____
7. bale	g. _____	17. smelt	q. _____	27. held	A. _____
8. bake	h. _____	18. small	r. _____	28. heel	B. _____
9. bait	i. _____	19. smack	s. _____	29. heat	C. _____
10. ball	j. _____	20. smart	t. _____	30. helm	D. _____

Write a paragraph about a phone call you have made. Use "contact" as a verb.

_____
_____
_____
_____
_____
_____
_____
_____

Arranging Proper Names in Alphabetical Order

People's names are arranged alphabetically by the last name.
When two people have the same last name, order is decided by
the first name.

EXAMPLE:

a. Felix Lynn	Allen, Roger
b. Mike Cook	Brown, Alex
c. Roger Allen	Cook, Mike
d. Alex Brown	Lynn, Felix

* Arrange each group of words in alphabetical order.

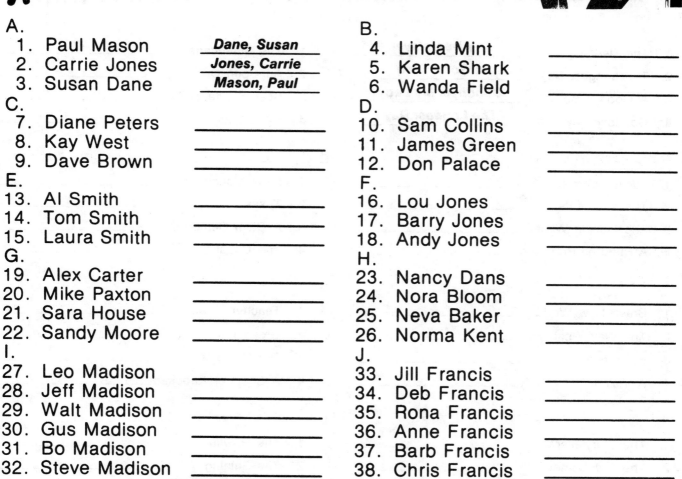

A.
1. Paul Mason
2. Carrie Jones
3. Susan Dane

Dane, Susan
Jones, Carrie
Mason, Paul

B.
4. Linda Mint
5. Karen Shark
6. Wanda Field

C.
7. Diane Peters
8. Kay West
9. Dave Brown

D.
10. Sam Collins
11. James Green
12. Don Palace

E.
13. Al Smith
14. Tom Smith
15. Laura Smith

F.
16. Lou Jones
17. Barry Jones
18. Andy Jones

G.
19. Alex Carter
20. Mike Paxton
21. Sara House
22. Sandy Moore

H.
23. Nancy Dans
24. Nora Bloom
25. Neva Baker
26. Norma Kent

I.
27. Leo Madison
28. Jeff Madison
29. Walt Madison
30. Gus Madison
31. Bo Madison
32. Steve Madison

J.
33. Jill Francis
34. Deb Francis
35. Rona Francis
36. Anne Francis
37. Barb Francis
38. Chris Francis

COMPOSITION EXERCISE

List the first and last names of 10 of your friends. Then put your list in alphabetical order.

1. _____ 6. _____
2. _____ 7. _____
3. _____ 8. _____
4. _____ 9. _____
5. _____ 10. _____

1. _____ 6. _____
2. _____ 7. _____
3. _____ 8. _____
4. _____ 9. _____
5. _____ 10. _____

Unit 101 cont'd →

Arranging Titles Alphabetically

Titles are arranged alphabetically according to the first word of the title. However, if the words "a," "an," or "the" begin the title, go to the second word to determine the order.

EXAMPLES:

1. Tex	*A Bright Life*
2. A Bright Life	*The Red Pony*
3. The Red Pony	*Smoky*
4. Smoky	*Tex*

Arrange each list of titles in alphabetical order.

A.
1. The Deerslayer
2. The Longest Day
3. A Good Time
4. Goodbye, My Lady

The Deerslayer
A Good Time
Goodbye, My Lady
The Longest Day

B.
1. Lucky Laura
2. The Innocents
3. The Lion in Winter
4. A Hundred Promises

C.
1. Brave New World
2. The Way West
3. Builders
4. A Vision

D.
1. The Storyteller
2. The Old Demon
3. Beauty Is Truth
4. The Pasture

E.
1. Long River
2. A Last Glance
3. She Grows Up
4. A Visit

F.
1. The Americans
2. An Open Door
3. Special Effects
4. Deep Waters

G.
1. Slow Motion
2. Texas
3. A Calm Center
4. The Guest

H.
1. Teacher, Teacher
2. Green Hills
3. Our Universe
4. A Stranger Knocked

I.
1. The Howling
2. The Shining
3. After Hours
4. Only Yesterday

J.
1. Of Mice and Men
2. The Stranger Within
3. The Listener
4. Listen to the Wind

Guide Words

In each box is a set of guide words. Underline on what page each word would appear in a dictionary.

93	
dark	date

94	
daughter	daze

95	
dead	deal

1. deadline	before 93	on 93	on 94	<u>on 95</u>	after 95
2. dash	before 93	on 93	on 94	on 95	after 95
3. dare	before 93	on 93	on 94	on 95	after 95
4. dear	before 93	on 93	on 94	on 95	after 95
5. darkness	before 93	on 93	on 94	on 95	after 95
6. deadly	before 93	on 93	on 94	on 95	after 95
7. daughter	before 93	on 93	on 94	on 95	after 95
8. day	before 93	on 93	on 94	on 95	after 95
9. death	before 93	on 93	on 94	on 95	after 95
10. danger	before 93	on 93	on 94	on 95	after 95
11. dart	before 93	on 93	on 94	on 95	after 95
12. dawn	before 93	on 93	on 94	on 95	after 95
13. deaf	before 93	on 93	on 94	on 95	after 95

156	
rear	recall

157	
receive	recess

158	
recite	record

14. reach	before 156	on 156	on 157	on 158	after 158
15. receiver	before 156	on 156	on 157	on 158	after 158
16. recount	before 156	on 156	on 157	on 158	after 158
17. rebel	before 156	on 156	on 157	on 158	after 158
18. recreation	before 156	on 156	on 157	on 158	after 158
19. react	before 156	on 156	on 157	on 158	after 158
20. recommend	before 156	on 156	on 157	on 158	after 158
21. reason	before 156	on 156	on 157	on 158	after 158
22. read	before 156	on 156	on 157	on 158	after 158
23. recent	before 156	on 156	on 157	on 158	after 158
24. recovery	before 156	on 156	on 157	on 158	after 158
25. recognize	before 156	on 156	on 157	on 158	after 158

Unit 102 cont'd

More Guide Words

Each box contains a set of guide words. On which page would each word appear?

accident	20	actress

21	1. adventure	___	6. ace
___	2. act	___	7. adjust
___	3. address	___	8. active
___	4. adopt	___	9. admit
___	5. again	___	10. acquire

add	21	against

___	11. after	___	16. actor
___	12. admire	___	17. against
___	13. acorn	___	18. acting
___	14. action	___	19. acre
___	15. advice	___	20. activity

do	35	dot

___	21. done	___	26. dock
___	22. double	___	27. dragon
___	23. drip	___	28. dome
___	24. dog	___	29. dove
___	25. draw	___	30. doll

double	36	drive

___	31. down	___	36. dress
___	32. doctor	___	37. door
___	33. drag	___	38. dot
___	34. dream	___	39. dozen
___	35. doodle	___	40. dolphin

fold	53	for

___	41. forget	___	46. fold
___	42. food	___	47. follow
___	43. form	___	48. force
___	44. fool	___	49. fond
___	45. for	___	50. forgive

force	54	forward

___	51. forehead	___	56. forward
___	52. foot	___	57. forest
___	53. fork	___	58. football
___	54. folk	___	59. fort
___	55. fortune	___	60. follower

lace	78	large

___	61. land	___	66. ladder
___	62. last	___	67. late
___	63. lamp	___	68. lane
___	64. lay	___	69. large
___	65. lazy	___	70. lead

last	79	leave

___	71. law	___	76. lap
___	72. lady	___	77. leader
___	73. leaf	___	78. lake
___	74. laugh	___	79. lamb
___	75. language	___	80. layer

table	96	tape

___	81. team	___	86. teach
___	82. tea	___	87. tap
___	83. talker	___	88. tan
___	84. tail	___	89. task
___	85. target	___	90. tablet

tar	97	tease

___	91. take	___	96. taxi
___	92. taste	___	97. tale
___	93. talk	___	98. tear
___	94. tax	___	99. tank
___	95. talent	___	100. teacher

The Guide Words

At the top of each page in a dictionary are the guide words.
The guide words name the first and last entry words found on
that particular page of the dictionary.

 Read the following sets of guide words. Then write the page number on
which each of the following words would be found.

bird	15	blame		blank	16	block		blond	17	board
boast	18	booth		border	19	boundary		bow	20	breed

breeze	21	broil		brown	22	brute

_15_	1. birth	___	26. boat	___	51. birthday	___	76. book
___	2. blush	___	27. blemish	___	52. brick	___	77. bottom
___	3. brutal	___	28. blame	___	53. bread	___	78. brush
___	4. boil	___	29. blister	___	54. blow	___	79. both
___	5. blaze	___	30. brain	___	55. brim	___	80. brown
___	6. branch	___	31. black	___	56. blot	___	81. bleach
___	7. blend	___	32. bounce	___	57. box	___	82. broad
___	8. bridge	___	33. bleed	___	58. bit	___	83. brake
___	9. blink	___	34. blest	___	59. bring	___	84. booth
___	10. borrow	___	35. bitter	___	60. body	___	85. boy
___	11. bough	___	36. bishop	___	61. bore	___	86. bomb
___	12. blue	___	37. bless	___	62. bride	___	87. bruise
___	13. bison	___	38. blank	___	63. bolt	___	88. broil
___	14. boot	___	39. bone	___	64. blouse	___	89. boss
___	15. brief	___	40. bird	___	65. board	___	90. border
___	16. brass	___	41. bleak	___	66. brew	___	91. brand
___	17. bite	___	42. blast	___	67. blade	___	92. bluff
___	18. bonnet	___	43. break	___	68. block	___	93. blood
___	19. brute	___	44. blond	___	69. blur	___	94. bottle
___	20. born	___	45. boundary	___	70. bowl	___	95. brave
___	21. blanket	___	46. blind	___	71. bound	___	96. bold
___	22. bloom	___	47. bow	___	72. blunt	___	97. boom
___	23. bright	___	48. breed	___	73. boast	___	98. blunder
___	24. breeze	___	49. bother	___	74. bossy	___	99. bond
___	25. breath	___	50. booklet	___	75. boost	___	100. boar

Unit 103 cont'd →

Guide Word Practice

Guide words appear at the top of each page. They are the same as the first and last words on the dictionary page.

A Underline the words which would appear on a page with the following guide words.

above	anxious

1. <u>account</u>
2. aardvark
3. about
4. address
5. age
6. adventure
7. alone
8. agony
9. able
10. airport
11. appreciate
12. afterward
13. against
14. active
15. among
16. ahead
17. ant
18. angel
19. abolish
20. awful

B Each box contains a set of guide words. On which of these pages would each of the following words appear?

calf	16	crawl

distance	18	drum

creek	17	dime

eagle	19	exact

_16_ 1. candle
____ 2. creek
____ 3. driver
____ 4. escape
____ 5. deadline
____ 6. darkness
____ 7. either
____ 8. call
____ 9. capture
____ 10. distant
____ 11. equipment
____ 12. college
____ 13. castle
____ 14. drum
____ 15. decorate

____ 16. crowd
____ 17. danger
____ 18. contest
____ 19. eagle
____ 20. drill
____ 21. calf
____ 22. chance
____ 23. drug
____ 24. drown
____ 25. curl
____ 26. election
____ 27. capitol
____ 28. enjoy
____ 29. dill
____ 30. clothing

____ 31. celebrate
____ 32. earn
____ 33. exact
____ 34. daughter
____ 35. calm
____ 36. cruel
____ 37. distance
____ 38. career
____ 39. deadly
____ 40. crawl
____ 41. edit
____ 42. divide
____ 43. damage
____ 44. crab
____ 45. especially

____ 46. education
____ 47. dice
____ 48. captain
____ 49. doll
____ 50. dream
____ 51. course
____ 52. dime
____ 53. chatter
____ 54. dead
____ 55. evenly
____ 56. case
____ 57. draw
____ 58. cellar
____ 59. catch
____ 60. effort

250

The V-C-C-V Pattern

Words with a V-C-C-V pattern are usually divided between the consonants.

EXAMPLES: a. *journey*   jour ney
            b. *follow*   fol low
            c. *budget*   bud get

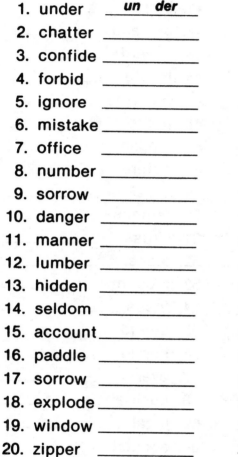

A Divide each word into syllables.

1. under __un der__	21. confuse _____	41. follow _____
2. chatter _____	22. advice _____	42. airport _____
3. confide _____	23. suggest _____	43. bargain _____
4. forbid _____	24. wisdom _____	44. combine _____
5. ignore _____	25. zigzag _____	45. collapse _____
6. mistake _____	26. collect _____	46. garden _____
7. office _____	27. hurry _____	47. slender _____
8. number _____	28. letter _____	48. surround _____
9. sorrow _____	29. hammer _____	49. tunnel _____
10. danger _____	30. battle _____	50. forgot _____
11. manner _____	31. except _____	51. adjust _____
12. lumber _____	32. insect _____	52. nonsense _____
13. hidden _____	33. effort _____	53. sturdy _____
14. seldom _____	34. motto _____	54. wisdom _____
15. account _____	35. market _____	55. offer _____
16. paddle _____	36. kettle _____	56. cartoon _____
17. sorrow _____	37. normal _____	57. infant _____
18. explode _____	38. unless _____	58. yonder _____
19. window _____	39. attract _____	59. basket _____
20. zipper _____	40. escape _____	60. conclude _____

B Underline the words which follow the V-C-C-V pattern.

1. <u>forward</u>	6. cattle	11. easy	16. music
2. magnet	7. gossip	12. defeat	17. clatter
3. collide	8. rejoice	13. pardon	18. ruin
4. contest	9. neon	14. person	19. funnel
5. nurse	10. sudden	15. money	20. formal

Unit 104 cont'd

The V-C-V Pattern

Words with a V-C-V pattern are usually divided before the consonants.

EXAMPLES: a. *defend*   de   fend
           b. *tiger*   ti   ger
           c. *notice*   no   tice

A Divide each word into syllables.

1. resign _re sign_	21. secure _____	41. before _____
2. decide _____	22. pretend _____	42. demand _____
3. amend _____	23. detain _____	43. reward _____
4. ideal _____	24. because _____	44. locate _____
5. license _____	25. apart _____	45. precise _____
6. silent _____	26. seven _____	46. polite _____
7. behave _____	27. delay _____	47. slogan _____
8. around _____	28. bonus _____	48. nature _____
9. result _____	29. adult _____	49. vocal _____
10. retire _____	30. remain _____	50. famous _____
11. became _____	31. open _____	51. virus _____
12. return _____	32. radar _____	52. alone _____
13. favor _____	33. record _____	53. recount _____
14. beyond _____	34. deserve _____	54. focus _____
15. major _____	35. zero _____	55. stupid _____
16. recall _____	36. repeat _____	56. humid _____
17. protect _____	37. defense _____	57. over _____
18. item _____	38. later _____	58. beside _____
19. notice _____	39. equip _____	59. legal _____
20. again _____	40. twilight _____	60. against _____

B Underline the words which follow the V-C-V pattern.

1. <u>habit</u>	6. become	11. fluid	16. hero
2. receive	7. create	12. vacate	17. enjoy
3. border	8. preview	13. humid	18. among
4. deceit	9. swallow	14. obey	19. trust
5. kitten	10. result	15. message	20. regard

Syllable Breaks

RULE 1

Words with a V-C-C-V pattern are usually divided between the consonants.

    EXAMPLE: cotton   cot   ton

RULE 2

Words with a V-V pattern are divided between the vowels.

    EXAMPLE: neon   ne   on

RULE 3

Words with a V-C-V pattern are divided before the consonant.

    EXAMPLE: believe   be   lieve

mit ten
tri al
pre fer

 Write the number of the rule each word follows.

_2_ 1. diet	___ 26. army	___ 51. unique	___ 76. quiet
___ 2. written	___ 27. college	___ 52. lion	___ 77. prepare
___ 3. protect	___ 28. riot	___ 53. reserve	___ 78. inform
___ 4. forward	___ 29. direct	___ 54. renounce	___ 79. refer
___ 5. expand	___ 30. motion	___ 55. intend	___ 80. little
___ 6. chaos	___ 31. narrate	___ 56. curtain	___ 81. paper
___ 7. receive	___ 32. sudden	___ 57. locust	___ 82. ocean
___ 8. murmur	___ 33. predict	___ 58. fluid	___ 83. income
___ 9. ruin	___ 34. remark	___ 59. detail	___ 84. blossom
___ 10. music	___ 35. supply	___ 60. effect	___ 85. middle
___ 11. puzzle	___ 36. depend	___ 61. profit	___ 86. liar
___ 12. accord	___ 37. rotten	___ 62. button	___ 87. always
___ 13. border	___ 38. even	___ 63. enrich	___ 88. delay
___ 14. enter	___ 39. below	___ 64. trial	___ 89. helmet
___ 15. report	___ 40. flavor	___ 65. produce	___ 90. request
___ 16. minor	___ 41. create	___ 66. adult	___ 91. husband
___ 17. village	___ 42. error	___ 67. wallet	___ 92. escape
___ 18. amend	___ 43. dagger	___ 68. approve	___ 93. giant
___ 19. funnel	___ 44. renew	___ 69. correct	___ 94. below
___ 20. equal	___ 45. comment	___ 70. repay	___ 95. warden
___ 21. cruel	___ 46. monkey	___ 71. fuel	___ 96. accept
___ 22. award	___ 47. license	___ 72. order	___ 97. unit
___ 23. absent	___ 48. perfect	___ 73. channel	___ 98. famous
___ 24. pattern	___ 49. tiger	___ 74. pirate	___ 99. until
___ 25. divide	___ 50. science	___ 75. number	___ 100. triumph

Unit 105 cont'd ⟶

Dividing Words into Syllables

Each sound within a word is called a syllable.

EXAMPLES:
  a. captain   cap   tain   c. journey   jour   ney
  b. deadline   dead   line   d. hospital   hos   pi   tal

A Divide each word into syllables.

1. hungry **hun gry**	21. itself _____	41. forward _____
2. excuse _____	22. greedy _____	42. collect _____
3. became _____	23. newspaper _____	43. tomato _____
4. tunnel _____	24. pleasant _____	44. useful _____
5. vacation _____	25. protection _____	45. mistake _____
6. straight _____	26. market _____	46. outline _____
7. nonsense _____	27. seldom _____	47. question _____
8. telephone _____	28. remember _____	48. laugh _____
9. wisdom _____	29. zoo _____	49. practice _____
10. guide _____	30. sorrow _____	50. wonderful _____
11. promise _____	31. umbrella _____	51. normal _____
12. separate _____	32. difficult _____	52. change _____
13. angry _____	33. enormous _____	53. key _____
14. freedom _____	34. idea _____	54. easy _____
15. adventure _____	35. daughter _____	55. habit _____
16. crowd _____	36. welcome _____	56. surprise _____
17. return _____	37. opinion _____	57. reason _____
18. important _____	38. accident _____	58. island _____
19. forget _____	39. decide _____	59. hurry _____
20. ghost _____	40. signature _____	60. ocean _____

A closed syllable is one ending in a consonant. An open syllable is one ending in a vowel.

                  closed   **open**
EXAMPLES: a. es   cape   a. si   lent
                  b. lead   ing   b. fa   mous

B Write "c" if the underlined syllable is a closed syllable. Write "o" if the underlined syllable is an open syllable.

c 1. o <u>pen</u>	__ 7. <u>fun</u> nel	__ 13. <u>of</u> fice	__ 19. <u>he</u> ro
__ 2. <u>dai</u> ly	__ 8. <u>pro</u> tect	__ 14. <u>list</u>	__ 20. sud <u>den</u>
__ 3. air <u>port</u>	__ 9. <u>no</u> where	__ 15. <u>ab</u> sent	__ 21. <u>ex</u> plain
__ 4. <u>own</u> er	__ 10. <u>test</u>	__ 16. <u>con</u> test	__ 22. i <u>de</u> a
__ 5. <u>re</u> main	__ 11. <u>plen</u> ty	__ 17. <u>a</u> part	__ 23. <u>mu</u> sic
__ 6. <u>rea</u> son	__ 12. <u>sun</u> shine	__ 18. <u>ham</u> mer	__ 24. <u>grab</u>

Comprehension Check

(A) Write each list of names in alphabetical order.

1. Carmen Jones   a. *Jones, Carla*
2. Carla Jones   b. _____
3. Ken Jones   c. _____
4. Cheryl Jones   d. _____
5. Sara Jones   e. _____

6. Jill Jennings   f. _____
7. Marty Boyd   g. _____
8. Lisa Fisher   h. _____
9. Eva Donne   i. _____
10. Shay Elison   j. _____

(B) Write each list of titles in alphabetical order.

1. The Storyteller   a. *A Far Road*
2. A Far Road   b. _____
3. Over the Mountain   c. _____
4. To a Friend   d. _____
5. A Lost River   e. _____

6. Time after Time   f. _____
7. The Big Story   g. _____
8. Another Sister!   h. _____
9. An Angry God   i. _____
10. A Goodbye   j. _____

(C) Each box contains a set of guide words. Write the page number on which each word in the list would be found.

saber 117 sake	sauce 120 scalp	seal 125 self

set 128 shame	show 131 silk	sit 132 sky

- **128** 1. set
- ___ 2. silence
- ___ 3. savage
- ___ 4. sable
- ___ 5. seaweed
- ___ 6. sew
- ___ 7. save
- ___ 8. shrub
- ___ 9. secure
- ___ 10. saddle
- ___ 11. select
- ___ 12. scald
- ___ 13. Seattle
- ___ 14. shall
- ___ 15. shutter
- ___ 16. settle
- ___ 17. sail
- ___ 18. sign

- ___ 19. shy
- ___ 20. safe
- ___ 21. seven
- ___ 22. say
- ___ 23. shut
- ___ 24. second
- ___ 25. sewer
- ___ 26. sight
- ___ 27. sacred
- ___ 28. shag
- ___ 29. sixth
- ___ 30. saint
- ___ 31. skate
- ___ 32. shady
- ___ 33. sizzle
- ___ 34. safety
- ___ 35. sixty
- ___ 36. ski

- ___ 37. saw
- ___ 38. shower
- ___ 39. sack
- ___ 40. sedan
- ___ 41. saucer
- ___ 42. sick
- ___ 43. Savannah
- ___ 44. sauna
- ___ 45. signal
- ___ 46. seldom
- ___ 47. sawmill
- ___ 48. seventh
- ___ 49. secret
- ___ 50. skeleton
- ___ 51. sake
- ___ 52. section
- ___ 53. skip
- ___ 54. skull

- ___ 55. sag
- ___ 56. see
- ___ 57. scale
- ___ 58. sad
- ___ 59. shun
- ___ 60. sausage
- ___ 61. seed
- ___ 62. side
- ___ 63. sawdust
- ___ 64. shade
- ___ 65. sage
- ___ 66. size
- ___ 67. shadow
- ___ 68. seem
- ___ 69. shake
- ___ 70. sailor
- ___ 71. site
- ___ 72. skill

Test 21 cont'd →

Comprehension Check (continued)

(D) Underline the words which follow the V-C-C-V pattern.

1. <u>mitten</u>
2. nurse
3. airport
4. funnel
5. lady
6. winter
7. any
8. office
9. body
10. insect
11. effort
12. idea
13. kitten
14. hero
15. ignore
16. sudden
17. apart
18. advice
19. wisdom
20. decide
21. forward
22. reason
23. contest
24. easy
25. music
26. number
27. neon
28. bargain
29. formal
30. ruin

(E) Underline the words which follow the V-C-V pattern.

1. <u>over</u>
2. enjoy
3. regard
4. obey
5. sorrow
6. become
7. person
8. adult
9. resign
10. create
11. favor
12. trust
13. habit
14. trial
15. result
16. deceit
17. major
18. motto
19. nature
20. focus
21. bonus
22. infant
23. record
24. neon
25. alone
26. polite
27. demand
28. contest
29. secure
30. silent

(F) Divide each word into syllables.

1. airport _____*air   port*_____
2. captain _____
3. ghost _____
4. protect _____
5. resign _____
6. signature _____
7. ocean _____
8. hurry _____
9. reason _____
10. practice _____
11. famous _____
12. office _____
13. major _____
14. humid _____
15. ruin _____
16. repay _____
17. create _____
18. island _____
19. treasure _____
20. legal _____
21. again _____
22. mask _____
23. favor _____
24. accept _____

(G) Underline the open syllables.

1. <u>de</u> cide
2. sen a tor
3. dai ly
4. mu sic
5. re main
6. men tion
7. use ful
8. to ma to
9. hap py
10. trea son
11. fun nel
12. cru el

Write a paragraph about a book you have read. Be sure to underline the book's title.

_____
_____
_____
_____
_____
_____
_____
_____

Dividing Words

Each sound within a word is called a syllable.

EXAMPLES: a. absent   ab sent
            b. peace   peace

 Divide each word into syllables if possible.

1. newspaper _news paper_
2. mistake _____
3. answer _____
4. key _____
5. invite _____
6. although _____
7. nightmare _____
8. often _____
9. became _____
10. nonsense _____
11. cause _____
12. country _____
13. habit _____
14. globe _____
15. return _____
16. daughter _____
17. misplace _____
18. job _____
19. difficult _____
20. knock _____
21. replace _____
22. education _____
23. suddenly _____
24. uncertain _____
25. laugh _____
26. quite _____
27. surprise _____
28. clearing _____
29. enormous _____
30. sentence _____
31. before _____
32. famous _____
33. through _____

34. chance _____
35. blanket _____
36. practice _____
37. normal _____
38. statement _____
39. forget _____
40. income _____
41. office _____
42. bowl _____
43. breakfast _____
44. promise _____
45. captain _____
46. reward _____
47. easy _____
48. smart _____
49. itself _____
50. lonesome _____
51. wrong _____
52. yourself _____
53. correct _____
54. machine _____
55. together _____
56. spent _____
57. example _____
58. rabbit _____
59. farmer _____
60. young _____
61. different _____
62. unless _____
63. clue _____
64. vacation _____
65. enjoy _____
66. straight _____
67. combine _____

68. protection _____
69. folks _____
70. bashful _____
71. business _____
72. careful _____
73. question _____
74. reason _____
75. distrust _____
76. collect _____
77. guest _____
78. remember _____
79. crowd _____
80. excellent _____
81. ticket _____
82. wisdom _____
83. rush _____
84. suggest _____
85. deadline _____
86. weigh _____
87. parachute _____
88. forward _____
89. sleep _____
90. tunnel _____
91. hidden _____
92. wonderful _____
93. important _____
94. frown _____
95. thick _____
96. voice _____
97. hungry _____
98. soon _____
99. understand _____
100. now _____

Unit 106 cont'd

Dividing Longer Words

When there are two consonants at the syllable break, the division comes between the consonants.

When there are two vowels at the syllable break, the division comes between the vowels.

When there is a vowel and a consonant at the syllable break, the division usually comes after the vowel.

EXAMPLES:
a. *information*   in for ma tion
b. *tomorrow*   to mor row
c. *consonant*   con so nant

 Divide each word into syllables.

1. carpenter	car pen ter	26. difficult _____
2. occupy _____		27. enormous _____
3. stadium _____		28. helium _____
4. adventure _____		29. surrender _____
5. protection _____		30. hibernate _____
6. remember _____		31. attractive _____
7. condition _____		32. accident _____
8. identify _____		33. recognize _____
9. almanac _____		34. quietly _____
10. entertain _____		35. creative _____
11. finally _____		36. bewilder _____
12. incident _____		37. happiness _____
13. commonly _____		38. expansion _____
14. skeleton _____		39. wonderful _____
15. equipment _____		40. excellent _____
16. cruelty _____		41. suggestion _____
17. hospital _____		42. possessive _____
18. suddenly _____		43. holiday _____
19. estimate _____		44. gigantic _____
20. intelligent _____		45. ambition _____
21. attention _____		46. familiar _____
22. vacation _____		47. abandon _____
23. normally _____		48. important _____
24. wilderness _____		49. significant _____
25. yesterday _____		50. medium _____

Counting Syllables

A Underline the one-syllable words.

1. <u>peace</u>
2. greed
3. exam
4. truth
5. laugh
6. final
7. engage
8. cause
9. kick
10. quite
11. voice
12. urge
13. unless
14. fright
15. visual
16. shut
17. bowl
18. knob
19. night
20. device
21. foreign
22. none
23. ghost
24. wrong
25. leaf
26. measure
27. triumph
28. knock
29. threat
30. grief
31. smart
32. young
33. rejoice
34. usual
35. lawn
36. squeeze
37. ideal
38. globe
39. battle
40. count

B Underline the two-syllable words.

1. <u>fragile</u>
2. surprise
3. remedy
4. modern
5. equip
6. significant
7. partner
8. shrewd
9. itself
10. honest
11. occupy
12. absent
13. movies
14. ignore
15. pledge
16. journey
17. legal
18. forbidden
19. quiet
20. anxious
21. giant
22. nonsense
23. luxury
24. career
25. explode
26. similar
27. lonesome
28. daughter
29. bewilder
30. motto
31. nuisance
32. machine
33. needy
34. fierce
35. persuade
36. ignorance
37. minute
38. question
39. chatter
40. eternal

C Underline the words which contain three or more syllables.

1. <u>ambition</u>
2. distinct
3. happiness
4. confused
5. securely
6. welcome
7. wonderful
8. plunder
9. flexible
10. xylophone
11. condemn
12. idea
13. tragic
14. exercise
15. identify
16. television
17. vanish
18. penalty
19. combine
20. publisher
21. conquer
22. favorite
23. impossible
24. separate
25. wisdom
26. zone
27. outstanding
28. bleach
29. zigzag
30. furious
31. opinion
32. ruin
33. piano
34. vacant
35. decision
36. hesitate
37. skeleton
38. yummy
39. value
40. interesting

Unit 107 cont'd

Word Syllables

Each sound within a word is called a syllable.

EXAMPLES: a. prepare ➡ pre pare
b. baseball ➡ base ball
c. attention ➡ at ten tion

A Underline each word that has more than one syllable.

1. <u>paper</u>
2. office
3. cause
4. suddenly
5. allow
6. finally
7. even
8. lawn
9. together
10. night
11. hospital
12. giant
13. gain
14. accident
15. safe
16. prize
17. possible
18. weigh
19. folks
20. terrible
21. anxious
22. juice
23. favorite
24. separate
25. license
26. career
27. quite
28. medium
29. history
30. magic
31. wisdom
32. telephone
33. voice
34. none
35. return
36. job
37. umbrella
38. ghost
39. piano
40. desk
41. straight
42. mistake
43. comma
44. modern
45. strong
46. through
47. guess
48. exercise
49. own
50. television
51. holiday
52. key

B How many syllables are in each word?

__3__ 1. universe
____ 2. although
____ 3. guest
____ 4. wonderful
____ 5. explain
____ 6. early
____ 7. match
____ 8. honest
____ 9. language
____ 10. information
____ 11. sleep
____ 12. reason
____ 13. reward
____ 14. tooth
____ 15. journey
____ 16. neighbor
____ 17. nonsense
____ 18. welcome
____ 19. bowl
____ 20. forever
____ 21. secret
____ 22. knock
____ 23. freedom
____ 24. tomato
____ 25. melt
____ 26. leaf
____ 27. machine
____ 28. peace
____ 29. protection
____ 30. wrong
____ 31. tunnel
____ 32. habit
____ 33. raw
____ 34. vacation
____ 35. laugh
____ 36. adventure
____ 37. bold
____ 38. famous
____ 39. thought
____ 40. zero
____ 41. important
____ 42. between
____ 43. shape
____ 44. unless
____ 45. rush
____ 46. person
____ 47. visit
____ 48. sentence
____ 49. remember
____ 50. itself
____ 51. pleasure

Pronunciations

A Match each respelling with the word it describes.

1. bûrth′ dā	monkey	21. woolf	world
2. mung′ kē	money	22. wûrd	word
3. brīt	bicycle	23. wûrk	work
4. mun′ ē	birthday	24. wûrld	wolf
5. bī′ sik əl	bright	25. wûrm	worm
6. plēz	please	26. val′ yoo	verb
7. plen′ tē	practice	27. vûrb	value
8. pub′ lik	pocket	28. vīn	vine
9. prak′ tis	plenty	29. vōt	visit
10. pok′ it	public	30. viz′ it	vote
11. yir	yacht	31. hap′ ē	honest
12. yel′ ō	young	32. haz	has
13. yung	year	33. hav	happy
14. yoo	you	34. hap′ ən	happen
15. yot	yellow	35. on′ ist	have
16. skōr	serve	36. fol′ ō	fruit
17. sûrv	score	37. rông	follow
18. shad′ ō	street	38. ī dē′ a	island
19. sīn	sign	39. ī′ lənd	idea
20. strēt	shadow	40. froot	wrong

B Write the word described by each respelling.

1. pen′ səl	_pencil_	11. pāj	_____
2. stud′ ē	_____	12. roo′ lər	_____
3. wô′ tər	_____	13. pûr′ sən	_____
4. nīf	_____	14. yooz	_____
5. dûrt	_____	15. tī′ nē	_____
6. kab′ in	_____	16. stō′ rē	_____
7. kwik	_____	17. ruf	_____
8. boks	_____	18. pär′ tē	_____
9. drīv	_____	19. bild	_____
10. noo	_____	20. ə buv′	_____

Unit 108 cont'd

Respellings

In the dictionary a respelling tells you how a word is pronounced.

EXAMPLES.　a.　/ĕn′ jən/　　*engine*
　　　　　　b.　/ə lōn′/　　　*alone*

 Read the definition and respelling for each word. Then write the word.

DEFINITION	RESPELLING	WORD
1. the season between summer and winter	/ô′ təm/	*autumn*
2. road bordered by trees	/ăv′ ə nōō/	
3. to think highly of	/ə prē′ shē āt/	
4. a limiting line	/boun′ dər ē/	
5. two things of the same kind	/kŭp′ əl/	
6. a female child	/dô′ tər/	
7. knowledge gained through training	/ĕj′ ōō kā′ shən/	
8. the one liked very much	/fā′ vər ĭt/	
9. to watch over; to take care of	/gärd/	
10. fair; truthful; not cheating	/ŏn′ ĭst/	
11. to form a picture in the mind	/ĭ măj′ ən/	
12. meaning much; significant	/ĭm pôr′ tənt/	
13. bring or put together	/join/	
14. flat piece of metal with sharp edge	/nīf/	
15. not active or willing to work	/lā′ zē/	
16. put together; stir together	/mĭks/	
17. person who lives near another	/nā′ bər/	
18. way one thing follows another	/ôr′ dər/	
19. person who steers an airplane	/pī′ lət/	
20. that can happen or be done	/pŏs′ ə bəl/	
21. coin worth twenty-five cents	/kwôr′ tər/	
22. cause or explanation	/rē′ zən/	
23. to look at again	/rĭ vyōō′/	
24. figure with four equal sides	/skwâr/	
25. not known, seen, or heard before	/strānj/	
26. in the direction of	/tə wôrd′/	
27. get the meaning of	/ŭn dər stănd′/	
28. if not	/ŭn lĕs′/	
29. low land between mountains	/văl′ ē/	
30. make a clear, shrill sound	/hwĭs′ əl/	

More Respellings

The respelling shows how to pronounce a word.

EXAMPLES: a. līf   life
                b. ə wā´   away
                c. sik   sick

  Write the word described by each respelling.

1. lā´dē _____lady_____
2. mōōv _____
3. hap´ē _____
4. dôg _____
5. frunt _____
6. tā´bəl _____
7. kwik _____
8. ə buv´ _____
9. grēn _____
10. ō´vər _____
11. win´do _____
12. wīz _____
13. stud´ē _____
14. sāf _____
15. kab´ən _____
16. boks _____
17. drēm _____
18. wôk _____
19. pāj _____
20. hav _____
21. lēf _____
22. sôlt _____
23. ə pon´ _____
24. ēst _____
25. frōōt _____
26. haz _____
27. nōō _____
28. lok _____
29. strēt _____
30. un´dər _____
31. pen´səl _____
32. bild _____
33. fûrst _____

34. snō _____
35. drīv _____
36. grāt _____
37. flud _____
38. kul´ər _____
39. häf _____
40. hous _____
41. lō _____
42. ō´pən _____
43. ruf _____
44. shad´ō _____
45. vōt _____
46. mun´ē _____
47. ī´lənd _____
48. on´ist _____
49. blō _____
50. tung _____
51. vīn _____
52. pik _____
53. moun´tən _____
54. plēz _____
55. pub´lik _____
56. yir _____
57. zē´rō _____
58. pō´nē _____
59. brīt _____
60. sûrv _____
61. thôt _____
62. wûrk _____
63. wûrd _____
64. jûr´nē _____
65. bod´ē _____
66. skōr _____
67. yot _____

68. viz´it _____
69. bûrth´dā _____
70. rōō´lər _____
71. sīn _____
72. hap´ən _____
73. tī´nē _____
74. ī dē´ə _____
75. mung´kē _____
76. vûrb _____
77. pûr´sən _____
78. wŏŏlf _____
79. fō´tō _____
80. plen´tē _____
81. yōō _____
82. tôk _____
83. val´yōō _____
84. pok´it _____
85. yōōz _____
86. wô´tər _____
87. rông _____
88. hōm _____
89. kôl _____
90. prak´tis _____
91. stōr _____
92. tûr´kē _____
93. wag´ən _____
94. prīz _____
95. yung _____
96. wā _____
97. yel´ō _____
98. stik _____
99. bī´sik əl _____
100. kwī´ət _____

Unit 109 cont'd →

Respelling Practice

In a dictionary the respelling shows how to pronounce a word.

EXAMPLES: a. chēz   cheese
            b. hid′ən   hidden
            c. chānj   change

  Write the word for each respelling.

1. pub′lik __public__	34. un′yən _____	67. in vīt′ _____
2. kwī′ət _____	35. prə tekt′ _____	68. mes′ij _____
3. kroud _____	36. skärf _____	69. lō′kāt _____
4. en′i _____	37. flou′ər _____	70. mer′ē _____
5. puz′əl _____	38. tou′əl _____	71. pärt′nər _____
6. yung _____	39. ug′lē _____	72. ôr′chərd _____
7. pē an′ō _____	40. wô′tər _____	73. nā′chər _____
8. sāf _____	41. pō′əm _____	74. prīz _____
9. ī′lənd _____	42. ə lou′ _____	75. risk _____
10. nē′dəl _____	43. bā′ker _____	76. tik′əl _____
11. di sīd′ _____	44. kloz′it _____	77. hwis′əl _____
12. kwēn _____	45. en′ə mē _____	78. wiz′dəm _____
13. lim′it _____	46. froun _____	79. dich _____
14. rông _____	47. hir′ō _____	80. ē′gər _____
15. koun′tē _____	48. jü′əl _____	81. fif′tē _____
16. sē′krit _____	49. gärd _____	82. gōl′dən _____
17. kich′ən _____	50. jī′ənt _____	83. hel′mit _____
18. mach _____	51. grō _____	84. lā′bər _____
19. ī′təm _____	52. in vent′ _____	85. kou′boi _____
20. plā _____	53. man′ər _____	86. chüz _____
21. ə grē′ _____	54. ə līv′ _____	87. kan′yən _____
22. kuz′ən _____	55. kab′ən _____	88. ek′ō _____
23. fā′vər _____	56. dif′ər _____	89. frō′zən _____
24. noun _____	57. jen′təl _____	90. hun′drəd _____
25. pō′it _____	58. pub′lish _____	91. nīt _____
26. gras _____	59. līt _____	92. juj _____
27. lōf _____	60. fing′gər _____	93. prom′is _____
28. myül _____	61. jump _____	94. rī′fəl _____
29. tun′əl _____	62. nā′tiv _____	95. on′ər _____
30. sum′ər _____	63. prob′ləm _____	96. man′ij _____
31. welth _____	64. ri zult′ _____	97. plan′it _____
32. yü′nit _____	65. sin _____	98. snēk _____
33. wėrld _____	66. tėrn _____	99. sē′zən _____
		100. wôl′nut _____

264

The Accented Syllable

Unit 110

A word that has two or more syllables usually has one syllable which is said harder than the other(s). To show which syllable is said hardest, write an accent mark (').

EXAMPLES: a. *person*   per´son   d. *famous*   fa´ mous
                b. *became*   be came´   e. *adventure*   ad ven´ture
                c. *journey*   jour´ney   f. *vacation*   va ca´ tion

 Divide each word into syllables. Then place an accent mark over the syllable that is said harder than the other(s).

1. return	*re turn´*	34. office		67. understand	
2. question		35. useful		68. reason	
3. lonely		36. practice		69. vacant	
4. machine		37. hurry		70. forever	
5. freedom		38. itself		71. angry	
6. follow		39. welcome		72. nobody	
7. wisdom		40. surprise		73. tomato	
8. opinion		41. mistake		74. hungry	
9. excuse		42. defend		75. valley	
10. blanket		43. absent		76. center	
11. daughter		44. remember		77. ticket	
12. perhaps		45. outline		78. umbrella	
13. license		46. minute		79. nonsense	
14. selfish		47. number		80. zero	
15. plastic		48. notebook		81. although	
16. history		49. final		82. deliver	
17. difficult		50. captain		83. inform	
18. danger		51. ambition		84. adult	
19. rejoice		52. budget		85. signal	
20. ignore		53. transfer		86. nectar	
21. deadline		54. simple		87. ruthless	
22. balance		55. delay		88. suggest	
23. almanac		56. bashful		89. bicycle	
24. missing		57. enormous		90. stupid	
25. correct		58. intern		91. talent	
26. approve		59. splendid		92. voyage	
27. pretend		60. awkward		93. dungeon	
28. pencil		61. measure		94. ashamed	
29. important		62. mermaid		95. nightmare	
30. sentence		63. disgraceful		96. obey	
31. liberty		64. because		97. rumble	
32. garden		65. statement		98. suffer	
33. alphabet		66. better		99. surround	

Unit 110 cont'd

Stressed Syllables

A word that has two or more syllables usually has one syllable which is said harder than the other(s). To show which syllable is said hardest, write an accent mark (′).

 Break each word into syllables. Then place an accent mark (′) over the stressed syllable.

1. airport	*air′ port*	35. winter	68. backward
2. itself		36. sugar	69. awful
3. zebra		37. along	70. certain
4. easy		38. awkward	71. final
5. against		39. forget	72. hero
6. journey		40. able	73. happy
7. wagon		41. receive	74. combine
8. normal		42. secret	75. useless
9. became		43. eagle	76. freedom
10. market		44. escape	77. habit
11. yellow		45. woman	78. vacant
12. heavy		46. obey	79. movie
13. under		47. seldom	80. study
14. candy		48. except	81. hidden
15. machine		49. sorrow	82. visit
16. collect		50. include	83. color
17. captain		51. hungry	84. teacher
18. practice		52. extra	85. mother
19. garden		53. famous	86. enjoy
20. begin		54. surprise	87. seven
21. center		55. arrive	88. police
22. question		56. morning	89. leader
23. number		57. after	90. welcome
24. about		58. silent	91. zero
25. story		59. ticket	92. honest
26. nonsense		60. favor	93. wisdom
27. reason		61. tunnel	94. hurry
28. country		62. fellow	95. simple
29. danger		63. because	96. watching
30. person		64. children	97. hungry
31. cartoon		65. today	98. singing
32. summer		66. around	99. over
33. decide		67. unless	100. window
34. return			

Comprehension Check

Test 22

(A) How many syllables are in each word?

_4_	1. watermelon	___	11. vacancy	___	21. breeze	___	31. decision
___	2. number	___	12. bicycle	___	22. carpenter	___	32. identify
___	3. remember	___	13. stainless	___	23. several	___	33. advertise
___	4. coupon	___	14. lunch	___	24. classroom	___	34. driveway
___	5. newspaper	___	15. author	___	25. freedom	___	35. bookcase
___	6. laundry	___	16. uncover	___	26. digest	___	36. membership
___	7. brought	___	17. horrible	___	27. rapid	___	37. capitalization
___	8. wonderful	___	18. reorganize	___	28. generation	___	38. handsome
___	9. thermometer	___	19. abandon	___	29. clockwork	___	39. gentlemen
___	10. demonstrate	___	20. immediate	___	30. horizon	___	40. motorcycle

(B) Divide each word into syllables.

1. adventure _ad ven ture_
2. birthday _____
3. journal _____
4. purchase _____
5. nowadays _____
6. railway _____
7. earthquake _____
8. marvelous _____
9. receive _____
10. scheme _____

11. guarantee _____
12. explain _____
13. microphone _____
14. development _____
15. logical _____
16. borrow _____
17. illustration _____
18. hazardous _____
19. famous _____
20. heretofore _____

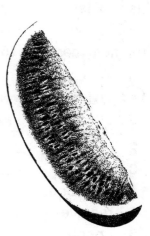

(C) Write the word described by each respelling.

1. ō′ pən _open_
2. nām _____
3. kōld _____
4. gō _____
5. ē′ zē _____
6. pīn _____
7. fat _____
8. lāt _____
9. sō′ də _____
10. jōk _____
11. rōz _____
12. lā′ zē _____
13. sāf _____

14. but′ ər _____
15. jī ənt _____
16. of′ is _____
17. kwiz _____
18. hob′ ē _____
19. fēld _____
20. nī′ lon _____
21. laf _____
22. men′ ē _____
23. fyu′ əl _____
24. up′ ər _____
25. shīn _____
26. kēp _____

27. ō′ shən _____
28. sel′ ər ē _____
29. nē′ dəl _____
30. di liv′ ər _____
31. siz′ ərz _____
32. eks′ trə _____
33. nēs _____
34. flou′ ər _____
35. rī′ vəl _____
36. mə shēn′ _____
37. in vīt′ _____
38. pāv′ mənt _____
39. tem′ pər _____
40. hwen _____

Test 22 cont'd ➡

Comprehension Check (continued)

(D) Complete each sentence with the word described in the parentheses.

(chok′ə lit)   1. I have a craving for ___*chocolate*___ cake.

(un dər stand′)   2. Did you _____ the assignment?

(ek′sər sīz)   3. Everyone should get plenty of _____ .

(kwol′ə tē)   4. _____ is more important than quantity.

(moun′tən)   5. This weekend Al and I are going _____ climbing.

(wāst′bas kit)   6. Throw this paper in the _____ .

(di sizh′ ən)   7. All of us will stand behind your _____ .

(sin′ ə nim)   8. "Look" is a _____ for "see."

(ken′əl)   9. Our dog is staying in a _____ this weekend.

(nā′ bər)   10. Ms. Russell, our _____ , is an attorney.

(bak′āk)   11. I have a _____ from lifting those boxes.

(tel′ə fōn)   12. Will you answer the _____ for me?

(fam′ə lē)   13. The _____ is important.

(poz′ə tiv)   14. You must think _____ about the race.

(ri mem′ bər)   15. Did Joyce _____ to call Dr. Winters?

(E) Divide each word into syllables. Then mark the accented syllable.

1. breakfast	_*break′ fast*_	11. absent	_____	21. exam	_____
2. include	_____	12. popcorn	_____	22. chocolate	_____
3. winter	_____	13. money	_____	23. ready	_____
4. bathroom	_____	14. driver	_____	24. confuse	_____
5. receive	_____	15. whistle	_____	25. paper	_____
6. noodle	_____	16. newspaper	_____	26. reward	_____
7. mustard	_____	17. regret	_____	27. message	_____
8. student	_____	18. hospital	_____	28. inside	_____
9. travel	_____	19. siren	_____	29. carefully	_____
10. diet	_____	20. music	_____	30. homeward	_____

Write a paragraph about your favorite kind of music. Why do you prefer it over other kinds?

_____

_____

_____

_____

_____

_____

_____

Definitions

Some words in the dictionary have more than one meaning.
Each meaning is numbered.

 Use the following dictionary entries to identify the meanings of the underlined words.

_n_   1. Joe wrote a <u>check</u> for the bicycle.
_v1_   2. You must learn to <u>check</u> your temper.
_v2_   3. <u>Check</u> your answers.

> **check** (chĕk), *v., n.* —v. 1 hold back; control. 2 prove true by comparing. —n. written order for payment of money.

____   4. <u>Draw</u> a picture of a horse.
____   5. The car is <u>drawing</u> nearer.
____   6. The game ended in a <u>draw</u>.
____   7. The events <u>draw</u> big crowds.
____   8. Ted will <u>draw</u> up the papers.
____   9. <u>Draw</u> some water from the well.

> **draw** (drô), *v., n.* —v. 1 pull out; take out. 2 attract. 3 make a picture with a pen. 4 write. 5 move. —n. tie.

____ 10. Anna <u>leads</u> a quiet life.
____ 11. We <u>lead</u> the state in production.
____ 12. Studying <u>leads</u> to good grades.
____ 13. <u>Lead</u> us to the treasure.

> **lead** (lēd), *v.,* 1 show the way by going in front of. 2 be first among. 3 be a way or road. 4 pass or spend time in some special way.

____ 14. Strike a <u>match</u> so we can see.
____ 15. Those two are a good <u>match</u>.
____ 16. The <u>match</u> is between the Hawks and the Eagles.

> **match** (măch), *n.,* 1 a pair that fits. 2 the coming together of two sides for a contest. 3 a device used for starting a fire.

____ 17. He plans to <u>practice</u> medicine.
____ 18. I'm out of <u>practice</u> at jogging.
____ 19. Nancy needs to <u>practice</u> playing the piano.

> **prac/tice** (prăk′tĭs), *n., v.* —n. the skill gained by experience. —v. 1 do some act over and over to learn to do it well. 2 to follow as a profession.

____ 20. Will you read my <u>rough</u> draft?
____ 21. We sailed through the <u>rough</u> weather.
____ 22. She bought the <u>rough</u> diamonds.
____ 23. The surface of a sidewalk is <u>rough</u>.
____ 24. Living in the desert is a <u>rough</u> life.

> **rough** (rŭf), *adj.,* 1 not smooth. 2 stormy. 3 without luxury and ease. 4 without polish or fine finish. 5 done as a first try.

Unit 111 cont'd ⟶

Looking Up Definitions

bill (bil) *n.* **1** a list of things for which money is owed **2** a piece of paper money **3** a law proposed to a body of lawmakers *v.* to send a list of charges to: I will bill you every week.

clear (klēr) *adj.* **1** easy to see through **2** bright; a clear day **3** easy to see **4** easy to understand *v.* **1** to free: clear of any guilt **2** to become clear

date (dāt) *n.* **1** the time when something happens such as March 12, 1985 **2** a period of time to which something belongs like a date in history **3** an appointment like a date to go to the show *v.* **1** to mark with a date **2** to belong to a certain period in time

nurse (nėrse) *n.* **1** a woman or man hired to take care of someone who is ill **2** a woman hired to care for someone's child *v.* to tend the sick

pock et (pok´ it) *n.* **1** a small bag sewn into clothing **2** a condition in the atmosphere: The airplane hit an air pocket. *adj.* that which will fit in a pocket, like a pocket calculator *v.* to put in a pocket

qui et (kwī´ ət) *adj.* **1** silent **2** without motion like a quiet sea **3** peaceful **4** gentle: a gentle voice *n.* **1** silence **2** peacefulness *v.* to make or become silent or still

re ward (ri wôrd´) *n.* **1** something given in return for something else **2** money given or offered *v.* to give a reward to

trail (trāl) *v.* **1** to pull along behind **2** to follow behind **3** to follow the tracks of *n.* a track or scent

voice (vois) *n.* **1** the sound made by a person speaking, singing, etc. **2** the ability to make sounds through the mouth **3** an expressed opinion *v.* to express: Henry voices his opinion on everything.

For each entry word in the dictionary, you will find listed the part of speech. Some words may be more than one part of speech.

A noun names a person, place, or thing. The abbreviation "n." stands for "noun."

A verb shows action. The abbreviation "v." stands for "verb."

An adjective tells how many, which one, or what kind; it describes a noun. The abbreviation "adj." stands for "adjective."

❋ **Answer each question by using the list of entry words on this page.**

1. What is the verb definition of the word "nurse"? *to tend the sick*

2. What are the noun definitions of the word "quiet"? _____

3. How many adjective definitions are given for the word "clear"? _____

4. What parts of speech are given for the word "pocket"? _____

5. What is the verb definition for the word "reward"? _____

6. What is the noun definition for the word "trail"? _____

7. What is the verb definition of the word "voice"? _____

8. What is the adjective definition of the word "pocket"? _____

9. How many noun definitions are given for the word "bill"? _____

10. Are any definitions given for "date" as an adjective? _____

11. What is the verb definition of the word "bill"? _____

12. What are the verb definitions of the word "clear"? _____

Words with More Than One Meaning

Sometimes a word may have more than one definition. The definition may determine how the word is to be used in a sentence.

 Match the definitions with the sentences which best illustrate them.

I. count
   a. to name numbers
   b. to number things
   c. to depend on
   d. to be of importance

1. I am counting on you to help me.
2. In an emergency every minute counts.
3. Count from one to fifty.
4. Bobby counted his pennies.

II. step
   e. putting one foot before another
   f. degree or rank
   g. a short distance
   h. measure or action
   i. place for foot on ladder

5. The process can be done in three steps.
6. Step forward.
7. He is one step below a captain.
8. We live one step from the store.
9. Each step on the ladder was broken.

III. weak
   j. lacking authority
   k. unable to bear strain
   l. lacks physical strength

10. The illness left him weak.
11. Charles was a weak president.
12. The chair was too weak to hold him.

IV. heart
   m. organ that pumps blood
   n. central part
   o. one's feelings

13. She lives in the heart of town.
14. The heart is a muscle.
15. The old woman had a kind heart.

V. keen
   p. sharp edge
   q. mentally alert
   r. sensitive

16. The eagle has keen eyesight.
17. The knife had a keen edge.
18. We need someone with keen intelligence.

VI. fail
   s. neglect
   t. lose strength
   u. not to succeed

19. I tried to win but failed.
20. The man's hearing was failing.
21. He failed to do his duties.

VII. ground
   v. surface of the earth
   w. foundation

22. On what grounds are these charges based?
23. The ground was frozen.

Unit 112 cont'd ⟶

Changing Parts of Speech

Sometimes the same word can function as different parts of speech. It may have to take on additional prefixes and suffixes, but its part of speech is determined by its use in a sentence.

EXAMPLE: *Notice how the word "order" changes from a noun to a verb to an adjective in these three sentences:*
I gave you an order.
Kevin did order the tuna salad.
Fill out the order blank.

✱ **Identify the part of speech of each underlined word. Write "1" for noun, "2" for verb, and "3" for adjective.**

_1_ 1. A small <u>crowd</u> gathered around us.
_3_ 2. I felt uncomfortable in the <u>crowded</u> room.
_2_ 3. Ten people <u>crowded</u> into the elevator.

____ 4. He is an <u>escaped</u> convict.
____ 5. The prisoners planned their <u>escape</u>.
____ 6. The man <u>escaped</u> on July 22.

____ 7. The incident <u>troubled</u> Dan.
____ 8. I think we're in <u>trouble</u>.
____ 9. Jill gave me a <u>troubled</u> look.

____ 10. The <u>reward</u> money was stolen.
____ 11. The winner was <u>rewarded</u> .
____ 12. The <u>reward</u> was fifty dollars.

____ 13. Gilda has a good <u>suggestion</u>.
____ 14. Mr. Price <u>suggested</u> we think it over.
____ 15. Put your idea in the <u>suggestion</u> box.

____ 16. <u>Welcome</u> our guests.
____ 17. Tim was given a warm <u>welcome</u>.
____ 18. Mother bought a new <u>welcome</u> mat.

____ 19. Frank <u>changed</u> his mind again.
____ 20. Everyone was ready for a <u>change</u>.
____ 21. My <u>change</u> purse has a hole in it.

____ 22. The <u>scale</u> is broken.
____ 23. Isaac did a <u>scale</u> drawing.
____ 24. Mark <u>scaled</u> the wall.

____ 25. Eric <u>promised</u> to bring the book.
____ 26. The deal sounds <u>promising</u>.
____ 27. I never break a <u>promise</u>.

____ 28. Call the <u>police</u>.
____ 29. The army <u>policed</u> the area carefully.
____ 30. I've never ridden in a <u>police</u> car.

____ 31. <u>Storms</u> frighten me.
____ 32. We slept in the <u>storm</u> cellar.
____ 33. It <u>stormed</u> again last night.

____ 34. Joan <u>watered</u> the flowers.
____ 35. The <u>water</u> buffalo lives there.
____ 36. The <u>water</u> was cool and refreshing.

____ 37. The captain <u>commanded</u> his troops to stop.
____ 38. The singer gave a <u>command</u> performance.
____ 39. He disobeyed your <u>command</u>.

____ 40. We <u>surprised</u> you.
____ 41. Kelly gave Sue a <u>surprise</u> party.
____ 42. This is a pleasant <u>surprise</u>!

____ 43. She <u>headed</u> the ship for home.
____ 44. Phil is the <u>head</u> officer.
____ 45. Move your <u>head</u> to the right.

____ 46. Ms. Young <u>graded</u> our tests.
____ 47. Vera always makes good <u>grades</u>.
____ 48. The teacher lost her <u>grade</u> book.

Recognizing Misspelled Words

Unit 113

 In each row underline the word that is spelled incorrectly. Then write it correctly in the blank.

1. (a) war (b) <u>battel</u> (c) captain (d) peace (e) _battle_
2. (a) dificult (b) easy (c) exam (d) test (e) _____
3. (a) remember (b) memory (c) forgit (d) think (e) _____
4. (a) food (b) starve (c) stuffed (d) hungree (e) _____
5. (a) sample (b) exampul (c) picture (d) illustrate (e) _____
6. (a) reason (b) cause (c) eksplain (d) show (e) _____
7. (a) amung (b) between (c) beside (d) upon (e) _____
8. (a) someone (b) knobody (c) anybody (d) everybody (e) _____
9. (a) funny (b) sad (c) jokke (d) tear (e) _____
10. (a) smell (b) taste (c) touch (d) sownd (e) _____
11. (a) seldom (b) never (c) uzual (d) often (e) _____
12. (a) agen (b) also (c) include (d) repeat (e) _____
13. (a) lazy (b) wurk (c) employ (d) play (e) _____
14. (a) purhaps (b) maybe (c) suddenly (d) chance (e) _____
15. (a) telephone (b) doorbell (c) camera (d) televizion (e) _____
16. (a) dokter (b) lawyer (c) teacher (d) professor (e) _____
17. (a) aged (b) old (c) yung (d) teen (e) _____
18. (a) spreng (b) summer (c) fall (d) winter (e) _____
19. (a) withowt (b) with (c) from (d) away (e) _____
20. (a) square (b) line (c) circul (d) rectangle (e) _____
21. (a) permit (b) lisense (c) allow (d) able (e) _____
22. (a) empty (b) complete (c) sufficient (d) enuf (e) _____
23. (a) roof (b) windo (c) lawn (d) porch (e) _____
24. (a) large (b) littel (c) huge (d) small (e) _____
25. (a) begining (b) opening (c) closing (d) finished (e) _____
26. (a) after (b) middle (c) befor (d) behind (e) _____
27. (a) Monday (b) Friday (c) Saterday (d) Sunday (e) _____
28. (a) week (b) munth (c) year (d) decade (e) _____
29. (a) misstake (b) error (c) correct (d) wrong (e) _____
30. (a) possibul (b) impossible (c) probably (d) always (e) _____
31. (a) quiet (b) quite (c) quitt (d) quick (e) _____
32. (a) ignore (b) knowledge (c) undurstand (d) intelligent (e) _____
33. (a) holliday (b) favorite (c) visit (d) day (e) _____
34. (a) dinner (b) lunch (c) snak (d) breakfast (e) _____
35. (a) voyage (b) trip (c) jurney (d) vacation (e) _____

Unit 113 cont'd →

Correcting Misspelled Words

 In each row underline the word that is spelled correctly. Then write it in the sentence.

1. (a) <u>career</u>   (b) carear   (c) kareer   Sam wants a ___career___ in medicine.
2. (a) kei   (b) key   (c) kee   Here is the _____.
3. (a) night   (b) nit   (c) niht   The opposite of morning is _____.
4. (a) reeturn   (b) retirn   (c) return   Did you _____ the call?
5. (a) uther   (b) other   (c) othur   You can have the _____ one.
6. (a) lonely   (b) lonley   (c) lonlee   The puppy looked cold and _____.
7. (a) hospitel   (b) hospital   (c) hospetal   My aunt works in the _____.
8. (a) danger   (b) dangur   (c) danjer   We will not be in any _____ here.
9. (a) accidint   (b) accident   (c) acident   Did anyone see the _____?
10. (a) widd   (b) wyde   (c) wide   The bridge is not _____ enough.
11. (a) holiday   (b) holliday   (c) holaday   Thanksgiving is a _____.
12. (a) cussin   (b) cousin   (c) cousen   Matthew is my _____.
13. (a) everbody   (b) everybody   (c) everbode   _____ is invited to come.
14. (a) arrport   (b) airpurt   (c) airport   We took my uncle to the _____.
15. (a) town   (b) toun   (c) towen   I grew up in a small _____.
16. (a) funnee   (b) funny   (c) funy   That was a _____ joke.
17. (a) ouner   (b) owner   (c) ownir   The _____ is Ms. Arnold.
18. (a) magic   (b) magik   (c) majic   I don't believe in _____.
19. (a) exciting   (b) exsiting   (c) excitin   The game was very _____.
20. (a) kompany   (b) company   (c) compeny   They have _____ for dinner.
21. (a) inturest   (b) interrest   (c) interest   She has no _____ in sports.
22. (a) banana   (b) bannana   (c) bananna   May I have a _____?
23. (a) usually   (b) usualy   (c) ussually   We _____ have a test on Friday.
24. (a) chanse   (b) chance   (c) chence   Let's give him another _____.
25. (a) famus   (b) fammous   (c) famous   Twain is a _____ writer.
26. (a) together   (b) togither   (c) tugether   You and I can work _____.
27. (a) accross   (b) across   (c) akross   Walk slowly _____ the room.
28. (a) chaced   (b) chased   (c) chassed   The lion _____ the deer.
29. (a) ennemy   (b) enamy   (c) enemy   We must outwit the _____.
30. (a) middel   (b) middle   (c) midle   He stood in the _____ of the circle.
31. (a) outlaw   (b) owtlaw   (c) outlow   Jesse James was an _____.
32. (a) language   (b) langauge   (c) langage   Can you speak a foreign _____?
33. (a) evining   (b) evenen   (c) evening   The meeting is this _____.
34. (a) titel   (b) title   (c) titil   What is the _____ of the book?
35. (a) finish   (b) finnish   (c) finesh   Did you _____ your work?

Practice Using the Dictionary

Unit 114

Each entry word in a dictionary gives the following information.

1. *the spelling of the word*
2. *the word divided into syllables*
3. *the pronunciation of the word*
4. *the part of speech of the word*
5. *the meaning or meanings of the word*

 Use the following dictionary entries to answer the questions.

---

a/bove (ə bŭv'), *adv., adj., prep.* —*adv.* 1 In a higher place. 2 more than.
—*adj.* being above.
—*prep.* in a higher place than.

age (āj), *n., v.* —*n.* 1 time of life. 2 in a particular period of life. 3 a period in history.
—*v.* grow old.

air/port (âr'pōrt'), *n.,* place where airplanes land and take off.

al/though (ôl thō'), *conj.,* even if: *Although it looks like rain, we will go.*

ar/rive (ə rīv'), *v.,* reach the end of a journey: *We will arrive home Monday.*

at/tack (ə tăk'), *v., n.* —*v.* 1 set upon to hurt. 2 go at with vigor.
—*n.* use of forceful language in order to harm.

at/tend (ə tĕnd'), *v.,* 1 be present at. 2 wait on: *the maid will attend the queen.*

---

1. How is "attack" divided into syllables?
   _____at___tack_____ How many syllables? ___*two*___
2. How is "airport" divided into syllables?
   _____ How many syllables? _____
3. Which of the entry words has only one syllable? _____
4. What is the sound of the "i" in "arrive"?
   _____
5. What is the sound of the "e" in "attend"? _____
6. Which syllable in "although" is stressed?
   _____
7. What parts of speech are listed for "above"?
   _____
8. What part of speech is listed for "airport"?
   _____
9. What is the definition for "above" as an adjective? _____
10. What is the definition for "age" as a verb?
    _____
11. How many definitions are listed for "attend" as a verb? _____
12. What part of speech is listed for "although"?
    _____
13. How many definitions are listed for "age" as a noun? _____
14. What example of usage is given for "arrive"?
    _____
15. What is the definition for "airport"? _____
    _____

Unit 114 cont'd →

Using a Dictionary

ab sent (ab′sənt) *adj.* not present; missing: Who is absent? (ab sent′) *v.* to take or keep (oneself) away

broom (brüm) *n.* a brush for sweeping: Sweep the floor with a broom.

cause (kôz) *n.* **1** something which produces a result **2** an activity which people are interested in and support *v.* to make happen; bring about; He did cause the accident.

ea gle (ē′gəl) *n.* any of a number of large, strong birds of prey

grab (grab) *v.* to seize or snatch suddenly *n.* a sudden seizing or snatching

har vest (här′vist) *n.* the season when grain, fruit, etc., are gathered in *v.* to reap and gather in

hol i day (hol′ə dā) *n.* **1** a day of freedom from work: Easter is a holiday. **2** a vacation: We went to Ohio for the holidays.

knee (nē) *n.* the joint between the thigh and the lower part of a person's leg

lone some (lōn′səm) *adj.* lonely

nail (nāl) *n.* **1** a slender piece of metal with a sharp point **2** the thin growth at the end of a finger or toe *v.* **1** to attach with a nail **2** to make certain

of fi cer (ôf′ə sər) *n.* **1** a person in position of authority **2** a policeman

pack age (pak′ij) *n.* **1** a bundle of things; parcel, like a package of books **2** the thing in which something is packed

Your dictionary is a book containing the words of a language. Look at the sample list of entry words on this page. What does the dictionary tell you about each entry word?

1. The entry word is divided into syllables.
2. An accent mark shows you the stressed syllable.
3. The respelling shows you how to pronounce the word.
4. Diacritical marks show the sounds of the vowels.
5. Sometimes a picture illustrates the entry word.
6. The definition tells you the meaning of the word. Some words may have more than one meaning.

 Answer each question by using the list of entry words on this page.

1. How is "harvest" divided into syllables?
   _____*har   vest*_____

2. How is "officer" divided into syllables?
   _____

3. What is the sound of the first vowel in "eagle"? _____

4. Which entry word begins with a silent letter? _____

5. Which syllable is stressed in "lonesome"? _____

6. What is the respelling of "nail"?
   _____

7. How many definitions are listed under "grab"? _____

8. Which word on this page is illustrated with a picture? _____

9. What two pronunciations are given for "absent"? _____

10. What is the sound of the "c" in "cause"? _____

Unscrambling Letters to Make Words

The letters which make a word are arranged in a definite order.

EXAMPLES:
a. selfti ___itself___
b. reaht ___heart___
c. tnaeru ___nature___
d. nynfu ___funny___

A Arrange each set of letters to make a word.

1. saetnb ___absent___
2. esepla _____
3. spstro _____
4. wldro _____
5. bcani _____
6. wdmsio _____
7. thghtuo _____
8. rrwead _____
9. daegr _____
10. weelj _____
11. aihtb _____
12. sstdeer _____
13. zoend _____
14. tquei _____
15. etclos _____
16. outbelr _____
17. memsur _____
18. rnoht _____
19. shfferi _____
20. unhert _____

21. ecpae _____
22. sviti _____
23. fofcie _____
24. wblo _____
25. cvoie _____
26. nmalro _____
27. fsokl _____
28. pttooa _____
29. uenssl _____
30. ryruh _____
31. oprsime _____
32. tcreen _____
33. cfta _____
34. sreano _____
35. rshea _____
36. tmcha _____
37. ndaec _____
38. wnse _____
39. mnerub _____
40. gdeui _____

41. ntnlue _____
42. cweelom _____
43. rkmeat _____
44. srmat _____
45. wonre _____
46. usllayu _____
47. otgsh _____
48. ctsere _____
49. theors _____
50. gynou _____
51. gmica _____
52. eyoujrn _____
53. poplee _____
54. stcale _____
55. fela _____
56. tlounei _____
57. slinad _____
58. wntire _____
59. betask _____
60. hgrynu _____

B Here are some really tough ones. Arrange the letters to make words.

1. vtenadeur ___adventure___
2. tvseelioni _____
3. cvtnioaa _____
4. dsdnlyue _____
5. wdfluoenr _____
6. ffltdiicu _____
7. aistrtgh _____
8. ewapnpers _____

9. soloenem _____
10. rlleumba _____
11. exresiec _____
12. tinesingret _____
13. rmmeeerb _____
14. sioniced _____
15. prgroma _____
16. btphaael _____

17. ffeidernt _____
18. nsoeenns _____
19. caonitdue _____
20. tonuqesi _____
21. eioafvrt _____
22. vyigeerthn _____
23. eaarfstkb _____
24. lllyaesb _____

Unit 115 cont'd ➡

Recognizing Word Groups

A noun names a person, place, or thing.
A noun may be common or proper. A noun may be singular or plural.

A pronoun is a noun substitute. It may be singular or plural.

A verb shows action or state of being. It may be written in present, past, or future tense.

An adjective tells which one, what kind, or how many.

An adverb tells when, where, why, or how.

※ Underline the word in each group which does not fit in with the others in the group.
What kind of words make up the group?

1. chocolate
   <u>frequently</u>
   strawberry
   vanilla
   ___**nouns**___

2. chase
   quit
   select
   general
   _____

3. mine
   she
   voice
   you
   _____

4. kindness
   business
   lonely
   nonsense
   _____

5. safely
   always
   modern
   often
   _____

6. penny
   ran
   holiday
   machine
   _____

7. vacation
   journey
   is
   accident
   _____

8. quietly
   now
   today
   blue
   _____

9. curly
   dessert
   interesting
   favorite
   _____

10. it
    yourself
    like
    ours
    _____

11. tomorrow
    quickly
    evenly
    beautiful
    _____

12. cute
    newspaper
    angry
    magical
    _____

13. are
    zoo
    wisdom
    promise
    _____

14. ordered
    discover
    practice
    ghost
    _____

15. understand
    truth
    market
    surprise
    _____

16. they
    I
    people
    we
    _____

17. our
    protect
    buy
    defend
    _____

18. suddenly
    usually
    broken
    never
    _____

19. laughed
    raw
    crowded
    vacant
    _____

20. sleep
    cried
    wonderful
    talked
    _____

Comprehension Check

(A) Use the dictionary entry to identify the meaning of each underlined word. Write "n" or "v," followed by the number of the correct definition, in the blanks. The definitions may be used more than one time.

_**v1**_ 1. She <u>dropped</u> the valuable vase.

____ 2. <u>Drops</u> of water covered the glasses.

____ 3. We gave the baby a <u>drop</u> of aspirin.

____ 4. There was a <u>drop</u> in car sales.

____ 5. Don't <u>drop</u> the crystal!

____ 6. Eva's eye <u>drops</u> stung her eyes.

____ 7. Mike <u>dropped</u> into his recliner.

____ 8. The parachute <u>drop</u> was successful.

____ 9. Sean <u>dropped</u> his voice to a whisper.

____ 10. The stock market is <u>dropping</u>.

> **drop** (drŏp) *n.* 1. The smallest quantity of liquid heavy enough to fall in a round or pear-shaped mass. 2. A small quantity. 3. drops. Liquid medicine given in such quantity. 4. The act of falling. 5. A swift decline or decrease. —*v.* dropped, dropping. 1. To fall or let fall from a higher to a lower place. 2. To become less in number, intensity, etc.; decrease. 3. To descend. 4. To sink into a state of exhaustion. 5. To lower the level of (the voice).

(B) Answer the questions about the two dictionary entries.

> **fall** (fôl) *v.* 1. To move under the influence of gravity. 2. To come down; collapse. 3. To hang down: *Her hair falls in long curls.* 4. To divide naturally: *They fall into three categories.* —*n.* 1. The act of falling: *He took a fall on the stairs.* 2. Autumn. 3. An overthrow or collapse: *the fall of a government.* 4. A decline or reduction: *Did school attendance fall?*

1. Which word has two syllables? _____ *present*
2. How many noun definitions are given for "fall"? _____
3. Write the respelling for "present." _____
4. Which syllable is stressed in "present"? _____
5. How many definitions are given for "fall"? _____
6. How many definitions are given for "present"? _____
7. Write the third verb definition for "fall." _____
   _____
8. Write the first example for "present." _____
   _____

> **present** (prĭ zĕnt´) *v.* 1. To introduce. 2. To bring before the public: *present a play.* 3. To offer formally: *present one's opinion.*

9. Which definition of "present" is used in this sentence: "May I present Mr. Harris"? _____
10. Which definition of "fall" is used in this sentence: "Don't fall on the ice"? _____
11. Is there a definiton for "fall" used in this sentence: "He went over the falls in his canoe"? _____
12. Write the third definition for "present." _____
    _____

13. Use the dictionary entries to identify the meaning of "fall" and "present" in these sentences.

____ a. The play was <u>presented</u> in the evening.

____ b. The weather turns cooler in the <u>fall</u>.

____ c. Darrell <u>presented</u> his report to the class.

____ d. The <u>fall</u> of Nicaragua was no surprise.

____ e. "C" <u>falls</u> between "B" and "D."

____ f. The baby was <u>presented</u> to his grandparents.

____ g. Anna had a bad <u>fall</u> on the slippery floor.

____ h. Did the building <u>fall</u> down last year?

Test 23 cont'd ➤

Comprehension Check (continued)

Ⓒ **Match each definition with the sentence which best illustrates it.**

I. appeal
   a. an earnest request
   b. the transfer of a court case
   c. to be attractive or interesting

1. Does this color appeal to you?
2. I appeal to your sense of fair play.
3. Mr. Millard won his appeal.

II. conduct
   d. to lead or guide
   e. to behave oneself
   f. the way a person acts.

4. Conduct yourself in a courteous manner.
5. How was your conduct this semester.
6. Will you conduct the choir?

III. grand
   g. large and impressive
   h. principal; main
   i. complete

7. What is the grand plan?
8. The building was grand.
9. Missy gave us the grand total.

Ⓓ **Identify the part of speech of each underlined word. Write "n" for noun, "v" for verb, and "a" for adjective.**

_n_ 1. The air feels cool.
___ 2. Air up the flat tires.
___ 3. The truck has an air horn.
___ 4. We play our opponents at 7:30 p.m.
___ 5. The play was exciting
___ 6. Lean to the left.
___ 7. This is lean steak.
___ 8. I think there is an air leak.
___ 9. Did the air leak?
___ 10. Carla leaked the secret.

Ⓔ **Underline each correctly spelled word.**

1. (a) reccord   (b) record   (c) recorrd
2. (a) driving   (b) driveing   (c) drivving
3. (a) defense   (b) difense   (c) defence
4. (a) sucess   (b) success   (c) succes
5. (a) commplete   (b) complite   (c) complete
6. (a) cought   (b) caught   (c) coutt
7. (a) field   (b) feeld   (c) feald
8. (a) magic   (b) majec   (c) magec
9. (a) serprise   (b) surprise   (c) surprize
10. (a) enamy   (b) enimy   (c) enemy
11. (a) through   (b) throogh   (c) throgh
12. (a) shineing   (b) shining   (c) shinning

Write a paragraph telling how to cook something. Use the word "cook" as a noun and as a verb.

_____
_____
_____
_____
_____
_____
_____
_____

Base Words

The base word is the word to which prefixes and suffixes are added. Every word contains a base word.

EXAMPLES:
a. freedom _____free_____
b. recover _____cover_____
c. finally _____final_____
d. greedy _____greed_____
e. keys _____key_____
f. bicycle _____cycle_____

A Write the base word of each word.

1. lonesome _lone_	26. misspell _____	51. useful _____
2. voices _____	27. easily _____	52. owner _____
3. careful _____	28. knocking _____	53. written _____
4. asked _____	29. rework _____	54. undivided _____
5. exchange _____	30. biting _____	55. truthful _____
6. recount _____	31. talked _____	56. courts _____
7. unable _____	32. ponies _____	57. suggestion _____
8. equipment _____	33. carried _____	58. building _____
9. laughing _____	34. tricycle _____	59. distrust _____
10. asleep _____	35. farmer _____	60. ashamed _____
11. incorrect _____	36. valuable _____	61. statement _____
12. different _____	37. seventy _____	62. uninvited _____
13. confession _____	38. healthy _____	63. prosperous _____
14. misplace _____	39. unkind _____	64. helpless _____
15. clothes _____	40. battles _____	65. clearing _____
16. boldness _____	41. hidden _____	66. honest _____
17. accidentally _____	42. countries _____	67. backward _____
18. jewelry _____	43. graded _____	68. following _____
19. artist _____	44. lucky _____	69. secretly _____
20. suddenly _____	45. visitor _____	70. nonsense _____
21. latest _____	46. inches _____	71. magical _____
22. reordered _____	47. modernize _____	72. straighten _____
23. weight _____	48. selfish _____	73. whom _____
24. teacher _____	49. shortage _____	74. obedience _____
25. reheat _____	50. fifteen _____	75. lower _____

B Which of the words are base words? Underline them.

1. words   wordy   <u>word</u>   wordless
2. tell   untold   told   telling
3. opening   open   reopen   opened
4. used   unused   reuse   use
5. homes   homely   home   homeward
6. small   smaller   smallest   smallness
7. farmer   farms   farm   farmland
8. renew   newer   newly   new
9. doing   do   done   does
10. take   mistake   taken   taking

Unit 116 cont'd

Derived Words

A derived word is a base word plus a prefix and/or suffix.

EXAMPLES:
1. be   (a) <u>being</u>   (b) bee   (c) <u>been</u>   (d) beekeeper
2. slow   (a) <u>low</u>   (b) <u>slowly</u>   (c) <u>slower</u>   (d) soft
3. work   (a) walk   (b) <u>reword</u>   (c) <u>rework</u>   (d) <u>worker</u>
4. laugh   (a) <u>laughed</u>   (b) <u>laughs</u>   (c) smile   (d) <u>laughing</u>

 At the beginning of each row is a base word. Underline the derived words which have been formed from that base word.

1. do   (a) <u>doing</u>   (b) <u>done</u>   (c) doom   (d) <u>does</u>   (e) <u>did</u>
2. sit   (a) <u>sat</u>   (b) see   (c) <u>sitting</u>   (d) shall   (e) <u>sits</u>
3. hurry   (a) hurt   (b) <u>hurried</u>   (c) <u>hurriedly</u>   (d) <u>hurries</u>   (e) heart
4. leave   (a) <u>left</u>   (b) lease   (c) leaf   (d) <u>leaving</u>   (e) <u>leaves</u>
5. safe   (a) <u>unsafe</u>   (b) <u>safer</u>   (c) salve   (d) <u>safely</u>   (e) <u>safest</u>
6. night   (a) knight   (b) <u>nights</u>   (c) <u>tonight</u>   (d) <u>nightly</u>   (e) not
7. please   (a) peace   (b) <u>pleasant</u>   (c) <u>pleases</u>   (d) plus   (e) <u>pleased</u>
8. use   (a) <u>reuse</u>   (b) us   (c) <u>useless</u>   (d) unless   (e) <u>uses</u>
9. own   (a) on   (b) <u>owner</u>   (c) <u>owned</u>   (d) <u>owns</u>   (e) only
10. turn   (a) <u>return</u>   (b) <u>turning</u>   (c) tune   (d) <u>turned</u>   (e) ton
11. wise   (a) was   (b) <u>wisdom</u>   (c) <u>wisely</u>   (d) wish   (e) <u>wiser</u>
12. you   (a) young   (b) <u>your</u>   (c) <u>yourself</u>   (d) youth   (e) <u>yours</u>
13. change   (a) chance   (b) chase   (c) <u>changes</u>   (d) exchange   (e) <u>changing</u>
14. care   (a) <u>careful</u>   (b) <u>caring</u>   (c) card   (d) <u>uncaring</u>   (e) car
15. gain   (a) <u>regain</u>   (b) <u>gained</u>   (c) <u>gaining</u>   (d) giant   (e) general
16. collect   (a) <u>recollect</u>   (b) correct   (c) collar   (d) <u>collected</u>   (e) <u>collects</u>
17. honest   (a) <u>honestly</u>   (b) honey   (c) <u>dishonest</u>   (d) home   (e) hunt
18. spend   (a) <u>spent</u>   (b) <u>spending</u>   (c) spin   (d) <u>spends</u>   (e) spun
19. visit   (a) advise   (b) <u>visitor</u>   (c) <u>visited</u>   (d) vice   (e) <u>visits</u>
20. magic   (a) <u>magical</u>   (b) <u>magician</u>   (c) made   (d) make   (e) <u>magically</u>
21. rain   (a) <u>raining</u>   (b) <u>rained</u>   (c) reign   (d) <u>rains</u>   (e) rein
22. sleep   (a) sheep   (b) asleep   (c) <u>sleeps</u>   (d) sheet   (e) <u>sleeping</u>
23. worth   (a) <u>worthy</u>   (b) word   (c) <u>unworthy</u>   (d) <u>worthless</u>   (e) work
24. kind   (a) kite   (b) <u>unkind</u>   (c) <u>kindly</u>   (d) <u>kinder</u>   (e) kin
25. pay   (a) <u>repay</u>   (b) <u>paid</u>   (c) pale   (d) <u>paying</u>   (e) paper
26. build   (a) <u>building</u>   (b) big   (c) <u>rebuild</u>   (d) <u>builds</u>   (e) <u>built</u>
27. act   (a) <u>actor</u>   (b) ask   (c) apt   (d) <u>acting</u>   (e) <u>react</u>
28. friend   (a) <u>friendly</u>   (b) <u>unfriendly</u>   (c) afraid   (d) <u>friends</u>   (e) free
29. write   (a) right   (b) <u>rewrite</u>   (c) <u>written</u>   (d) wrong   (e) <u>writes</u>
30. long   (a) <u>longer</u>   (b) log   (c) <u>longest</u>   (d) lone   (e) longwise

Adding Prefixes

Prefixes are letters added to the beginnings of words. They have
definite meanings and change the meanings of the words to
which they are added.

EXAMPLES: Study the following list of prefixes and their meanings.

a.	inter-	between	h.	fore-	front	o.	mis-	wrong
b.	re-	again	i.	trans-	across	p.	post-	after
c.	sub-	under	j.	pre-	before	q.	non-	not
d.	bi-	two	k.	super-	above	r.	com-	with
e.	semi-	half	l.	dis-	opposite	s.	tri-	three
f.	intra-	within	m.	anti-	against	t.	ex-	out of
g.	ab-	away	n.	multi-	many	u.	auto-	self

 Using the list of prefixes, write the word described by each definition.

1. half a circle ____semi-____
2. front of head _____
3. within states _____
4. to work again _____
5. opposite of agree _____
6. across the Atlantic _____
7. to come between _____
8. against rust _____
9. to contend with another _____
10. soil under the surface soil _____
11. many syllables _____
12. not poisonous _____
13. three feet _____
14. before school _____
15. opposite of believer _____
16. to pay before due _____
17. to mix with another _____
18. front of the deck _____
19. against slavery _____
20. to build again _____

21. two wheels _____
22. between states _____
23. underwater _____
24. before the war _____
25. against communism _____
26. to carry away wrongfully _____
27. once in two months _____
28. opposite of honor _____
29. door leading out _____
30. hero above all others _____
31. story about oneself _____
32. not having a profit _____
33. to lead wrong _____
34. train under the ground _____
35. three times a week _____
36. to spell wrong _____
37. opposite of approve _____
38. across the border _____
39. to breathe out _____
40. half finished _____

COMPOSITION EXERCISE

Write a word beginning with each prefix listed in the examples.

1. _____
2. _____
3. _____
4. _____
5. _____
6. _____

8. _____
9. _____
10. _____
11. _____
12. _____
13. _____

15. _____
16. _____
17. _____
18. _____
19. _____
20. _____

Unit 117 cont'd

Prefixes

A prefix is added to the beginning of a word.

EXAMPLES: a. un + happy = **unhappy**
b. dis + obey = **disobey**

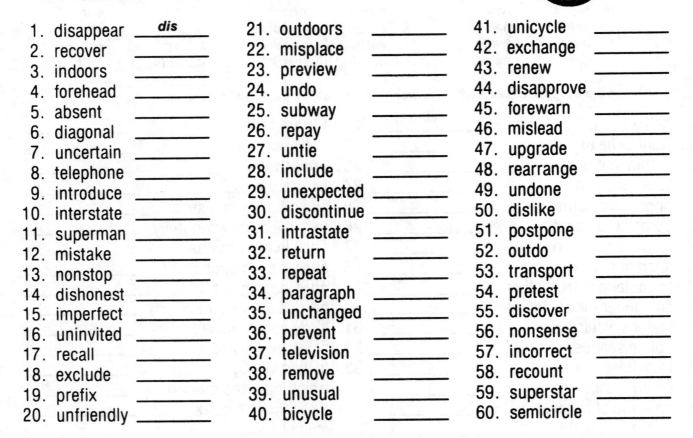

A Write the prefix of each word in the blank.

1. disappear __dis__	21. outdoors _____	41. unicycle _____
2. recover _____	22. misplace _____	42. exchange _____
3. indoors _____	23. preview _____	43. renew _____
4. forehead _____	24. undo _____	44. disapprove _____
5. absent _____	25. subway _____	45. forewarn _____
6. diagonal _____	26. repay _____	46. mislead _____
7. uncertain _____	27. untie _____	47. upgrade _____
8. telephone _____	28. include _____	48. rearrange _____
9. introduce _____	29. unexpected _____	49. undone _____
10. interstate _____	30. discontinue _____	50. dislike _____
11. superman _____	31. intrastate _____	51. postpone _____
12. mistake _____	32. return _____	52. outdo _____
13. nonstop _____	33. repeat _____	53. transport _____
14. dishonest _____	34. paragraph _____	54. pretest _____
15. imperfect _____	35. unchanged _____	55. discover _____
16. uninvited _____	36. prevent _____	56. nonsense _____
17. recall _____	37. television _____	57. incorrect _____
18. exclude _____	38. remove _____	58. recount _____
19. prefix _____	39. unusual _____	59. superstar _____
20. unfriendly _____	40. bicycle _____	60. semicircle _____

B Add a prefix to each word.

1. __pre__ view	11. ____ place	21. ____ trust	31. ____ cycle
2. ____ side	12. ____ look	22. ____ do	32. ____ marine
3. ____ equal	13. ____ cover	23. ____ finished	33. ____ healthy
4. ____ build	14. ____ plore	24. ____ work	34. ____ gram
5. ____ courage	15. ____ likely	25. ____ real	35. ____ nounce
6. ____ safe	16. ____ ample	26. ____ told	36. ____ covery
7. ____ break	17. ____ fair	27. ____ tire	37. ____ crease
8. ____ write	18. ____ aware	28. ____ agree	38. ____ easy
9. ____ use	19. ____ dress	29. ____ clude	39. ____ tract
10. ____ prove	20. ____ written	30. ____ decided	40. ____ load

Prefixes Signal Verbs

A All the verbs in this exercise were formed by the addition of a permanent verb prefix to a root word. Write the prefixes and the roots for each verb in the proper spaces. Follow the example.

		Prefix	Root
EXAMPLE:	rewrite	re	write

		Prefix	Root
1.	encircle	*en*	*circle*
2.	enact		
3.	enable		
4.	behold		
5.	begrudge		
6.	belabor		
7.	redecorate		
8.	rebound		
9.	rebuild		
10.	reappear		
11.	rework		
12.	refreeze		
13.	remix		
14.	rediscover		
15.	undress		
16.	untie		
17.	unzip		
18.	withdraw		
19.	withhold		
20.	withstand		

B Mark an "x" on the line next to each sentence that has a verb with a prefix.

__x__ 1. Lee withdraws her money from the bank.
_____ 2. Mom put the phone on the receiver.
_____ 3. A rebozo is a long scarf worn by Spanish women.
_____ 4. The company recalled all 1973 cars.
_____ 5. That baby has a lot of energy.
_____ 6. Mother mailed the letter.
_____ 7. I remade my bed.
_____ 8. The race car driver sighed in relief after the race.

Unit 118 cont'd

Verb Prefixes

Prefixes are letters added to the beginnings
of words. Each prefix has a definite meaning
and changes the meaning of the word to which
it is added.

Many verbs begin with prefixes. The most common
verb prefixes include "re," "dis," "con," "ex," and "de."
Notice the meaning of each prefix.

re-	repeat, again	con-	with
dis-	away from	ex-	out of, formerly
de-	away, down		

EXAMPLES: a. The teacher <u>dis</u>missed the class.
b. John <u>con</u>firmed my suspicions.
c. You <u>de</u>livered the wrong package.
d. I must <u>re</u>turn the call immediately.
e. We will <u>ex</u>plore the cave tomorrow.

 Complete each sentence by adding a prefix to the verb.
Choose from those prefixes listed in the box.

1. You must <u>con</u>trol your temper.
2. Janet ____clined the invitation.
3. No one was ____cused to go home.
4. Alex ____voted his time to studying.
5. Dad finally ____sented to let me go.
6. We ____cussed plans for the picnic.
7. The lawyer ____fended his client.
8. Jason was ____pelled from school.
9. Henry and I ____changed gifts.
10. He is an ____-president.
11. The country ____ports rice and wheat.
12. The ghost ____appeared.
13. We were ____layed at the airport.
14. The jewels were never ____covered.
15. Why did you ____ceive me?
16. She ____approves of my friends.
17. ____count the money.
18. You'll ____turb the next class.
19. Would you ____peat the statement?
20. The building was ____demned.

21. The army was ____feated.
22. ____nect wire "A" with wire "B."
23. The acid ____solved the tablet.
24. ____main calm in an emergency.
25. Pam ____plained the problem.
26. Columbus ____covered America.
27. ____sult a dictionary.
28. Adam ____hearsed his part in the play.
29. I ____agree with you.
30. The train will ____part at noon.
31. Allen ____assured us.
32. The building was ____molished.
33. Did you ____place the light bulb?
34. The bomb ____ploded.
35. The man was ____fronted by reporters.
36. Did you ____examine the contents?
37. I couldn't ____member his name.
38. ____tinue working on your assignment.
39. He ____considered his opinion.
40. ____write the sentence correctly.

The Prefix "un"

A prefix is added to the beginning of a word.
The letters "un" make a prefix.
"Un" means "not."

EXAMPLE: not lucky ➡ unlucky

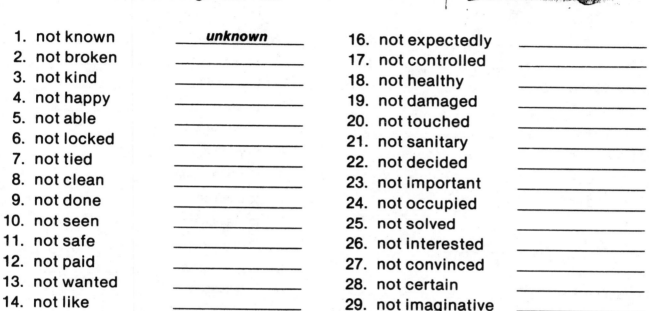

A Write the words which begin with "un."

1. not known	_**unknown**_	16. not expectedly	_____
2. not broken	_____	17. not controlled	_____
3. not kind	_____	18. not healthy	_____
4. not happy	_____	19. not damaged	_____
5. not able	_____	20. not touched	_____
6. not locked	_____	21. not sanitary	_____
7. not tied	_____	22. not decided	_____
8. not clean	_____	23. not important	_____
9. not done	_____	24. not occupied	_____
10. not seen	_____	25. not solved	_____
11. not safe	_____	26. not interested	_____
12. not paid	_____	27. not convinced	_____
13. not wanted	_____	28. not certain	_____
14. not like	_____	29. not imaginative	_____
15. not cooked	_____	30. not invited	_____

B Complete each sentence with a word from part A.

1. Read this and delete any ____**unimportant**____ facts.
2. I am _____ as to what I want to do on my vacation.
3. Bengie was _____ in Rudolph's speech on the sun.
4. The seat next to Mr. Rollins was _____.
5. That house is _____ any other house I've ever seen.
6. Although Rob was _____, he attended the party.
7. After sixty years the mystery is still _____.
8. Jerry was _____ with Janet's answer to the last question.
9. My dog Alfie _____ all our shoelaces.
10. Although the box had fallen from the train, its contents were _____.
11. The teacher was _____ to read the student's handwriting.
12. The door to Dr. Franklin's office was _____.

Unit 119 cont'd ➡

The Prefix "re"

A prefix is added to the beginning of a word.

The letters "re" make a prefix.

"Re" means "back" or "again."

EXAMPLES: to pay back ➜ repay
                to do again ➜ redo

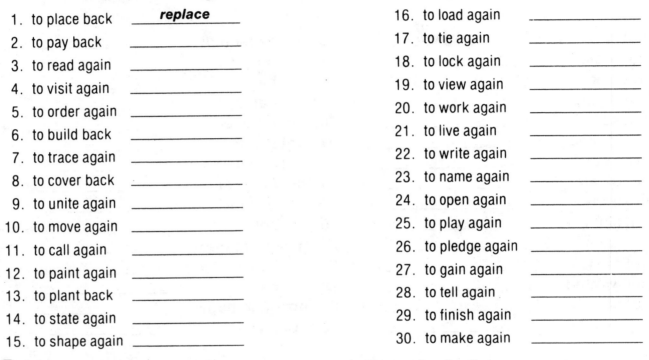

A Write the words which begin with "re."

1. to place back   ___replace___
2. to pay back   _____
3. to read again   _____
4. to visit again   _____
5. to order again   _____
6. to build back   _____
7. to trace again   _____
8. to cover back   _____
9. to unite again   _____
10. to move again   _____
11. to call again   _____
12. to paint again   _____
13. to plant back   _____
14. to state again   _____
15. to shape again   _____

16. to load again   _____
17. to tie again   _____
18. to lock again   _____
19. to view again   _____
20. to work again   _____
21. to live again   _____
22. to write again   _____
23. to name again   _____
24. to open again   _____
25. to play again   _____
26. to pledge again   _____
27. to gain again   _____
28. to tell again   _____
29. to finish again   _____
30. to make again   _____

B Complete each sentence with the word in the parentheses plus "re."

(arrange)   1. Jody began to ___rearrange___ the flowers.

(schedule)   2. We must _____ the meeting for next week.

(locate)   3. I am trying to _____ the shipment.

(charge)   4. You will have to _____ the batteries.

(examine)   5. The doctor wants to _____ the patient.

(phrase)   6. Let me _____ my question.

(grade)   7. Ms. Nest will _____ my essay tonight.

(estimate)   8. Will you _____ the cost of repair.

(claim)   9. Mr. Jamison came to _____ the package.

(word)   10. Try to _____ the sentence so its meaning is clear.

(capture)   11. The police will _____ the escaped prisoners.

(organize)   12. You need to _____ your report.

Suffixes

A suffix is added to the end of a word.

EXAMPLES: a. *assign + ment = assignment*
   b. *care + ful = careful*

A **Write the suffix of each word in the blank.**

1. rudeness **ness**	17. childhood _____	34. foolish _____
2. colorless _____	18. inward _____	35. dangerous _____
3. shameful _____	19. blinded _____	36. neighbors _____
4. friendly _____	20. narrower _____	37. building _____
5. worthy _____	21. happiness _____	38. insecticide _____
6. clearing _____	22. guards _____	39. fearless _____
7. roughest _____	23. penniless _____	40. suddenly _____
8. frighten _____	24. lawyer _____	41. expected _____
9. childish _____	25. careless _____	42. kindness _____
10. bashful _____	26. thicker _____	43. action _____
11. booklet _____	27. quietly _____	44. cowardly _____
12. lovable _____	28. easiest _____	45. peaceful _____
13. younger _____	29. hopeless _____	46. greediness _____
14. darkness _____	30. joyful _____	47. counting _____
15. dentist _____	31. owner _____	48. lucky _____
16. worthless _____	32. protection _____	49. tickets _____
	33. lonely _____	50. safely _____

B **Add a suffix to each word to make a new word.**

1. Add "ness" to "sad." **sadness**	13. Add "ful" to "forget." _____
2. Add "ly" to "different." _____	14. Add "er" to "farm." _____
3. Add "ment" to "govern." _____	15. Add "y" to "trick." _____
4. Add "er" to "new." _____	16. Add "s" to "monkey." _____
5. Add "ing" to "surround." _____	17. Add "ing" to "stand." _____
6. Add "hood" to "adult." _____	18. Add "es" to "match." _____
7. Add "ward" to "home." _____	19. Add "ment" to "state." _____
8. Add "less" to "use." _____	20. Add "ed" to "follow." _____
9. Add "y" to "greed." _____	21. Add "ish" to "green." _____
10. Add "ly" to "honest." _____	22. Add "ly" to "correct." _____
11. Add "ing" to "laugh." _____	23. Add "ing" to "sleep." _____
12. Add "s" to "license." _____	24. Add "es" to "branch." _____
	25. Add "ed" to "trust." _____

Unit 120 cont'd →

Suffixes Point to Nouns

Some suffixes form nouns.

EXAMPLES:
a.	*ment*	*government*	c.	*er*	*miner*	e.	*ist*	*scientist*
b.	*ness*	*kindness*	d.	*or*	*inventor*	f.	*al*	*arrival*

 Column 1 lists words that were formed by adding the suffixes in column 2. Draw a line from each word in column 1 to its suffix in column 2.

1	2
1. prominence	A. acy
2. supremacy	B. age
3. bakery	C. al
4. assistant	D. ance
5. actor	E. ence
6. worker	F. ant
7. direction	G. ard
8. survival	H. dom
9. breakage	I. er
10. drunkard	J. or
11. performance	K. ery
12. failure	L. hood
13. happiness	M. ure
14. kingdom	N. ion
15. brotherhood	O. ty
16. hardship	P. ism
17. management	Q. ment
18. cruelty	R. ness
19. health	S. ship
20. patriotism	T. th

290

Comprehension Check

Ⓐ Underline the base word of each derived word.

1. <u>gain</u>ed	11. unworthy	21. crossly
2. walking	12. uses	22. nights
3. talked	13. exchange	23. undo
4. untie	14. collects	24. safer
5. reunite	15. unwise	25. sitting
6. asked	16. actor	26. hurrying
7. friendly	17. builds	27. visitor
8. rebuild	18. repay	28. yours
9. longer	19. wishing	29. magically
10. turned	20. return	30. owned

Ⓑ Underline each word which has a prefix.

1. <u>dis</u>trust	11. unwilling	21. newer
2. trusting	12. preview	22. telegram
3. increase	13. unfriendly	23. tricycle
4. subtract	14. reason	24. suffix
5. adding	15. unsafe	25. nonsense
6. exclude	16. reheat	26. multiple
7. include	17. safely	27. unusual
8. redress	18. reload	28. usually
9. smarter	19. unload	29. foreground
10. teacher	20. loading	30. prefix

Ⓒ Match each prefix with its definition.

1. inter-	a. under
2. sub-	b. away
3. fore-	c. between
4. ab-	d. front
5. pre-	e. before
6. re-	f. opposite
7. com-	g. again
8. dis-	h. with
9. intra-	i. three
10. tri-	j. within
11. bi-	k. many
12. multi-	l. wrong
13. auto-	m. after
14. mis-	n. two
15. post-	o. self
16. ex-	p. out of
17. semi-	q. not
18. un-	r. across
19. trans-	s. not
20. non-	t. half
21. anti-	u. above
22. super-	v. against

Ⓓ Put a check (✓) beside each sentence which contains a word which has a prefix.

✓___ 1. The children learned to subtract.
___ 2. The country has a new government.
___ 3. Our puppy is unhappy.
___ 4. Uncle Bud is arriving soon.
___ 5. We saw a submarine.
___ 6. I planted the acorn here.
___ 7. The headline is misleading.
___ 8. That large truck travels intrastate.
___ 9. Is Myra's work finished?
___ 10. Rewrite your theme before lunch.
___ 11. We'll have to postpone the concert.
___ 12. There is a measles outbreak.
___ 13. We're using red and green tinsel.
___ 14. Will they rebuild the church?
___ 15. Mrs. Akers gave us a pretest.
___ 16. Eating too much sugar is unhealthy.
___ 17. What is an unwritten law?
___ 18. Don't discourage her efforts.
___ 19. Talking to you is useless!
___ 20. The kitten followed Eve home.
___ 21. Please untie the string for me.
___ 22. There was an increase in sales.
___ 23. Chris placed the boundary for us.
___ 24. Write three paragraphs about forests.

Test 24 cont'd ➡

Comprehension Check (continued)

Ⓔ Underline each word which has a suffix.

1. <u>shameful</u>	11. kingdom	21. restate
2. sadness	12. useful	22. incorrect
3. uncaring	13. useless	23. statement
4. careless	14. unmatched	24. adulthood
5. entrust	15. farmer	25. greedy
6. cruelty	16. unformed	26. honest
7. trusting	17. correctly	27. thicken
8. actor	18. greenish	28. joyful
9. react	19. mismanage	29. unusual
10. bakery	20. undoing	30. usually

Ⓕ Write the suffix of each word.

1. worthy	_y_	11. greenery	_____
2. careful	_____	12. patriotism	_____
3. homeward	_____	13. assistant	_____
4. useless	_____	14. accuracy	_____
5. bluish	_____	15. hardship	_____
6. talking	_____	16. churches	_____
7. monkeys	_____	17. childhood	_____
8. honestly	_____	18. lovable	_____
9. walked	_____	19. cleanest	_____
10. older	_____	20. homeless	_____

Ⓖ Write the base word and the prefix and/or suffix for each underlined word.

	base word	prefix	suffix
1. I heard Terri <u>laughing</u>.	_laugh_	_____	_ing_
2. The sunset was a <u>reddish</u> color.	_____	_____	_____
3. I <u>trusted</u> you!	_____	_____	_____
4. The business failed due to <u>mismanagement</u>.	_____	_____	_____
5. Craig jumped into the <u>swimming</u> pool.	_____	_____	_____
6. This is our <u>easiest</u> test.	_____	_____	_____
7. The sudden <u>darkness</u> was scary.	_____	_____	_____
8. Is Linda <u>unhappy</u> with the results?	_____	_____	_____
9. Jimmy <u>reorganized</u> his room.	_____	_____	_____
10. May we <u>review</u> our homework?	_____	_____	_____
11. The basketball <u>rebounded</u> into Ed's hands.	_____	_____	_____
12. Did you hear the <u>telephone</u>?	_____	_____	_____

Write a paragraph about a hard test you have taken. Underline each word which has either a prefix or a suffix.

_____

_____

_____

_____

_____

_____

_____

Suffixes for Words Ending in "e"

When words end in silent "e," we usually drop the "e" before adding a suffix which begins with a vowel.

   EXAMPLE: *bake + ing = baking*

When words end in silent "e," we usually keep the "e" when adding a suffix which begins with a consonant.

   EXAMPLE: *late + ly = lately*

A Add each word and suffix, and write the new word.

1. strange + er = _____*stranger*_____

2. surprise + ing = _____

3. promise + ed = _____

4. hate + ful = _____

5. fierce + ly = _____

6. please + ant _____

7. freeze + ing = _____

8. hike + ing = _____

9. notice + ed = _____

10. hope + less = _____

11. serve + ant = _____

12. state + ment = _____

13. choose + ing = _____

14. wave + ed = _____

15. wire + less = _____

16. escape + ing = _____

17. joke + er = _____

18. balance + ing = _____

19. love + ly = _____

20. rude + ness = _____

B Complete each sentence by writing the word in the parentheses plus a suffix.

(announce)   1. Dr. Adams will make the ___*announcement*___ today.

(estimate)   2. I _____ the amount of the damages.

(rule)   3. Measure the paper with a _____.

(postpone)   4. The meeting was _____ until Wednesday.

(increase)   5. The cost of living is _____.

(grade)   6. Ms. Booth had not _____ our science test.

(office)   7. The _____ are located on the sixth floor.

(recognize)   8. No one _____ me with my hair cut.

(safe)   9. Everyone made it home _____.

(charge)   10. The man was _____ with larceny.

Unit 122 cont'd ➡

Suffixes and the Final Silent "e"

A suffix is added to the end of a word.
When a word ends in a silent "e," drop the "e" before adding a suffix that begins with a vowel.
When a word ends in a silent "e," keep the "e" before adding a suffix that begins with a consonant.

EXAMPLES: care + ful   a. **Be careful when you cross the street.**
              hope + ed   b. **I had hoped to see him before he left.**
              bake + er   c. **My uncle is a baker.**
              hike + ing. d. **I enjoy hiking in the woods.**

   Complete each sentence by adding the word plus the suffix.

1. use + less
   It would be _____useless_____ to try again.
2. dance + ing
   _____ is very good exercise.
3. invite + ed
   Everyone is _____ to attend.
4. write + er
   Hemingway is my favorite _____.
5. argue + ment
   Let's not have an _____.
6. love + ly
   Everything looks _____.
7. home + ward
   This plane is _____ bound.
8. escape + ed
   Two prisoners have _____.
9. office + s
   All of the _____ are locked.
10. value + able
    Diamonds are _____.
11. safe + ly
    The plane landed _____.
12. peace + ful
    The winds were calm and _____.
13. minute + s
    It will take only a few _____.

14. joke + s
    His _____ are never funny.
15. grade + ed
    Mrs. Morris has _____ our papers.
16. wise + est
    She is the _____ woman I know.
17. change + ing
    Stop _____ your mind.
18. hide + en
    The money was _____ in the cave.
19. dive + er
    The _____ hurt his hand.
20. believe + ed
    No one _____ her.
21. late + er
    I'll see you _____.
22. announce + ment
    Mr. Aldon has an_____.
23. persuade + ed
    Rick _____ Ken to go.
24. polite + ly
    Thomas excused himself _____.
25. imagine + ation
    Paul has an excellent _____.
26. leave + ing
    Diane is _____ for Boston.

Suffixes and the Final "y"

A suffix is added to the end of a word.

When a word ends in a consonant plus "y," change the "y" to "i" before adding a suffix unless the suffix begins with "i."

When a word ends in a vowel plus "y," keep the "y" and add the suffix.

EXAMPLES: a. fry + ing = frying c. lazy + ly = lazily
  b. stay + ed = staying d. day + s = days

A Add each word and the suffix, and write the new word.

1. play + ing   *playing*
2. easy + ly   _____
3. monkey + s   _____
4. beauty + ful   _____
5. study + ed   _____
6. funny + est   _____
7. marry + ed   _____
8. way + s   _____

9. dry + ed   _____
10. obey + s   _____
11. carry + ed   _____
12. try + ing   _____
13. happy + est   _____
14. key + s   _____
15. sky + es   _____
16. say + ing   _____

17. busy + er   _____
18. story + es   _____
19. turkey + s   _____
20. angry + er   _____
21. family + es   _____
22. party + es   _____
23. buy + ing   _____
24. occupy + ed   _____

B Complete each sentence by adding the word plus the suffix in the parentheses.

1. (disobey + ed)
You have ___*disobeyed*___ my orders.
2. (dry + ing)
Brad is _____ the dishes.
3. (study + ing)
We are _____ for our math test.
4. (lovely + er)
Today was _____ than yesterday.
5. (delay + ed)
The train was _____ for two hours.
6. (hurry + ed)
Everyone _____ to see the ship.
7. (fry + ed)
Nick ordered _____ fish.
8. (lazy + est)
Luther is the _____ dog of all.

9. (silly + est)
That's the _____ story I've ever heard.
10. (try + ed)
We _____ to warn you.
11. (marry + ed)
My sister _____ an actor.
12. (cry + ing)
Why are you _____?
13. (play + s)
Quincy _____ the piano.
14. (happy + er)
Steve has never looked _____.
15. (penny + es)
I counted thirty-six _____.
16. (pretty + er)
Kelly is _____ than Karen.

Unit 123 cont'd

Words Ending in a Consonant Plus "y"

How do you add a suffix which begins with "i" to a word which ends with a consonant plus "y"?

You simply add the suffix to the word.

     EXAMPLE: study + ing = studying

How do you add a suffix which begins with any letter but "i" to a word which ends with a consonant plus "y"?

You change the "y" to "i" and add the suffix.

     EXAMPLE: study + ed = studied

    Add each word and suffix, and write the new word.

1. apply + ing =   *applying*
2. funny + er =   _____
3. gloomy + ly =   _____
4. pry + ing =   _____
5. pity + ful =   _____
6. envy + ous =   _____
7. carry + ing =   _____
8. happy + ness = _____
9. study + ing =   _____
10. bury + ing =   _____
11. apply + ed =   _____
12. fly + ing =   _____
13. weary + ly =   _____
14. busy + ly =   _____
15. ordinary + ly = _____
16. identify + ing = _____
17. marry + ed =   _____
18. cry + ed =   _____
19. luxury + ous = _____
20. dry + ing = _____
21. vary + ous =   _____
22. imply + ing =   _____
23. pretty + est = _____

24. lazy + ness =   _____
25. justify + ed =   _____
26. hurry + ing =   _____
27. penny + less =   _____
28. clumsy + ly =   _____
29. plenty + ful =   _____
30. worry + ed =   _____
31. angry + ly =   _____
32. carry + ed =   _____
33. drowsy + ness = _____
34. silly + est =   _____
35. lonely + ness = _____
36. duty + ful =   _____
37. try + ed =   _____
38. greedy + ly =   _____
39. ready + ness =   _____
40. cozy + ness =   _____
41. heavy + est =   _____
42. fancy + ful =   _____
43. necessary + ly = _____
44. fry + ing =   _____
45. merry + ly =   _____
46. empty + ness =   _____

Doubling Final Consonants

When a word ends in a short vowel followed by a consonant, double the consonant before adding a suffix which begins with a vowel.

EXAMPLE: chop + ed = chopped

A Add the suffix "ed" to each word.

1. plan ___*planned*___	6. stop _____	11. plot _____
2. beg _____	7. hop _____	12. slip _____
3. pop _____	8. grab _____	13. map _____
4. trip _____	9. pin _____	14. fit _____
5. rip _____	10. drop _____	15. cap _____

B Add the suffix "ing" to each word.

1. stir ___*stirring*___	6. spin _____	11. put _____
2. cut _____	7. run _____	12. dig _____
3. stop _____	8. get _____	13. quit _____
4. shut _____	9. win _____	14. beg _____
5. plan _____	10. sit _____	15. let _____

C Complete each sentence by writing the word in the parentheses plus a suffix.

(permit)   1. No one was ___*permitted*___ to speak during the film.

(occur)   2. The accident _____ at seven o'clock.

(prefer)   3. My mother _____ the green one.

(scan)   4. I _____ the story hurriedly.

(commit)   5. Betsy had never _____ a crime.

(regret)   6. I am _____ what I said to you yesterday.

(submit)   7. The paper was _____ by an anonymous writer.

(refer)   8. Are you _____ to the article on page six?

(wrap)   9. The package was _____ in orange paper.

(trim)   10. We _____ the tree with popcorn and berries.

(stir)   11. Jason was _____ the soup with a wooden spoon.

(admit)   12. The man has _____ to stealing the money.

Unit 124 cont'd

Final Consonants

A suffix is added to the end of a word.

To add a suffix to a one-syllable word that ends in a single consonant after a single vowel, double the final consonant before adding a suffix that begins with a vowel.

EXAMPLE: a. stop   stopped   stopping
            b. pick   picked   picking

A Add "ed," and "ing," to each word.

1. chin	_chinned_	_chinning_		16. chop	_____	_____
2. ask	_____	_____		17. wash	_____	_____
3. dip	_____	_____		18. call	_____	_____
4. sign	_____	_____		19. clear	_____	_____
5. pop	_____	_____		20. can	_____	_____
6. pin	_____	_____		21. jump	_____	_____
7. beg	_____	_____		22. wrap	_____	_____
8. rob	_____	_____		23. train	_____	_____
9. end	_____	_____		24. want	_____	_____
10. hug	_____	_____		25. rip	_____	_____
11. hop	_____	_____		26. ship	_____	_____
12. rain	_____	_____		27. grab	_____	_____
13. burn	_____	_____		28. spell	_____	_____
14. look	_____	_____		29. tag	_____	_____
15. step	_____	_____		30. obey	_____	_____

B Complete each sentence by adding either "ed" or "ing" to the word in parentheses.

(let) 1. You're ___letting___ him get away.

(trip) 2. I _____ on the rug.

(begin) 3. It is _____ to snow.

(work) 4. Ellen is _____ on her paper.

(swim) 5. Fran is _____ across the lake.

(wish) 6. Everyone _____ them luck.

(map) 7. We _____ our course carefully.

(chip) 8. All the dishes were _____.

(learn) 9. I'm _____ French.

(push) 10. Who _____ the button?

(plan) 11. The class _____ the picnic.

(put) 12. He is _____ it in the garage.

(watch) 13. No one is _____ the game.

(rip) 14. You _____ my paper.

(eat) 15. I am _____ my lunch.

(flip) 16. We _____ a coin.

(bet) 17. Ben is _____ that we'll lose.

(regret) 18. He _____ his decision.

(hum) 19. Carl was _____ a sad song.

(rub) 20. Ann was _____ her arm.

COMPOSITION EXERCISE

Choose 10 verbs from part A. Write a sentence with each.

1. _____
2. _____
3. _____
4. _____
5. _____

6. _____
7. _____
8. _____
9. _____
10. _____

Recognizing Synonyms

Synonyms are words with similar meanings.

EXAMPLES:
a. worth   value
b. enjoy   like
c. gather   collect

A Draw a line to connect each set of synonyms.

1. amend	daybreak	11. night	frequently
2. start	help	12. result	evening
3. aid	change	13. novel	end
4. wrong	begin	14. often	book
5. drawn	incorrect	15. absent	away
6. unclean	behind	16. woman	lady
7. after	quiet	17. sound	desire
8. cause	come	18. angry	mad
9. arrive	dirty	19. wish	present
10. silent	reason	20. gift	noise

B Match the synonyms.

_d_ 1. center	___ 16. careful	a. clear	p. cautious
___ 2. distinct	___ 17. echo	b. thin	q. comfortable
___ 3. slender	___ 18. conclusion	c. persuade	r. visitor
___ 4. cozy	___ 19. guest	d. middle	s. clumsy
___ 5. cruel	___ 20. forward	e. increase	t. quilt
___ 6. smear	___ 21. freedom	f. slogan	u. repeat
___ 7. convince	___ 22. gain	g. liberty	v. reason
___ 8. awkward	___ 23. blanket	h. vacation	w. pretty
___ 9. drenched	___ 24. quit	i. untrue	x. cunning
___ 10. false	___ 25. purpose	j. stop	y. needed
___ 11. perish	___ 26. necessary	k. unkind	z. smudge
___ 12. shrewd	___ 27. motto	l. ending	A. permit
___ 13. cute	___ 28. license	m. die	B. courteous
___ 14. polite	___ 29. hurry	n. ahead	C. perhaps
___ 15. maybe	___ 30. holiday	o. soaked	D. rush

Unit 125 cont'd

Words with Similar Meanings

Synonyms are words that have similar meanings.

EXAMPLES: a. wet   damp
            b. small   little
            c. cool   chilly

A Write a synonym for each word.

1. vacant	_empty_	9. plead	_____	17. peaceful	_____
2. hope	_____	10. alike	_____	18. legal	_____
3. believe	_____	11. near	_____	19. honest	_____
4. novice	_____	12. rule	_____	20. pace	_____
5. double	_____	13. root	_____	21. ill	_____
6. happy	_____	14. easy	_____	22. cut	_____
7. discover	_____	15. autumn	_____	23. insect	_____
8. wrestle	_____	16. scare	_____	24. road	_____

B In each pair of sentences underline the set of synonyms.

1. We must <u>stop</u> Nick from leaving. You must <u>prevent</u> it.
2. The Tigers were the champions. The victors won a trophy.
3. Thomas chose the one on the left. Eric picked the green one.
4. The man finally confessed. George admitted stealing the money.
5. I will try harder next time. I will attempt to do better next time.
6. That is a terrific idea. I have a marvelous idea.
7. The baby was crying. The mother rocked the infant.
8. Will you open the door for me? Please unlock the door.
9. He was a brave man. She was a courageous fighter.
10. Don't forget to take a coat. Wear a jacket if it's cold outside.
11. I had a nightmare last night. I had a dream about snakes.
12. How did you unravel the mystery? Can you solve the riddle?
13. You mustn't be so rude. He is never impolite.
14. The gems are in the safe. The jewels are safe.
15. Jean was aware of the changes. She was alert to any change.
16. Al suggested I talk to Don. I advise you to wait.
17. The battle had just begun. The fight began.
18. Give her one more chance. You have the opportunity of a lifetime.

Comprehension Check

Ⓐ Complete each sentence with the verb in the parentheses plus a suffix.

(cook)   1. Mom is __*cooking*__ chicken soup.

(walk)   2. We _____ all over town.

(read)   3. James _____ everything.

(need)   4. The people _____ food.

(want)   5. I _____ to help them.

(drive) 6. Ted has never _____ a bus.

(move)   7. The Smiths are _____ to Dallas.

(hope)   8. Marcie _____ to finish soon.

(talk)   9. Who is _____ to Sam?

(look) 10. It _____ like an eagle.

(count) 11. Carl _____ the money.

(sink) 12. The boat was _____ quickly.

(stop) 13. No one _____ for us.

(end)   14. The movie _____ too abruptly.

(make) 15. Bob _____ good grades.

(paint) 16. Who _____ the chair orange?

(open) 17. Estelle _____ the door.

(help) 18. You _____ me.

(live) 19. Mr. Martin _____ there.

(use)   20. It _____ unleaded gas.

(park) 21. He _____ the car.

(know) 22. Sandra _____ the number.

(smell) 23. Your shirt _____ fishy.

(hide) 24. It was _____ under the bed.

(drop) 25. Jill _____ her books.

(wait) 26. Ann was _____ for Gilbert.

(sell) 27. My uncle _____ used cars.

(wish) 28. Cameron _____ for a bike.

(crush) 29. Dave _____ my hat.

(have) 30. Are you _____ a good time?

Ⓑ Add each word and suffix and write the new word.

1. write + en   __*written*__
2. say + ing   _____
3. care + ful   _____
4. seat + ed   _____
5. smile + s   _____
6. soon + er   _____
7. kind + ness   _____
8. sugar + less _____
9. music + al   _____
10. ride + ing   _____
11. close + est   _____
12. hope + less   _____
13. child + hood _____
14. fly + s   _____
15. sing + er   _____
16. walk + ed   _____
17. box + es   _____
18. quick + ly   _____
19. run + ing   _____
20. gold + en   _____

Ⓒ Which of these words would drop the final silent "e" when adding the suffix "-ing"? Underline them.

1. <u>note</u>
2. save
3. rule
4. fade
5. use
6. hide
7. imitate
8. trade
9. write
10. drive
11. make
12. live
13. bathe
14. have
15. believe
16. operate

Ⓓ Add "-ed" to each of these words that end in "y."

1. stay   __*stayed*__
2. fry   _____
3. copy   _____
4. pray   _____
5. try   _____
6. hurry _____
7. stray _____
8. carry _____
9. cry   _____
10. pry   _____
11. marry _____
12. bray _____
13. bury _____
14. prey _____
15. candy _____
16. display _____

Test 25 cont'd ⟶

Comprehension Check (continued)

E) Place a check (✓) beside each pair of words that are synonyms.

✓ 1. fold ... bend
____ 2. path ... trail
____ 3. importance ... worth
____ 4. question ... answer
____ 5. note ... letter
____ 6. recipe ... instructions
____ 7. rob ... steal
____ 8. quiet ... noisy
____ 9. paw ... foot
____ 10. sweet ... sour
____ 11. study ... sleep
____ 12. holiday ... vacation
____ 13. buzz ... hum
____ 14. hint ... suggest
____ 15. passenger ... rider

____ 16. popular ... unknown
____ 17. wrong ... incorrect
____ 18. knit ... weave
____ 19. darkness ... lightness
____ 20. land ... earth
____ 21. fearless ... helpful
____ 22. object ... thing
____ 23. package ... parcel
____ 24. relax ... rest
____ 25. poor ... penniless
____ 26. cost ... price
____ 27. rough ... rugged
____ 28. needed ... wanted
____ 29. slumber ... sleep
____ 30. tour ... journey

F) Complete each sentence with a synonym of the word in the parentheses.

(topic) 1. What is the __*subject*__ of your theme?

(shore) 2. His house is on the _____ .

(false) 3. Your story is _____ .

(stop) 4. The captain shouted, " _____ !"

(wetness) 5. The plant needs _____ .

(practice) 6. Play _____ is at three.

(hurried) 7. Everyone _____ out.

(meal) 8. _____ was delicious.

(journey) 9. We took a _____ to Paris.

(changed) 10. The plan had been _____ .

(work) 11. I want a _____ at Anderson's.

(faith) 12. Do you _____ my judgment?

(remedy) 13. Is there a _____ for diabetes?

(note) 14. I will leave a _____ for Tina.

(chums) 15. We have been _____ for years.

(annually) 16. The race is a _____ event.

(freedom) 17. "Give me _____ , or give me death."

(sent) 18. I _____ the invitations yesterday.

(scared) 19. Brad was _____ of the snake.

(silent) 20. "Be _____ ," she whispered.

Write a paragraph about your best friend. Underline all synonyms you use for the word "friend."

_____
_____
_____
_____
_____
_____
_____
_____
_____

Synonyms

Synonyms are words with similar meanings.

EXAMPLES: a. hit   swat   c. halt   stop
           b. wet   moist   d. clue   hint

A Matching

_c_	1. blanket	a. lucky
____	2. cause	b. always
____	3. discover	c. quilt
____	4. twelve	d. dozen
____	5. honest	e. prohibit
____	6. rush	f. unusual
____	7. forever	g. shield
____	8. freedom	h. simple
____	9. separate	i. find
____	10. nonsense	j. exact
____	11. protect	k. silliness
____	12. strange	l. ask
____	13. forbid	m. split
____	14. vanish	n. reason
____	15. identify	o. truthful
____	16. consult	p. recognize
____	17. advice	q. victory
____	18. precise	r. part
____	19. damage	s. ship
____	20. balance	t. liberty
____	21. triumph	u. hurry
____	22. silent	v. polite
____	23. section	w. quiet
____	24. cozy	x. hurt
____	25. ought	y. disappear
____	26. courteous	z. suggestion
____	27. yacht	A. comfortable
____	28. fortunate	B. back
____	29. rear	C. equal
____	30. easy	D. should

B Complete each sentence with a synonym of the word in the parentheses.

(permit) 1. Will you ___*allow*___ me to explain?

(chance) 2. It is an excellent _____.

(huge) 3. The whale is _____.

(trip) 4. The _____ lasted four months.

(possess) 5. Does he _____ the store?

(stop) 6. _____ chewing your fingernails!

(error) 7. It was my _____.

(comprehend) 8. I cannot _____ why.

(pest) 9. That dog is becoming a _____.

(vacant) 10. The building was _____.

(combine) 11. _____ yellow and blue.

(delayed) 12. The meeting will be _____.

(perfect) 13. The diamond was _____.

(pretended) 14. Al _____ he saw a ghost.

(sure) 15. We must be _____ of it.

(rude) 16. There was no reason to be _____.

(purchase) 17. What did you _____?

(remedy) 18. I know the perfect _____.

(assist) 19. Why won't you let me _____ you?

(fake) 20. This money is _____.

(lawyer) 21. Mr. Andrews is my dad's _____.

(tan) 22. My new coat is _____ and black.

(evidence) 23. We have no _____.

(jail) 24. The man was sent to _____.

(frighten) 25. You are trying to _____ me.

(sketch) 26. I'll _____ you a map.

(scheme) 27. Listen to my _____.

(frequently) 28. Do you come here _____?

(sad) 29. The small child looked _____.

(hungry) 30. Some people in the world are _____.

Unit 126 cont'd

Using Synonyms

Synonyms are words that have similar meanings.

EXAMPLES:
a. shy — bashful
b. hike — walk
c. rude — impolite

A Draw a line to connect each set of synonyms.

1. marvelous	stay	11. enormous	tell
2. labor	wonderful	12. recount	wander
3. bewilder	confuse	13. locate	find
4. remain	work	14. roam	obey
5. secure	hint	15. separate	gigantic
6. section	part	16. follow	sleepy
7. always	blunder	17. stupid	apart
8. clue	forever	18. journey	limb
9. mistake	safe	19. branch	trip
10. carry	transport	20. drowsy	dumb

B Complete each sentence with a synonym of the word in the parentheses.

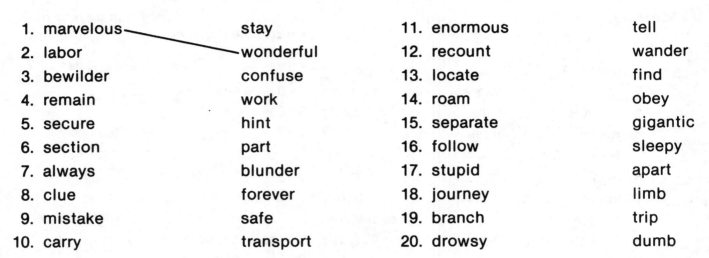

(delay) 1. We must ____postpone____ the game until Thursday.

(paused) 2. John _____ before entering the room.

(nuisance) 3. Kim's dog Alfie is a _____.

(glimpse) 4. I got a quick _____ at the President.

(important) 5. This letter contains a _____ clue.

(remember) 6. I don't _____ the man's name.

(greeted) 7. Ed stood at the door and _____ his guests.

(disappeared) 8. The ghost _____ before our eyes.

(smart) 9. Tina is an _____ girl.

(show) 10. We saw a _____ about World War II.

(perfect) 11. The diamond is _____.

(fake) 12. This money is _____.

(shy) 13. Jim was too _____ to ask her.

(pretend) 14. _____ you are on a deserted island.

(lost) 15. I have _____ my watch.

Recognizing Antonyms

Antonyms are words that have opposite meanings.

EXAMPLES: a. down   up
            b. here   there
            c. yes   no

A Draw a line to connect each set of antonyms.

1. better	last	11. sure	tame
2. first	ill	12. before	uncertain
3. strong	worse	13. wild	rich
4. healthy	sell	14. raise	after
5. buy	weak	15. poor	lower
6. now	cry	16. night	short
7. front	later	17. wide	day
8. laugh	cooked	18. dark	few
9. raw	thin	19. long	narrow
10. thick	back	20. many	light

B Match the antonyms.

_e_ 1. question	___ 16. content	a. dissatisfied	p. defend
___ 2. excellent	___ 17. interesting	b. discourage	q. withdraw
___ 3. normal	___ 18. seldom	c. safe	r. rejoice
___ 4. mourn	___ 19. asleep	d. falsehood	s. later
___ 5. remember	___ 20. truth	e. answer	t. rigid
___ 6. straight	___ 21. attack	f. lenient	u. crooked
___ 7. urge	___ 22. forbid	g. allow	v. dusk
___ 8. useful	___ 23. giant	h. abnormal	w. similar
___ 9. strict	___ 24. dawn	i. awake	x. contract
___ 10. different	___ 25. fearless	j. terrible	y. frequently
___ 11. advance	___ 26. inside	k. outside	z. simple
___ 12. flexible	___ 27. complex	l. backward	A. boring
___ 13. dangerous	___ 28. arrive	m. forget	B. depart
___ 14. expand	___ 29. sooner	n. cowardly	C. include
___ 15. forward	___ 30. exclude	o. dwarf	D. useless

Unit 127 cont'd ➔

Words with Opposite Meanings

Antonyms are words that have opposite meanings.

> EXAMPLES: a. *hot*   *cold*
> b. *wet*   *dry*
> c. *loud*   *soft*

A Write an antonym for each word.

1. more ____less____
2. learn _____
3. none _____
4. north _____
5. down _____
6. work _____
7. fresh _____
8. guest _____

9. spring _____
10. will _____
11. give _____
12. warm _____
13. sharp _____
14. open _____
15. active _____
16. fat _____

17. worried _____
18. empty _____
19. good _____
20. push _____
21. then _____
22. sweet _____
23. off _____
24. heavy _____

B In each sentence underline the set of antonyms.

1. These shoes are very <u>comfortable</u>. The boots felt <u>uncomfortable</u>.
2. Jim will distribute the papers. I will collect them tomorrow.
3. We support the amendment. Carl will protest the decision.
4. It is difficult to study in the lunchroom. The work was easy.
5. Ted carefully packed the glasses. He answered the question carelessly.
6. I forbid you to go. I cannot allow him to enter.
7. Our plans are definite. Chris is uncertain whether she will go.
8. No one saw us leave. Everyone waited patiently.
9. Betty was satisfied with the job. His discontent is obvious.
10. Their attempt ended in failure. The play proved a success.
11. Mark is our leader. We are his followers.
12. Dave has a high temperature. The price is in the low sixties.
13. Ms. Lewis arrived early. Don't be late for the party.
14. Summer is my favorite season. It is cold during the winter.
15. We have a problem. We must find a solution.
16. Samuel always finishes first. I never win.
17. The introduction was interesting. The conclusion was too long.
18. Several students were absent. I knew a few answers.
19. Ben admitted his guilt. Allen denied the charges.
20. I think he is innocent. Dennis thinks he is guilty.

Antonyms

Unit 128

Antonyms are words that have opposite meanings.

EXAMPLES: a. freeze melt   c. peace war
           b. most least   d. true false

A Matching

__g__	1. greedy	a.	forbid
____	2. absent	b.	proud
____	3. allow	c.	unusual
____	4. host	d.	guest
____	5. prefix	e.	simple
____	6. ashamed	f.	shout
____	7. forward	g.	generous
____	8. include	h.	strong
____	9. impossible	i.	normal
____	10. borrow	j.	often
____	11. punish	k.	suffix
____	12. seldom	l.	weakness
____	13. occupied	m.	applaud
____	14. patient	n.	light
____	15. boo	o.	present
____	16. smooth	p.	backward
____	17. subtract	q.	add
____	18. whisper	r.	reward
____	19. succeed	s.	loan
____	20. heavy	t.	fail
____	21. ordinary	u.	slave
____	22. awkward	v.	rough
____	23. remember	w.	forget
____	24. abnormal	x.	graceful
____	25. difficult	y.	vacant
____	26. fragile	z.	disorganize
____	27. organize	A.	possible
____	28. master	B.	happiness
____	29. sorrow	C.	omit
____	30. strength	D.	impatient

B Complete each sentence with an antonym of the word in the parentheses.

(toward) 1. The dog ran ___*away*___ from us.

(safe) 2. It is a _____ mission.

(adult) 3. The painting was done by a _____.

(careless) 4. Please be _____.

(enormous) 5. The flea is a _____ animal.

(cause) 6. What was the _____?

(escaped) 7. The prisoner was _____.

(specific) 8. Your outline is too _____.

(laugh) 9. The movie made me _____.

(modern) 10. My mother is very _____ .

(valuable) 11. This stone is _____.

(aged) 12. Mr. Sanders is a _____ man.

(appear) 13. The ghost will _____ if you talk.

(conquered) 14. The islanders _____.

(rude) 15. Joanne is always _____.

(flawed) 16. The diamond is _____.

(frown) 17. _____ for the camera.

(plural) 18. ''_____'' means ''one.''

(interesting) 19. His speech was _____.

(cheap) 20. She owns an _____ car.

(friend) 21. This man is our _____.

(doubt) 22. I _____ his judgment.

(different) 23. These two are _____.

(cruel) 24. Be _____ to the animals.

(beginning) 25. The _____ was surprising.

(won) 26. We _____ the tournament.

(summer) 27. _____ is the coldest season.

(stale) 28. Have a _____ donut.

(worse) 29. I've never had a _____ time.

(open) 30. The store is _____.

Unit 128 cont'd

Using Antonyms

Antonyms are words that have opposite meanings.

    EXAMPLES: a. **grow**   **shrink**
                  b. **left**   **right**
                  c. **true**   **false**

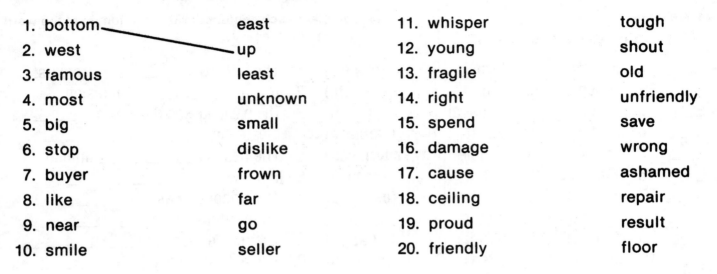

A Draw a line to connect each set of antonyms.

1. bottom	east	11. whisper	tough
2. west	up	12. young	shout
3. famous	least	13. fragile	old
4. most	unknown	14. right	unfriendly
5. big	small	15. spend	save
6. stop	dislike	16. damage	wrong
7. buyer	frown	17. cause	ashamed
8. like	far	18. ceiling	repair
9. near	go	19. proud	result
10. smile	seller	20. friendly	floor

B Complete each sentence with an antonym of the word in parentheses.

(allowed)   1. We were ___*forbidden*___ to speak to anyone.

(increased)   2. The funds were _____ by five per cent.

(vanished)   3. Suddenly three ghosts _____.

(legal)   4. Selling drugs is _____.

(greedy)   5. Dr. Price made a very _____ contribution.

(luxury)   6. Unfortunately, buying a car is a _____.

(discourage) 7. We must _____ him to do better.

(often)   8. Joey _____ has his assignment.

(penalty)   9. There is a _____ for hard work.

(question)   10. What is his _____?

(valuable)   11. All of these stones are _____.

(contrast)   12. _____ these with the ones on the table.

(safe)   13. That bridge looks too _____ to cross.

(smooth)   14. The surface of the sidewalk is very _____.

(singular)   15. Most _____ words end in "s."

Synonyms and Antonyms

Synonyms are words with similar meanings.

EXAMPLES: a. car   vehicle
           b. shirt   blouse

Antonyms are words with opposite meanings.

EXAMPLES: a. hate   love
           b. cold   hot

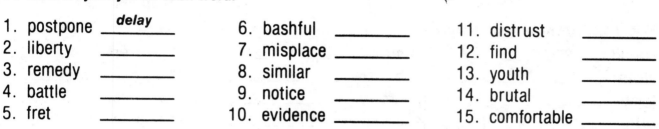

A Write a synonym for each word.

1. postpone _delay_
2. liberty _____
3. remedy _____
4. battle _____
5. fret _____

6. bashful _____
7. misplace _____
8. similar _____
9. notice _____
10. evidence _____

11. distrust _____
12. find _____
13. youth _____
14. brutal _____
15. comfortable _____

B Write an antonym for each word.

1. follower _leader_
2. agree _____
3. complete _____
4. borrow _____
5. able _____

6. defeat _____
7. equal _____
8. future _____
9. chaos _____
10. different _____

11. always _____
12. innocent _____
13. shrink _____
14. enter _____
15. smile _____

C Write 1 if the set of words is synonyms. Write 2 if the set of words is antonyms.

_1_ 1. obstinate   stubborn
____ 2. problem   solution
____ 3. importance   value
____ 4. tomorrow   yesterday
____ 5. recall   remember
____ 6. addition   subtraction
____ 7. combine   join
____ 8. amusement   entertainment
____ 9. organized   disorganized
____ 10. counterfeit   real

____ 11. blunder   mistake
____ 12. expensive   cheap
____ 13. create   destroy
____ 14. cautious   careful
____ 15. penalty   punishment
____ 16. thirst   quench
____ 17. united   together
____ 18. forgive   pardon
____ 19. satisfactory unsatisfactory
____ 20. vanish   disappear

Unit 129 cont'd

Distinguishing Between
Antonyms and Synonyms

Antonyms are words with opposite meanings.
  EXAMPLES: a. win   lose
              b. over   under

Synonyms are words with similar meanings.
  EXAMPLES: a. sack   bag
              b. invite ask

A **Write an antonym for each word.**

1. friend ___*enemy*___
2. victor _____
3. birth _____
4. offer _____
5. inner _____

6. short _____
7. borrow _____
8. pretty _____
9. soft _____
10. funny _____

11. even _____
12. real _____
13. finish _____
14. gain _____
15. love _____

B **Write a synonym for each word.**

1. build ___*construct*___
2. agenda _____
3. foolish _____
4. enough _____
5. found _____

6. suggestion _____
7. place _____
8. nearly _____
9. hurt _____
10. jump _____

11. rival _____
12. paint _____
13. pledge _____
14. fast _____
15. organization _____

C **Write "a" for antonyms and "s" for synonyms.**

___*a*___ 1. vacant   occupied
_____ 2. own   possess
_____ 3. visible   invisible
_____ 4. happiness   pleasure
_____ 5. familiar   unknown
_____ 6. wisdom   knowledge
_____ 7. needless   necessary
_____ 8. nobody   everybody
_____ 9. history   past
_____ 10. fragment   part
_____ 11. presently   today
_____ 12. worn   new

_____ 13. precise   exact
_____ 14. inform   tell
_____ 15. shy   bold
_____ 16. foreign   unknown
_____ 17. surprising   expected
_____ 18. pardon   excuse
_____ 19. steady   shakey
_____ 20. welcome   unwanted
_____ 21. outline   plan
_____ 22. ruin   destroy
_____ 23. male   man
_____ 24. useful   useless

Homonyms

Homonyms are words that sound alike.

> **EXAMPLES:** a. read   red
> b. see   sea
> c. bow   bough

 Underline the correct sentences.

0. whole . . . hole
   a. Dig the _**hole**_ here.
   b. I ate the _**whole**_ thing!

1. aloud . . . allowed
   a. Read the poem _____.
   b. We were not _____ to talk.

2. course . . . coarse
   a. This material feels _____.
   b. What _____ do you plan to take?

3. thrown . . . throne
   a. The king sat on his _____.
   b. He was _____ into the pool.

4. root . . . route
   a. Don't touch the _____ of the plant.
   b. What _____ should we take home?

5. urn . . . earn
   a. You broke the _____.
   b. I will _____ the money.

6. sail . . . sale
   a. The store is having a _____.
   b. The ship will _____ tomorrow.

7. flee . . . flea
   a. He tried to _____.
   b. I saw a _____.

8. minor . . . miner
   a. He is a coal _____.
   b. The repairs were _____.

9. dough . . . doe
   a. A _____ is a female deer.
   b. I watched the _____ rise.

10. wave . . . waive
    a. _____ good-bye.
    b. He will _____ the charges.

11. eye . . . aye
    a. If you agree, say _____.
    b. She has a black _____.

12. their . . . there
    a. They have _____ own cars.
    b. They live over _____.

13. affect . . . effect
    a. It will not _____ your grade.
    b. What _____ did that have?

14. principle . . . principal
    a. Mr. Barton is our _____.
    b. It's against his _____.

15. capitol . . . capital
    a. What is the _____ of Texas?
    b. The Senate meets at the _____.

16. colonel . . . kernel
    a. He is a retired _____.
    b. This is a _____ of corn.

17. stationery . . . stationary
    a. The letter was written on blue _____.
    b. These objects are _____.

18. isle . . . aisle
    a. Walk down the _____ slowly.
    b. We visited the _____ of Wight.

19. duel . . . dual
    a. They will fight a _____.
    b. The car had _____ exhausts.

20. council . . . counsel
    a. Do you need legal _____?
    b. The _____ met today.

21. kill . . . kiln
    a. Did you _____ the spider?
    b. Put the pottery in the _____.

22. sleigh . . . slay
    a. We are going on a _____ ride.
    b. The prince will _____ the dragon.

23. rain . . . reign
    a. It will _____ tomorrow.
    b. She will _____ over the ceremonies.

24. need . . . knead
    a. I watched her _____ the dough.
    b. Do you _____ any help?

25. been . . . bin
    a. I have _____ working.
    b. Put this in the red _____.

313

Unit 130 cont'd

Using Homonyms

Homonyms are words that sound alike.

> EXAMPLES: a. night   knight
> b. bread   bred
> c. feat   feet

 Underline the sentences with the correct homonyms.

1. a. Did you here anything?
   b. <u>Did you hear anything?</u>
2. a. What is the some of 2 + 2?
   b. What is the sum of 2 + 2?
3. a. She is heir to the throne.
   b. She is air to the throne.
4. a. I need two volunteers.
   b. I need to volunteers.
5. a. The store is having a sail.
   b. The store is having a sale.
6. a. You have big feat.
   b. You have big feet.
7. a. Draw a straight line.
   b. Draw a strait line.
8. a. I will earn the money.
   b. I will urn the money.
9. a. Wait in the haul.
   b. Wait in the hall.
10. a. They're arriving at noon.
    b. There arriving at noon.
11. a. The letter is for me.
    b. The letter is four me.
12. a. My ant is a truck driver.
    b. My aunt is a truck driver.
13. a. We have bin looking for you.
    b. We have been looking for you.
14. a. The birds flew away.
    b. The birds flue away.
15. a. They will fight a dual.
    b. They will fight a duel.
16. a. What did you buy?
    b. What did you bye?
17. a. We will wear our uniforms.
    b. We will ware our uniforms.

18. a. What's for desert?
    b. What's for dessert?
19. a. Mrs. Coggins is our principal.
    b. Mrs. Coggins is our principle.
20. a. We had stake for dinner.
    b. We had steak for dinner.
21. a. I bought a pair of shoes.
    b. I bought a pare of shoes.
22. a. My dog has flees.
    b. My dog has fleas.
23. a. I stepped in a whole.
    b. I stepped in a hole.
24. a. A female deer is a doe.
    b. A female deer is a dough.
25. a. What root did you take?
    b. What route did you take?
26. a. The plain landed safely.
    b. The plane landed safely.
27. a. I had a grate time.
    b. I had a great time.
28. a. The bear chased us.
    b. The bare chased us.
29. a. Steve was too weak.
    b. Steve was too week.
30. a. I will slay the dragon.
    b. I will sleigh the dragon.
31. a. Do you need anything?
    b. Do you knead anything?
32. a. Comb your hair.
    b. Comb your hare.
33. a. He's in the forth grade.
    b. He's in the fourth grade.

Comprehension Check

(A) Connect the synonyms.

1. foolish
2. also
3. smart
4. leap
5. branch

a. intelligent
b. silly
c. limb
d. too
e. jump

6. quick
7. shout
8. rock
9. woods
10. shut

f. stone
g. fast
h. close
i. yell
j. forest

(B) Connect the antonyms.

1. damage
2. clear
3. valuable
4. beautiful
5. brave

a. cloudy
b. ugly
c. repair
d. worthless
e. cowardly

6. succeed
7. life
8. noisy
9. laugh
10. take

f. quiet
g. fail
h. give
i. death
j. cry

(C) In each blank write an antonym of the word in parentheses.

(forget)   1. Did you __remember__ to brush your teeth?
(different) 2. We bought the _____ kind of car.
(honest)   3. The burglar is a _____ person.
(asleep)   4. Angie was _____ before 6:00 a.m.
(result)   5. What was the _____ of the fire?
(worse)   6. The patient feels _____ today.
(truth)   7. Did Janey tell us a _____ ?
(boring)   8. Science class was _____ today.
(danger)   9. The passengers jumped to _____ .
(entrance)   10. Leave the theater through the _____ .
(weak)   11. The weightlifter is _____ .
(many)   12. The students had _____ questions for the speaker.

(D) In each blank underline the synonym of the word in parentheses.

(arithmetic) 1. We have a (math, Spanish) lesson to complete.
(accept)   2. Will you (give, take) the money from me?
(buy)   3. They plan to (purchase, sell) a house this summer.
(wept)   4. The children (laughed, cried).
(lift)   5. (Raise, Lower) the garage door, please.
(easy)   6. Her method for painting the deck was (difficult, simple).
(huge)   7. She saw a (small, large) wolf in the forest.
(forbid)   8. Did Todd's parents (permit, prohibit) him from going?
(fast)   9. Ellen gave a (slow, quick) answer to the question.
(now)   10. Let's explore the cave (later, immediately).
(rear)   11. The (front, back) door is solid wood.
(split)   12. You must first (separate, connect) the wires.

Test 26 cont'd

Comprehension Check (continued)

E Write the correct homonym in each blank.

(route, root)   1. We'll take this _____route_____ to Jean's house.

(allowed, aloud)   2. Miss Markam read the poem _____ to the children.

(plain, plane)   3. The _____ paper should be used to wrap packages.

(hare, hair)   4. Another name for "rabbit" is "_____ ."

(urn, earn)   5. We'll have to _____ the money to go to the movie.

(Hall, Haul)   6. _____ the damaged furniture to the city dump.

(isle, aisle)   7. The middle _____ was waxed yesterday.

(desert, dessert) 8. I suggest cheesecake and strawberries for _____ .

(waive, wave)   9. The banker said we could _____ the paperwork.

(sale, sail)   10. The large discount store is having a _____ on Tuesday.

(coarse, course)   11. The _____ material will make a good laundry bag.

(Reign, Rein)   12. _____ in the horse before it runs away with you!

F Identify the sets of synonyms, antonyms, and homonyms. Write "s" for synonyms, "a" for antonyms, and "h" for homonyms. Then use one of each set in a sentence.

_h_ 1. their......there   The girls will sing _____their_____ song next.

____ 2. bashful ...shy   Barry is a _____ person.

____ 3. new......knew   I _____ you'd agree with me.

____ 4. good .....bad   Eating too many sweets can be _____ for you.

____ 5. like ......dislike   We _____ to see deep snow for our skiing.

____ 6. woman ...female   The young _____ has a new job.

____ 7. give .....take   Please _____ me your answer now.

____ 8. fur ....fir   The _____ tree is an evergreen.

____ 9. talk .....speak   We'll ask Mr. Harmon to _____ to our class.

____ 10. buy .....sell   Sharon saved her money to _____ new shoes.

____ 11. begin ....start   The play will _____ at 8:00 p.m.

____ 12. pane .....pain   The softball broke the big _____ of glass.

Write a paragraph describing your chores. Use at least two synonyms and underline them.

_____

_____

_____

_____

_____

_____

_____

Figures of Speech

The most common used figures of speech are the following:

simile -   *compares two entirely different things by the use of "like" or "as"*

metaphor -   *simply implies a comparison between two different things*

personification - *to give animals, nature, or inanimate objects the qualities of a person*

A Underline the two objects being compared in each sentence. These are called similes.

1. The <u>men</u> looked like <u>ants</u> on the ground.
2. The man's stomach looked like a balloon.
3. The hail was as big as a baseball.
4. The old man was as helpless as a kitten.
5. Huge buildings rose like mountains.
6. The answer was as plain as day.
7. Marcia is as thin as a toothpick.
8. Jason is acting like a clown today.
9. I'm as mad as a hornet.
10. The tall clouds looked like mountains.

B Underline the two objects being compared in each of these sentences. These are called metaphors.

1. My <u>father</u> was a <u>bear</u> when he awoke.
2. I am an island.
3. The moon is a smiling clown.
4. The heart is a lonely hunter.
5. She had a heart of gold.
6. Snowflakes are twirling ballerinas.
7. A graveyard is a ghost town.
8. Anger is a shouting voice.
9. Peace is a moonlit meadow.
10. Happiness is the last day of school.

C In the following sentences underline each object that is personified.

1. The <u>thunder</u> began to drum a song.
2. The raindrops played a lullaby on the roof.
3. The earth swallowed the village.
4. The clouds suddenly began to cry.
5. The tornado devoured everything in its path.
6. The old house was lonely.
7. The ocean clutched at the shore.
8. Our car gasped and then died.
9. The toys waited patiently for the child.
10. All four tires grabbed the road.

COMPOSITION EXERCISE

Write two examples each of a simile, a metaphor, and a personification.

simile _____

_____

metaphor _____

_____

personification _____

_____

Unit 131 cont'd ⟶

Interesting Sentences

SIMILE is a figure of speech that uses <u>like</u> or <u>as</u> or <u>as if</u> to compare two different things:
>The floor is as slick as glass.

METAPHOR is a figure of speech which simply implies the comparison between two different things:
>The sun is a ball of fire.

PERSONIFICATION is a figure of speech in which an inanimate object, an abstract quality, or one of the lower animals is spoken of as if it were a person:
>The shoe had hidden itself in the corner of the closet and had the impudence to stick its tongue out at me.

ALLUSION is a figure of speech that makes a casual reference to a famous historical or literary figure or event:
>Father is the local Scrooge.

Use the definitions and examples above to help you identify the figure of speech used in each of the following sentences. In the blank before each sentence, write "s" for simile, "m" for metaphor, "p" for personification, or "a" for allusion.

_P_ 1. The rain danced on the roof before sliding down the rain spout.

____ 2. The harsh words were arrows piercing my heart.

____ 3. Two huge oaks stood as sentinels guarding the entrance to the driveway.

____ 4. A clear little brook laughed and gurgled as it wandered down the hill.

____ 5. The snow crept in on little cat feet and silently spread a blanket of white over the town.

____ 6. The highway was a silver ribbon in the moonlight.

____ 7. They are the Beatles of Riverside High.

____ 8. Her presence was a ray of sunshine in the gloomy room.

____ 9. The untied shoe stared back at the small child like a beady-eyed old man with a drooping mustache.

____ 10. The red sunset, with narrow, black cloud strips like threats across it, lay on the curved horizon of the prairie.

____ 11. The pits in the road were the scars of gigantic bombs, their rawness already made a little natural by rain, seed, and time.

____ 12. The unending rattle of the conveyor belt, which in the confined space of the coal mine, is rather like the rattle of a machine gun.

____ 13. The man of facts is a mere container. His mind is a sponge, which takes up so much and gives it out again on a little squeezing.

____ 14. I (the Cloud) am the daughter of Earth and Water, And the nursling of the Sky, . . .

____ 15. He was able to stay on this Jack Sprat diet only one week.

____ 16. America is young: Her traditions are light bands around her heart and mind. She could easily break them, make profound changes, and quickly adjust herself to new policies.

____ 17. The moon had just risen, very golden, over the hill, and like a bright, watching spirit peered through the bars of an ash tree's naked boughs.

____ 18. The hurricane sobbed about the house, clutched at the eaves with frantic fingers, and devoured the chimney in one bite.

Writing Numbers

A hyphen is used in compound names of numbers from twenty-one through ninety-nine.

1 2 3

A Write the number name for each number.

1 - _one_	16 - _____	31 - _____	46 - _____
2 - _____	17 - _____	32 - _____	47 - _____
3 - _____	18 - _____	33 - _____	48 - _____
4 - _____	19 - _____	34 - _____	49 - _____
5 - _____	20 - _____	35 - _____	50 - _____
6 - _____	21 - _____	36 - _____	51 - _____
7 - _____	22 - _____	37 - _____	52 - _____
8 - _____	23 - _____	38 - _____	53 - _____
9 - _____	24 - _____	39 - _____	54 - _____
10 - _____	25 - _____	40 - _____	55 - _____
11 - _____	26 - _____	41 - _____	56 - _____
12 - _____	27 - _____	42 - _____	57 - _____
13 - _____	28 - _____	43 - _____	58 - _____
14 - _____	29 - _____	44 - _____	59 - _____
15 - _____	30 - _____	45 - _____	60 - _____

Ordinal numbers are words like "first," "second," or "third." To write some ordinal numbers, simply add "th" to the regular number words.

Here are some exceptions:

1. five — fifth
2. nine — ninth
3. twelve — twelfth
4. eight — eighth
5. number names that end in "y" but change the "y" to "i" and add "eth" (twenty — twentieth)

B Write the ordinal number name for each number.

1 - _first_	11 - _____	30 - _____
2 - _____	12 - _____	31 - _____
3 - _____	13 - _____	40 - _____
4 - _____	14 - _____	42 - _____
5 - _____	15 - _____	50 - _____
6 - _____	16 - _____	53 - _____
7 - _____	17 - _____	60 - _____
8 - _____	18 - _____	64 - _____
9 - _____	19 - _____	70 - _____
10 - _____	20 - _____	75 - _____

Unit 132 cont'd →

Writing the Names of the 50 States

Twenty-five (25) of the fifty (50) states are misspelled. Cross out the misspelled names, and write them correctly in the blanks.

1. *Alaska*	8. _____	14. _____	20. _____
2. _____	9. _____	15. _____	21. _____
3. _____	10. _____	16. _____	22. _____
4. _____	11. _____	17. _____	23. _____
5. _____	12. _____	18. _____	24. _____
6. _____	13. _____	19. _____	25. _____
7. _____			

"ie" and "ei" Words

Use "i" before "e" except after "c" or when sounded like /ā/ as in "neighbor."

EXAMPLES:
a. believe
b. receive
c. weigh

 Complete each word with either "ie" or "ei." Then write the word in the blank to complete the sentence.

a. cl _ie_ nt
b. aud ____ nce
c. dec ____ ve
d. ____ ghty
e. impat ____ nt
f. c ____ ling
g. fr ____ ght
h. p ____ ce
i. v ____ w
j. rec ____ ve
k. handkerch ____ f
l. ach ____ ve
m. sl ____ gh
n. n ____ ghbor
o. th ____ f
p. br ____ f
q. var ____ ty
r. ____ ght
s. p ____ r
t. rel ____ f
u. exper ____ nce
v. ch ____ f
w. n ____ ce
x. sh ____ ld
y. d ____ t
z. fr ____ nd
A. f ____ ld
B. disobed ____ nt
C. rev ____ w
D. w ____ ght

1. The lawyer defended his ____client____.
2. The _____ applauded the performers.
3. You can't _____ us.
4. Mr. Wilson is _____ years old today.
5. The principal is a very _____ man.
6. There is a spider on the _____.
7. We had to wait for the _____ train to pass.
8. May I have another _____ of apple pie?
9. The _____ from the mountaintop is beautiful!
10. Did you _____ a letter from Allen?
11. In his pocket was a bright yellow _____.
12. We should all try to _____ our goals.
13. We all went on a _____ ride.
14. My _____ has four dogs and ten cats.
15. The police caught the jewel _____.
16. Ms. Davis gave a _____ speech.
17. It's good to eat a _____ of vegetables.
18. _____ members attended the meeting.
19. Let's walk down to the _____ and watch the boats.
20. The medicine gave me some _____ from the pain.
21. Traveling is great _____.
22. The _____ ordered his men to stop.
23. His _____ is studying to be a doctor.
24. I had to _____ my eyes from the light.
25. I'm going on a _____ and lose this weight.
26. Georgie is my best _____.
27. Andy ran across the _____.
28. The mother punished the _____ child.
29. Tomorrow we will _____ for the test.
30. Write down your height and _____.

Unit 133 cont'd →

"ie" and "ei" Puzzle

friend

 Fill in the blanks. Then complete the puzzle.

Use "i" before "e,"
   Except after "c,"
Or when sounded as "a,"
   As in "neighbor" and "weigh."

achieve	relieve
believe	reprieve
eight	retrieve
feign	science
field	seine
forfeit	shield
frieze	shriek
grief	siege
grieve	soldier
height	vein
hygiene	view
lien	weigh
neighbor	weight
piece	wield
relief	yield

Down

1. _f_ _r_ _i_ _e_ _n_ _d_ a person who knows and likes another

2. _ _ _ _ _ _ _ act of making a person believe something that is false

3. _ _ _ _ _ _ a person who steals; robber

4. _ _ _ _ _ _ to think fit; to condescend

6. _ _ _ _ _ _ to make a god of; to worship as a god

7. _ _ _ _ _ _ the period of power of a ruler

9. _ _ _ _ _ _ _ what is held to be true or real

10. _ _ _ _ _ _ divine being; one of the gods worshipped by a tribe

11. _ _ _ _ _ has stopped living; stopped running

12. _ _ _ _ _ _ a false appearance; pretense

13. _ _ _ _ _ _ _ the sound made by a horse

14. _ _ _ _ _ daily; occurring every 24 hours

Across

1. _ _ _ _ _ _ an evil spirit; devil; addict

2. _ _ _ _ to stop living; to stop running or functioning

5. _ _ _ _ _ line fastened to a bridle or bit to guide a horse

8. _ _ _ _ _ _ daughter of one's brother or sister

15. _ _ _ _ something that is not true

16. _ _ _ _ _ usual kind of food or drink for a person or animal

17. _ _ _ _ _ structure built out over water

18. _ _ _ _ _ _ piece of land used for crops or pasture

322

Words That Are Spelled Alike

In a two-syllable word one syllable is usually said harder than the other. We call this syllable the stressed syllable and mark it with an accent mark (ʹ).

It is often possible to change the pronunciation of a word by stressing a different syllable. In such cases, the spelling of the word does not change. The meaning, however, does. For example, look at the word "record." "Record" may be pronounced as "rekʹ ərd" which means "a cylinder, disk, or roll prepared so as to reproduce sounds." "Record" may also be pronounced as "ri kordʹ" which means "to write down."

✳ Read each sentence. Then underline the pronunciation and meaning of the word which fits the use of the underlined word in the sentence.

1. Before us lay miles of endless <u>desert</u>.
   a. <u>dezʹərt</u>   <u>hot, dry region</u>
   b. di zûrtʹ   to abandon

2. The mayor will <u>address</u> the assembly.
   a. ə dresʹ   to speak to
   b. adʹres   residence of a person

3. The commercial lasted one <u>minute</u>.
   a. mi no͞otʹ   exceedingly small
   b. minʹit   the 60th part of an hour

4. I am the king, and you are the <u>subject</u>.
   a. subʹjikt   under power of another
   b. səb jektʹ   to offer for consideration

5. The essay <u>contest</u> was won by Nicholas.
   a. kən testʹ   to argue about
   b. konʹtest   competition

6. He is a <u>rebel</u> without a cause.
   a. ri belʹ   to resist authority
   b. rebʹəl   one who rises against

7. Marcus was <u>content</u> to stay at home.
   a. konʹtent   all that a thing contains
   b. kən tentʹ   satisfied

8. You must be <u>present</u> to win the contest.
   a. pri zentʹ   to introduce
   b. prezʹənt   being at hand

9. The students <u>protest</u> the war.
   a. pro͞oʹtest   the act of objecting
   b. prə testʹ   to object to

10. I <u>refuse</u> to answer that question.
    a. ri fyo͞ozʹ   to decline to do
    b. refʹyo͞os   anything worthless

11. Mr. Green signed a five-year <u>contract</u>.
    a. konʹtrakt   formal agreement
    b. kən traktʹ   to draw together

12. The two classes will <u>combine</u> their efforts.
    a. komʹbīn   machine used for harvesting
    b. kəm binʹ   to put together

13. <u>Contrast</u> a democracy and a dictatorship.
    a. kən trastʹ   to show dissimilarities
    b. konʹtrast   the unlikeness between two things

14. The meeting will <u>conflict</u> with our plans.
    a. kən fliktʹ   to be in mutual opposition
    b. konʹflikt   a struggle

Unit 134 cont'd ➜

Word Origins

Each short story contains three (3) misspelled words. Underline them. Then write the correct spellings in the blanks.

A umbrella

The <u>wurd</u> "umbrella" <u>coms</u> from the Latin words "**umbra**" and "**ella**." "Umbra" means "shade," and "ella" means "little." The <u>furst</u> umbrella was used in the sun. Now the umbrella is used in the rain.

word   *comes*   *first*
___   ___   ___

B July and August

The month of July was named in onor of Julius Caesar. The munth of August was named for Augustus Caesar. Both Julius and Augustus were Roman leeders.

___   ___   ___

C fool

The word "fool" comes from the Latin word "**follis**." In the begining "fool" ment "windbag." Latter the meaning changed to mean a "person who talks much, but says little."

___   ___   ___

D omnibus

Our word "bus" is a shortined form of the word "omnibus." In Latin "omnibus" means "four all." "Bus" has become the most populer form of the word.

___   ___   ___

E neighbor

The word "neighbor" is made up of too Old English words, "**neah**" and "**gebur**." "Neah" means "neerby." "Gebur" means "farmer." The meaning now encludes anyone who lives nearby.

___   ___   ___

F automobile

Automobile is maid from two words, "auto" and "mobile." "Auto" comes from the Greek "**autos**," witch means "self." "Mobile" comes from the Latin "**mobilis**," which means "movabel."

___   ___   ___

G manufacture

Before factory tooks over the production of goods, things were made by hand. The word "manufacture" comes from the Latin words "**manu**" and "**facture**." The orijinal meaning was "made by hand." The word now reffers to all production.

___   ___   ___

H sandwich

The sandwich was named for the Earl of Sandwich. When the Earl was bisy, he refused to stop for meels. He asked that bread and meat be brot to him, thus inventing the sandwich.

___   ___   ___

From "Advice" to "Hospitable"

---

advice   **advise**
    "Advice" means "an opinion." It is a noun.
    "Advise" means "to give counsel." It is a verb.

A Write "advice" or "advise" in each blank.

1. What is your ___advice___?
2. I would _____ you to wait.
3. Ask Dr. Roth for some _____.
4. May I offer some _____?
5. My dad likes to give _____.
6. Would you _____ him to try again?
7. I trust his _____.
8. The doctor will _____ you of the risk.

9. _____ me what to do.
10. Your _____ helped me.
11. Did he _____ you of the danger?
12. I need some _____.
13. Why did you _____ him to leave?
14. I don't like his _____.
15. My _____ is to keep trying.
16. What would you _____?

---

personal   **personnel**
    "Personal" has to do with a person's private affairs.
    "Personnel" refers to people employed in an organization.

B Write "personal" or "personnel" in each blank.

1. Mr. Benton liked to keep his ___personal___ life private.
2. You may fill out an application in the _____ office.
3. My dad is the _____ manager for a big company.
4. When she moved to Texas, she sold all her _____ property.
5. Put your _____ belongings in the safe.
6. How much money you have is your _____ business.
7. Joe went to the _____ office.
8. He did not ask us any _____ questions.

---

hospital   **hospitable**
    "Hospital" is a place for sick or injured persons.
    "Hospitable" refers to friendly treatment.

C Write "hospital" or "hospitable" in each blank.

1. When I broke my arm, I went to the ___hospital___.
2. You have been most _____ to our guests.
3. Surgery is done in the operating room in a _____.
4. The ambulance rushed him to the nearest _____.
5. The President and his family were _____ to the ambassador.
6. When Luther became ill, we took him to the _____.
7. Your _____ treatment of our visitors was appreciated.

Unit 135 cont'd ➡

From "Alter" to "Brake"

 Write the correct homonym in each blank.

---

alter   **altar**

To "alter" means "to change."
An "altar" is a place of worship.

---

1. We must ___*alter*___ our plans.
2. The man prayed at the _____.
3. Will you _____ the coat to fit me?
4. The _____ was decorated with flowers.
5. Can you _____ it some more?

6. They were married at the _____.
7. Would you _____ the dress for Fran?
8. She waited for us at the _____.
9. I will _____ the schedule.
10. The _____ was lit by candlelight.

---

aloud   **allowed**

"Aloud" means "loudly."
"Allowed" is the past-tense form of "allow." It means "permitted."

---

1. I read my story ___*aloud*___.
2. We were not _____ to talk.
3. Mark recited the poem _____.
4. They were not _____ to take pictures.
5. He _____ us to touch the stone.

6. You are _____ to ask questions.
7. Joe was _____ to leave early.
8. Read your answer _____.
9. Dogs are not _____ in the store.
10. Sue read her sentence _____.

---

board   **bored**

A "board" is a flat piece of wood.
"Bored" is an adjective meaning "disinterested."

---

1. Ann was ___*bored*___ with the movie.
2. Each _____ was painted a different color.
3. I am easily _____ by speeches.
4. Saw the _____ in halves.
5. You look _____.

6. Nail the _____ to the wall.
7. Are you _____ by commercials?
8. Everyone in the audience was _____.
9. Must you look so _____?
10. The _____ had a nail in it.

---

break   **brake**

"Break" means "to separate into pieces."
A "brake" is a device used for stopping.

---

1. Don't ___*break*___ the vase.
2. The _____ on my car doesn't work.
3. Glasses _____ easily.
4. The driver stepped on the _____.
5. The _____ is stuck.

6. Be careful not to _____ it.
7. This pedal is the _____.
8. The _____ needs fixing.
9. She'll _____ everything she touches.
10. How did you _____ your leg?

326

Comprehension Check

(A) Write the number name and the ordinal name for each number.

	number	ordinal
1.	one	first
2.		
3.		
10.		
19.		
20.		
29.		
31.		
40.		
45.		

(B) Put a check (✓) beside the name of each state which is spelled correctly.

✓	1. Montana		11. Oregon
	2. Wyoming		12. Missourri
	3. Ilinois		13. Alaska
	4. Calafornia		14. Ohio
	5. South Dakota		15. Washengton
	6. Arkansaw		16. Arrizona
	7. Utah		17. Kansas
	8. Mississippi		18. Gorgia
	9. Navada		19. Oklahoma
	10. Idaho		20. Texas

(C) Write "ei" or "ie" in each blank.

1. ch _ie_ f		13. v __ n	
2. ach __ ve		14. h __ r	
3. w __ ght		15. for __ gn	
4. p __ rce		16. n __ ther	
5. t __ r		17. ser __ s	
6. w __ ld		18. sh __ ld	
7. rel __ f		19. v __ w	
8. exper __ nce		20. s __ ge	
9. l __		21. bel __ ve	
10. c __ ling		22. dec __ t	
11. sc __ nce		23. perc __ ve	
12. __ ght		24. gr __ f	

(D) Match each word with its origin. Some words have two answers.

_c_	1. July	a.	from the Latin "follis"
	2. August	b.	"little shade"
	3. omnibus	c.	Julius Caesar
	4. sandwich	d.	"made by hand"
	5. manufacture	e.	"for all"
	6. neighbor	f.	the Earl of Sandwich
	7. automobile	g.	"autos mobilis"
	8. fool	h.	"nearby farmer"
	9. umbrella	i.	Augustus Caesar
		j.	"umbra ella"
		k.	"self movable"

(E) Tell whether the underlined word in each sentence should be accented on the first or on the second syllable. Write "1" for first syllable; write "2" for second syllable.

1. The material will <u>contract</u> if heated.   **2**
2. Will the other team <u>contest</u> the decision?   ____
3. "Space Exploration" is the <u>subject</u> of his report.   ____
4. Don't <u>desert</u> your friends when they need you.   ____
5. A peaceful <u>protest</u> will be held Sunday.   ____
6. A new corn <u>combine</u> is an expensive machine.   ____
7. A two-year-old child will <u>rebel</u> by saying "No!"   ____
8. I like the <u>contrast</u> between the two colors.   ____
9. Did Andy give Kara a birthday <u>present</u>?   ____
10. Tell me the basic <u>content</u> of your speech.   ____

Test 27 cont'd ➡

Comprehension Check (continued)

(F) Write the correct homonym in each blank.

(hospital, hospitable) 1. The injured woman was rushed to the ___hospital___ .

(advice, advise) 2. The counselor will _____ you about your courses.

(alter, altar) 3. I think that you should _____ your attitude.

(personal, personnel) 4. Military _____ must be ready to move on short notice.

(break, brake) 5. Did you _____ the mirror when you dropped it?

(advice, advise) 6. Linda's _____ was the best I'd ever received.

(bored, board) 7. The last _____ to be added was broken.

(alter, altar) 8. The _____ was covered with beautiful carnations.

(bored, board) 9. The movie was so exciting that we had no time to be _____ .

(hospital, hospitable) 10. Our neighbors to the north are very _____ .

(aloud, allowed) 11. Reading _____ in the library is very rude.

(break, brake) 12. Set the emergency _____ when you park on a hill.

(aloud, allowed) 13. Will you be _____ to use your family's car?

(personal, personnel) 14. My reasons for refusing to go are _____ .

(G) In the blanks write "s" for simile, "m" for metaphor, "p" for personification, and "a" for allusion.

__s__ 1. She was as mad as an old wet hen.

____ 2. Autumn is burning leaves.

____ 3. The chair groaned when Dad sat down.

____ 4. Her voice is beauty.

____ 5. Your teeth are like pearls.

____ 6. He was Romeo to her Juliet.

____ 7. The wind grabbed all the kites.

____ 8. Carl is as sly as a fox.

____ 9. Childhood is a sweet memory.

____ 10. King Henry VIII couldn't have been greedier than Uncle Ben.

____ 11. Flowers are jealous of her beauty.

____ 12. Their yard looks like *The Grapes of Wrath*.

Write a paragraph about a picnic you've gone on or would like to go on. Use at least one simile.

_____

_____

_____

_____

_____

_____

_____

_____

From "Counsel" to "Complement"

Write the correct homonym in each blank.

---

counsel   **council**
    To "counsel" means "to offer advice."
    A "council" is a body of persons.

---

1. The ___*council*___ meets this Friday.
2. My parents _____ students.
3. I'm a member of the _____.
4. The _____ elected a spokesman.
5. Howard served on the _____.

6. These women _____ children.
7. He is chairman of the _____.
8. The _____ will give its report.
9. What _____ did you give them?
10. I went to her for _____.

---

capital   **capitol**
    The "capital" is the chief city of a country or state.
    The "capitol" is the building where the legislature meets.

---

1. Little Rock is the ___*capital*___ of Arkansas.
2. The _____ is on State Street.
3. The _____ of Michigan is Lansing.
4. Do you know the _____ of France?
5. My father works at the _____.

6. The _____ closes on Sundays.
7. What is the _____ of Texas?
8. His picture hangs in the _____.
9. The _____ was remodeled.
10. Every state has a _____.

---

coward   **cowered**
A "coward" is a person lacking in courage.
"Cowered" is the past-tense of "cower"; it means "to tremble."

---

1. Everyone ___*cowered*___ in fear.
2. That man is a _____.
3. The people _____ at the mention of war.
4. He _____ behind the sofa.
5. My sister is not a _____.

6. Only a _____ would say that.
7. You are a _____!
8. We _____ at the sound of his voice.
9. The child _____ behind his mother.
10. I have never been a _____.

---

compliment   **complement**
    A "compliment" is an expression of praise.
    A "complement" is something which completes the whole.

---

1. He is a ___*complement*___ to the organization.
2. I _____ your excellent choice.
3. She accepted the _____ graciously.
4. Everyone enjoys a _____.
5. Your dessert will _____ the meal.

6. Mr. Ross gave me a _____.
7. I appreciate the _____.
8. The rice will _____ the main dish.
9. A _____ finishes a sentence.
10. I must _____ your hard work.

Unit 136 cont'd

From "Fewer" to "Between"

> **fewer**   **less**
> "Fewer" refers to number.
> "Less" refers to degree or quantity.

A **Write "fewer" or "less" in each blank.**

1. ___*Fewer*___ students are taking Latin.
2. There's more to do and _____ time to do it.
3. Give each student _____ work.
4. We have _____ members today.
5. They showed _____ enthusiasm.
6. _____ cars are sold on Mondays.
7. He received _____ votes.
8. Don has _____ support.

9. Don't settle for _____ quality.
10. _____ people are attending.
11. We are getting _____ complaints.
12. _____ workers will be hired.
13. There is _____ chance of fire.
14. They sold _____ tickets.
15. _____ money is available.
16. This book has _____ pages.

> **over**   **more than**
> "Over" refers to relationships in space.
> "More than" is used with numbers.

B **Write "over" or "more than" in each blank.**

1. The frog jumped ___*over*___ the rock.
2. There were _____ forty pieces.
3. We need _____ fifty dollars.
4. She wrote _____ twenty letters.
5. They own _____ 200 trucks
6. The horse jumped _____ the fence.
7. The bird flew _____ the ocean.
8. He has made _____ a million dollars.

9. _____ 200 people attended.
10. The plane flew _____ our house.
11. He fell _____ the box.
12. We raised _____ $500.
13. He threw the ball _____ home plate.
14. _____ thirty students were absent.
15. Its population is _____ 200,000.
16. Sara drove the car _____ the ice.

> **among**   **between**
> "Among" usually refers to more than two.
> "Between" refers to two.

C **Write "among" or "between" in each blank.**

1. You are ___*among*___ friends.
2. Sit _____ Frank and Bobby.
3. _____ the listeners sat my uncle.
4. Keep the secret _____ you and me.
5. It was distributed _____ the students.
6. Eric walked _____ Joe and Zeke.
7. The leftovers were divided _____ us.
8. It was hidden _____ the leaves.

9. It was divided _____ the members.
10. The money was split _____ Ed and Carl.
11. He walked _____ the spectators.
12. Put the meat _____ the bread.
13. It was handed out _____ the voters.
14. The sandwich was divided _____ four people.
15. She pressed the flower _____ the pages.
16. We planted daisies _____ the marigolds.

From "Gate" to "Hangar"

 Write the correct homonym in each blank.

> **gate**   **gait**
> A "gate" is an opening in a fence or wall.
> "Gait" is a manner of walking or stepping.

1. He walks with a steady __*gait*__.
2. Someone left the _____ open.
3. I can't keep pace with your _____.
4. Close the _____ behind you.
5. His _____ slowed.
6. We painted the _____ white.
7. The _____ will be locked at noon.
8. She walks with a brisk _____.
9. The _____ will close automatically.
10. Ned opened the _____ slowly.

> **groan**   **grown**
> "Groan" means "to utter a low sound of pain or sorrow."
> "Grown" is past participle of "grow."

1. I heard someone __*groan*__.
2. The tree has _____ three feet.
3. The _____ became louder.
4. The _____ came from in there.
5. It had _____ into a butterfly.
6. The plant had not _____ in a year.
7. The boy had _____ tall.
8. Did you hear a _____?
9. Why do you _____?
10. I had _____ ten inches.

> **great**   **grate**
> "Great" means "very large" or "excellent."
> "Grate" means "to reduce to small particles."

1. The dinosaur was a __*great*__ animal.
2. Will you _____ the cheese?
3. I had a _____ time.
4. He is a _____ football player.
5. Your idea sounds _____.
6. Use this to _____ eggs.
7. That was a _____ party.
8. The _____ room was empty.
9. I will _____ these for you.
10. The food tastes _____!

> **hanger**   **hangar**
> A "hanger" is a device on which something is hung, such as a coat.
> A "hangar" is a shelter for airplanes.

1. Planes are parked in a __*hangar*__.
2. The _____ was made of plastic.
3. My jacket fell from the _____.
4. A _____ is part of an airport.
5. I've never been in a _____.
6. Put your coat on a _____.
7. There's a _____ in the closet.
8. We took a tour of the _____.
9. The _____ lay on the floor.
10. My uncle works in a _____.

Unit 137 cont'd ⟶

From "Imply" to "Further"

imply   infer

A speaker "implies."
A hearer "infers."

A Write the correct form of "imply" or "infer" in each blank.

1. Mrs. Wordley ___*implied*___ that she was retiring.
2. I _____ that the party would be postponed.
3. I _____ that she was planning to run for President.
4. You have _____ that Alfred is guilty of cheating.
5. I _____ from his speech that he was against the amendment.
6. The speaker _____ that the trip would probably be cancelled.
7. Are you _____ that I am a coward?

reluctant   reticent

One who does not want to act is "reluctant."
One who does not want to speak is "reticent."

B Write "reluctant" or "reticent" in each blank.

1. Karen and Phil were ___*reluctant*___ to take part in the play.
2. Rex decided to remain _____ about his objections.
3. Why are you so _____ to volunteer for the project?
4. You should not be _____ about voicing your opinions.
5. Carla was _____ to give the officer her keys.
6. No matter what is said, Nancy always remains _____.
7. Mr. Knight was _____ to accept the job of driver.

farther   further

"Farther" refers to physical distance.
"Further" refers to something abstract, such as an idea.

C Write "farther" or "further" in each blank.

1. The bank is ___*farther*___ west than the post office.
2. Instead, Ken became _____ behind in his studies.
3. How much _____ is it to Los Angeles?
4. There have been no _____ developments.
5. Ellen lives _____ from the school than you.
6. Has there been any _____ news concerning the crisis?
7. John ran _____ than anyone in our class.

From "Kiln" to "Medal"

✱ **Write the correct homonym in each blank.**

---

kiln   **kill**

A "kiln" is an oven for baking products such as bricks.
To "kill" means "to cause the death of."

---

1. The man bought a new ___*kiln*___.
2. Take the bricks from the _____.
3. I will _____ the spider.
4. A _____ gets very hot.
5. Poison can _____ people and pets.

6. We tried to _____ the mosquitoes.
7. The _____ belongs to Mr. Marshall.
8. She placed the pottery in the _____.
9. _____ the bug before it bites me.
10. Our cats _____ mice.

---

manner   **manor**

"Manner" is the way of doing anything.
A "manor" is a nobleman's estate.

---

1. He is the lord of the ___*manor*___.
2. His _____ is sometimes strange.
3. She had an unusual _____ of speaking.
4. The _____ was open to visitors.
5. The old _____ was rebuilt.

6. We visited an English _____.
7. His _____ of dress is different to ours.
8. You must change your _____ of behavior.
9. The _____ was decorated in blue.
10. In which _____ should I begin?

---

morning   **mourning**

"Morning" is the early part of the day.
"Mourning" is the act of expressing grief.

---

1. The bus leaves in the ___*morning*___.
2. He is _____ the death of his dog.
3. I sleep late every _____.
4. The women are _____ the dead.
5. School begins tomorrow _____.

6. Black is a symbol of _____.
7. It rains every Monday _____.
8. The sun rises in the _____.
9. She is still _____ over her loss.
10. What time did you get up this _____?

---

metal   **medal**

"Metal" is a hard, heavy material used for making many products.
A "medal" is a small piece of metal used as an award.

---

1. She received a gold ___*medal*___.
2. The machine is made of _____.
3. The _____ was made of silver.
4. They awarded her a _____ for bravery.
5. A _____ building is cheaper to build.

6. The _____ hung around his neck.
7. I received a _____ for tennis.
8. _____ does not melt quickly.
9. Tim received a _____ of appreciation.
10. The window had _____ bars.

Unit 138 cont'd ➡

From "Knew" to "Need"

 Write the correct homonym in each blank.

---

knew   **new**
"Knew" is the past-tense form of "know." It means "to have knowledge of."
"New" is the opposite of "old."

---

1. Sam ___*knew*___ the answer.
2. I have a _____ bicycle.
3. Let's buy a _____ car.
4. Mother _____ all about it.
5. The _____ owner is Mr. Alberts.

6. No one _____ his name.
7. The family bought a _____ house.
8. Henry _____ what to do.
9. I want a _____ pair of skates.
10. She _____ everyone at the meeting.

---

know   **no**
"Know" means "to have knowledge of."
"No" is the opposite of "yes."

---

1. I ___*know*___ who he is.
2. _____, you cannot go.
3. We have _____ money.
4. Do you _____ how to fix it?
5. Jake has _____ brothers or sisters.

6. Did you _____ the answer?
7. There is _____ time to lose.
8. Liz doesn't _____ my address.
9. _____, I don't want any.
10. How did you _____ that?

---

knot   **not**
A "knot" is an interlacing of the parts of a string or rope.
"Not" means "in a no manner."

---

1. Tie the rope in a ___*knot*___.
2. I do _____ know how to ski.
3. It is _____ time to go.
4. You were _____ invited.
5. The _____ was tied securely.

6. Hank has _____ called yet.
7. The ribbon has a _____ in it.
8. I couldn't undo the _____.
9. Untie the _____.
10. Ginger will _____ tell anyone.

---

knead   **need**
"Knead" means "to mix."
"Need" means "to require" or "to be necessary."

---

1. ___*Knead*___ the dough for two minutes.
2. Do you _____ anything?
3. You _____ dough with your hands.
4. We all _____ friends.
5. I don't _____ any advice.

6. These men _____ jobs.
7. They _____ new coats of paint.
8. _____ the two clays together.
9. Does she _____ to see me?
10. I will _____ the dough.

From "Loan" to "Capability"

> **loan**   **borrow**
> You "loan" your possessions to someone else.
> You "borrow" a possession from someone else.

A Write "loan" or "borrow" in each blank.

1. I will ___*loan*___ you the money.
2. Willis wants to _____ my coat.
3. You may _____ her book.
4. No one would _____ him anything.
5. Terry will _____ Rick his uniform.
6. Did you _____ the wagon?
7. May I _____ your sweater?
8. _____ the key from Ms. Atkins.

9. He will _____ his dad's car.
10. Can you _____ me a dime?
11. _____ me your pen.
12. Did you _____ your aunt's toaster?
13. Ben will _____ us his bicycle.
14. We must _____ a tent from someone.
15. You shouldn't _____ him any money.
16. Ned wants to _____ a pencil.

> **agree to**   **agree with**
> You "agree to" a thing.
> You "agree with" a person.

B Write "agree to" or "agree with" in each blank.

1. Ted will ___*agree to*___ our plan.
2. She will _____ Arnold.
3. Do you _____ me?
4. He won't _____ those conditions.
5. Did Hank _____ the plan?
6. Did Lisa _____ Ollie?
7. Does she _____ the change in plans?
8. They never _____ each other.

9. I _____ Ms. Parker.
10. Would you _____ the idea?
11. No one will _____ Charles.
12. How could you _____ his idea?
13. No one will _____ the proposal.
14. Will Gene _____ the students?
15. I _____ the suggestion made by Alex.
16. We _____ you.

> **ability**   **capability**
> "Ability" is the skill to perform.
> "Capability" refers to mental power.

C Write "ability" or "capability" in each blank.

1. My brother Henry has the ___*ability*___ to fix any kind of car.
2. Not everyone has the _____ to learn a foreign language.
3. Connie does not have the _____ to understand math.
4. We need someone with the _____ to type fast.
5. Thomas lacks the _____ to think logically.
6. The _____ to make good decisions comes with experience.
7. We all have the _____ to do something well.
8. Paul has the _____ to build houses.

335

Unit 139 cont'd

From "Piece" to "Pray"

* **Write the correct homonym in each blank.**

piece	peace
A "piece" is a small part of a whole.	
"Peace" is a state of quiet.	

1. Give him a ____piece____ of cake.
2. I wish you _____ and happiness.
3. The _____ was interrupted by the explosion.
4. You can have a _____ of my bread.
5. Sherry brought me a _____ of pie.
6. I need a _____ of string.
7. The puzzle is missing a _____.
8. The world is never at _____.
9. May you find _____.
10. He fed the dog a _____ of meat.

picture	pitcher
A "picture" is a drawing, painting, or photograph.	
A "pitcher" is one who pitches a ball; it is also a container for liquids.	

1. The ___pitcher___ threw me the ball.
2. Look at this _____ of me.
3. That _____ is filled with water.
4. Gene will take our _____.
5. I dropped a _____ of tea.
6. Felix needs a _____ of a train.
7. Leroy is our _____.
8. The _____ was blurred.
9. Fill the _____ with milk.
10. May I be the _____?

pedal	peddle
A "pedal" is a lever operated by the foot.	
To "peddle" is to travel about selling small wares.	

1. Work the __pedal__ with your left foot.
2. My shoe stuck to the _____.
3. I fixed the _____ on the tricycle.
4. They _____ their goods on the roadside.
5. Push the _____ to the floor.
6. The _____ on my bike is broken.
7. You can't _____ without a license.
8. Can you _____ faster?
9. He wanted permission to _____ brushes.
10. Step on this _____ with your foot.

prey	pray
A "prey" is an animal seized by another for food.	
To "pray" is "to address a deity."	

1. The priest began to ___pray___.
2. He followed his _____ to the river.
3. The man pretended to _____.
4. He attacked his _____ from above.
5. The tiger cornered its _____.
6. The lion stalked its _____.
7. They bowed their heads to _____.
8. Its _____ tried to run away.
9. She walked to the altar to _____.
10. It stalks its _____ at night.

From "Preceding" to "Respectfully"

> **preceding**   **previous**
> "Preceding" means "to come before."
> "Previous" means "to come before at other times."

A Write "preceding" or "previous" in each blank.

1. The _____*preceding*_____ announcement was made by Dr. Reuben.
2. _____ announcements were recorded on tapes.
3. In June we raised more money than in the _____ month.
4. In August we collected more money than in the _____ months.
5. The year _____ 1955 was our worst.
6. The years _____ to 1970 were the worst.
7. All the _____ members have been men.

> **formally**   **formerly**
> "Formally" means "in a formal manner."
> "Formerly" means "in the past."

B Write "formally" or "formerly" in each blank.

1. Everyone at the dinner was _____*formally*_____ dressed.
2. _____ he was the representative from India.
3. When you go to a banquet, you should dress _____.
4. The job has _____ been left to the vice president.
5. Mrs. Collier and I have not been _____ introduced.
6. The President _____ accepted the gift from the ambassador.
7. _____ she was a member of the Peace Corps.

> **respectively**   **respectfully**
> "Respectively" means "in the order named."
> "Respectfully" means "in a courteous manner."

C Write "respectively' or "respectfully" in each blank.

1. They chose "A," "B," and "C" _____*respectively*_____.
2. Everyone welcomed the visitors _____.
3. We _____ voted for Anne, Kimberly, and Martha.
4. The winners of the race were Al, Joe, and Ben _____.
5. The members _____ saluted the flag.
6. The players _____ presented their coach with the trophy.
7. I _____ offer my congratulations.

Unit 140 cont'd →

From "Slay" to "Wood"

Write the correct homonym in each blank.

---

slay   **sleigh**

To "slay" means "to kill."
A "sleigh" is a vehicle used for traveling over snow.

---

1. The knight will __*slay*__ the dragon.
2. The horses pulled the _____.
3. _____ the beast!
4. The _____ was packed with toys.
5. I rode to school in a _____.

6. Let's go for a _____ ride.
7. He tried to _____ him with his sword.
8. Santa rides in a red _____.
9. The man tried to _____ the monster.
10. The _____ was painted blue.

---

stationary   **stationery**

"Stationary" means "remaining in one place."
"Stationery" refers to writing materials.

---

1. Bring me some __*stationery*__.
2. A house is a _____ object.
3. Joey likes the green _____ best.
4. A tree is _____.
5. This _____ is too expensive.

6. The _____ is on sale today.
7. I gave her a box of _____.
8. You cannot move a _____ object.
9. Lynn received four boxes of _____.
10. People write on _____.

---

waive   **wave**

"Waive" means "to give up or relinquish a claim to."
"Wave" means "to move freely back and forth or up and down."

---

1. I will __*waive*__ my right to object.
2. Tom will _____ the flag.
3. Don't _____ your right to vote.
4. Did you _____ at Paul?
5. The judge will _____ the charges.

6. They didn't _____ at us.
7. _____ your arms like a bird.
8. You can _____ your objection.
9. _____ at the police officer.
10. We must _____ our claims.

---

would   **wood**

"Would" refers to what might be expected.
"Wood" is the material of which trees are made.

---

1. The bowl is made of __*wood*__.
2. I _____ like to meet Charles.
3. _____ you help us?
4. This _____ scratches easily.
5. _____ you have come?

6. Don't carve your name in the _____.
7. What _____ you do?
8. I'll wax the _____ furniture.
9. He _____ have stopped them.
10. Kate is chopping _____.

Comprehension Check

(A) **Match each word with its definition.**

1. counsel   a   a body of persons
2. council   b. "to offer advice"

3. capital   a. the building where the legislature
                         meets
4. Capitol   b. the main city of a country or a state

5. coward   a. a person lacking in courage
6. cowered   b. past tense of "cower";
                         "to tremble"

7. compliment   a. an expression of praise
8. complement   b. something which completes
                         the whole

(B) **Fill in the blanks with words from part A.**

1. Ms. Lynch will ___*counsel*___ us.
2. The _____ meets tonight.
3. Austin is the _____ of Texas.
4. They met in the _____ building.

5. Is the dog a _____ ?
6. The kitten _____ under the chair.

7. The tie will _____ your suit.
8. Please accept my _____ .

(C) **Match each word with its definition.**

___*d*___ 1. fewer   a. used with numbers
_____ 2. less   b. refers to relationships in space
_____ 3. over   c. usually refers to more than two
_____ 4. more than   d. refers to number; things you can count
_____ 5. among   e. an opening in a fence or wall
_____ 6. between   f. refers to degree or quantity; things you can measure
_____ 7. gate   g. refers to two

_____ 8. gait   h. "very large" or "excellent"
_____ 9. groan   i. past participle of "grow"
_____ 10. grown   j. a device on which something is hung, such as a coat
_____ 11. great   k. a manner of walking or stepping
_____ 12. grate   l. a shelter for aircraft
_____ 13. hanger   m. "to utter a low sound of pain or sorrow"
_____ 14. hangar   n. "to reduce to small particles"

(D) **Fill in the blanks with words from part C.**

1. Add ___*less*___ water to the mixture.
2. The large puzzle has _____ 5,000 pieces.
3. There are _____ students this year.
4. Divide the candy _____ all students.
5. The lock on the _____ is broken.
6. She spent _____ $250.00.
7. The secret is _____ you and me.
8. _____ people voted in November.
9. Just _____ you and me, I agree.
10. Pass these out _____ the students.
11. The horse's _____ is unusual.
12. The small planes are in the _____ .
13. Molly tripped on a clothes _____ .
14. That's _____ !
15. His _____ slowed after ten minutes.
16. Please close the door to the _____ .
17. Karen will _____ the cheese.
18. The wind seemed to moan and _____ .
19. Put the jacket on a _____ .
20. The puppy is nearly _____ .

Test 28 cont'd →

Comprehension Check (continued)

(E) Complete each sentence with the correct word in the parentheses.

(imply, infer)   1. Did our teacher ___*imply*___ that we would have a test?

(reluctant, reticent)   2. Steve remained _____ about his objections.

(farther, further)   3. We'll speak _____ about the matter on Tuesday.

(manor, manner)   4. Her _____ of dress looks strange to us.

(mourning, morning)   5. Carla will call you on Saturday _____ .

(metal, medal)   6. Chris received a silver _____ as his award.

(knew, new)   7. I _____ you'd decide to go with us!

(know, no)   8. _____ , you aren't too late to ride the bus.

(knot, not)   9. Please untie the _____ in my necklace.

(knead, need)   10. You don't _____ to eat so much pizza.

(loan, borrow)   11. Greg filled out a _____ application to buy his car.

(agree to, agree with) 12. I can't _____ the plan you've proposed.

(F) Match each word with its definition.

_e_ 1. ability   a. mental power

___ 2. capability   b. a small part of a whole

___ 3. piece   c. a state of quiet

___ 4. peace   d. one who throws a ball; a container for liquids

___ 5. picture   e. the skill to perform

___ 6. pitcher   f. a drawing, painting, or photograph

___ 7. pedal   g. "in the past"

___ 8. peddle   h. "to address a deity"

___ 9. prey   i. to travel about selling small wares

___ 10. pray   j. "to come before"

___ 11. preceding   k. a lever operated by the foot

___ 12. formerly   l. an animal seized by another for food

Write a paragraph about your favorite car. Use at least three words from the sections of this test.

_____

_____

_____

_____

_____

_____

_____

From "Such As" to "Besides"

> **such as**   **like**
> Use "such as" for examples.
> Use "like" for resemblances.

A **Write "such as" or "like" in each blank.**

1. Large cities, _____*such as*_____ Detroit, have higher crime rates.
2. Tom resembles his father, but Betsy looks _____ her mother.
3. Big ships, _____ ocean liners, fascinate me.
4. The room looked _____ a cyclone had hit it.
5. Although Jenny and Kenny are twins, they do not look _____ each other.
6. I have always liked unusual animals, ____ _____ the aardvark.
7. Foreign countries _____ France are interesting to visit.
8. My brother Charles looks _____ my grandfather.

> **accept**   **except**
> "Accept" is a verb which means "to take or receive."
> "Except" is either a verb or a preposition; it means "exclude."

B **Write "accept" or "except" in each blank.**

1. All of us will ___*accept*___ your decision.
2. Everyone was there _____ John.
3. He won't _____ those conditions.
4. She took everything _____ her desk.
5. All the students are here _____ Vera.
6. Please _____ our thanks.
7. Nothing was missing _____ the money.
8. You should not _____ the reward.
9. I cannot _____ your idea.
10. She did not _____ my excuse.
11. I bought everything _____ milk.
12. Will you _____ my apology?
13. We have everything _____ socks.
14. They do not _____ checks.
15. Sherry liked everything _____ the spinach.
16. Did you _____ the gift?

> **beside**   **besides**
> "Beside" means "by the side of."
> "Besides" means "also" or "in addition to."

C **Write "beside" or "besides" in each blank.**

1. We ate our lunches ___*beside*___ the lake.
2. _____ jogging, we played tennis and went swimming.
3. The man in the blue suit sat _____ me on the bus.
4. _____ his cap and jacket, Bert forgot his gloves.
5. The dog walked patiently _____ his master.
6. I sat _____ a tall woman wearing a green hat.
7. _____ going to the park, we visited the zoo and the museum.
8. _____ math, I like English and science.

Unit 141 cont'd ➔

From "Suite" to "Steal"

 Write the correct homonym in each blank.

---

suite   **sweet**
"Suite" is an apartment in a hotel or office building.
"Sweet" has the flavor of sugar.

---

1. Candy is ___*sweet*___.
2. Her _____ is on the top floor.
3. He rents a _____ at the Hilton.
4. The fudge is too _____.
5. _____ is the opposite of sour.

6. The _____ was decorated in green.
7. The bread tastes _____.
8. Peter doesn't like _____ foods.
9. His _____ is next door.
10. I would like to rent a _____.

---

scene   **seen**
A "scene" is a place or a view.
"Seen" is the past participle of "see."

---

1. Have you ___*seen*___ the movie?
2. The _____ takes place in Italy.
3. Theo described the _____ of the accident.
4. The _____ is beautiful.
5. My brother has _____ the picture.

6. She has already _____ it.
7. Describe the next _____.
8. He has _____ the show four times.
9. You were _____ leaving the park.
10. This _____ shows the river.

---

seam   **seem**
A "seam" is a line where two pieces of cloth meet.
"Seem" means "to give the impression of being; appear."

---

1. The ___*seam*___ on my coat is ripped.
2. I can't _____ to do anything right.
3. Did he _____ to be hiding something?
4. The side _____ split.
5. The pictures _____ to look alike.

6. You _____ more tired than usual.
7. Stitch the _____ twice.
8. They _____ to go well together.
9. The top _____ was sewn with red thread.
10. You _____ to be on the right track.

---

steel   **steal**
"Steel" is a metal.
To "steal" means "to take without right."

---

1. These pipes are made of ___*steel*___.
2. I saw him _____ the money.
3. The _____ ball weighs ten pounds.
4. My dog likes to _____ shoes.
5. I put the money in a _____ box.

6. The frame is made of _____.
7. Did you _____ my pencil?
8. It is wrong to _____.
9. My father owns a _____ company.
10. Why did you _____ the car?

342

From "Weak" to "Hole"

Unit 142

 Write the correct homonym in each blank.

---

weak   **week**

"Weak" means "lacking strength."
A "week" consists of seven days.

---

1. Our class meets once a __week__.
2. The man felt _____ and hungry.
3. Next _____ is our math test.
4. He was too _____ to run.
5. The illness left her _____.

6. Sunday is the first day of the _____.
7. I was too _____ to answer him.
8. The meeting is this next _____.
9. Seven days make a _____.
10. You look _____.

---

write   **right**

To "write" means "to put words on paper."
"Right" is the opposite of "wrong." It is also the opposite of "left."

---

1. Turn __right__ at the corner.
2. Your answers are _____.
3. I must _____ a letter.
4. _____ the company.
5. That is not the _____ one.

6. _____ your name here.
7. I _____ with my _____ hand.
8. I want the hat on the _____.
9. Will you _____ her a note?
10. We turned _____ on Court Street.

---

wear   **where**

"Wear" means "to have on the person as a garment."
"Where" refers to place.

---

1. __where__ do you live?
2. Do you know _____ she went?
3. What will you _____ to the party?
4. Did he _____ that old hat?
5. I know _____ it is.

6. We will _____ our uniforms.
7. Show me _____ to go.
8. _____ is the bus station?
9. Did Jane _____ her coat?
10. _____ did you park the car?

---

whole   **hole**

"Whole" means "containing all the necessary parts; entire."
A "hole" is a "cavity in a solid body."

---

1. The dog dug a __hole__ for his bone.
2. The _____ thing is ruined.
3. The _____ needs to be bigger.
4. George ate the _____ pie.
5. I fell in the _____.

6. Two halves make a _____.
7. Ben covered the _____ with a board.
8. I dug a deep _____.
9. The _____ was filled with water.
10. The _____ room was filled with gifts.

Unit 142 cont'd →

Using "Who" and "Whom"

"Who" refers to the person who is the actor. It is a subject.

> EXAMPLES: a. *Who is that man?*
> b. *Tell me who did it.*

"Whom" refers to the person who has been acted upon. It is an object.

> EXAMPLES: c. *To whom do you wish to speak?*
> b. *For whom is the message?*

 Underline the correct sentences.

1. a. To who is the letter addressed?
   b. <u>To whom is the letter addressed?</u>

2. a. Who wrote <u>Huckleberry</u> <u>Finn</u>?
   b. Whom wrote <u>Huckleberry</u> <u>Finn</u>?

3. a. To who am I speaking?
   b. To whom am I speaking?

4. a. Who told who?
   b. Who told whom?

5. a. Who is he?
   b. Whom is he?

6. a. To who did you give the box?
   b. To whom did you give the box?

7. a. Who lives in the white house?
   b. Whom lives in the white house?

8. a. For who is the present?
   b. For whom is the present?

9. a. Do you know who she is?
   b. Do you know whom she is?

10. a. He's the one to who I spoke.
    b. He's the one to whom I spoke.

11. a. Who are you?
    b. Whom are you?

12. a. To who does this belong?
    b. To whom does this belong?

13. a. Sam is the one who told me.
    b. Sam is the one whom told me.

14. a. Who are you calling?
    b. Whom are you calling?

15. a. Who won the contest?
    b. Whom won the contest?

16. a. Who are you inviting?
    b. Whom are you inviting?

17. a. Who did you tell?
    b. Whom did you tell?

18. a. Who has finished his work?
    b. Whom has finished his work?

19. a. Who do you wish to see?
    b. Whom do you wish to see?

20. a. Who painted this picture?
    b. Whom painted this picture?

Sets of Three

Write the correct homonym in each blank.

> **pair**   **pare**   **pear**
> A "pair" is a set of two.
> To "pare" means "to cut off the covering."
> A "pear" is a fruit.

1. I bought a __*pair*__ of shoes.
2. Will you _____ the apples?
3. He was carrying a _____ of skis.
4. I lost a _____ of gloves.
5. The _____ was not ripe.
6. Ken ordered a _____ of glasses.
7. Send him a _____ of boots.

8. Walter was eating a _____.
9. Use this knife to _____ the orange.
10. You need a new _____ of socks.
11. The _____ tasted sweet.
12. I tried to _____ the apple with a fork.
13. A _____ is green.
14. Bring me a _____ of mittens.

> **scent**   **sent**   **cent**
> A "scent" is a smell.
> "Sent" is the past-tense form of "send."
> A "cent" is a penny.

1. You could recognize a skunk by the __*scent*__.
2. We _____ you a copy.
3. It costs one _____.
4. The dog followed the raccoon's _____.
5. She would not give a _____ more.
6. The package was _____ to Mr. Olson.
7. The envelope contained one _____.

8. Dee _____ the letter to my dad.
9. He gave a _____ too much.
10. Has anyone _____ him a card?
11. Linda needs one _____.
12. I _____ my mother some flowers.
13. No one noticed the _____ of perfume.
14. It was _____ to the wrong address.

> **by**   **bye**   **buy**
> "By" is a preposition.
> "Bye" is an expression of farewell.
> To "buy" means "to purchase."

1. What did you __*buy*__ at the store?
2. We said good-_____ at the station.
3. The train goes _____ my house.
4. _____ the one on the right.
5. I want to _____ a bicycle.
6. Let's sit _____ the window.
7. He cannot afford to _____ the car.

8. You must _____ a new coat.
9. Ned sits _____ me in class.
10. He waved good-_____ to everyone.
11. My mother stood _____ the table.
12. I helped her _____ the groceries.
13. Did you tell her good-_____?
14. Wait for me _____ the bus.

Unit 143 cont'd

Words Often Confused

A Write "then" or "than" in each blank.

1. We will go home __*then*__.
2. I am taller _____ Ronald.
3. Sam is smarter _____ Nick.
4. It is better _____ ours.
5. _____ I will help you.
6. The room is bigger _____ the garage.
7. _____ everyone went home.
8. I am shorter _____ Billie.
9. _____ what did you do?
10. Jill runs faster _____ Dan.
11. The bus is later _____ usual.
12. _____ the door opened.
13. Theodore is older _____ Brad.
14. What happened _____?
15. _____ I remembered the answer.
16. It was easier _____ I expected.

B Write "passed" or "past" in each blank.

1. We __*passed*__ the math test.
2. Hal ran _____ the store.
3. The train _____ the station.
4. He _____ the house.
5. I live _____ the fire station.
6. _____ troubles should be forgotten.
7. I _____ the science test.
8. The verb is in _____ tense.
9. Connie walked _____ the bakery.
10. The car _____ us.
11. She remembered _____ times.
12. I _____ the exam easily.
13. We walked _____ the old schoolhouse.
14. Lou hurried _____ the haunted house.
15. The truck _____ the bus.
16. He _____ me in the hallway.

C Write "later" or "latter" in each blank.

1. I arrived __*later*__ than Edward.
2. The _____ one is mine.
3. They were _____ than we.
4. The _____ car is a Chevrolet.
5. The _____ of the two is Jason.
6. Our bus arrived five hours _____.
7. The _____ bike was yellow.
8. Paula came _____ than Kim.
9. The _____ one is better.
10. The train is _____ than usual.
11. I will see him _____.
12. I choose the _____ of the two.
13. Schedule me for a _____ time.
14. I will take the _____ box of clothes.
15. The _____ of the two men is Mr. Jones.
16. She arrived _____ that evening.

How Important Is Listening?

Did you ever stop to think how much time you spend listening during the average day? You probably would be surprised at the amount. Studies have shown that on the average, 70% of our waking day is spent in verbal communication (reading, talking, listening, and writing). Look at the graph at the right of the page, and you will see that 45% of the time spent in verbal communication is spent in listening.

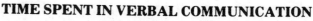

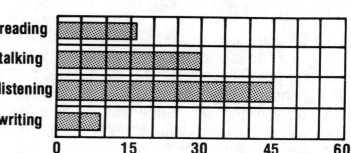

TIME SPENT IN VERBAL COMMUNICATION

People listening to people affects the lives of nearly everyone. What we eat, wear, read, and watch on television are all influenced by what we hear. As we look around, we see more and more how much we rely upon the way people listen. Surveys have shown that during political elections, the voters received most of their information from what they hear and are influenced by listening to other people. Our jury system depends entirely upon the listening ability of the jurors. In every trial by jury, twelve people listen to evidence in order to decide what is a just verdict. Reporters who write and tell the news receive much of their information from listening during interviews, speeches, and press conferences. If journalists are to be fair and accurate, they have to be the best of listeners. The success of businesses depends on good listening. Employers and employees must listen to each other in order to solve problems and develop new ideas. In the classroom the success or failure of students often depends upon good listening. Perhaps the most important use of listening is in the home where good communication can come about only if parents and children listen to each other with respect, love, and courtesy.

Listening is so important in our daily life that we should all strive toward developing effective skills that help us to meet the listening demands placed on us every day.

✱ **Place the letter of the best answer in the blank before each of the following questions. There may be more than one answer for each question.**

_A, C, D, E_ 1. What does the term "verbal communication" refer to? (a) talking (b) eating (c) reading (d) writing (e) listening

_____ 2. What percentage of our time is spent in verbal communication? (a) 20% (b) 70% (c) 16% (d) 45%

_____ 3. What percentage of our time is spent in listening? (a) 45% (b) 16% (c) 9% (d) 30%

_____ 4. Are any of the following things influenced by what we listen to? (a) our clothes (b) the food we like (c) the movies we see (d) the books we read (e) the toys we buy (f) the people we like

_____ 5. Where do voters receive most of their information? (a) from newspapers (b) by listening (c) from magazines (d) from books

_____ 6. How do jurors arrive at a just verdict? (a) by listening to evidence (b) by reading newspapers (c) from police files (d) from TV newscasts

_____ 7. How do reporters receive their information? (a) reading newspapers (b) listening to press conferences (c) at interviews (d) listening to speeches

_____ 8. How is listening used in businesses? (a) to solve problems (b) to entertain (c) between employers and employees (d) to develop new ideas

_____ 9. How is listening used in the home? (a) to show love (b) to show respect (c) for good communication (d) to show courtesy

Unit 144 cont'd ➡

How Well Do You Listen?

Listening is an art. To be well performed, it requires more than just letting sound waves enter your ears. Good listening demands alert and active participation and is developed through training and practice.

1. Do you listen between the lines? A good listener applies his spare thinking to what is being said and is attentive at all times.
2. Do you concentrate? It is not easy to concentrate; therefore, it is necessary to remove distractions from the path of your listening.
3. Do you give your full attention while listening? A wandering mind or being easily distracted can detract from your listening power. A good listener disciplines himself.
4. Do you participate when you listen? A speaker should have the chance to present all the facts without interruptions. The good listener must be alert to find something interesting in what is being said and attempts to keep the discussion moving by asking questions or adding something constructive to the situation.
5. Do you understand and grasp the true idea or meaning of what is said? To understand fully, it is necessary to be interested in what is being said and to avoid distractions.
6. Do you evaluate when you listen? Reacting thoughtfully to the spoken word is one of the most important goals in listening skills. Thinking beyond the speaker's words, weighing what has been said, and applying your own knowledge of the subject will help you develop critical listening skills.

If you were able to answer a sincere yes to all of the above questions, you're an excellent listener. If any of your answers was no, make a point to try to improve upon them. When you have conquered all the listening skills, you will be rewarded by the ability to better understand and enjoy the world around you.

Place a check mark in the blank beside each of the following sentences that you think shows good listening skills.

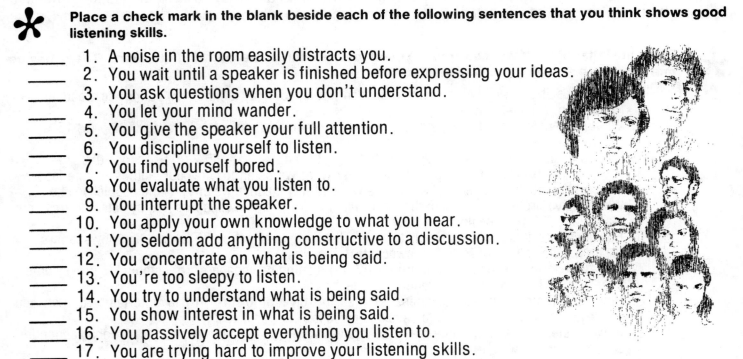

____ 1. A noise in the room easily distracts you.
____ 2. You wait until a speaker is finished before expressing your ideas.
____ 3. You ask questions when you don't understand.
____ 4. You let your mind wander.
____ 5. You give the speaker your full attention.
____ 6. You discipline yourself to listen.
____ 7. You find yourself bored.
____ 8. You evaluate what you listen to.
____ 9. You interrupt the speaker.
____ 10. You apply your own knowledge to what you hear.
____ 11. You seldom add anything constructive to a discussion.
____ 12. You concentrate on what is being said.
____ 13. You're too sleepy to listen.
____ 14. You try to understand what is being said.
____ 15. You show interest in what is being said.
____ 16. You passively accept everything you listen to.
____ 17. You are trying hard to improve your listening skills.

Taking Notes

When you write down information in class, you are taking notes. Write down only important information. With practice, you can learn to recognize the main ideas of a lesson. Write each main idea on your paper. List related topics under each main idea. Don't try to write down everything that's said. You should spend more time listening than you spend writing. Otherwise, you may miss some important information.

Try to develop your own form of shorthand. This will help you to spend less time writing and more time listening. You can practice your "shorthand" daily to gain speed. You can fill in more information after class if you need to. As you listen for the main ideas for your notes, you will find that you're paying closer attention to what is being said in class.

Keep all your notes on each subject together in one notebook, or keep your notes in a section of a large notebook. Look at your notes regularly. This will help you prepare for class. It will also help you prepare for tests. To get the full benefit from your notes, use good penmanship.

A Put a check (✓) beside each statement or suggestion which agrees with the lesson above.

✓ 1. Use good penmanship.
___ 2. Try to write down everything.
___ 3. Notes have little value.
___ 4. Organizing notes is important.
___ 5. You must listen carefully.
___ 6. Spend more time writing than listening.
___ 7. Select the main ideas.
___ 8. Don't bother studying your notes.
___ 9. Develop your own shorthand.
___ 10. Notes can help you prepare for class.

___ 11. Read over your notes regularly.
___ 12. Your notes can help you study for tests.

B Read the main idea. Underline each topic which relates to it.

Main idea: Baseball is an important sport in the United States.

1. U.S. fans fill baseball parks.
2. I think crowds get too noisy.
3. Sharon's uncle plays baseball.
4. Our baseball players sometimes become heroes.
5. Our TV networks broadcast many games.

6. Local companies often have their own teams.
7. Baseball is very popular in Japan.
8. Foul balls are often hit.
9. Players "warm up" in the bull pen.
10. U.S. newspapers give complete game details.

Unit 145 cont'd

Deciding What's Important

Write important information in your notes for class.

EXAMPLES: a. *The War of 1812 ended in 1814.*
This is important information.
b. *We studied that last year.*
This is not important information.

A Put a check (✓) beside each statement that would be important enough to write down.

✓ 1. The Mississippi River flows south.

___ 2. Our school has a game next week.

___ 3. It's raining today.

___ 4. Reading about rockets is interesting.

___ 5. Cells have different shapes.

___ 6. California's gold rush began in 1848.

___ 7. They may win the World Series.

___ 8. Cliff sprained his wrist.

___ 9. John Glenn was the first American in orbit.

___ 10. Jefferson City is the capital of Missouri.

___ 11. Our President once grew a beard.

___ 12. Scott Carpenter was the second American in orbit.

___ 13. The wind spreads seeds.

___ 14. The Grand Canyon is in Arizona.

___ 15. We had a windstorm last night.

___ 16. A fable is a story that teaches a lesson.

___ 17. Flies are insects.

___ 18. Salt can be found in water, soil, and rocks.

___ 19. Australia is the smallest continent.

___ 20. Rice and wheat are grains.

___ 21. Ocean water rises and falls.

___ 22. David is a good surfer.

___ 23. March is the third month of the year.

___ 24. Lana's birthday is in March.

___ 25. Americans have freedom of speech.

___ 26. Andy talks too much in class.

___ 27. A sentence must have a noun and a verb.

___ 28. Most Canadians speak English and French.

B Read the lesson below. Underline the sentences which you wouldn't write in your notes.

The earth travels around the sun. You already know that. The North Pole faces the sun for six months. Then the South Pole faces the sun for six months. The pole which faces the sun has only daylight for six months. The other pole has only darkness during that time. Wouldn't that be strange? The sun shines at the North Pole from March 21 to September 21. What a long day! The sun shines at the South Pole from September 21 to March 21. The tilt of the earth is the cause of the midnight sun.

COMPOSITION EXERCISE

Copy a paragraph from a textbook or an encyclopedia. Underline the words or sentences which you would not write in your notes.

_____

_____

_____

_____

_____

_____

_____

_____

Comprehension Check

Ⓐ Match each word with its definition; then use the word correctly in a sentence.

1. such as ——	a.	use for examples
2. like	b.	use for resemblances
3. except	c.	"to take or receive"
4. accept	d.	"exclude"
5. beside	e.	"also" or "in addition to"
6. besides	f.	"by the side of"
7. suite	g.	the flavor of sugar
8. sweet	h.	an apartment or a room
9. scene	i.	a place or a view
10. seen	j.	past participle of "see"
11. steel	k.	a metal
12. steal	l.	"to take without right"
13. wear	m.	refers to place
14. where	n.	"to have on one's person"
15. write	o.	"to put words on paper"
16. right	p.	opposite of "wrong" and "left"

The table looked ___*like*___ an antique.

Hobbies _____ stamp collecting are interesting.

Everyone's invited _____ Norm.

Please _____ my apology, Jim.

Sit _____ me while we talk.

_____ cake, we baked a pie and cookies.

The caramel pie is too _____ .

We rented a _____ at the hotel.

She hasn't been _____ since Friday.

Barry, can you paint this _____ ?

They had to _____ some moments for privacy.

Use a _____ pipe under the sink.

Did Andrew _____ his white jacket?

_____ is the candy machine?

Did Mary _____ her term paper?

I think you have the _____ idea.

Ⓑ Complete each sentence with "who" or "whom."

1. To ___*whom*___ did you point?
2. _____ is calling?
3. _____ are you calling?
4. Shari's the one to _____ I spoke.
5. Who told _____ ?
6. Jane's the one _____ told me.
7. _____ finished the job?
8. To _____ do you wish to speak?
9. _____ cleaned the carport?
10. Did you know _____ called?
11. Do you know _____ she is?
12. To _____ shall we speak?
13. By _____ should we sit?
14. _____ is building the fence?

Ⓒ Underline the correct words.

1. He (<u>passed</u>, past) me the basketball.
2. Sit (by, bye, buy) the assistant.
3. A (pair, pare, pear) is a fruit.
4. I smell the (cent, sent, scent) of oranges.
5. We (than, then) called Richard.
6. I chose the (latter, later) question.
7. Walk (passed, past) the window.
8. Ted (scent, sent, cent) me a note.
9. Please (pair, pare, pear) the apples.
10. Ed is taller (than, then) Terry.
11. We'll discuss this (latter, later).
12. Did you (by, bye, buy) more candy?
13. Here's your (pair, pare, pear) of shoes.
14. You may (than, then) go home.

Test 29 cont'd →

Comprehension Check (continued)

(D) **Put a check (✓) beside each suggestion that is a good listening or note-taking skill.**

__✓__ 1. Read over your notes regularly.

____ 2. Listen carefully in class.

____ 3. Try to write down everything.

____ 4. Let your mind wander.

____ 5. Select the main ideas.

____ 6. Don't bother studying your notes.

____ 7. Develop your own shorthand.

____ 8. Use good penmanship.

____ 9. Interrupt the speaker regularly.

____ 10. Use your notes to prepare for class.

____ 11. Show interest in what is being said.

____ 12. Organize your notes.

____ 13. Write down only important information.

____ 14. Spend more time writing than listening.

(E) **Put a check (✓) beside each statement that would be important enough to write in your notes.**

__✓__ 1. Halley's Comet arrives every 75-77 years.

____ 2. There are other heavenly bodies.

____ 3. Mark Twain died in 1910.

____ 4. Edgar Allan Poe was born in 1809.

____ 5. We watched a science show last night.

____ 6. Halley's Comet was first seen in 240 B.C.

____ 7. The comet was named for Edmund Halley.

____ 8. Halley lived from 1656 to 1742.

____ 9. We bought a new telescope.

____ 10. Halley's Comet reappeared in 1986.

____ 11. Thomas Edison invented the phonograph.

____ 12. March is the month of Lana's birthday.

____ 13. March is the third month.

____ 14. Super Bowl Sunday is always interesting.

____ 15. Flies are insects.

____ 16. The wind damaged our garage door.

____ 17. We have an electric door opener.

____ 18. Water freezes at 32° F.

____ 19. Water boils at 212° F.

____ 20. The temperature is dropping now.

Write a paragraph describing your listening skills. Are you a good listener or a poor listener?

_____

_____

_____

_____

_____

_____

_____

_____

Putting Sentence Groups Together

*Information on the same subject should be
grouped together.*

A Put a check beside each sentence which would belong with information about the history of dancing.

✓ 1. The waltz began in Germany.
___ 2. Even young children can dance.
___ 3. Some steps are hard to learn.
___ 4. Dancing is good exercise.
___ 5. What is your favorite music?
___ 6. Dance styles have changed often.
___ 7. Almost anyone can learn to dance.
___ 8. Dancing is a big part of our past.
___ 9. Cruise ships have large dance floors.
___ 10. A polka calls for a great deal of energy.
___ 11. Dancing has been popular throughout history.
___ 12. Ancient people danced to honor their gods.
___ 13. Romans copied dances from other countries.
___ 14. The square dance came from an English dance.
___ 15. Cave paintings of people dancing have been found.
___ 16. Many new dances have been introduced since 1900.
___ 17. Primitive people danced to celebrate marriages.
___ 18. Modern people dance to celebrate marriages.
___ 19. More people marry in June than in any other month.
___ 20. People started taking dance lessons in the Middle Ages.
___ 21. Your parents' dance steps may look funny to you.
___ 22. The steps to the waltz are easy to learn and to remember.

B Read the following information about the state of Washington. Put the information into groups by writing a "c" beside information which is about the climate. Put an "h" beside information about history, an "s" beside information about schools, and an "r" beside information about resources.

r 1. Washington has a good water supply.
___ 2. Seattle University is located in Seattle.
___ 3. Public schools opened in 1895.
___ 4. Washington became a state on Nov. 11, 1889.
___ 5. Parts of the state get a great deal of rain.
___ 6. Nearly 24 million acres of the state are forest land.
___ 7. Lewis and Clark explored Washington.
___ 8. Washington was part of the Oregon Territory.
___ 9. Eastern and western Washington have different weather.
___ 10. Walla Walla College is located in Washington.
___ 11. Rainbow trout are found in the rivers.
___ 12. Many Indian tribes lived in Washington.

Unit 146 cont'd

Organizing Your Material

When you organize, you put ideas into a working order. The better you organize your material before you write, the easier your writing will be.

A Read the list of notes about space-age careers. Put a check beside each sentence which you could use in a report on that subject.

✓   1. An astronaut explores space.

____ 2. Denny's aunt met John Glenn.

____ 3. Engineers design spacecraft.

____ 4. Scientists prepare space experiments.

____ 5. Some people learn to repair spacecraft.

____ 6. New fuels are discovered by chemists.

____ 7. Children play with toy rockets.

____ 8. The first moon landing was in 1969.

____ 9. Doctors keep a close watch on the astronauts.

____ 10. Scientists examined the moon rocks.

____ 11. Researchers constantly develop new equipment.

____ 12. Office workers are necessary to manage NASA offices.

____ 13. Office workers are necessary in other industries.

____ 14. Someone must build new space equipment.

____ 15. The U.S. Government has space career information.

____ 16. Some people work with weather satellites.

____ 17. Space equipment must be taken care of by workers.

____ 18. Companies employ people to make equipment.

____ 19. Engineers design and build instruments for space.

____ 20. Science and math are important for future scientists.

B The facts below are about South America. Put "c" beside each statement which is about the climate, "n" beside each statement about natural resources, and "a" beside each statement about animals.

n   1. Pine trees are found in South America.

____ 2. The anaconda snake may grow to 30 feet.

____ 3. Winters last from June to September.

____ 4. Some rodents may grow to three feet long.

____ 5. Land near the equator is hot and humid.

____ 6. The Amazon is South America's longest river.

____ 7. South America's rivers are filled with piranha fish.

____ 8. The climate is always cold in the Andes mountains.

____ 9. The largest cat is the cougar.

____ 10. Angel Falls is the world's highest waterfall.

____ 11. Parrots and storks are found in South America.

____ 12. Silver is mined in Peru.

____ 13. The Brazil-nut tree can grow to 150 feet.

____ 14. The tapir is the largest wild animal.

____ 15. Colombia gets heavy rainfall.

____ 16. Pineapples grow in humid areas.

____ 17. Most areas are warm throughout the year.

____ 18. Brazil is very hot in January.

____ 19. The Amazon River basin has many animals.

____ 20. Argentina has wide grasslands.

____ 21. Summer lasts from December to March.

____ 22. Petroleum is an important resource.

____ 23. Turtles grow very large in some areas.

____ 24. There are more than 2,500 kinds of trees.

C Draw a line from each subject to a sentence which relates to that subject.

1. mining
2. people
3. climate
4. holidays
5. industry
6. language
7. land
8. rivers
9. family life

a. English is the international language.
b. The average rainfall is 26 inches.
c. Coal is mined in West Virginia.
d. Florida has many miles of coastline.
e. Shoes are made in many southern states.
f. There are many single-parent families in the U.S.
g. The Mississippi River is 2,350 miles long.
h. There are many immigrants from Southeast Asia.
i. We celebrate our independence on July 4th.

Facts or Opinions?

A fact is a true statement about a subject.
EXAMPLE: Texas is larger than Delaware.

An opinion is someone's belief about a subject.
EXAMPLE: Texas is the best state in the U.S.

A Write "f" beside each fact. Write "o" beside each opinion.

__f__ 1. Arizona has a dry climate.
____ 2. Paris is the capital of France.
____ 3. The painting is by Rockwell.
____ 4. Parrots make nice pets.
____ 5. The museum is interesting to visit.
____ 6. Our football team won Friday.
____ 7. Your paragraph is boring.
____ 8. Mark has a new job.
____ 9. The parade is Saturday.
____ 10. My canary sings very well.
____ 11. Ellen speaks too softly.
____ 12. Janis has a poodle.

____ 13. Paris is called the "City of Light."
____ 14. The library is closed.
____ 15. Andrew is a good painter.
____ 16. You're my best partner.
____ 17. A collie is the friendliest dog.
____ 18. New Mexico has a good climate.
____ 19. Cassie has a passport.
____ 20. Parakeets have feathers.
____ 21. Jackie is our best player.
____ 22. I've waited too long for you.
____ 23. The July 4th parade was great.
____ 24. Your voice is too loud.

B Each statement below is either a fact or an opinion. Rewrite each fact as an opinion. Rewrite each opinion as a fact.

1. My brother lost his job.   _His job loss was his fault._
2. Mickey is in college.   _____
3. Mr. Brown is our new science teacher.   _____
4. Rhonda yawned.   _____
5. Jonathan's dog is lost.   _____
6. Eric ate a peach.   _____
7. Our new chair is blue.   _____
8. The television is on.   _____
9. A potato chip contains ten calories.   _____
10. World War II ended in 1945.   _____
11. The game ended at 10:00 p.m.   _____
12. Monica is tired.   _____

COMPOSITION EXERCISE

Write a paragraph about one of your school subjects. Underline each statement which is an opinion.

_____
_____
_____
_____
_____
_____
_____
_____

Unit 147 cont'd

Conclusions Based on Facts

A conclusion should be based on fact rather than on opinion.

EXAMPLE: Matt left the classroom.
      a. He needed to be elsewhere.   This conclusion is based on fact.
      b. He wasn't prepared for the test.   This conclusion is based on opinion.

A Read each statement. Underline the conclusion which is based on fact rather than on opinion.

1. Mary is frowning.
   a. Mary has a headache.
   b. <u>Something is bothering Mary.</u>

2. The dog ate his food.
   a. The dog was hungry.
   b. That was his favorite food.

3. Turn left at the light.
   a. That is the correct direction to turn.
   b. The road on the right is bumpy.

4. The apples are bruised.
   a. The apples have been handled roughly.
   b. All apples are bruised.

5. There is smoke in the house.
   a. The TV is on fire.
   b. Something may be burning.

6. Melissa started the car.
   a. Melissa is probably going somewhere.
   b. Melissa is the only one who can drive.

7. Al took an aspirin.
   a. Al needs pain relief.
   b. Al takes aspirins constantly.

8. She didn't buy the brown shoes.
   a. She hates brown shoes.
   b. The shoes were not suitable.

9. Amy dialed a number.
   a. Amy is making a phone call.
   b. She is calling her parents.

10. Tricia took her cat to the vet.
   a. The cat needs medical attention.
   b. Her cat has a serious illness.

11. Joe is running for class president.
   a. Joe wants to be class president.
   b. Joe wants a political career.

12. Denise types fast.
   a. She wants to be a secretary.
   b. She has practiced her skill.

B Write a conclusion for each statement. Base the conclusion on fact and not on opinion.

1. Thunder boomed constantly.   *A storm was building.* _____
2. Jimmy is late for the meeting. _____
3. Angela smiled at Ronald. _____
4. Barry ate three hamburgers. _____
5. The cows are on the highway. _____
6. Darrell saddled his horse. _____
7. The police siren blew. _____
8. Alice turned the TV to channel five. _____
9. The baby is crying. _____

The Topic Sentence

The topic sentence tells the main idea of a paragraph.
It is often the first sentence of a paragraph.

EXAMPLE: *My dog is very lazy. He sleeps most of the day. He wants me to bring his food to him. He won't even chase cats. Have you ever heard of a lazier dog?*

 Underline the topic sentence of each paragraph.

1.   <u>Alex is so clumsy today.</u> He dropped all of his books. Then he tripped over his shoelaces. Next he spilled cola on his new shirt. He'll be glad when this day is over.

2.   We need to discuss your report. You need to make some changes. Move the paragraphs down on the first page. Write more about your second topic. Add a conclusion. These changes should be made by Friday.

3.   We should be allowed to attend the dance. Larry earned the money for admission. Al borrowed his brother's car. We promised the girls we'd take them. Won't you reconsider?

4.   I want to tell you why I'm late. It really wasn't my fault. The traffic delayed me. Then I had to buy Jenny something to eat. Later, I had to go back to get my math book. Please don't be angry.

5.   Jill is very upset with you. There are three reasons why she is upset. You forgot to call her last night. She heard that you went to a movie. You haven't spoken to her today. Maybe you should talk to her.

6.   This is a good book. The main character has an exciting life. The plot keeps my interest. Reading the book makes me feel good. Would you like to borrow it?

7.   I think we need to buy a new car. Our car has several problems. The tires are worn. The paint is cracked. A brake job is needed. Let's go car shopping!

8.   That restaurant is a good place to eat. The food is delicious. It is served quickly. The waiters and waitresses are friendly. Let's eat there tonight.

9.   Sheila is a good friend. There are several reasons why I like her. She understands my problems. She always listens when I want to talk. I can trust her with my secrets. I hope we'll always be friends.

Unit 148 cont'd

Choosing Your Main Topic

A topic sentence states the subject of a paragraph.

A Read each paragraph. Write a topic sentence for each paragraph.

1. _____

The cat won't eat. She sleeps most of the time. She won't play with me. I hope she gets well soon.

2. _____

She smiled when she got her report card. She ran to tell her parents about her grades. Melissa's been in a good mood all day.

3. _____

She sings very well. Her dancing is outstanding. The audience seems to like her act. I hope Sharon wins the talent contest.

4. _____

All my friends are here. I get to learn about many subjects. School prepares me for a career. I enjoy school more each year.

5. _____

She is a good leader. She's had experience as a class officer. Her plans for our class sound interesting. I hope Gina is elected president of our class.

B Put a check (✓) beside each sentence which could be a topic sentence.

✓ 1. Alison gets to do whatever she wants.
____ 2. Then he called his best friend.
____ 3. Finally, the cab driver drove away.
____ 4. This is the best car I've ever had.
____ 5. She has a good sense of humor.
____ 6. The picnic was fun.

____ 7. There are three reasons why I can't go.
____ 8. We'll have a busy vacation.
____ 9. Karen wants to be a doctor.
____ 10. I've always wanted to see Paris.
____ 11. This is my favorite kind of music.
____ 12. I lost the keys this morning.

COMPOSITION EXERCISE

Write a paragraph; use one of the sentences from part B as the topic sentence.

_____
_____
_____
_____
_____
_____
_____

Weeding Out Unnecessary Thoughts

***Each sentence in a paragraph should relate to the
subject of the paragraph.***

 Read each paragraph. Underline the sentence in each paragraph which does not stay on the subject.

1.   Labor Day was created to honor working people. The holiday was the idea of Peter J. McGuire. The first Labor Day was celebrated in 1882 in New York City. Labor Day became a national holiday in 1894. Life is not always easy for working people. Labor Day falls on the first Monday of September each year.

2.   Memorial Day is not a happy celebration. It is a day on which we honor Americans who have died while defending their country. My uncle was killed in World War II. Memorial Day is the last Monday in May.

3.   Halloween is the night that ghosts and goblins walk among us. Halloween began long, long ago. People believed in ghosts and built bonfires to protect themselves. Some of their customs became part of our Halloween. My little sister is too scared to trick or treat. Halloween is also celebrated in Ireland, England, and Scotland.

4.   Thanksgiving is truly an American holiday. It began in 1621. The Pilgrims set aside a day to give thanks for their blessings. They had survived the long ocean voyage. They had a good harvest that first year. The Pilgrims and their Indian guests feasted for three days. I wonder what the Indians thought of the settlers. In 1863, President Lincoln set aside the last Thursday in November to be celebrated each year as Thanksgiving Day.

5.   England has a holiday which celebrates an event that never happened. The holiday is called Guy Fawkes Day. In 1605, Guy Fawkes and his followers planned to blow up England's king and government leaders. Guy Fawkes was caught before he carried out his plan. He was hanged the next year. November 5 is Guy Fawkes Day. The United States also has a holiday in November.

COMPOSITION EXERCISE

Write a paragraph about a holiday you have celebrated. Write one sentence which doesn't belong with the paragraph. Underline the unnecessary sentence.

_____

_____

_____

_____

_____

_____

_____

_____

Unit 149 cont'd

Staying on the Subject

Each sentence in a paragraph should relate to the subject of the paragraph.

A Put a check (✓) beside each sentence which would belong in a paragraph about kinds of birds. Seven groups are named. Underline the name of each group.

✓ 1. <u>Perching birds</u> include sparrows and robins.

_____ 2. Some birds eat seeds.

_____ 3. The heron has a bill shaped like a spear.

_____ 4. Parakeets make good pets.

_____ 5. Some birds can fly for days without rest.

_____ 6. Water birds are found near the water.

_____ 7. There are more land birds than water birds.

_____ 8. Owls, eagles, and hawks are birds of prey.

_____ 9. Some birds eat insects that harm crops.

_____ 10. Ducks and geese are game birds.

_____ 11. All birds are hatched from eggs.

_____ 12. All birds have wings.

_____ 13. Ostriches and penguins are flightless birds.

_____ 14. Many birds migrate each year.

_____ 15. Owls hunt at night.

_____ 16. There are more tropical birds than any other kind.

_____ 17. Parrots live in the tropics.

_____ 18. There are about 9,000 kinds of birds.

_____ 19. Most birds like worms.

_____ 20. Hummingbirds feed on nectar in flowers.

B Each paragraph contains one sentence which does not support the subject of the paragraph. Underline each sentence which does not belong in its paragraph.

1.　　Birds have a language of their own. They call to warn other birds to stay away. They may also call out to warn other birds that an enemy is nearby. Birds are usually afraid of cats. Birds may sing to attract another bird. Each bird has a different song.

2.　　Most birds build nests. Rats and mice also have nests. Owls may dig tunnels for their nests. Oriole nests look like pouches. Woodpeckers use their bills to cut holes in trees. Then they build nests in the holes. Swallows combine straw with mud to make a strong nest.

3.　　Birds have different types of beaks. A spear beak is used to catch fish. Prober beaks are used by birds that eat insects. Birds that eat seeds have cracker beaks. Cracker beaks are strong enough to break hard shells. Many birds eat seeds.

4.　　Birds have ways of protecting themselves. Most of them can fly to escape enemies. Fast runners, such as an ostrich, can outrun their enemies. Ostriches are strange-looking birds. Some brave birds actually attack their enemies. Many birds colors allow them to blend with their surroundings. Then an enemy cannot see the bird.

Writing Your Topic Sentence

A topic sentence states the subject of a paragraph. It is often the first sentence in a paragraph.

A Underline each sentence which states the subject of its paragraph.

1.   There are many explanations for the disappearance of dinosaurs. They may have died from diseases. Their eggs may have been eaten by other animals. Their water supply may have dried up. The real reason may always be a mystery.

2.   A rodeo presents many exciting events. Bull riding is dangerous and difficult. Calf roping calls for great skill. A cowboy uses no reins in bareback riding. A good cowboy can wrestle a steer to the ground in less than eight seconds.

3.   There are several kinds of ships. Cargo ships carry products such as wheat and corn. Oil and other liquids are carried by tankers. Ocean liners carry passengers. They are usually very luxurious. Some ships carry products which have to be refrigerated.

4.   Different kinds of spiders have different habits. Some spiders are good jumpers. Others can walk backward. One spider tracks its prey, an insect. The water spider builds its web under the water. Some spiders are poisonous to people.

5.   A lawn needs care in order to be healthy. Diseases can be cured by the use of chemicals. Weeds can also be stamped out with chemicals. Lawn food is called fertilizer. The lawn should be watered regularly. Some insects are enemies of lawns. There are products which will kill these insects.

B The first sentence below is a topic sentence. Put a check (✓) beside each sentence that would support the topic sentence.

Topic sentence: The Statue of Liberty is very large.

✓___ 1. Nineteen bright lamps light the torch.
___ 2. Many people visit the statue each year.
___ 3. The statue is 151 feet high.
___ 4. The torch is 305 feet above the base.
___ 5. Steel columns support the statue.
___ 6. The Statue of Liberty welcomes immigrants.
___ 7. There are stairs inside the statue.
___ 8. Large lights shine on the base.
___ 9. The copper and steel statue weighs 450,000 pounds.
___ 10. France gave the U.S. the statue in 1884.

Unit 150 cont'd

Phrasing Your Topic Sentence

The topic sentence tells what the paragraph will discuss.

A Read the two topic sentences. Read the paragraph under them. Decide which topic sentence best states the subject and underline it.

I. a. Lightning can be beautiful.
    b. Follow safety rules when you see lightning.

Try to get inside a closed car or a steel-frame building which has lightning rods. Outside, lie down on low ground. Never stand under a tree. Avoid bodies of water. Indoors, stay away from open windows and doorways. Do not touch anything electrical.

II. a. There are several forms of lightning.
    b. Lightning often occurs in spring and summer.

Ball lightning can travel on the ground. Heat lightning has faint flashes. Chain lightning seems to go from side to side. It may divide into fork shapes. Sheet lightning has a bright flash which lights the sky.

III. a. Our water comes from various sources.
     b. Salt can be removed from sea water.

Lakes and rivers supply some of our water. Few people depend on rain water. Sea water can be converted into fresh water in small amounts. Water is often stored to be used when necessary. There is water in the ground which can be tapped.

IV. a. Trees can give us shelter.
    b. Trees supply us with many products.

Some of our food is grown on trees. Tree wood provides us with paper products. Our houses and furniture may be made of wood. Even perfume and dye are created from parts of trees.

B Read the following supporting sentences. Write a topic sentence which states the subject of the paragraph.

_____ .

Unplug electrical appliances when you're not using them. Don't overload outlets. Never use flammable liquids to start fires. Store matches in a safe place. Inspect wiring regularly. Never leave a stove untended. You can prevent fires in the home.

Comprehension Check

(A) Put a check beside each statement which would belong with information about the kinds of spiders and their habits.

✓   1. Crab spiders can move backwards.
____ 2. Many persons fear spiders.
____ 3. The black widow spider is poisonous.
____ 4. Webs are very strong.
____ 5. The water spider spins a web under water.
____ 6. Female spiders often kill their mates.
____ 7. A crab spider doesn't make a web.
____ 8. A trap-door spider digs a burrow.
____ 9. Trisha is afraid of spiders.

____ 10. The wolf spider stalks insects.
____ 11. Jumping spiders leap on their prey.
____ 12. Wasps are spiders' enemies.
____ 13. Spiders get their name from a Greek myth.
____ 14. Tarantulas are usually very large.
____ 15. Many creatures like to eat spiders.
____ 16. The wolf spider doesn't build a web.
____ 17. The water spider collects air bubbles.
____ 18. Wasps sting spiders.
____ 19. Most crab spiders are white or yellow.
____ 20. The female spider usually spins the web.

(B) Write "f" beside each fact. Write "o" beside each opinion.

f   1. The football game is over.
____ 2. Denver is the capital of Colorado.
____ 3. Denver is my favorite city.
____ 4. I don't have enough time.
____ 5. The student failed his test.
____ 6. Arizona has a good climate.
____ 7. Erin is Tim's sister.
____ 8. The dog ran away.
____ 9. Cheesecake is delicious.
____ 10. The war ended in 1814.

____ 11. Snow is fun.
____ 12. These are running shoes.
____ 13. Your voice is too soft.
____ 14. This is the best brand.
____ 15. I can't wait any longer.
____ 16. Mike doesn't have permission.
____ 17. You stayed too late.
____ 18. The store closes at 9:00 p.m.
____ 19. This was our best parade.
____ 20. The parade is Thursday.

(C) Put a check (✓) beside each sentence which could be a topic sentence.

✓   1. Allan can cook these foods.
____ 2. We discussed several subjects.
____ 3. I hope you recover soon.
____ 4. Here are my three reasons.
____ 5. Then we replaced the wire.
____ 6. Follow these instructions.
____ 7. Must you leave now?
____ 8. I made several mistakes on the test.
____ 9. Do you know why I like Ms. Hanner?
____ 10. Next add the cup of flour.
____ 11. We should vote for Edwin.
____ 12. Finally, put a stamp on it.

____ 13. You need to make several changes.
____ 14. Your last job is to mop the floors.
____ 15. Here are your jobs for today.
____ 16. It is served quickly.
____ 17. Listen to these suggestions.
____ 18. I want you to solve these problems.
____ 19. We promised the students.
____ 20. I agree with four of your ideas.
____ 21. Then I spilled the orange juice.
____ 22. Read these three books.
____ 23. You forgot to call me!
____ 24. Study these chapters.

Test 30 cont'd →

Comprehension Check (continued)

(D) Underline the sentences which do not belong in each paragraph.

1. People have wandered all over the world for many reasons. Some were searching for food. They also wandered out of curiosity. Cats are also very curious. They wanted to know what was on the other side of the water, so they set sail to new lands.

2. In the South American countries of Peru and Bolivia, the Incas built a great empire high in the mountains. They built their empire a long time before Columbus sailed to America. Columbus and his men had a difficult voyage. Where did Columbus actually land? The Incas grew crops on the sides of mountains. Everyone worked very hard, including children and elderly people.

3. The Black Death was a terrible illness. It killed about one-third of all the people in Asia and Europe. It was called the "plague." Other plagues have killed many people. The Black Death reached England in 1348. By that time, it had already killed twenty-five million people.

4. Napoleon was a powerful French military leader. He lead defeats of the English and Spanish navies in the late 1700's. He and his soldiers won many battles in Italy. He decided to invade Egypt. There are pyramids in Egypt. France became the leading power in Europe under Napoleon's leadership.

5. The ancient Egyptians believed that the bodies of the dead went to heaven. That is why they tried to preserve the bodies as mummies. Children sometimes dress as mummies on Halloween. They buried food for the soul to use.

Write a paragraph describing a school activity. Underline your topic sentence.

_____

_____

_____

_____

_____

_____

_____

_____

_____

_____

Supporting Sentences

Supporting sentences explain the topic sentence.

✳ **Read each topic sentence. Read the sentences below each topic sentence. Put a check (✓) beside each sentence which supports the topic sentence.**

1. Topic sentence: Some fish have unusual habits.

  ✓   a. Some fish appear to be kissing.
_____ b. Fish have gills and fins.
_____ c. One fish can puff up to twice its size.
_____ d. Fish is a good source of protein.
_____ e. The "flying" fish can glide for short distances.

_____ f. Another kind of fish can climb on tree roots.
_____ g. My cousin won a fishing contest.
_____ h. A "walking" fish has fins which serve as legs.
_____ i. Trout are good to eat.
_____ j. A barracuda looks mean.

2. Topic sentence: The U.S. flag has undergone changes.

_____ a. The Flag of 1795 had fifteen stars and stripes.
_____ b. The Stars and Bars was a Confederate flag.
_____ c. Most Boy Scout troops own a flag.
_____ d. The Flag of 1861 had thirty-four stars.
_____ e. The Great Star Flag of 1818 had twenty stars.

_____ f. Show respect for the flag.
_____ g. Did Betsy Ross really make our first flag?
_____ h. The Alamo flag of 1836 was red, white, and green.
_____ i. The color red stands for courage.
_____ j. Today's flag has fifty stars and thirteen stripes.

3. Topic sentence: Flowers bloom at different times of the year.

_____ a. Goldenrod is seen in late summer.
_____ b. Roses scent the summer air.
_____ c. Wild geraniums bloom in spring and early summer.
_____ d. I have a friend named Daisy.
_____ e. Asters are autumn flowers.

_____ f. Tulips make springtime bright.
_____ g. Mountain lilies bloom in spring, too.
_____ h. Lana wore an iris corsage.
_____ i. Snapdragon is a funny name.
_____ j. Some wild flowers are considered to be pests.

4. Topic sentence: Wild flowers grow in many places.

_____ a. Alpine plants grow high in the mountains.
_____ b. Many wild flowers are bright red and orange.
_____ c. Cactus plants are found in the desert.
_____ d. Sagebrush covers the prairie.

_____ e. Insects are attracted to blossoms.
_____ f. Cacti often have large flowers.
_____ g. Water lilies grow in water.
_____ h. Wild roses dot sunny meadows.
_____ i. Some flowers bloom only at night.
_____ j. Willows and cattails are swamp plants.

Unit 151 cont'd →

Supporting Your Topic

Each sentence in a paragraph should support the topic sentence.

✳ Read the supporting sentences in each paragraph below. Then write a topic sentence for each paragraph.

1. Topic sentence: _____
   Whales' tail fins are horizontal. Fishes' tail fins are vertical. Whales have lungs and must breathe air. Fish have gills and must always live in water. Whales are mammals, and their babies are born live. Fish lay eggs, which are hatched later.

2. Topic sentence: _____
   The silver maple has beautiful silver and green leaves. Sugar maples have sugary sap that is turned into maple syrup. The red maple is used for lumber. Mountain maples grow in the northern areas of the U.S.

3. Topic sentence: _____
   First, state the problem. Then try to form an explanation. Next, observe and experiment. Then explain the outcome of the experiment. Last, draw conclusions about the outcome. Those are the five steps of the scientific method.

4. Topic sentence: _____
   Some people use sharks for food. Leather can be made from shark skin. The shark's liver is a source of vitamin pills. Some parts of the shark are used to make fertilizer.

5. Topic sentence: _____
   The proteins in milk help build blood and tissue. The fat in milk contains four important vitamins. Milk sugar provides energy. The calcium in milk helps build bone tissue. The vitamins and minerals in milk are important nutrients.

COMPOSITION EXERCISE

Write a paragraph about the importance of pets. Underline the topic sentence.

_____
_____
_____
_____
_____
_____
_____
_____

Details

A detail sentence tells more about the topic sentence.

A Read each topic sentence. Put a check beside each sentence which gives further details about the topic sentence.

I. Topic sentence: Our school library contains various materials for our use.

✓ a. We have a good selection of art books.
____ b. The library opens at 8:15 a.m.
____ c. There are 10 sets of encyclopedia.
____ d. New fiction books are added each year.
____ e. The library receives four newspapers daily.

____ f. Our librarian is Ms. Holmes.
____ g. The library is in the west wing.
____ h. The record collection is kept up-to-date.
____ i. Almanacs are in the reference section.
____ j. We can check out our favorite magazines.

II. Topic sentence: Jack should be elected our class president.

____ a. He has experience in that position.
____ b. Jack is a natural leader.
____ c. Last year he went to camp.
____ d. He took a course in bookkeeping.
____ e. Jack wants to be a good officer.

____ f. He would represent the views of the class.
____ g. He is a good soccer player.
____ h. He is levelheaded in a crisis.
____ i. He has an interest in politics.
____ j. Jack has an "A" in art class.

III. Topic sentence: Ellen should be allowed to fly to California to visit her grandmother.

____ a. Ellen is old enough to travel alone.
____ b. She can go during school vacation.
____ c. California is in the West.
____ d. Ellen has saved her money for the trip.
____ e. She wants to see her grandmother.
____ f. Ellen's parents promised her the trip.

____ g. She enjoys reading poetry.
____ h. Ellen's grandmother wants to see her.
____ i. Planes fly at all hours of the day and night.
____ j. Ellen can remain calm in an emergency.

B Read the topic sentence and write six detail sentences which would support it.

Topic sentence: Pets are important to many people.

1. _____
2. _____
3. _____
4. _____
5. _____
6. _____

Unit 152 cont'd

General Ideas or Details?

Detail sentences explain the topic sentence.

A Read each paragraph. The first sentence of each paragraph is its topic sentence. Underline the sentences in each paragraph which explain the topic sentence.

1. Our school cafeteria is too small. Students must eat in shifts. Many school cafeterias are too small. Students who bring their lunches do not have a place to sit. We are served hamburgers each Monday.

2. Lake Powell has excellent camping areas. Bonner Lake does, too. Each camping area has a picnic table. Showers are available for the campers. We plan to go to Lake Powell in June.

3. We won't be able to go swimming today. My brother can't drive us to the lake. It looks as if it might rain. I have an appointment early this afternoon. I think we'd better plan to go another time.

4. There are rules for nominating candidates for the Hall of Fame for Great Americans. A candidate must have been a U.S. citizen. A candidate must have been dead for at least twenty-five years. A majority of the electors must vote for the candidate. The Hall of Fame is located at New York University.

B Write "t" beside each topic sentence. Write "d" beside each detail sentence.

_t_ 1.	Here are the rules for the game.	____ 11.	You can then polish the chrome.
____ 2.	These are my reasons.	____ 12.	The final question is on page four.
____ 3.	First, use the proper tools.	____ 13.	Your new puppy needs special care.
____ 4.	Your last job is to rake the leaves.	____ 14.	Break in the engine in this manner.
____ 5.	Follow these directions.	____ 15.	Next, remove the paint.
____ 6.	These are my favorite poets.	____ 16.	There are four major steps.
____ 7.	Then put the car in "neutral."	____ 17.	Then use fine sandpaper.
____ 8.	There are many sights to see in Paris.	____ 18.	Now add sugar to the eggs.
____ 9.	We visited three European countries.	____ 19.	Here are the final plans.
____ 10.	Last, put the cap on the bottle.	____ 20.	Push the red button on the right.

COMPOSITION EXERCISE

Write four topic sentences; write one detail sentence for each topic sentence.

1. _____   _____
2. _____   _____
3. _____   _____
4. _____   _____

The Concluding Sentence

The concluding sentence is usually the last sentence in a paragraph.

A Underline the concluding sentence in each paragraph.

1. Sondra loves winter sports. She likes to swoosh down a snow-covered mountain. Ice-skating is one of her favorite pastimes. She likes to try her hand with a hockey stick. Winter is Sondra's favorite season.

2. We shouldn't have homework on weekends. We need time to relax. Most sports events and concerts are on the weekend. Weekends are a good time for pursuing hobbies. We need to have weekends free from homework.

3. There are some rules you can follow to maintain good health. A balanced diet will help your body build and repair tissues. Regular exercise builds your muscles and aids in blood circulation. Sleep is important for helping the body repair worn tissue and grow properly. Those are three important rules to follow for the maintenance of good health.

4. Helicopters are useful aircraft. The armed forces use helicopters for transportation and other missions. Industries use them to do a variety of jobs. Even farmers use helicopters in caring for their crops. Helicopters perform many tasks very well.

5. Tornadoes have powerful winds that are destructive. Their strong winds can drive cornstalks through wooden doors. The winds can rip wool from the backs of sheep. Tornadoes suck up everything in their path, including people and animals. Tornadoes can cause much damage wherever they touch down.

B Put a check (✓) beside each sentence which could serve as the concluding sentence of a paragraph.

✓	1. Those are the main reasons.	___ 11.	That is my favorite story.
___	2. First, eat a good breakfast.	___ 12.	Our final answer was given.
___	3. These ideas are only a beginning.	___ 13.	We finally pulled in and stopped.
___	4. Now you're ready to start the engine.	___ 14.	Vail, CO, is a great ski area.
___	5. Then turn the key.	___ 15.	Traffic signals are important.
___	6. Be sure you understand each step.	___ 16.	Our last picture was the loveliest.
___	7. Now you can shift the gears.	___ 17.	The engineers solved the problems.
___	8. Enjoy your trip!	___ 18.	Interstate highways connect large cities.
___	9. Our first stop was London.	___ 19.	Next, push the blue button.
___	10. You're ready to share your knowledge.	___ 20.	Those questions puzzled scientists.

Unit 153 cont'd →

Reaching Logical Conclusions

Each detail sentence in your paragraph should lead to a logical, reasonable conclusion.

EXAMPLE: *In the following paragraph, each detail sentence leads to a logical conclusion. The concluding sentence is underlined.*

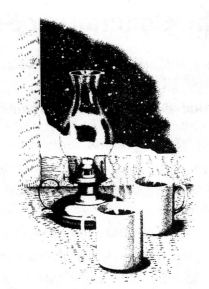

> *I think the coffee is ready. The coffeemaker's noise has stopped. The light that signals the end of the cycle is lighted. The coffee has stopped dripping. <u>The coffee is ready to drink.</u>*

A Write a logical conclusion for each paragraph.

1.   The dog might be hungry. He's barking at his master. He's standing beside his food dish. He hasn't been fed yet today.   *The dog is hungry.* _____

2.   There may be a burglar in the house. I heard footsteps downstairs. Something fell to the floor just now. The dog is growling. _____

3.   Snow may soon begin falling. The temperature is perfect for snow. "Snow clouds" are overhead. The weatherperson predicted snow for today. _____
     _____

4.   I think Jeff failed to do his homework. He isn't taking his paper from his notebook. He has a worried expression. He is trying to hide behind George. _____
     _____

5.   The car isn't running right. The engine "misses" when I press the accelerator. The engine nearly "dies" when I slow down. There is very little power when the car goes uphill. _____
     _____

6.   I don't think I'll have time to watch my favorite show tonight. We are having guests from 6:00 p.m. to 9:00 p.m. I have to help prepare dinner. Two hours of homework will be waiting for me. _____

COMPOSITION EXERCISE

Write a paragraph containing a topic sentence, three detail sentences, and a concluding sentence. Underline the conclusion.

_____
_____
_____
_____
_____
_____
_____
_____

The Paragraph's Parts

A correctly written paragraph contains a topic sentence, detail sentences, and a conclusion. The topic sentence states the subject of the paragraph. Each detail sentence relates to and develops the topic sentence. The last sentence is a logical conclusion to the paragraph.

A Read each topic sentence. Put a check (✓) beside each sentence which relates to and develops the topic sentence.

1. Topic sentence: This is a good movie.

✓___ 1. The actors and actresses are good.　　___ 6. It seems very lifelike.
___ 2. The plot is interesting　　　　　　　　　___ 7. It's been out for three weeks.
___ 3. My cousin brought me to the movie.　　 ___ 8. I saw a good movie last week, too.
___ 4. Some parts are very exciting.　　　　　 ___ 9. It keeps me laughing.
___ 5. I've seen a movie similar to it.　　　　 ___ 10. I can understand the story.

2. Topic sentence: I think I'll have a good grade in science this quarter.

✓___ 1. I've turned in all my homework.　　　　 ___ 6. The teacher liked my ideas.
___ 2. I really like science.　　　　　　　　　 ___ 7. My lab work was good.
___ 3. My test scores are high.　　　　　　　　 ___ 8. Jenny broke a test tube.
___ 4. My dad made good grades in　　　　　　 ___ 9. We had a fire drill during class.
　　　science.　　　　　　　　　　　　　　　 ___ 10. I watched the assigned PBS science
___ 5. I've answered questions in class.　　　　　　　 programs.

B Put a check beside each sentence which would be a logical conclusion to the topic and detail sentences in part A.

1. Topic sentence: This is a good movie.

___ 1. This is one of the best movies I've seen.　　___ 3. I'm truly enjoying this movie.
___ 2. I hope you like it.　　　　　　　　　　　　___ 4. My uncle must see it.

2. Topic sentence: I think I'll have a good grade in science this quarter.

___ 1. My grade in science should be　　　　　 ___ 3. Science is neat.
　　　high.　　　　　　　　　　　　　　　　 ___ 4. I've worked hard in science to make a
___ 2. I want a better grade than Jan's.　　　　　　　good grade.

COMPOSITION EXERCISE

Select a topic sentence, detail sentences, and a concluding sentence from parts A and B. Write them in correct order in a paragraph.

_____
_____
_____
_____
_____
_____
_____

Unit 154 cont'd

Arranging Parts in Order

The topic sentence is usually the first sentence in a paragraph.
The detail sentences follow the topic sentence. The concluding
sentence is usually the last sentence in a paragraph.

A Use the information above and the information on page 371 to match the paragraph parts with their descriptions.

c = concluding sentence   t = topic sentence   d = detail sentence

_d_ 1. follows the topic sentence
___ 2. usually the last sentence
___ 3. relates to the topic sentence
___ 4. ends the paragraph
___ 5. usually the first sentence

___ 6. the end of the paragraph
___ 7. develops the topic sentence
___ 8. logically closes the paragraph
___ 9. states the subject of the paragraph
___ 10. located between the topic and the concluding sentence

B Read each paragraph and then tell which kind of sentence is missing from the paragraph.

1. First, set the oven on 300°. Then mix all ingredients. Bake the brownies for 35-40 minutes. Soon you'll have a delicious treat!

What is missing? _____

2. Follow these steps when dusting the furniture. Find a soft cloth. Spray the furniture polish on the cloth. Carefully wipe the wood parts of the furniture.

What is missing? _____

3. There are three reasons why I like you. You're a friendly person. You're very loyal. Those are the reasons why I like you.

What is missing? _____

COMPOSITION EXERCISE

Write a paragraph describing your favorite elementary schoolteacher. Write "t" over the first word of the topic sentence. Write "d" over the first word of each detail sentence. Write "c" over the first word of the concluding sentence.

_____
_____
_____
_____
_____
_____
_____
_____

Arranging by Time

The sentences in a paragraph should follow one another in a natural and logical order. Connective words will keep the sentences in order.

The box contains connective words. Underline each connective word in the paragraphs.

first	today
second	yesterday
third	tomorrow
last	then
next	at the same time
now	immediately
until	finally
before	as soon as
during	when
after	afterward
meanwhile	later
soon	

1. We shopped at the mall yesterday. First we shopped for new jeans. Then we went to the record store. We finally decided to have lunch. After shopping all day, we drove home tiredly.

2. Gayle couldn't find her Christmas presents anywhere. After her family left for the theater, she searched in all the closets. Next she looked in the storage building. The last place she looked was under the beds. When she heard the family returning, she quickly grabbed a book and began reading it.

3. I will now give you an easy recipe for delicious butter cookies. You should first put the flour, sugar, and margarine on the cabinet. Melt 1½ sticks of margarine until it is liquid. Then add ¾ cup of sugar, stirring at the same time. Next add two cups of flour and stir until the mixture becomes dough. After the mixture becomes dough, roll it into small balls and then place them on a cookie sheet. Then press the cookies until they are flat. Bake the cookies at 350° until they begin to brown. As soon as they are somewhat browned, remove them from the oven and immediately take them off the cookie sheet. After the cookies are cool, store them in an airtight container until you are ready to eat them.

COMPOSITION EXERCISE

Write a paragraph explaining how to do something. Use at least three connective words and underline them.

_____

_____

_____

_____

_____

_____

_____

_____

Unit 155 cont'd

Sequence of Events

Connective words are used to help sentences follow one another in natural order.

A Number the sentences in natural order. Underline the connective word(s).

1. _1_ 1. We wanted to go to a movie today.
   ___ 2. The theater was closed for repairs.
   ___ 3. Then we looked in the newspaper.
   ___ 4. No one answered the phone.
   ___ 5. We called the theater first.
   ___ 6. Finally we chose a movie.
   ___ 7. We drove to the theater.
   ___ 8. We read the movie ads.

2. _1_ 1. Today Jill tried out for the team.
   ___ 2. After talking to the coach, Jill tried out.
   ___ 3. Afterward, the coach put her on the team.
   ___ 4. She practiced until the coach arrived.
   ___ 5. First she found her gym clothes.
   ___ 6. Next she "warmed up" on the gym floor.

3. _1_ 1. Tomorrow we're beginning our vacation.
   ___ 2. After leaving the Grand Canyon, we'll drive west.
   ___ 3. We'll be at Disneyland by Thursday.
   ___ 4. Our goal is Disneyland.
   ___ 5. We'll first drive to the Grand Canyon.
   ___ 6. We'll stay at the Grand Canyon until Tuesday.

4. _1_ 1. We decorated our Christmas tree yesterday.
   ___ 2. Finally, Janey flung the icicles on the tree.
   ___ 3. Lights were the first thing we put on the tree.
   ___ 4. While we strung the lights, Ann found the icicles.
   ___ 5. Next, we added the shiny ornaments.
   ___ 6. After the ornaments were hung, we laced the garland.

B Underline the sentence which is out of order in each paragraph.

1.   Karen's tooth began to hurt. She called the dentist's office today. She first gave her name. Then she described her problem. When she called the dentist's office, the receptionist answered. After she described her problem, she was given an appointment.

2.   Jack saw a car he wanted to buy. First he asked the price of the car. He finally drove away in his new car. Then he checked his bank account. As soon as he saw the balance, he decided he could afford to buy the car.

COMPOSITION EXERCISE

Write one of the sets of sentences in part A in paragraph form.

_____
_____
_____
_____
_____
_____
_____
_____
_____

Comprehension Check

(A) Match the paragraph parts with their descriptions. Write "t" for topic sentence, "s" for supporting sentence, and "c" for concluding sentence.

_c_ 1. ends the paragraph

____ 2. develops the topic sentence

____ 3. logically closes the paragraph

____ 4. follows the topic sentence

____ 5. states the subject of the paragraph

____ 6. relates to the topic sentence

____ 7. usually the first sentence

____ 8. the end of the paragraph

____ 9. located between the topic and the concluding sentence

____ 10. usually the last sentence

(B) Read each topic sentence. Put a check beside each sentence which supports the topic sentence.

1. Topic sentence: Computers can perform many tasks.

_✓_ 1. Computers prepare payrolls for businesses.

____ 2. They are used to identify criminals.

____ 3. Library information can be stored in computers.

____ 4. Mom uses a home computer.

____ 5. My grandfather dislikes computers.

____ 6. Computers can listen to voices and reply.

____ 7. A computer must be told what to do.

____ 8. Mom's computer plans menus.

____ 9. Robots can be controlled by computers.

____ 10. A computer can't think for itself.

2. Topic sentence: Many of our possessions are made of plastic.

____ 1. A toothbrush's handle and bristles are plastic.

____ 2. We put food in plastic sandwich bags.

____ 3. Helmets are made of very hard plastic.

____ 4. My sister's doll is made of soft plastic.

____ 5. Paper is made from wood.

____ 6. Toy phones and real phones are plastic.

____ 7. Some car parts are made of plastic.

____ 8. Gasoline is made from crude oil.

____ 9. Plastic doesn't rust.

____ 10. Even some furniture is plastic.

3. Topic sentence: Benjamin Franklin contributed much to our country.

____ 1. Franklin printed a very successful newspaper.

____ 2. He helped Canada set up a mail system.

____ 3. He established the first subscription library.

____ 4. Franklin invented the lightning rod.

____ 5. Franklin organized the first city hospital.

____ 6. Bifocal lenses were Franklin's invention.

____ 7. Franklin refused to patent his inventions.

____ 8. He represented the American colonies in Europe.

____ 9. Franklin was a minister to France.

____ 10. He helped to write the Declaration of Independence.

4. Topic sentence: There are eight basic courses offered in industrial arts.

____ 1. Woodworking helps students learn to build.

____ 2. Boys and girls take industrial arts.

____ 3. Ceramics can become a hobby.

____ 4. Electricity skills can be useful.

____ 5. Drawing and design are usually taught.

____ 6. General metal covers several areas.

____ 7. Auto mechanics is very practical.

____ 8. Many students enjoy industrial arts.

____ 9. Plastics is a fairly new branch.

____ 10. Printing can lead to various careers.

Test 31 cont'd →

Comprehension Check (continued)

Ⓒ **Number the sentences 1-5 in natural order. Write "x" beside each sentence which doesn't support the topic sentence.**

1. __1__ a. Sandy decided to sell her bike.
   _____ b. Then she posted signs at school.
   _____ c. The bike is red and white.
   _____ d. Last, she put a sign on her bike.
   _____ e. She's waiting for someone to buy the bike.
   _____ f. The bike is in good condition.
   _____ g. She got the bike for her birthday.
   _____ h. She first placed a newspaper ad.

2. _____ a. Marie decided to give a party.
   _____ b. Her parties are usually fun.
   _____ c. She's ready for her guests.
   _____ d. Next she planned her menu.
   _____ e. She gives three parties each year.
   _____ f. Her first job was to send invitations.
   _____ g. I like to attend parties.
   _____ h. Last she bought and prepared the food.

Ⓓ **Underline each connective word.**

Listen to this quick and easy recipe for microwave fudge. <u>First</u>, sift together one pound of confectioner's sugar and one-half cup of cocoa powder into a two-quart bowl. Then add one-fourth cup of evaporated milk. Next break up a stick of margarine and place it in the bowl. Then cook the mixture in your microwave for 2½ minutes or until the margarine is melted. Meanwhile, line an 8x8x2-inch baking pan with aluminum foil. When the mixture is cooked, add two teaspoons of vanilla. Then stir the mixture. Next pour the mixture into the foil-lined pan. Place it in the freezer for ten minutes. As soon as the fudge is set, remove it from the freezer. Finally, cut the fudge into small squares. Add pecans if you wish.

Write a paragraph explaining how to do something. Underline your topic sentence.

_____
_____
_____
_____
_____
_____
_____
_____
_____
_____

Giving Reasons

The main idea in a paragraph may be developed by giving reasons for a certain belief or point of view.

Read each paragraph; answer the questions about each one.

A.   I like to play my electronic keyboard for several reasons. One reason is that I enjoy creating the sounds. My keyboard can make the sounds of twenty different instruments. I also enjoy trying to play my favorite songs. The music of the early Beatles era is a challenge. Another reason why I like to play my keyboard is that I can entertain my family and friends with my music. Sometimes we sing together for hours. I hope to develop my talent into a musical career someday.

1. Write the topic sentence. _____

_____

2. Write the first reason. _____

_____

3. Write the second reason. _____

_____

4. Write the third reason. _____

_____

5. What is the concluding sentence? _____

_____

B.   Television watching can be the cause of poor grades. Some students watch television instead of doing their homework. Others try to watch television while doing their homework. They can't concentrate on their lessons while watching television. A few students stay up very late on school nights to watch television. Then they're too tired to do their work at school. Television watching can affect a student's grades.

1. What is one way television watching can cause poor grades? _____

_____

2. Write the concluding sentence. _____

_____

COMPOSITION EXERCISE

Write a paragraph about the length of your school day. Support your topic sentence with at least three reasons.

_____

_____

_____

_____

_____

_____

_____

_____

Unit 156 cont'd

How-to-Do Arrangement

Write how-to-do information in natural order.

A **Read the lists of steps to follow; number the steps 1-5. Write a paragraph with the sentences, putting them in correct order.**

I. ____ a. Arrange to be at home when the repairman arrives.
   ____ b. The person who answers your call will arrange for repair service.
   ____ c. The number is usually found on the first page of the telephone directory.
   ____ d. Find the number of your local telephone company's repair service.
   ____ e. Sometime you may need to call for telephone repair service.

Write a paragraph.

_____
_____
_____
_____
_____
_____
_____
_____

II. ____ a. Go to the post office and get a change-of-address form.
    ____ b. Your mail should now be forwarded to your new address.
    ____ c. If you change your address, you should fill out a change-of-address card.
    ____ d. Give the completed form to a postal worker.
    ____ e. Read the form carefully and fill in the information.

Write a paragraph.

_____
_____
_____
_____
_____
_____
_____

B **List some questions you might find on a change-of-address form.**

1. _____
2. _____
3. _____

Giving Directions

Give directions in the natural time order.

❋ **Put a check (✓) beside each sentence that gives a step to follow.**

✓ 1. Mix the ingredients.

____ 2. Those are the steps to follow to make brownies.

____ 3. Read the recipe carefully.

____ 4. You can smell them as they bake.

____ 5. Bake at 350° for 25 minutes.

____ 6. Next, put all ingredients on the cabinet.

____ 7. Brownies are Jeff's favorite treat.

____ 8. Then prepare the oven dish.

____ 9. Pour the batter into the oven dish.

____ 10. This is how to bake brownies.

Write a paragraph using 8 of the sentences above. Remember to write a topic sentence as well as a conclusion.

_____

_____

_____

_____

_____

_____

_____

_____

_____

✓ 1. Last, hold the camera still and snap the picture.

____ 2. I like to take pictures of mountains.

____ 3. Next, set the distance and light controls.

____ 4. Photography is Sara's hobby.

____ 5. Then look through the viewfinder.

____ 6. That is the way to take good pictures.

____ 7. Pets make good subjects for pictures.

____ 8. First, remove the lens cap.

____ 9. Follow these steps to take good pictures.

____ 10. Center the subject in the viewfinder.

Write a paragraph using 7 of the sentences above. Remember to write a topic sentence as well as a concluding sentence.

_____

_____

_____

_____

_____

_____

_____

_____

Unit 157 cont'd ➜

Words That Tell Order

Order words will keep information in the correct place.

A **Choose words from the following list to write as order words in the paragraphs.**

first	then	next	second	third	final	last	finally

1. You may sometime have to help control bleeding from a wound. __*First*__ , get a clean cloth to use as a pressure pack. _____ , fold the cloth tightly and place it over the wound. _____ , press the pack firmly against the wound until the bleeding stops. You may wish to call for medical attention after the bleeding stops.

2. There are several steps to follow to stop a nosebleed. _____ , sit in an upright position and tilt your head slightly backward. _____ , press your nostrils together firmly for several minutes. _____ , place a wet, cold cloth over your nose. Call a doctor if the bleeding does not stop soon.

3. Treat burns carefully. _____ , put a clean cloth over the burn. _____ , apply more dressings over the cloth. Your _____ job is to secure the dressing loosely over the burn. Call a doctor if the burn is large or severe.

4. It is possible to get relief from insect bites. You should _____ apply cold water to the bite. You can _____ apply a paste made of baking soda and cold cream. _____ , you could apply ice to get more relief. If the swelling covers a large area, seek medical attention.

5. An animal bite requires special care. _____ , wash the area immediately with soap and water. _____ , call a doctor. _____ , try to locate and confine the animal. The animal must be watched for signs of rabies.

B **Rewrite the following paragraph. Use order words in your paragraph.**

You must act quickly to help a child who is choking. Hold the child with his head downward. Tap the child firmly on the back. If this fails, seek help from a person who is skilled in first aid. A person with first aid training will know what to do next.

_____

_____

_____

_____

_____

_____

_____

Writing a Description

When writing a description, tell what you see as well as what you think about the object of your description.

❋ **Study the picture; answer the questions about the picture.**

1. What is the first thing that catches your attention? _____
_____

2. What is the man doing? _____
_____

3. List the objects on the desk. _____
_____

4. Whose picture is on the desk? _____
_____

5. What kind of expression does the woman have? _____
_____

6. What do you see that tells you how the man feels? _____
_____
_____
_____

7. How does the man feel? _____
_____

8. If you asked the man a question, what might he say or do? _____
_____

9. What might have made the man act as he is acting? _____
_____

10. What will he do next? _____
_____

COMPOSITION EXERCISE

Write a paragraph describing the picture and your thoughts about it.

_____
_____
_____
_____
_____
_____
_____
_____

Unit 158 cont'd ➡

Describing Yourself

Most people find it difficult to write a description of themselves. Maybe the best way to start is by making lists of your likes, dislikes, activities, appearance, and personality.

A Underline each adjective which describes you. Then write ten more adjectives which describe you.

1. friendly	11. quiet	a. _____
2. generous	12. young	b. _____
3. happy	13. silly	c. _____
4. lonely	14. loud	d. _____
5. loyal	15. busy	e. _____
6. short	16. smart	f. _____
7. strong	17. tall	g. _____
8. handsome	18. sad	h. _____
9. pretty	19. tough	i. _____
10. nice	20. gentle	j. _____

B Write "l" beside the items that you like. Write "d" beside the items that you dislike. Then list 10 more of your likes and dislikes.

____ 1. country music	a. _____
____ 2. science	b. _____
____ 3. the beach	c. _____
____ 4. school	d. _____
____ 5. mountains	e. _____
____ 6. animals	f. _____
____ 7. TV	g. _____
____ 8. holidays	h. _____
____ 9. sewing	i. _____
____ 10. cooking	j. _____

C Put a check (✓) beside each activity which appeals to you. Then list 10 more activities that appeal to you.

____ 1. participating in sports	a. _____
____ 2. writing letters	b. _____
____ 3. taking walks	c. _____
____ 4. reading fiction books	d. _____
____ 5. studying a new subject	e. _____
____ 6. shopping for clothes	f. _____
____ 7. playing video games	g. _____
____ 8. travelling to new places	h. _____
____ 9. dancing to rock music	i. _____
____ 10. meeting new people	j. _____

COMPOSITION EXERCISE

Use the lists in parts A, B, and C to write a description of yourself.

_____

_____

_____

_____

_____

_____

_____

_____

_____

Describing Your Family

In order to describe your family, you must consider each individual person as well as the entire family as a group.

A List each member of your family, and describe each person's likes and dislikes. Include yourself.

	likes	dislikes
1.		
2.		
3.		
4.		
5.		

B List each family member again and describe each person's appearance.

1. _____
2. _____
3. _____
4. _____
5. _____

C Put a check (✓) beside each activity your family enjoys. Then explain in detail how your family shares each one.

____ 1. shopping _____
____ 2. TV _____
____ 3. meals _____
____ 4. vacations _____
____ 5. movies _____
____ 6. holiday traditions _____
____ 7. pets _____
____ 8. visiting relatives _____
____ 9. sports _____
____ 10. work _____

COMPOSITION EXERCISE

Write a description of your family.

_____
_____
_____
_____
_____
_____
_____

Unit 159 cont'd →

Describing a Friend

Your friends are the people with whom you choose to associate. Therefore, there are reasons why you select certain people to be your friends. Once you identify those reasons, you can use them to describe your friends.

A Decide which friend you would like to describe, and answer the questions about him or her.

1. What are some activities your friend enjoys? _____
   _____

2. Where was your friend born? _____

3. Where is his/her favorite place to live? _____

4. What are his/her favorite foods? _____

5. What is your favorite memory of him/her? _____

6. What is your friend's favorite possession? _____

7. How did you and your friend meet? _____
   _____

8. How often do you see each other? _____

9. List some activities you and your friend enjoy together. _____
   _____

10. Describe his/her physical appearance. _____
    _____
    _____

B Write a short explanation of your friend's attitudes toward the following.

1. homework _____
2. school _____
3. movies _____
4. animals _____
5. cigarettes _____
6. politics _____
7. his/her family _____
8. you _____

C Underline the words which describe your friend. Then write 8 more descriptions of your friend.

1. loyal   a. _____
2. friendly   b. _____
3. cute   c. _____
4. smart   d. _____
5. witty   e. _____
6. popular   f. _____
7. nervous   g. _____
8. polite   h. _____

COMPOSITION EXERCISE

Write a description of your friend.

_____
_____
_____
_____
_____
_____

Describing an Animal

Before writing a descriptive paragraph, gather as much information as possible about the subject. Then choose the information you wish to include in the description.

A Put a check (✓) beside each animal you've seen "in person."

——— 1. rhinoceros	——— 11. lion	——— 21. wolf
——— 2. gorilla	——— 12. peacock	——— 22. sheep
——— 3. parakeet	——— 13. polar bear	——— 23. horse
——— 4. rat	——— 14. tiger	——— 24. hippopotamus
——— 5. snake	——— 15. penguin	——— 25. alligator
——— 6. fox	——— 16. skunk	——— 26. orangutan
——— 7. duck	——— 17. kangaroo	——— 27. zebra
——— 8. eel	——— 18. buffalo	——— 28. giraffe
——— 9. deer	——— 19. shark	——— 29. octapus
——— 10. monkey	——— 20. elephant	——— 30. tortoise

B Select an animal from the list in part A or of your own choosing, and answer the questions about it.

1. What is the animal? _____

2. Where did you see it? _____

3. Where does it live? _____

4. If you saw it in a zoo, where is its natural home? _____

5. Describe the animal's physical appearance. _____

   a. size _____

   b. color _____

   c. shape _____

   d. unusual features _____

   e. skin (feathers, fur, etc.) _____

6. Does it make a sound? _____ If so, describe it. _____

_____

7. Do people like or dislike the animal? _____ Why or why not? _____

_____

8. What would its skin, etc. feel like? _____

COMPOSITION EXERCISE

Use the information in part B to write a description of the animal.

_____

_____

_____

_____

_____

_____

Unit 160 cont'd ⟶

Describing a Place

Read each situation and picture it in your mind. Answer the questions about each one.

1. You are searching a semi-dark movie theater for a friend.
   a. What do you see? _____
   _____

   b. What do you hear? _____
   _____

   c. What do you smell? _____
   _____

   d. Describe what you might touch. _____
   _____

   e. Describe the walls and the ceiling. _____
   _____

   f. Describe the floor and the screen. _____
   _____

2. You are standing near the only exit at the zoo. Someone shouts that a ferocious gorilla has escaped.
   a. What do you see? _____
   _____

   b. What do you hear? _____
   _____

   c. What do you smell? _____
   _____

   d. Describe what you might touch. _____
   _____

   e. Describe the zoo one hour later. _____
   _____

3. Today is the last day of school before summer vacation! The final bell rang one minute ago, and you are standing beside your locker.
   a. What do you see? _____
   _____

   b. What do you hear? _____
   _____

   c. What do you smell? _____
   _____

   d. Describe what you might touch. _____
   _____

   e. Describe what you might taste. _____
   _____

   f. Describe the hall one hour later. _____
   _____

Comprehension Check

(A) Put a check (✓) beside each sentence that gives a step to follow.

1. ✓ a. First, pour the gelatin powder into a bowl.
   ___ b. The gelatin will make a tasty treat.
   ___ c. Then add two cups of hot water.
   ___ d. After adding hot water, stir briskly.
   ___ e. Pour the mixture into a 9x13 dish.
   ___ f. I'll tell you how to make gelatin.
   ___ g. The gelatin will set in two hours.
   ___ h. Third, add two cups of cold water.

2. ___ a. Put the car in gear when you turn off the engine.
   ___ b. Move the gear shift to "first."
   ___ c. Learning to shift gears takes practice.
   ___ d. Many cars have an automatic shift.
   ___ e. Push in on the clutch while turning the key.
   ___ f. Slowly let out on the clutch as you accelerate.
   ___ g. Don't "ride" the clutch with your foot.
   ___ h. Push in on the clutch each time you change gears.

3. ___ a. Set the channel to be taped.
   ___ b. Taping on your VCR is easy.
   ___ c. Set the timer control.
   ___ d. Turn on the "power" switch.
   ___ e. Push the "record" button.
   ___ f. A VCR can provide hours of entertainment.
   ___ g. Insert the VCR tape.
   ___ h. The "power" and "record" lights should be on.

(B) Underline each order word.

1. <u>Before</u> we went shopping, Leah and I made a list of items that we needed to buy.
2. Our first stop was at the gas station.
3. Then we went to a discount store to buy film, plastic forks, and paper plates.
4. Leah then decided to buy a new cassette tape at the music shop.
5. Next we ate lunch at our favorite fast-food restaurant.
6. While we ate lunch, we discussed our plans for the afternoon.
7. After lunch we went to the grocery store.
8. The first items in our shopping cart were chips, cookies, and colas.
9. Then we added lettuce, cheese, bread, hot dogs, and mustard.
10. We were finally ready to return home.

(C) Underline each word which could appropriately describe each subject.

1. fire	a. <u>hot</u>	b. <u>yellow</u>	c. cool	d. soft
2. silk	a. soft	b. smooth	c. expensive	d. rough
3. snow	a. white	b. soft	c. cold	d. plaid
4. fur	a. brittle	b. firm	c. silky	d. soft
5. mountains	a. majestic	b. liquid	c. tall	d. skinny
6. stars	a. distant	b. twinkling	c. blue	d. furry
7. eggshell	a. white	b. tender	c. noisy	d. brittle
8. milk	a. cold	b. white	c. warm	d. hard
9. shirt	a. fluid	b. plaid	c. striped	d. red
10. engine	a. scaly	b. powerful	c. small	d. dirty

Test 32 cont'd →

Comprehensive Check (continued)

Ⓓ **Read the paragraph and answer the questions about it.**

There are several reasons why I like to vacation in Florida. First, my grandparents live in Florida. They live on the east side of the state. Their home is close to the Kennedy Space Center. Another reason is that I like to visit Disney World. A new marine exhibit opened at Epcot in early 1986. It's my favorite exhibit. A third reason why I like to go to Florida is that I can go deep-sea fishing. Last year I caught a huge marlin. We even spotted a school of sharks far from shore. I was terrified, but we were safe on our boat. For these and several other reasons, I enjoy visiting Florida.

1. What is the topic sentence? *There are several reasons why I like to vacation in Florida.*

2. Write the first reason. _____

3. Write the second reason. _____

4. Write the third reason. _____

5. What is the concluding sentence. _____

6. Write the three connective words. _____

7. Underline the descriptive words: a. deep-sea   b. reasons   c. new
    d. fishing   e. huge   f. safe   g. enjoy   h. home   i. marine   j. far   k. east

Write a paragraph describing an object or a person in your classroom.

_____

_____

_____

_____

_____

_____

_____

_____

Using Your Senses

Use your senses of sight, hearing, touch, taste, and smell to observe. Then write about how your senses were affected.

 Picture each object in your mind. Then write a description which would appeal to the senses of sight, hearing, touch, taste, and smell.

1. a car
   a. sight ___ *rusted, faded red, small, broken windshield* ___
   b. hearing _____
   c. touch _____
   d. taste _____
   e. smell _____

2. a dog
   a. sight _____
   b. hearing _____
   c. touch _____
   d. taste _____
   e. smell _____

3. your lunch
   a. sight _____
   b. hearing _____
   c. touch _____
   d. taste _____
   e. smell _____

4. a bakery
   a. sight _____
   b. hearing _____
   c. touch _____
   d. taste _____
   e. smell _____

COMPOSITION EXERCISE

Choose one of the objects listed above and write a paragraph describing it. Use your lists of descriptions of that object.

_____
_____
_____
_____
_____
_____
_____
_____

Unit 161 cont'd

Writing with Your Senses

You can describe the world around you by observing how it
affects your senses of sight, hearing, smell, taste, and touch.

A Read each topic and identify one sense it could appeal to. Write "sight," "hearing," "smell," "taste," or "touch" in the first blank. Describe the ways in which your senses are affected.

1. a parade   *hearing*   *bands playing loud music; crowds of people cheering*
2. a dill pickle _____ _____
3. your favorite video _____ _____
4. a fire _____ _____
5. a river _____ _____
6. a storm _____ _____
7. a concert _____ _____
8. a basketball game _____ _____
9. a traffic jam _____ _____
10. a farm _____ _____
11. your locker _____ _____
12. a blanket _____ _____

B Observe the activity in your classroom. Describe how your senses are affected.

1. What do you see? _____

2. What do you hear? _____

3. What do you smell? _____

4. What do you taste? _____

5. What are you touching? How does it feel? _____

COMPOSITION EXERCISE

Use the descriptions you wrote in part B to write a paragraph describing your classroom.

_____
_____
_____
_____
_____
_____
_____
_____

Writing a Note

Read the two notes below.

I.

Dear Mrs. Brady,

    Thank you for the alarm clock. It's very pretty and is just what I need for college next year. I like the large numbers and the loud buzzer. Now I'll have no excuse for not getting to class on time.

    You were very thoughtful to remember me with such a nice graduation gift.

                   Sincerely,

                   Marcia

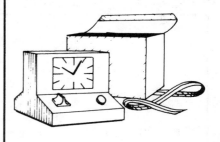

II.

Dear Carla,

    Are you ready for a surprise? Mom said I may invite you down for the homecoming dance on Friday, November 8. My sister, Angie, can pick you up at 5:00 p.m. that Friday on her way home for the weekend. She can also take you home on Sunday afternoon.

    You'll need to bring a formal dress and high heels. You'll also need some casual clothes for a picnic on Saturday.

    Please write me back as soon as possible. I can't wait to tell all our friends that you'll be here for the weekend. Hope you can come!

                   Love,

                   Lynette

✳ Answer the following questions about the two notes.

1. Which note is an invitation? _____

2. Which note was written to a close friend? _____

3. Which note needs a reply? _____

4. Which note is a thank-you note? _____

COMPOSITION EXERCISE

On your own paper, write either a thank-you note or an invitation. Write your rough draft on the lines below.

_____

_____

_____

_____

_____

_____

_____

Unit 162 cont'd →

Writing a Friendly Letter

A friendly letter is a message you send to someone you like.

A Read the following friendly letter.

heading {
1009 Meadow Lane
Austin, TX
July 29, 1985

Dear Rhonda, ← greeting

I'm waiting to hear about your new home. All of us really miss you and hope you're happy in Dallas. Please write me soon. } body

closing ➡ **Love,**

signature ➡ *Andrea*

B Answer these questions about the friendly letter above. Underline your answers.

1. Who wrote the letter?	a. <u>Andrea</u>	b. Rhonda
2. Who received the letter?	a. Andrea	b. Rhonda
3. Where does Andrea live?	a. Dallas	b. Austin
4. Where does Rhonda live?	a. Dallas	b. Austin
5. What is the closing?	a. Please write me soon.	b. Love,
6. What is the greeting?	a. Love,	b. Dear Rhonda,
7. "July 29, 1985" is part of the	a. body	b. heading.

C Write a reply to the letter. Use the correct punctuation for each section.

The Parts of a Letter

A business letter has a heading, inside address, greeting, body, closing, and signature.

heading {
383 Reed Cove
Dayton, Ohio 72101
August 5, 1985

Wood Products Corp.
Customer Service Dept.
891 Timber Lane
Elmville, Vermont 88211 } inside address

Dear Customer Service Director: ← greeting

    On June 3, 1985, I placed a telephone order for a stereo cabinet. I was told that the cabinet would be shipped on June 4. I waited two weeks before calling to check on the shipment. An employee named Brian King told me he'd check into the problem.

    The cabinet was charged to my credit card account on June 20. I still haven't received the shipment. The model number for the cabinet is ST-5-396. I ordered it from your sale catalog. } body

    Please check into this matter for me.

closing →   Sincerely,

signature →   *Alex Meyers*

    Alex Meyers

✳ Complete the following.

1. Who wrote the letter? _____ *Alex Meyers* _____
2. Where does he live? _____
3. When was the letter written? _____
4. Where is Wood Products Corp. located? _____
5. Write the closing. _____
6. Write the greeting. _____
7. Why wasn't the letter addressed to a particular person? _____
_____
8. Is this a friendly letter or a business letter? _____

On your own paper, write a reply to the letter. Pretend that you are the customer service director.

Unit 163 cont'd →

A Business Letter

A business letter consists of the heading, inside address, greeting, body, closing, and signature.

heading {
512 Crenshaw Rd.
Marysville, KY 80812
June 18, 1985

Ms. Janet Baldwin
Credit Department
800 S. Main St.
Memphis, TN 36892
} inside address

Dear Ms. Baldwin: ← greeting

Thank you for correcting the error in my account. I appreciate your prompt attention to this matter. } body

closing → Sincerely,

signature → *Marian Henley*

Marian Henley

A Read the letter and answer the questions about it.

1. Who wrote the letter?
   Marian Henley
   _____

2. To whom was the letter written?
   _____
   _____

3. When was the letter written?
   _____
   _____

4. Write the closing.
   _____
   _____

5. Write the greeting.
   _____
   _____

6. Write the inside address.
   _____
   _____
   _____
   _____

B Correct the spelling and punctuation in these parts of the business letter. Then identify the name of each part.

1. dear ms baldwin   This part of the letter is called the ____*greeting*____ .

2. sincerely   This part of the letter is called the _____ .

3. "thank you for correcting the error...."   This is part of the _____ .

4. marysville ky 80812   This is part of the _____ .

5. 800 s main st   This is part of the _____ .

6. *Marian henley*   This is the _____ .

On your own paper, write a business letter to a company requesting a copy of the company's catalog.

394

The Envelope

An envelope contains the address of the person who is sending the letter and the address of the person who will receive the letter. The address in the middle of the envelope tells who will receive the letter. The address in the upper left-hand corner tells who is sending the letter. It is called the return address.

Jill Wren
509 Broadway
Decatur, IL 33001

Anne Turner
31 S. Wood Ave.
Chicago, IL 33599

1. Write the address of the person sending the letter.

_____

_____

_____

2. Write the address of the person receiving the letter.

_____

_____

_____

3. Address the envelope below to Mr. Allen Wade, 210 N. Wynne St., Mayberry, CO 52681. The return address is Sharon Corbet, 8214 Westbury, Aberdeen, TX 61201. Draw a square where the stamp should be placed.

4. Address the envelope below to Ms. Roberta Ross, Credit Department, 1005 S. Watson, Fort Lee, VA 22001. The return address is Richard Kane, 217 Rosemond St., Anise, OH 41121. Draw a square for the stamp.

5. Address the envelope below to a friend. Use your return address. Draw a square for the stamp.

6. Address the envelope below to your favorite singer. Use your return address. Draw a square for the stamp.

Unit 164 cont'd

Answering a Letter

Keep each letter that you intend to answer. You can read each letter again to get ideas for writing your answer.

A Read the following sentences from a friendly letter. Pretend you are answering the letter and write a possible response to each sentence.

1. We went to Disney World last month.

What did you enjoy most at Disney World?
_____

2. We have a new puppy.

_____

3. School is hard this year.

_____

4. My parents gave me money for my birthday.

_____

5. I plan to look for a job this summer.

_____

6. I hope I can go to the dance next Friday.

_____

7. I'd like to visit you soon.

_____

8. I'm trying to get tickets to the concert.

_____

9. We have a new student in English class.

_____

10. We hope to take a bike trip.

_____

11. Have you made any plans for the holidays?

_____

12. Do you have a part-time job this year?

_____

B Below is the body of a friendly letter. On your own paper, write a reply to the letter.

What do you plan to do this summer? I'm going to fly to Florida to visit my grandmother. She promised to take me to all the great places. I don't know yet when I'll go.

Our school will be out in three weeks. We're having an end-of-school dance next Friday. I hope I get to go.

Write and tell me what you've been doing. I'll be waiting to hear from you.

Writing for Pleasure

Many famous people, including Mark Twain and Thomas Jefferson, kept a diary in which they recorded the events of their lives. You might enjoy writing down what happens to you and how you feel about it. Some people keep diaries, or journals, for the pleasure of writing. Others wish to record information to be read and enjoyed in the future.

A Think about some events that have occurred in your life during the past week. Write down a few of them, including those that seem very unimportant. Beside each event, write how it made you feel.

1. _____   _____
2. _____   _____
3. _____   _____
4. _____   _____
5. _____   _____

Combine the events and your feelings about them to write a diary entry in paragraph form. Write today's date at the beginning of the entry.

_____
_____
_____
_____
_____
_____
_____
_____

Have you ever had a pen pal? A pen pal is someone with whom you exchange letters. Some pen pals never meet each other in person.

B The questions below are some that a pen pal might ask you. Write your answers in complete sentences.

1. What is your name? _____
2. How old are you? _____
3. Where do you live? _____
4. Where do you go to school? _____
5. What are your hobbies? _____
6. What are some of your other interests? _____
7. Describe your family. _____
8. Describe your appearance. _____
9. Describe your personality. _____
10. Write your complete address. _____

Unit 165 cont'd

Being Creative

A Match the general topics, a. - i., with the specific word pictures which could complete them. Your answers may be different from those of other students.

a. Freedom is ...   b. Summer is ...   c. Love is ...   d. Beauty is ...   e. Fear is ...

f. Peace is ...   g. Winter is ...   h. Sadness is ...   i. Kindness is ...

_a_ 1. being able to say "no."	_____ 11. being at home alone.
_____ 2. an empty mailbox.	_____ 12. silent snow.
_____ 3. a quiet meadow.	_____ 13. thinking of the other person first.
_____ 4. helping a new student.	_____ 14. rapid heartbeats.
_____ 5. dancing eyes.	_____ 15. a friendly welcome.
_____ 6. bare trees and dead leaves.	_____ 16. newborn puppies.
_____ 7. walking hand-in-hand.	_____ 17. a deserted house.
_____ 8. shining stars.	_____ 18. wet feet and cold noses.
_____ 9. fun and sun.	_____ 19. a pat on the back.
_____ 10. waiting for the doctor's report.	_____ 20. a mother rocking her baby.

B Write two more word pictures for a. - i. in part A.

1. Freedom is ...   _____   _____
2. Summer is ...   _____   _____
3. Love is ...   _____   _____
4. Beauty is ...   _____   _____
5. Fear is ...   _____   _____
6. Peace is ...   _____   _____
7. Winter is ...   _____   _____
8. Sadness is ...   _____   _____
9. Kindness is ...   _____   _____

C Underline the more appropriate ending for each idea.

1. Wisdom is ...	a. giggles.	b. having plenty of firewood.
2. Loyalty is ...	a. keeping secrets.	b. telling secrets.
3. Motherhood is ...	a. bright lights.	b. sleepless nights.
4. Happiness is ...	a. a purring kitten.	b. gritting your teeth.
5. Security is ...	a. a teddy bear at night.	b. a rocking boat.
6. Friendship is ...	a. listening to her problems.	b. a slamming door.
7. School is ...	a. homework.	b. diving into a pool.
8. Work is ...	a. sleeping late.	b. constant demands.
9. July 4th is ...	a. rockets and firecrackers.	b. sleigh bells.
10. Wonder is ...	a. a giant redwood tree.	b. a page in a book.
11. Loneliness is ...	a. a good, close friend.	b. a silent telephone.
12. Hate is ...	a. a screaming siren.	b. sunshine.
13. Autumn is ...	a. the scent of burning leaves.	b. new-mown grass.
14. War is ...	a. rat-a-tat-tat.	b. beautiful harp music.

398

Comprehension Check

(A) Match each item with the sense that it would <u>most likely</u> appeal to. Write "sight," "hearing," "touch," "smell," or "taste" in each blank.

1. ice _____touch_____
2. oranges _____
3. a dill pickle _____
4. sandpaper _____
5. fur _____

6. water _____
7. sugar _____
8. a radio _____
9. flames _____
10. a sunset _____

(B) Identify each part of a business letter by writing "heading," "inside address," "greeting," "closing," "body," and "signature" in the blanks.

_____heading_____ { 812 Richmond St.
Savannah, GA 00911
April 8, 1986

Allen's Bike Shop
811 Oak Grove Ave.   } _____
Tampa, FL 32106

Dear Mr. Allen: _____

I ordered a Raston bicycle from your shop on March 15. Your phone order clerk told me that the bike would be shipped immediately, but it hasn't arrived yet.

The catalog number is RS-W1147. The bike appears on page 17 of your catalog. It sells for $185.00.   } _____

Please check into this matter for me. My phone number is 308-882-5610.

_____
_____   Very truly yours,
Janna Jenkins
Janna Jenkins

(C) Correct the spelling and punctuation as you rewrite parts of the business letter.

1. allen's Bike shop   _____*Allen's Bike Shop*_____
2. very Truly Yours   _____
3. "please check into ... "   _____

4. dear mr allen   _____
5. savannah ga   _____
6. april 8 1986   _____

Test 33 cont'd ➡

Comprehension Check (continued)

D Address an envelope for the letter in part B on page 399. Draw a square where the stamp should be placed.

[blank envelope box]

E Read the following friendly letter and answer the questions about it.

101 Dale St.
Austin, TX 72302
March 3, 1986

Dear Mary Beth,

I'm so glad you can visit me next weekend! Mom said we could have a party Friday. We'll go shopping on Saturday and go to a movie Saturday night.

I can't wait until Friday!

Always,

Jeanne

1. Who wrote the letter? _*Jeanne*_____
2. Write the greeting. _____
_____
3. Write the closing. _____
4. When was the letter written? _____
_____
5. What is Jeanne's address? _____
_____
6. When will Mary Beth arrive at Jeanne's? _____
7. What will Mary Beth and Jeanne do on Saturday? _____
_____

Write a thank-you note for a gift you have received from a friend or relative.

_____
_____
_____
_____
_____
_____
_____